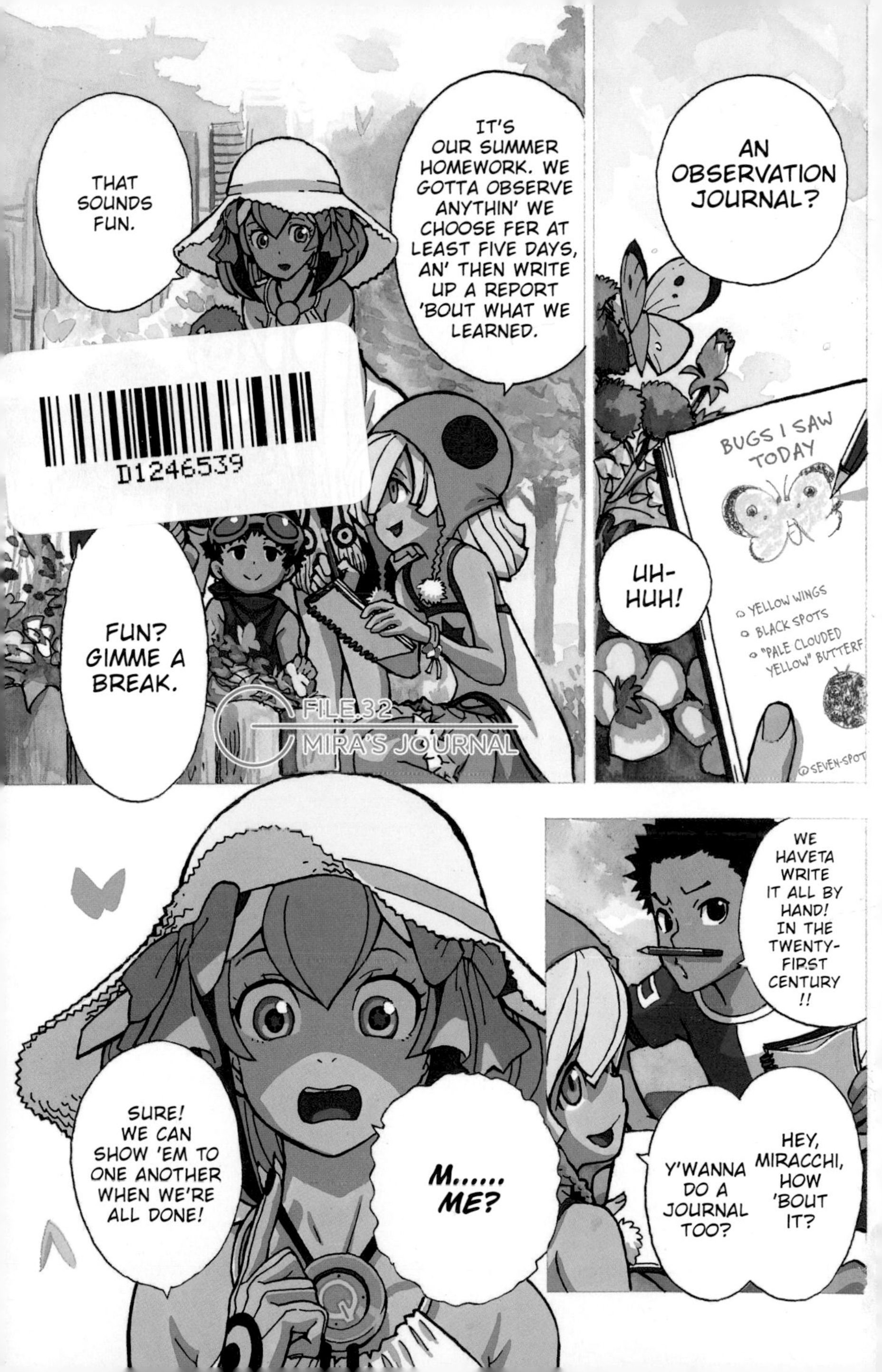
AN OBSERVATION JOURNAL?
BUGS I SAW TODAY
YELLOW WINGS
BLACK SPOTS
"PALE CLOUDED YELLOW" BUTTERF
SEVEN-SPOT
UH-HUH!
IT'S OUR SUMMER HOMEWORK. WE GOTTA OBSERVE ANYTHIN' WE CHOOSE FER AT LEAST FIVE DAYS, AN' THEN WRITE UP A REPORT 'BOUT WHAT WE LEARNED.
THAT SOUNDS FUN.
FUN? GIMME A BREAK.
FILE.32 MIRA'S JOURNAL
WE HAVETA WRITE IT ALL BY HAND! IN THE TWENTY-FIRST CENTURY!!
HEY, MIRACCHI, HOW 'BOUT IT?
Y'WANNA DO A JOURNAL TOO?
M...... ME?
SURE! WE CAN SHOW 'EM TO ONE ANOTHER WHEN WE'RE ALL DONE!

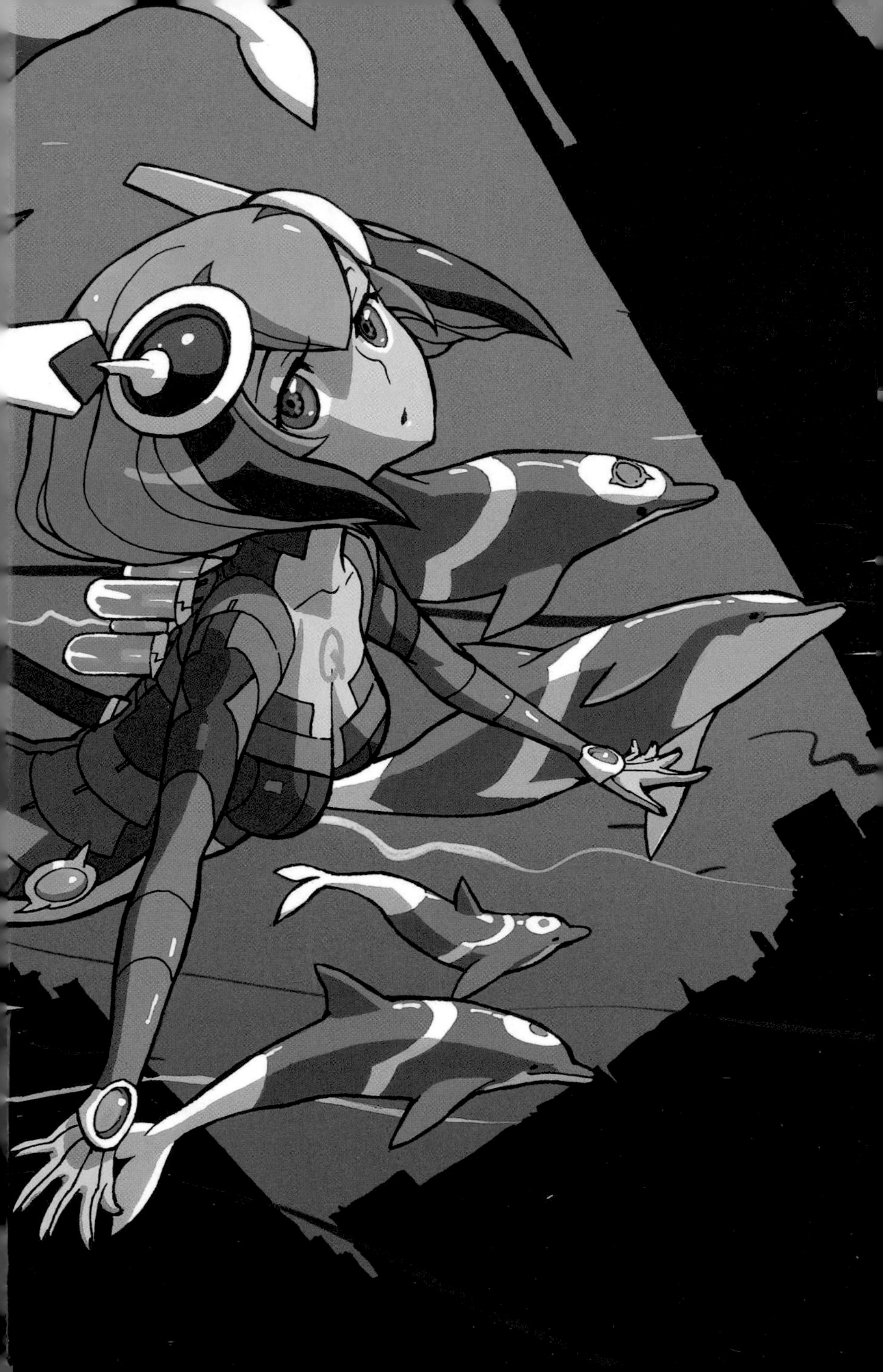

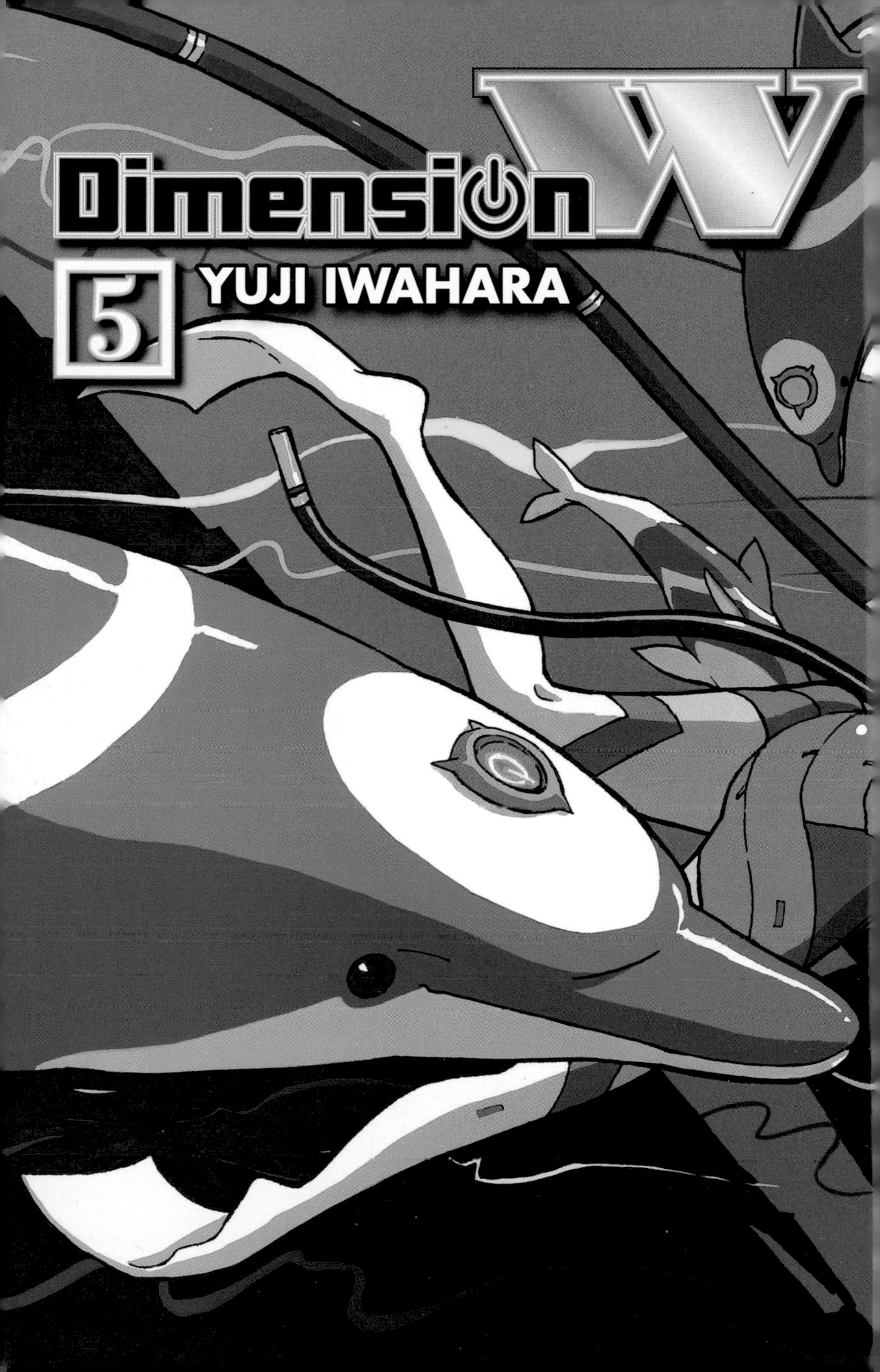
Dimension W
5
YUJI IWAHARA

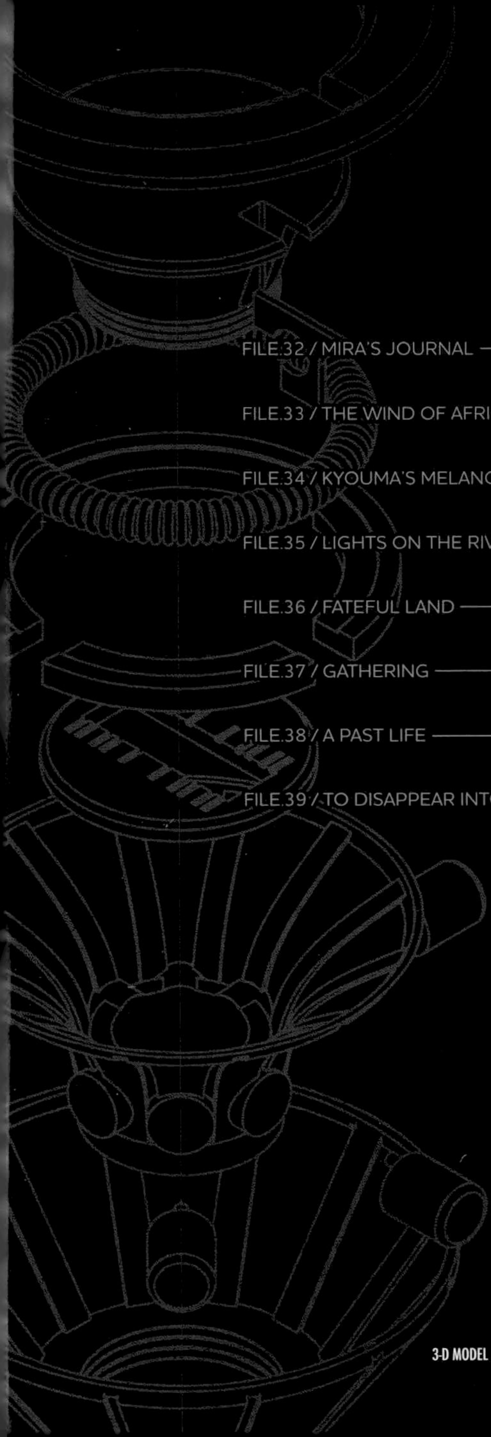

CONTENTS

3-D MODEL DESIGN: TOSHIKAZU SENBA

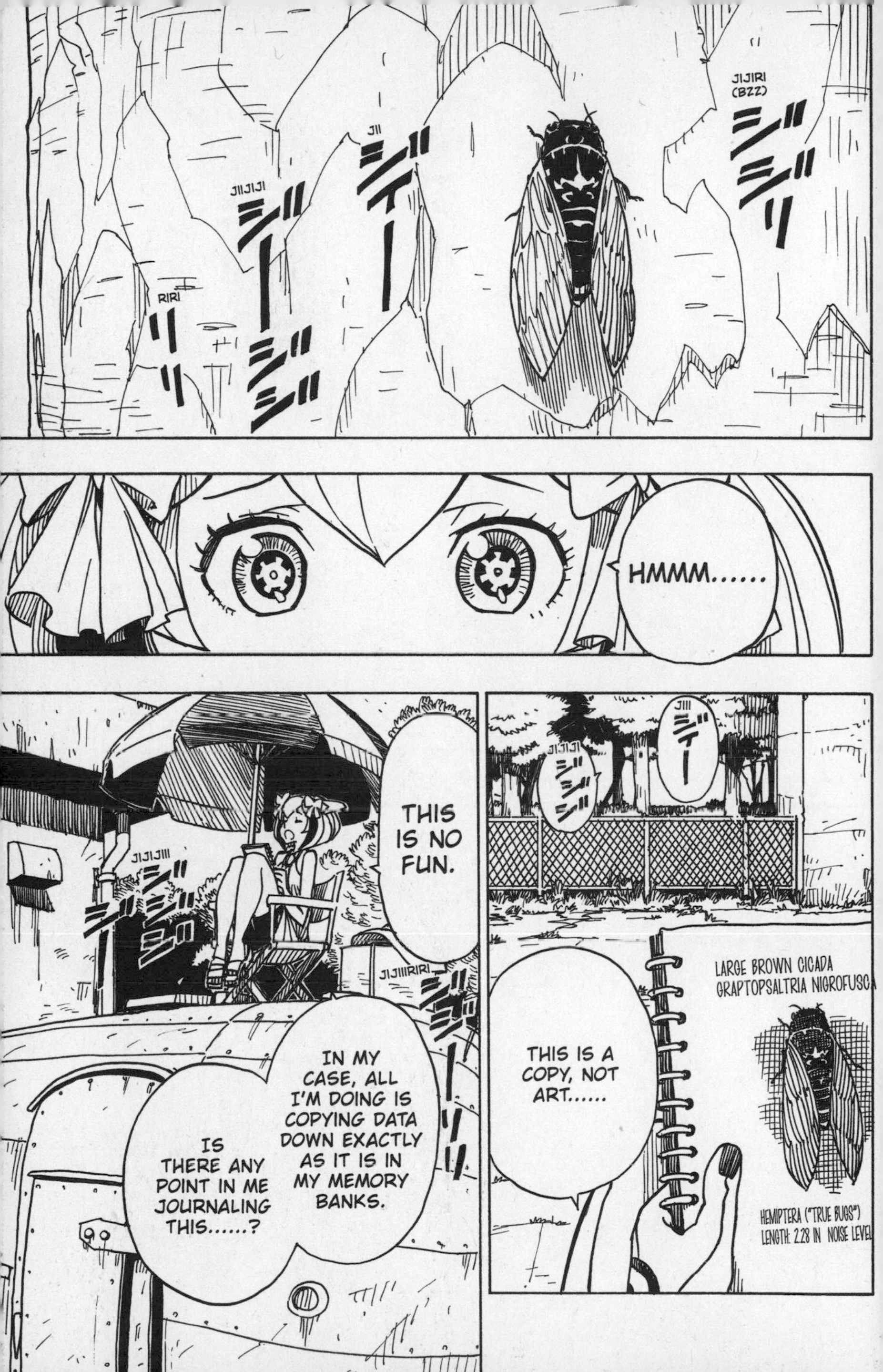
JIJIRI (BZZ)
JII
JIIJIJI
RIRI
HMMM......
JIII
JIJIJI
THIS IS A COPY, NOT ART......
LARGE BROWN CICADA GRAPTOPSALTRIA NIGROFUSCA
HEMIPTERA ("TRUE BUGS")
LENGTH: 2.28 IN NOISE LEVEL
THIS IS NO FUN.
JIJIJIII
JIJIIIRIRI
IN MY CASE, ALL I'M DOING IS COPYING DATA DOWN EXACTLY AS IT IS IN MY MEMORY BANKS.
IS THERE ANY POINT IN ME JOURNALING THIS......?

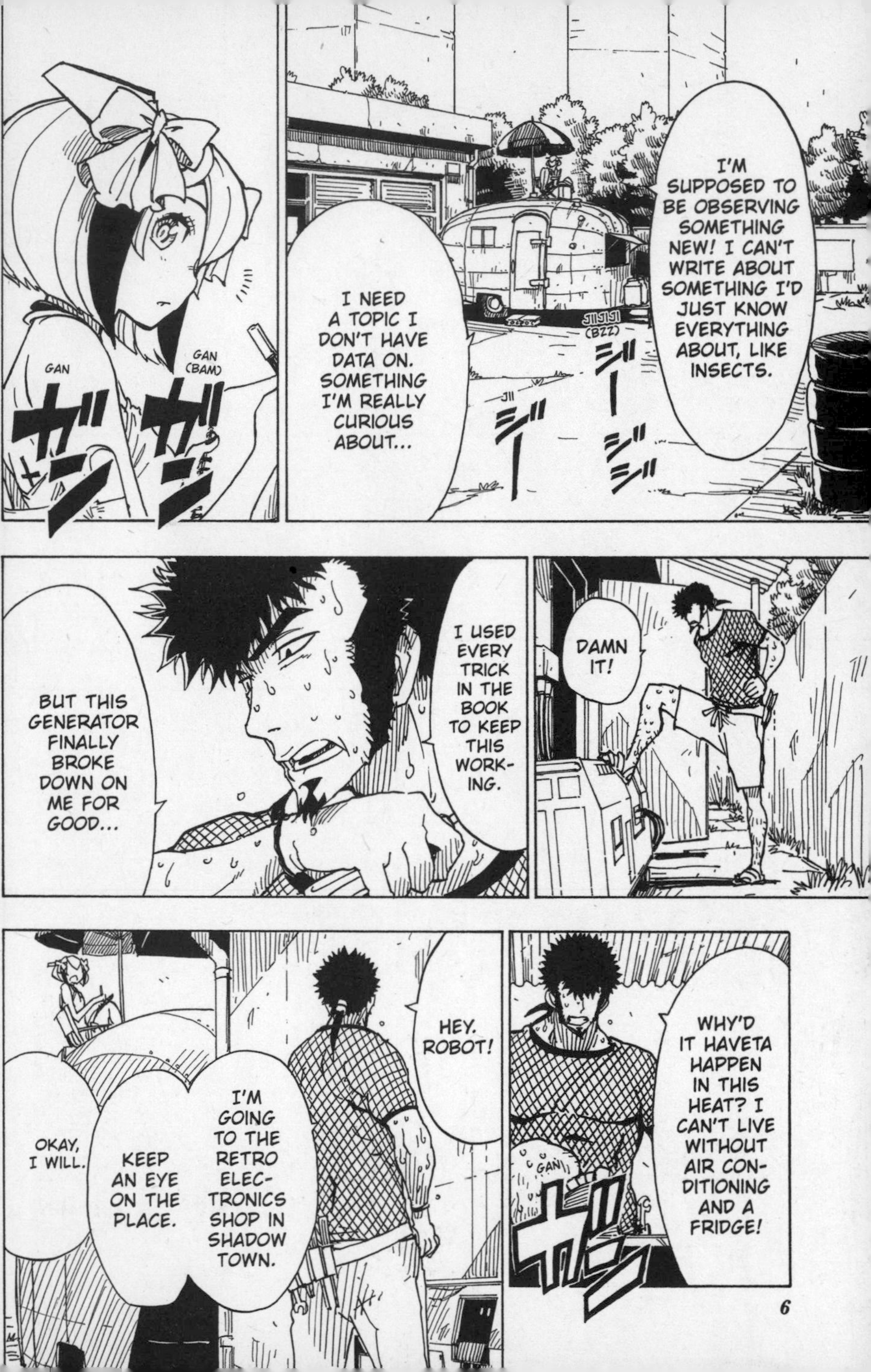

I'M SUPPOSED TO BE OBSERVING SOMETHING NEW! I CAN'T WRITE ABOUT SOMETHING I'D JUST KNOW EVERYTHING ABOUT, LIKE INSECTS.
I NEED A TOPIC I DON'T HAVE DATA ON. SOMETHING I'M REALLY CURIOUS ABOUT...
JIIJIJI (BZZ)
JII
GAN (BAM)
GAN
DAMN IT!
I USED EVERY TRICK IN THE BOOK TO KEEP THIS WORKING.
BUT THIS GENERATOR FINALLY BROKE DOWN ON ME FOR GOOD...
WHY'D IT HAVETA HAPPEN IN THIS HEAT? I CAN'T LIVE WITHOUT AIR CONDITIONING AND A FRIDGE!
GAN
HEY. ROBOT!
I'M GOING TO THE RETRO ELECTRONICS SHOP IN SHADOW TOWN.
KEEP AN EYE ON THE PLACE.
OKAY, I WILL.

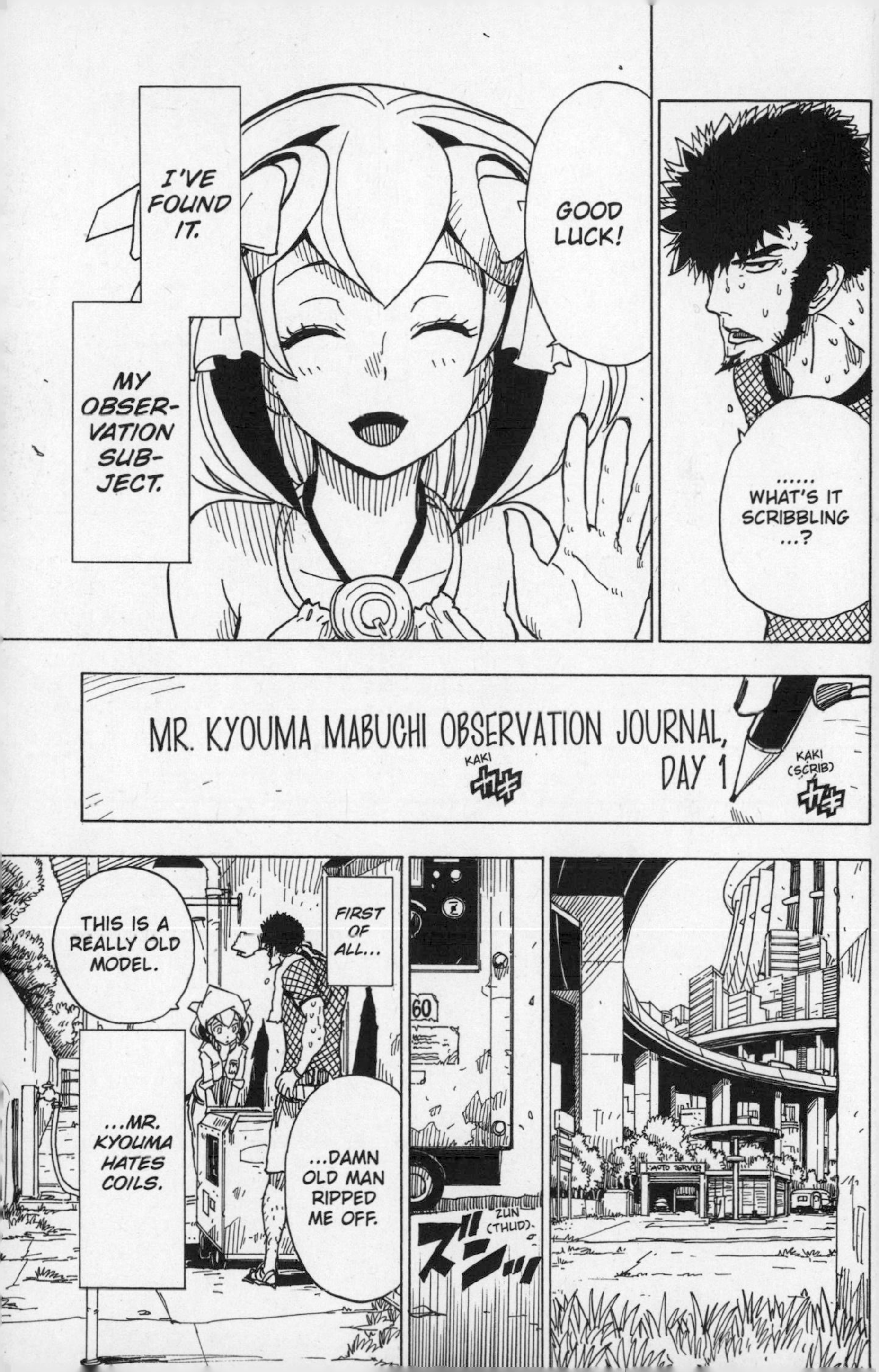

...... WHAT'S IT SCRIBBLING ...?
GOOD LUCK!
I'VE FOUND IT.
MY OBSERVATION SUBJECT.
MR. KYOUMA MABUCHI OBSERVATION JOURNAL, DAY 1
KAKI (SCRIB)
KAKI
ZUN (THUD)
60
FIRST OF ALL...
THIS IS A REALLY OLD MODEL.
...DAMN OLD MAN RIPPED ME OFF.
...MR. KYOUMA HATES COILS.

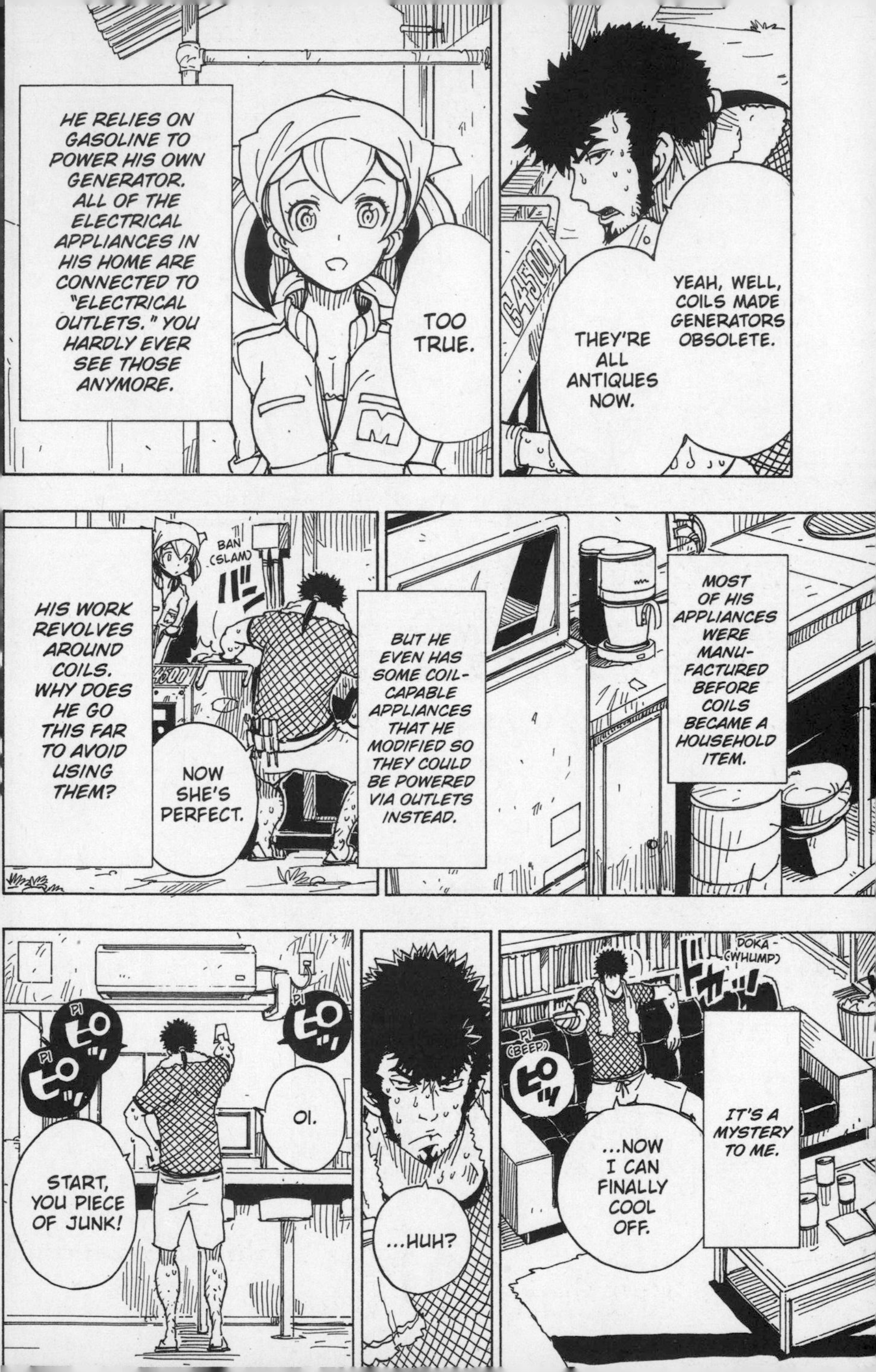
YEAH, WELL, COILS MADE GENERATORS OBSOLETE.
THEY'RE ALL ANTIQUES NOW.
TOO TRUE.
HE RELIES ON GASOLINE TO POWER HIS OWN GENERATOR. ALL OF THE ELECTRICAL APPLIANCES IN HIS HOME ARE CONNECTED TO "ELECTRICAL OUTLETS." YOU HARDLY EVER SEE THOSE ANYMORE.
MOST OF HIS APPLIANCES WERE MANU-FACTURED BEFORE COILS BECAME A HOUSEHOLD ITEM.
BUT HE EVEN HAS SOME COIL-CAPABLE APPLIANCES THAT HE MODIFIED SO THEY COULD BE POWERED VIA OUTLETS INSTEAD.
BAN (SLAM)
NOW SHE'S PERFECT.
HIS WORK REVOLVES AROUND COILS. WHY DOES HE GO THIS FAR TO AVOID USING THEM?
DOKA (WHUMP)
IT'S A MYSTERY TO ME.
PI (BEEP)
...NOW I CAN FINALLY COOL OFF.
...HUH?
PI
OI.
PI
PI
START, YOU PIECE OF JUNK!

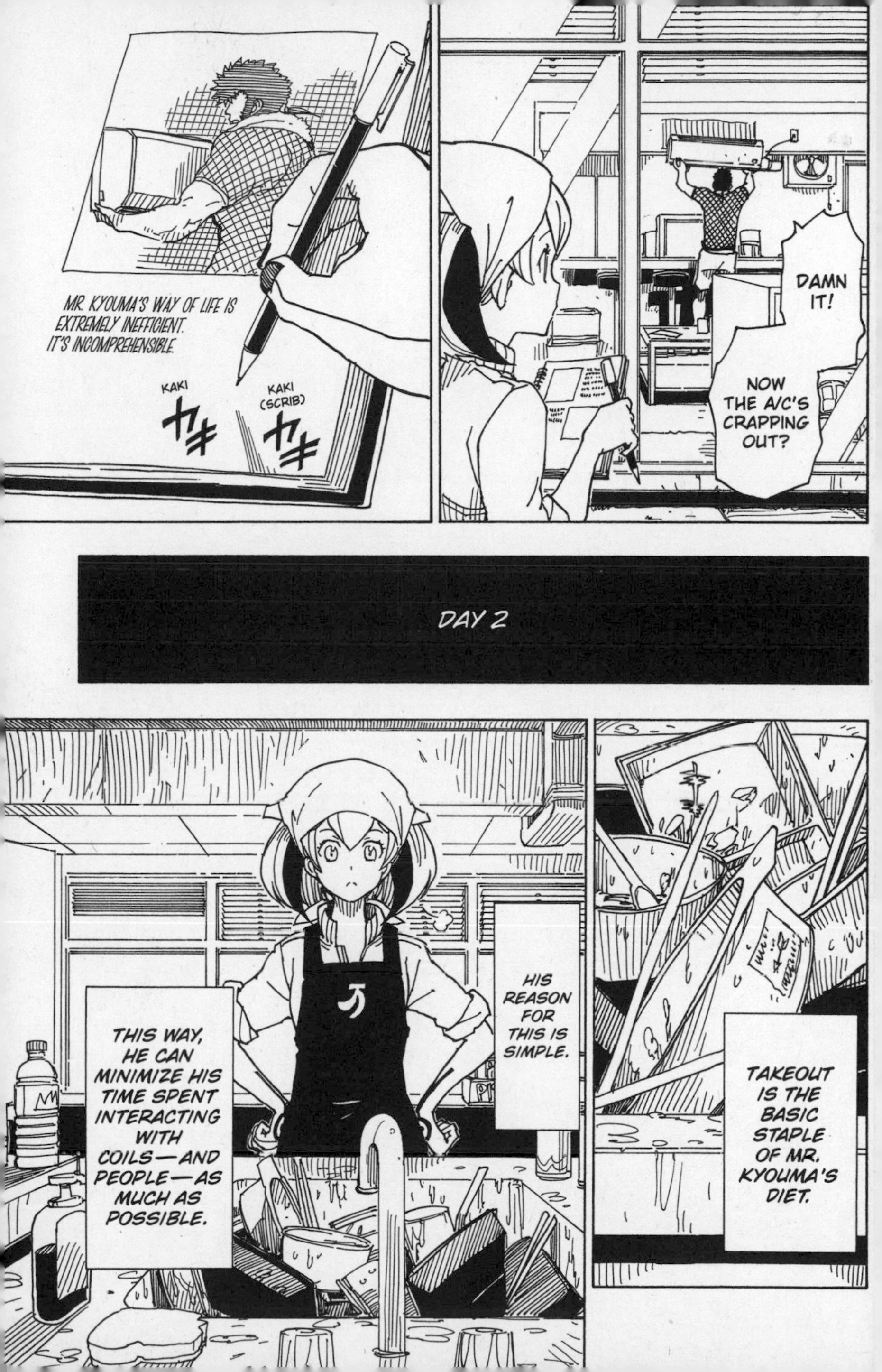
DAMN IT!
NOW THE A/C'S CRAPPING OUT?
MR. KYOUMA'S WAY OF LIFE IS EXTREMELY INEFFICIENT. IT'S INCOMPREHENSIBLE.
KAKI
KAKI (SCRIB)
DAY 2
TAKEOUT IS THE BASIC STAPLE OF MR. KYOUMA'S DIET.
HIS REASON FOR THIS IS SIMPLE.
THIS WAY, HE CAN MINIMIZE HIS TIME SPENT INTERACTING WITH COILS—AND PEOPLE—AS MUCH AS POSSIBLE.

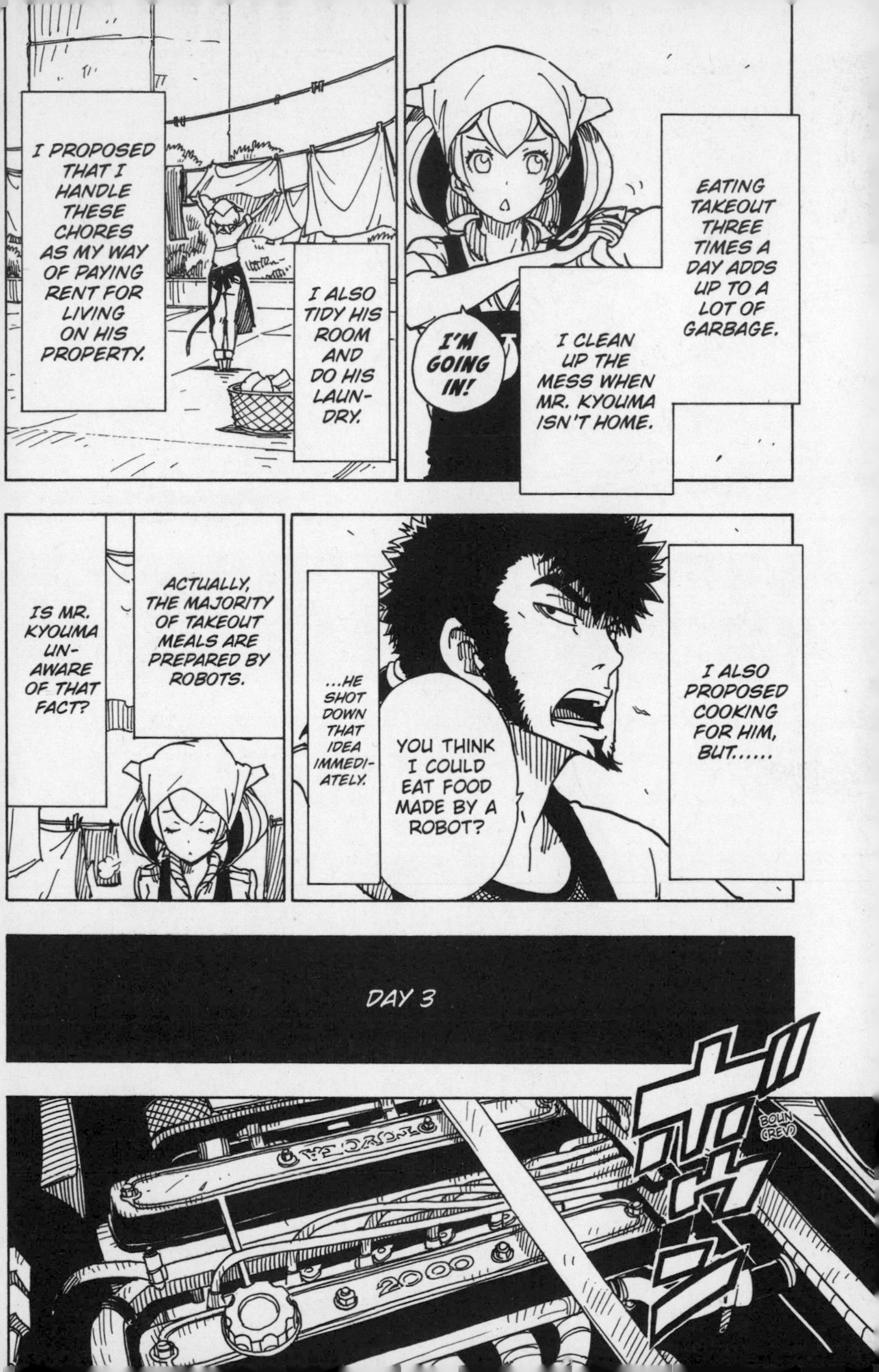
EATING TAKEOUT THREE TIMES A DAY ADDS UP TO A LOT OF GARBAGE.
I CLEAN UP THE MESS WHEN MR. KYOUMA ISN'T HOME.
I'M GOING IN!
I ALSO TIDY HIS ROOM AND DO HIS LAUNDRY.
I PROPOSED THAT I HANDLE THESE CHORES AS MY WAY OF PAYING RENT FOR LIVING ON HIS PROPERTY.
I ALSO PROPOSED COOKING FOR HIM, BUT......
YOU THINK I COULD EAT FOOD MADE BY A ROBOT?
...HE SHOT DOWN THAT IDEA IMMEDIATELY.
ACTUALLY, THE MAJORITY OF TAKEOUT MEALS ARE PREPARED BY ROBOTS.
IS MR. KYOUMA UNAWARE OF THAT FACT?
DAY 3
BOUN (REV)
2000

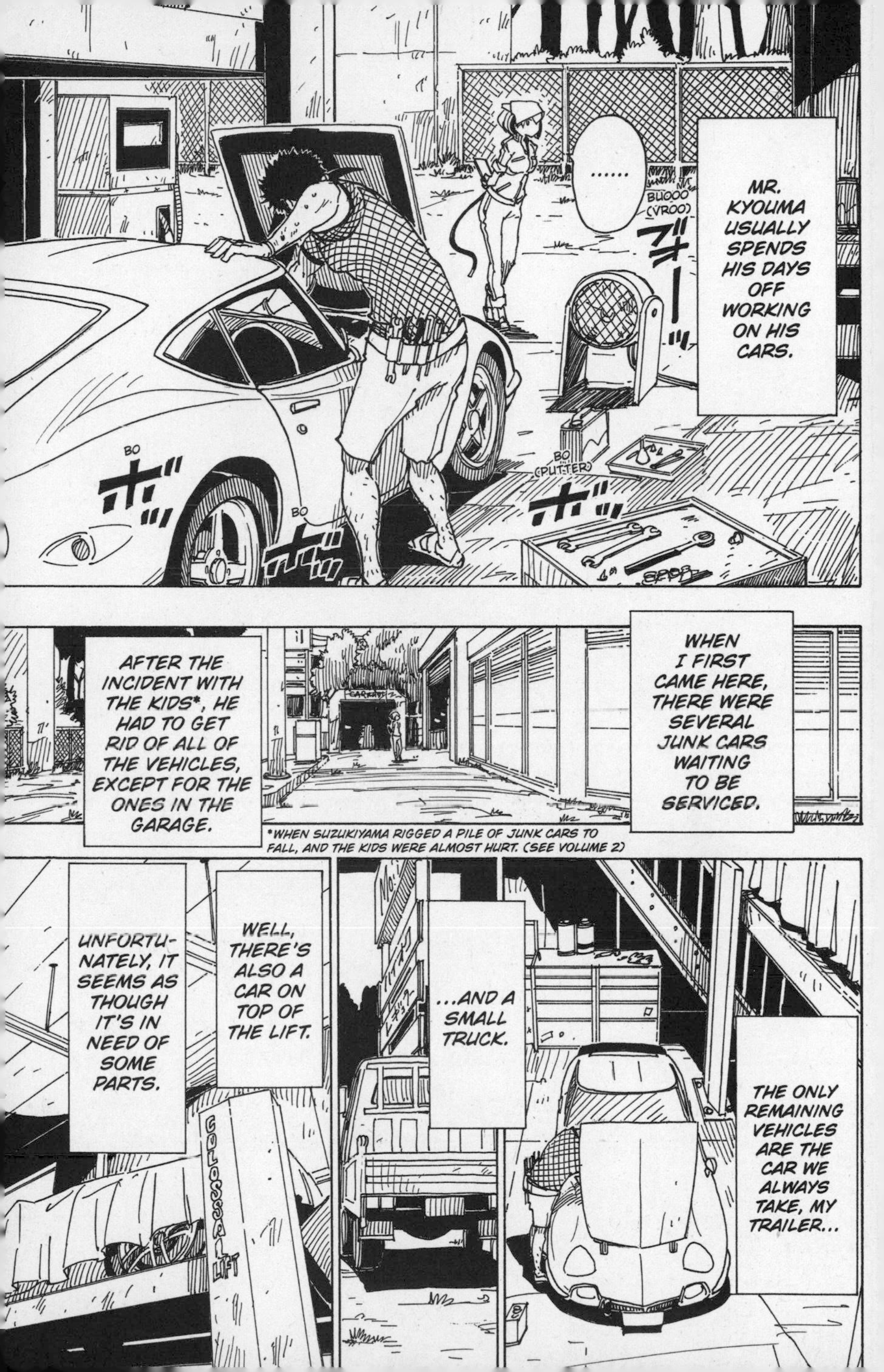
MR. KYOUMA USUALLY SPENDS HIS DAYS OFF WORKING ON HIS CARS.
......
BUOOO (VROO)
BO (PUTTER)
BO
BO
WHEN I FIRST CAME HERE, THERE WERE SEVERAL JUNK CARS WAITING TO BE SERVICED.
AFTER THE INCIDENT WITH THE KIDS*, HE HAD TO GET RID OF ALL OF THE VEHICLES, EXCEPT FOR THE ONES IN THE GARAGE.
*WHEN SUZUKIYAMA RIGGED A PILE OF JUNK CARS TO FALL, AND THE KIDS WERE ALMOST HURT. (SEE VOLUME 2)
THE ONLY REMAINING VEHICLES ARE THE CAR WE ALWAYS TAKE, MY TRAILER...
...AND A SMALL TRUCK.
WELL, THERE'S ALSO A CAR ON TOP OF THE LIFT.
UNFORTU-NATELY, IT SEEMS AS THOUGH IT'S IN NEED OF SOME PARTS.
COLOSSAL LIFT

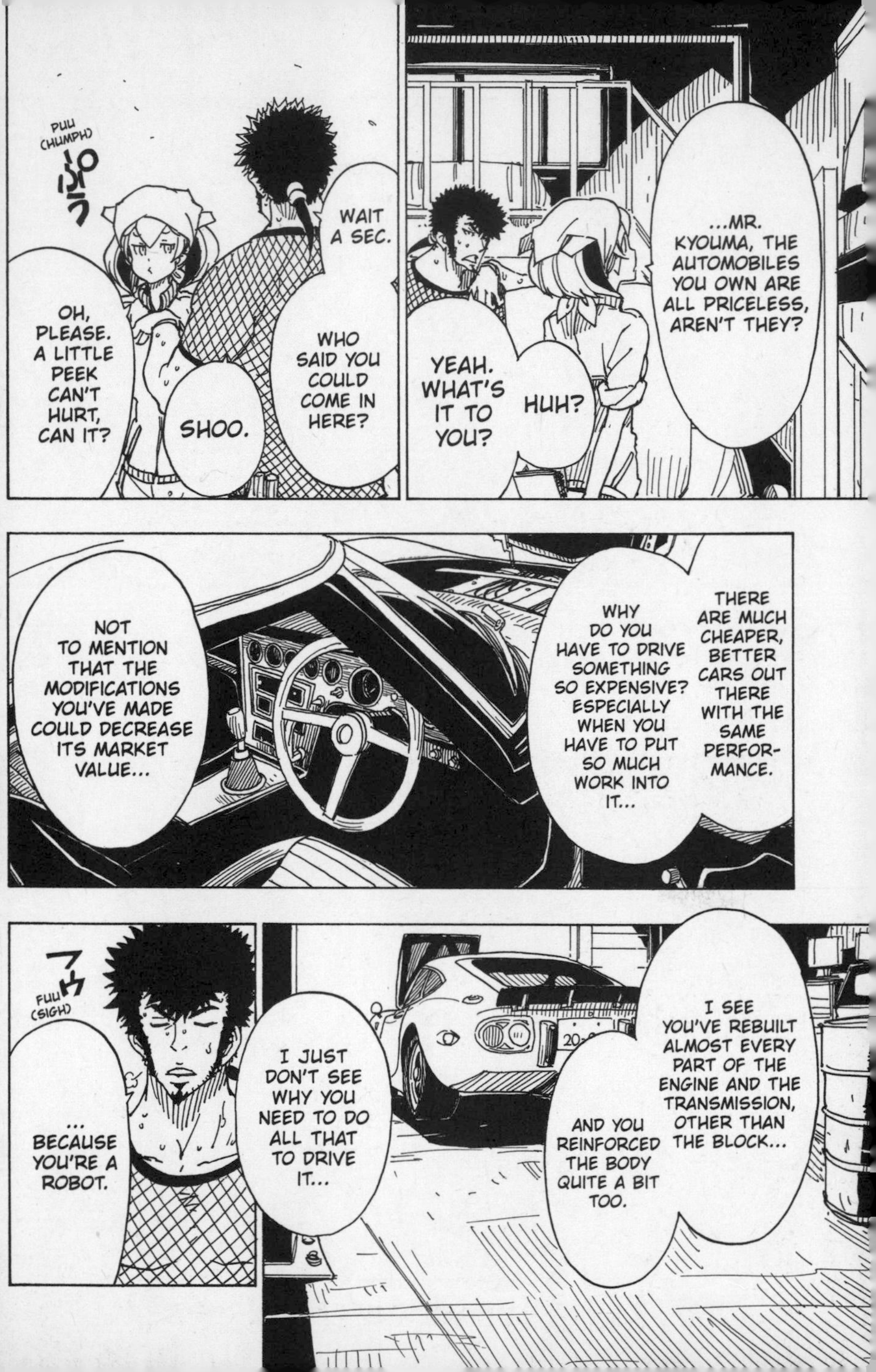
...MR. KYOUMA, THE AUTOMOBILES YOU OWN ARE ALL PRICELESS, AREN'T THEY?
HUH?
YEAH. WHAT'S IT TO YOU?
WAIT A SEC.
WHO SAID YOU COULD COME IN HERE?
SHOO.
PUU (HUMPH)
OH, PLEASE. A LITTLE PEEK CAN'T HURT, CAN IT?
THERE ARE MUCH CHEAPER, BETTER CARS OUT THERE WITH THE SAME PERFORMANCE.
WHY DO YOU HAVE TO DRIVE SOMETHING SO EXPENSIVE? ESPECIALLY WHEN YOU HAVE TO PUT SO MUCH WORK INTO IT...
NOT TO MENTION THAT THE MODIFICATIONS YOU'VE MADE COULD DECREASE ITS MARKET VALUE...
I SEE YOU'VE REBUILT ALMOST EVERY PART OF THE ENGINE AND THE TRANSMISSION, OTHER THAN THE BLOCK...
AND YOU REINFORCED THE BODY QUITE A BIT TOO.
I JUST DON'T SEE WHY YOU NEED TO DO ALL THAT TO DRIVE IT...
FUU (SIGH)
... BECAUSE YOU'RE A ROBOT.

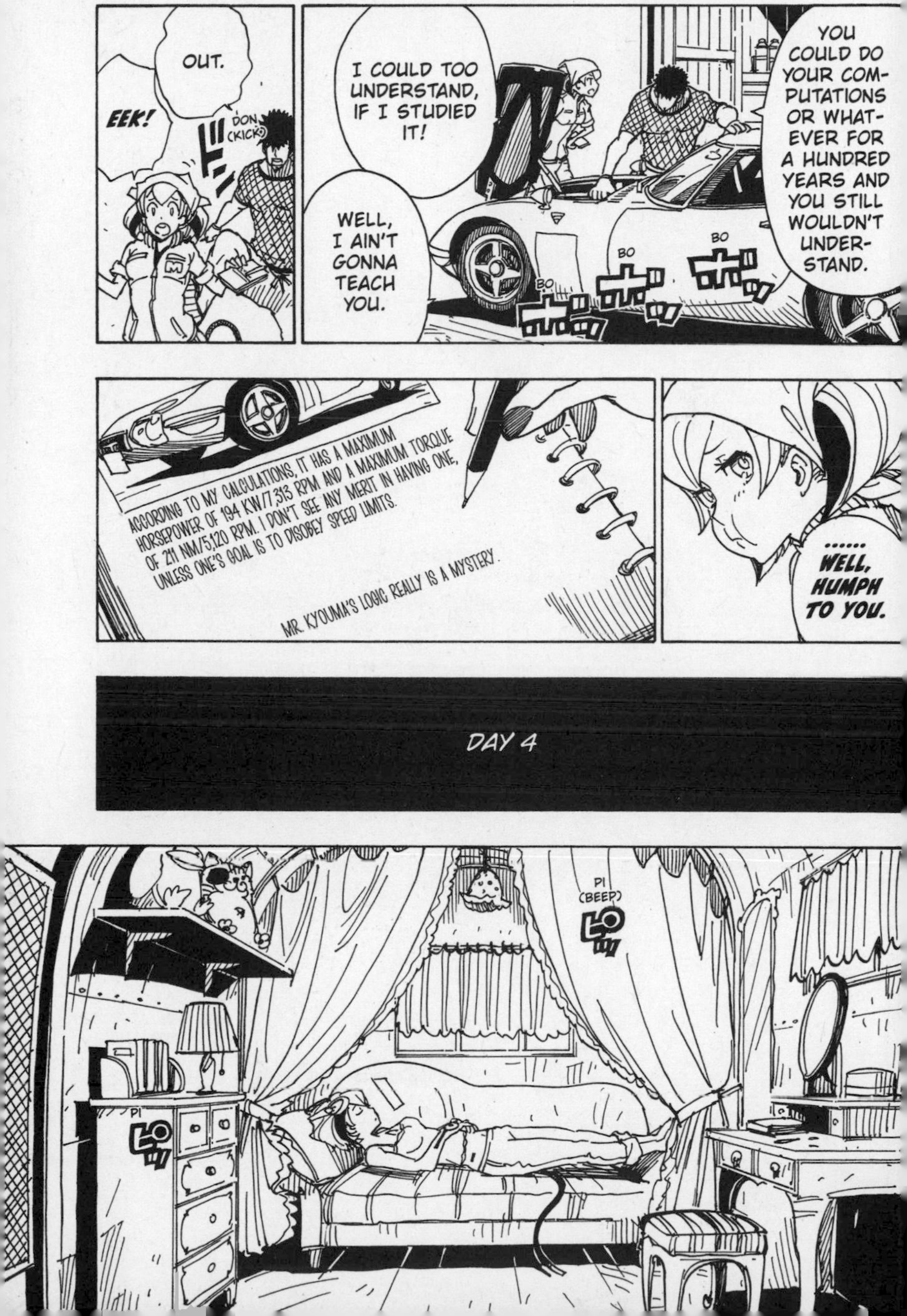
YOU COULD DO YOUR COMPUTATIONS OR WHATEVER FOR A HUNDRED YEARS AND YOU STILL WOULDN'T UNDERSTAND.
I COULD TOO UNDERSTAND, IF I STUDIED IT!
WELL, I AIN'T GONNA TEACH YOU.
BO
BO
BO
OUT.
DON (KICK)
EEK!
...... WELL, HUMPH TO YOU.
ACCORDING TO MY CALCULATIONS, IT HAS A MAXIMUM HORSEPOWER OF 194 KW/7,313 RPM AND A MAXIMUM TORQUE OF 211 NM/5,120 RPM. I DON'T SEE ANY MERIT IN HAVING ONE, UNLESS ONE'S GOAL IS TO DISOBEY SPEED LIMITS.
MR. KYOUMA'S LOGIC REALLY IS A MYSTERY.
DAY 4
PI (BEEP)
PI

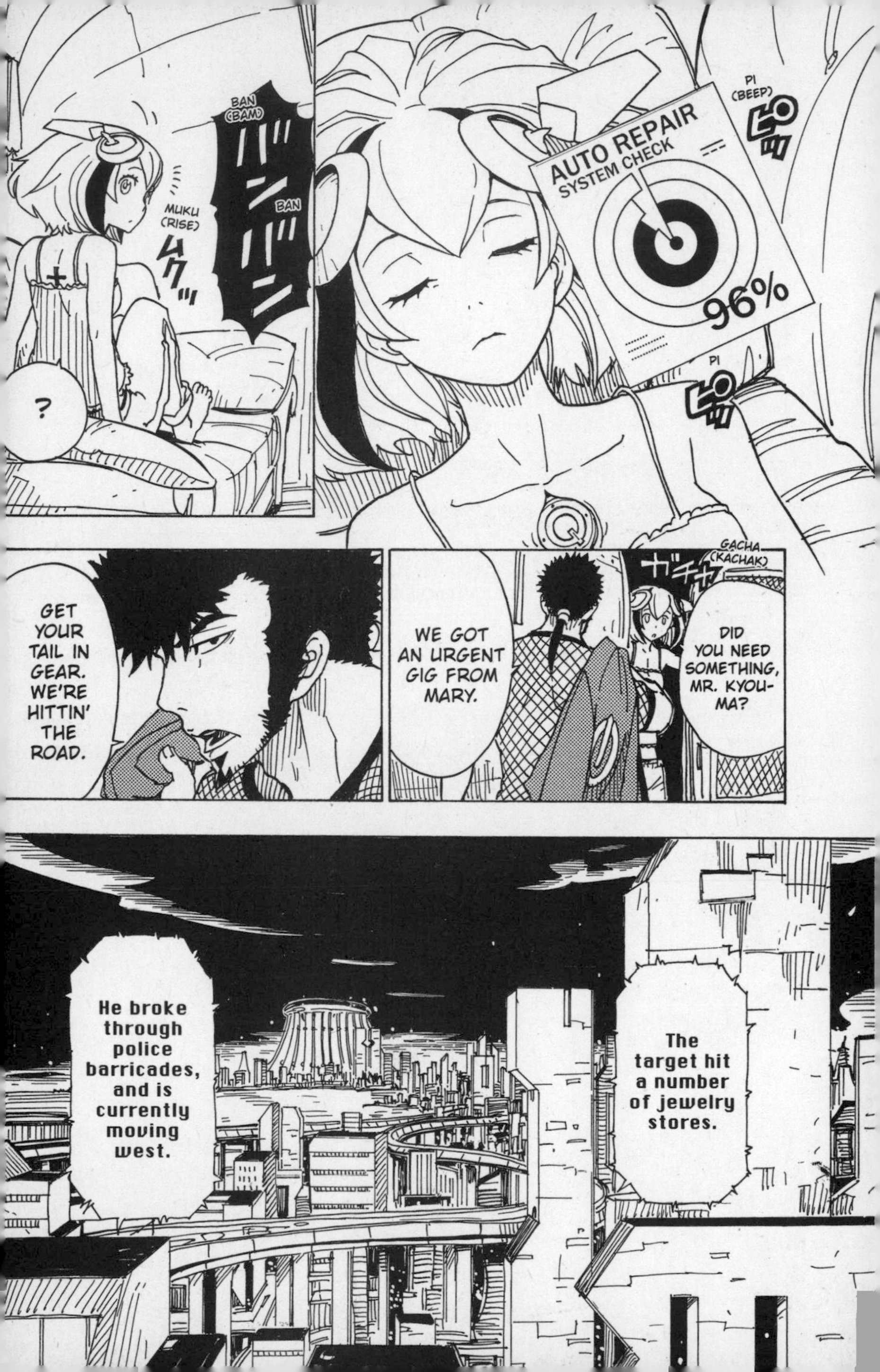

PI (BEEP)
ピッ
AUTO REPAIR
SYSTEM CHECK
96%
PI
ピッ
BAN (BAM)
バン
BAN
バン
MUKU (RISE)
ムクッ
?
GACHA (KACHAK)
ガチャ
DID YOU NEED SOMETHING, MR. KYOU-MA?
WE GOT AN URGENT GIG FROM MARY.
GET YOUR TAIL IN GEAR. WE'RE HITTIN' THE ROAD.
The target hit a number of jewelry stores.
He broke through police barricades, and is currently moving west.

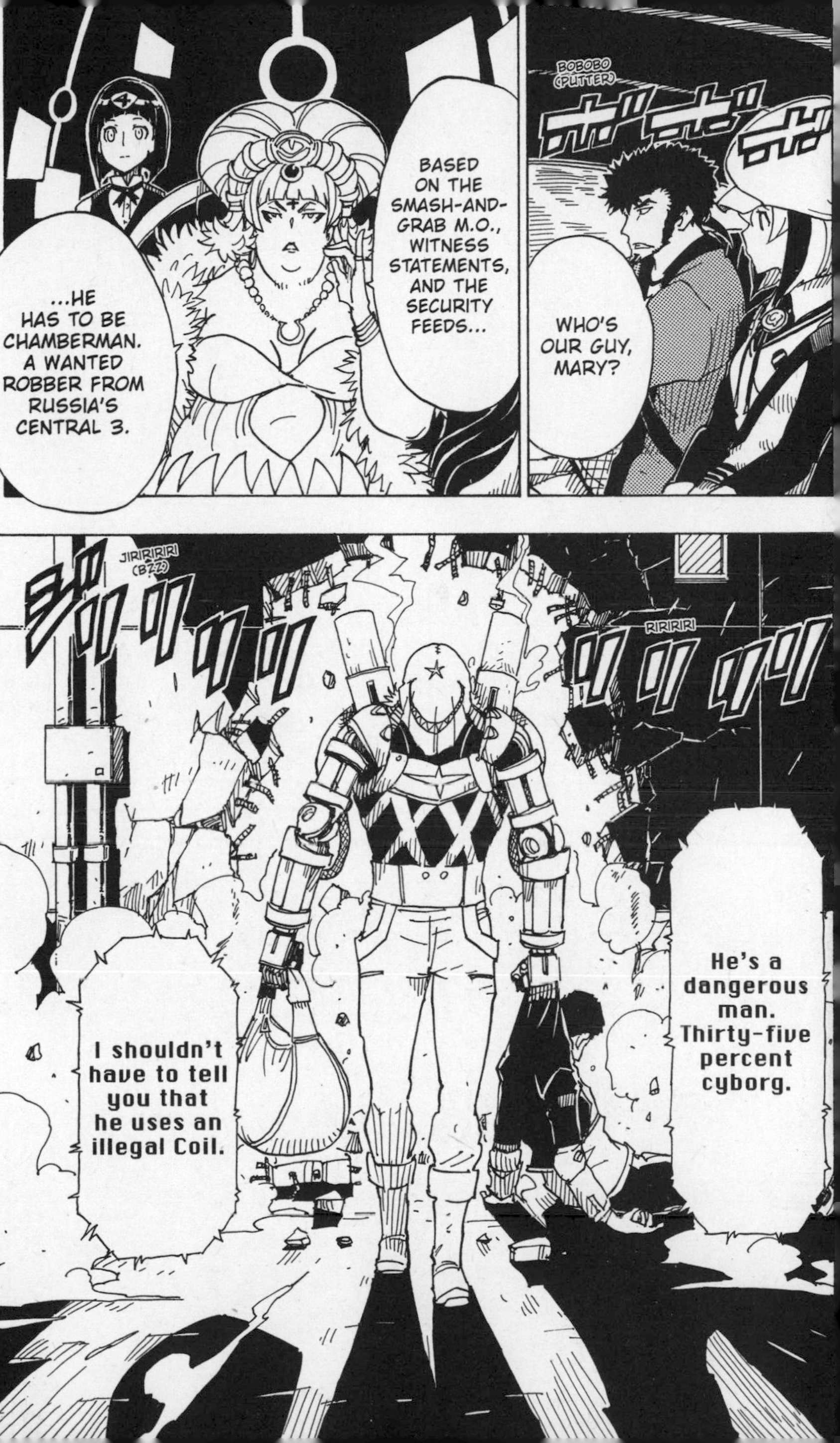
BOBOBO (PUTTER)
WHO'S OUR GUY, MARY?
BASED ON THE SMASH-AND-GRAB M.O., WITNESS STATEMENTS, AND THE SECURITY FEEDS...
...HE HAS TO BE CHAMBERMAN. A WANTED ROBBER FROM RUSSIA'S CENTRAL 3.
JIRIRIRI (BZZ)
RIRIRIRI
He's a dangerous man. Thirty-five percent cyborg.
I shouldn't have to tell you that he uses an illegal Coil.

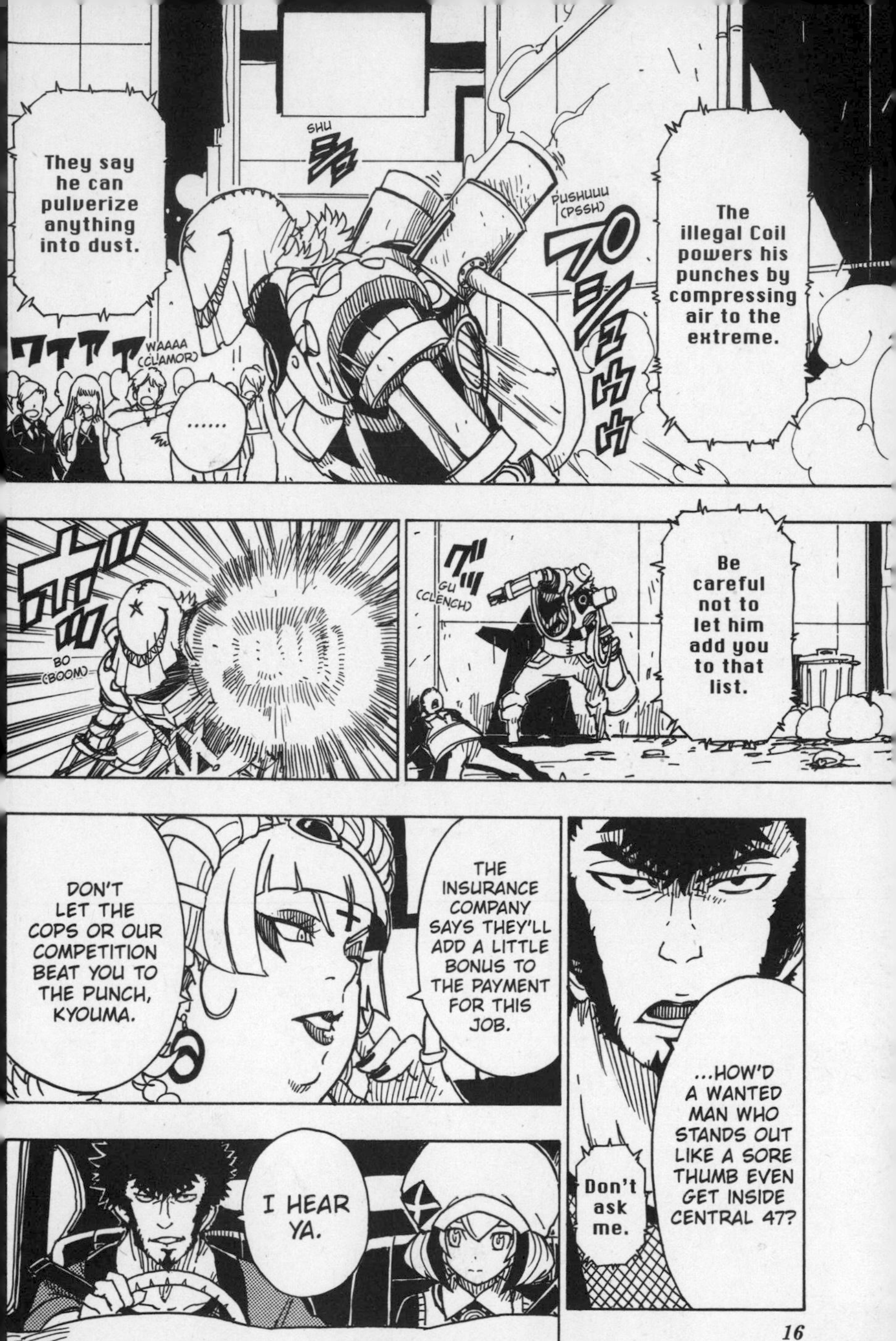

The illegal Coil powers his punches by compressing air to the extreme.
PUSHUUU (PSSH)
SHU
They say he can pulverize anything into dust.
WAAAA (CLAMOR)
......
Be careful not to let him add you to that list.
GU (CLENCH)
BO (BOOM)
...HOW'D A WANTED MAN WHO STANDS OUT LIKE A SORE THUMB EVEN GET INSIDE CENTRAL 47?
Don't ask me.
THE INSURANCE COMPANY SAYS THEY'LL ADD A LITTLE BONUS TO THE PAYMENT FOR THIS JOB.
DON'T LET THE COPS OR OUR COMPETITION BEAT YOU TO THE PUNCH, KYOUMA.
I HEAR YA.

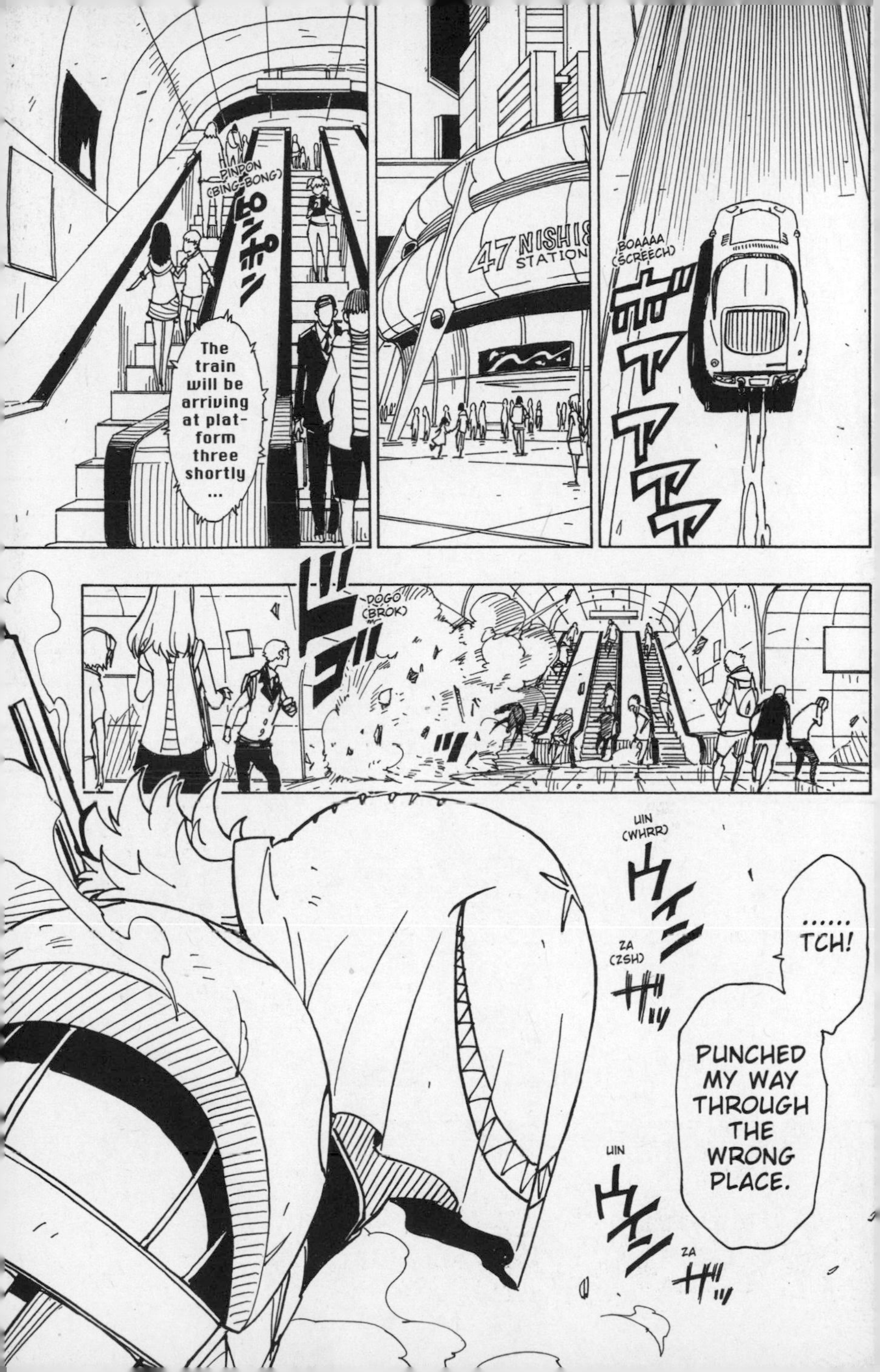

BOAAAA (SCREECH)
47 NISHI8 STATION
PINPON (BING-BONG)
The train will be arriving at plat-form three shortly ...
DOGO (BROK)
UIN (WHRR)
......TCH!
ZA (ZSH)
PUNCHED MY WAY THROUGH THE WRONG PLACE.
UIN
ZA

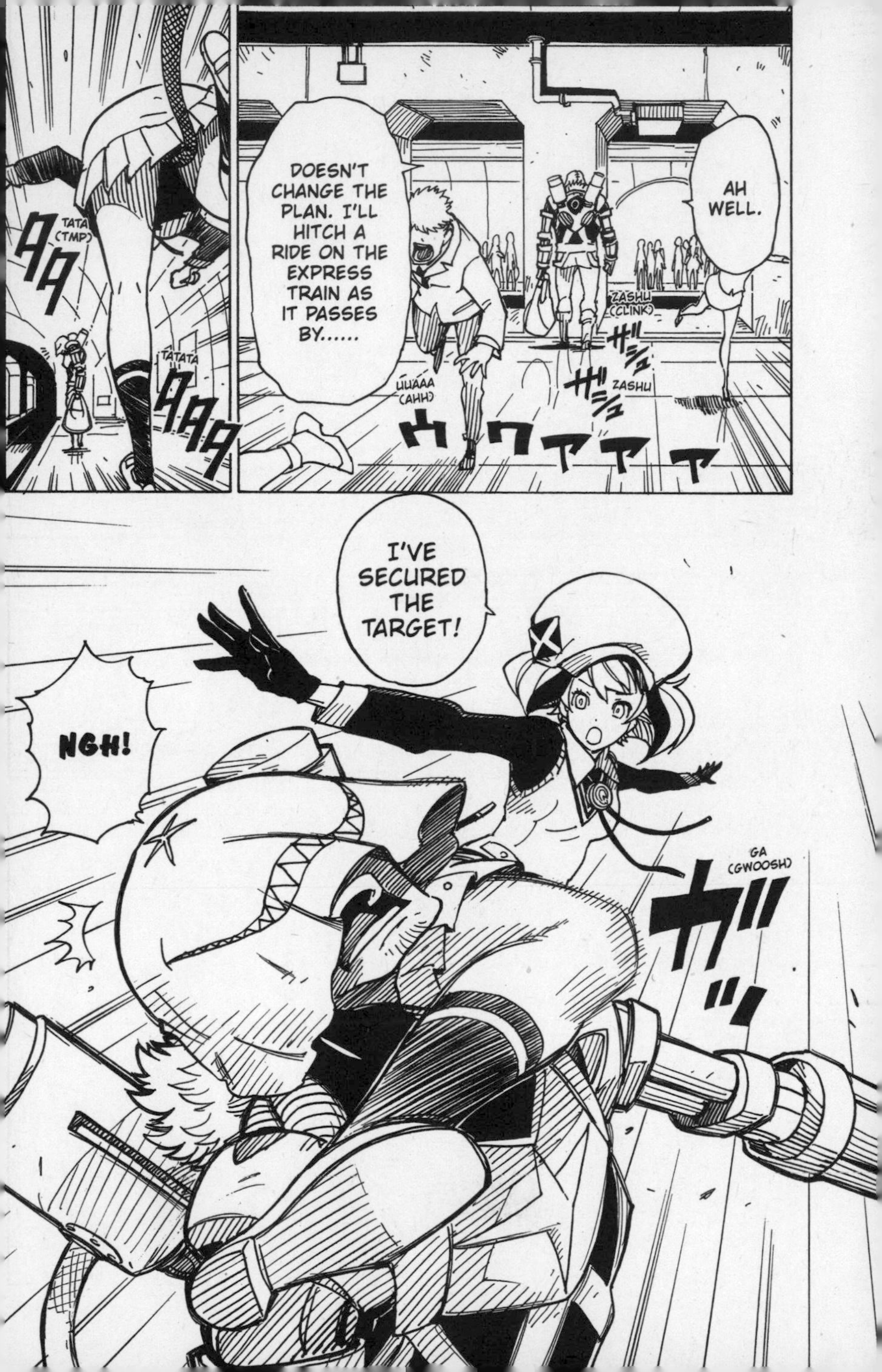
AH WELL.
DOESN'T CHANGE THE PLAN. I'LL HITCH A RIDE ON THE EXPRESS TRAIN AS IT PASSES BY......
ZASHU (CLINK)
ザシュ
ザシュ
ZASHU
UUAAA (AHH)
ウワアアア
TATA (TMP)
タタ
TATATA
タタタ
I'VE SECURED THE TARGET!
GA (GWOOSH)
ガッ
NGH!

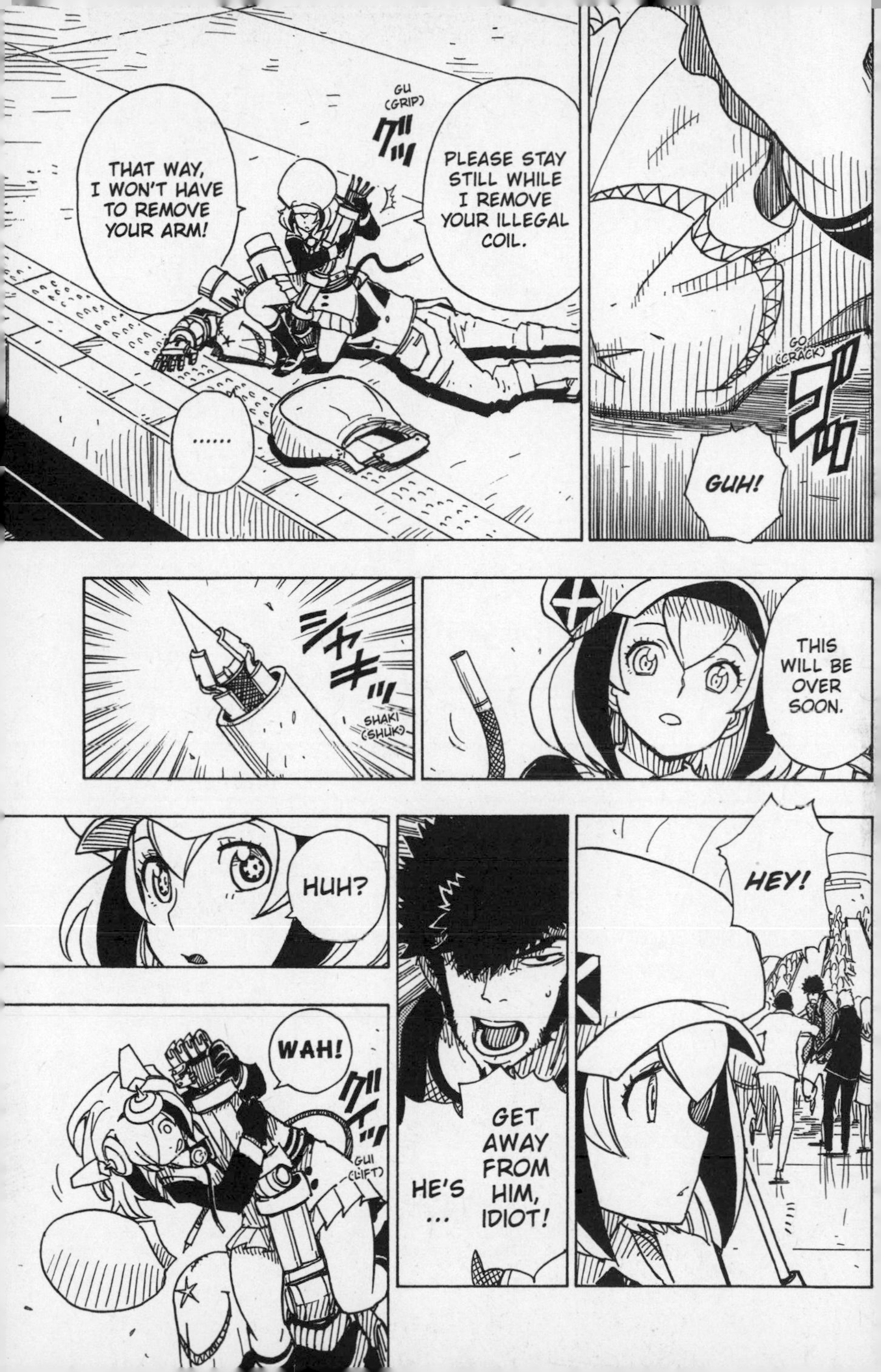
GO
(CRACK)
GUH!
GU
(GRIP)
PLEASE STAY STILL WHILE I REMOVE YOUR ILLEGAL COIL.
THAT WAY, I WON'T HAVE TO REMOVE YOUR ARM!
......
THIS WILL BE OVER SOON.
SHAKI
(SHUK)
HEY!
GET AWAY FROM HIM, IDIOT!
HE'S ...
HUH?
WAH!
GUI
(LIFT)

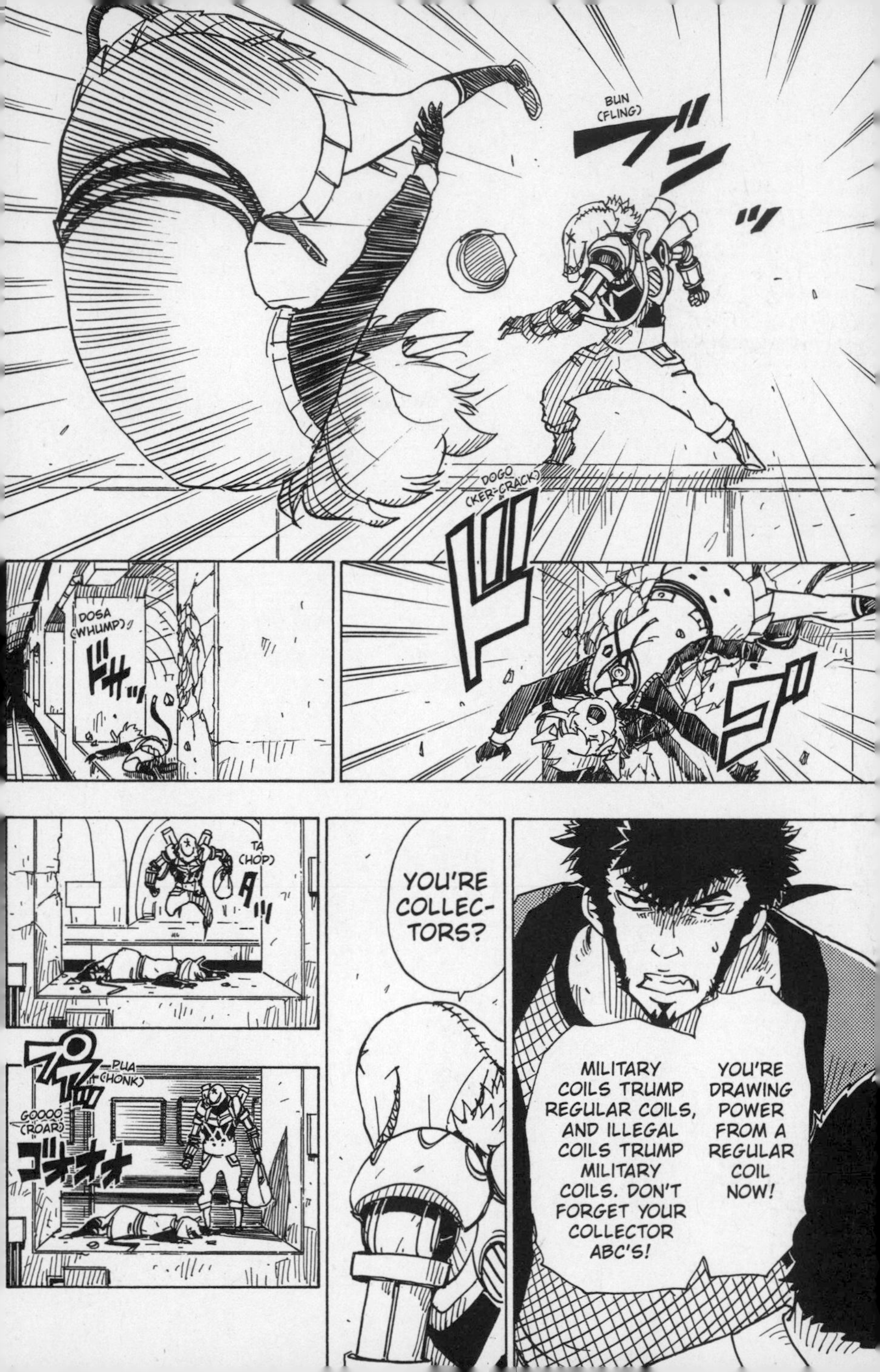
BUN (FLING)
DOGO (KER-CRACK)
DOSA (WHUMP)
YOU'RE DRAWING POWER FROM A REGULAR COIL NOW!
MILITARY COILS TRUMP REGULAR COILS, AND ILLEGAL COILS TRUMP MILITARY COILS. DON'T FORGET YOUR COLLECTOR ABC'S!
YOU'RE COLLECTORS?
TA (HOP)
PUA (HONK)
GOOOO (ROAR)

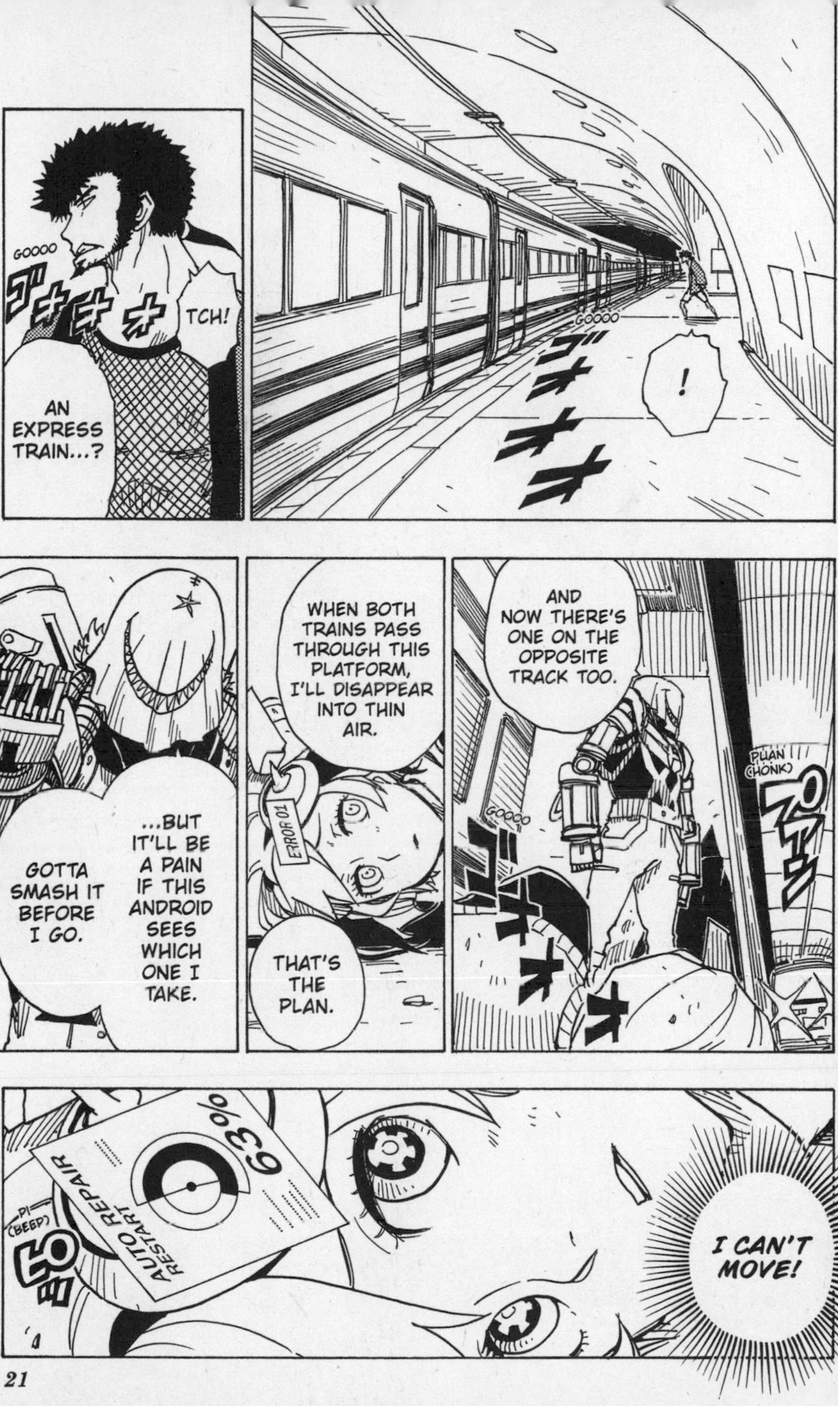
GOOOO
!
GOOOO
TCH!
AN EXPRESS TRAIN...?
AND NOW THERE'S ONE ON THE OPPOSITE TRACK TOO.
PUAN (HONK)
GOOOO
WHEN BOTH TRAINS PASS THROUGH THIS PLATFORM, I'LL DISAPPEAR INTO THIN AIR.
ERROR 01
THAT'S THE PLAN.
...BUT IT'LL BE A PAIN IF THIS ANDROID SEES WHICH ONE I TAKE.
GOTTA SMASH IT BEFORE I GO.
I CAN'T MOVE!
63%
AUTO REPAIR
RESTART
PI (BEEP)

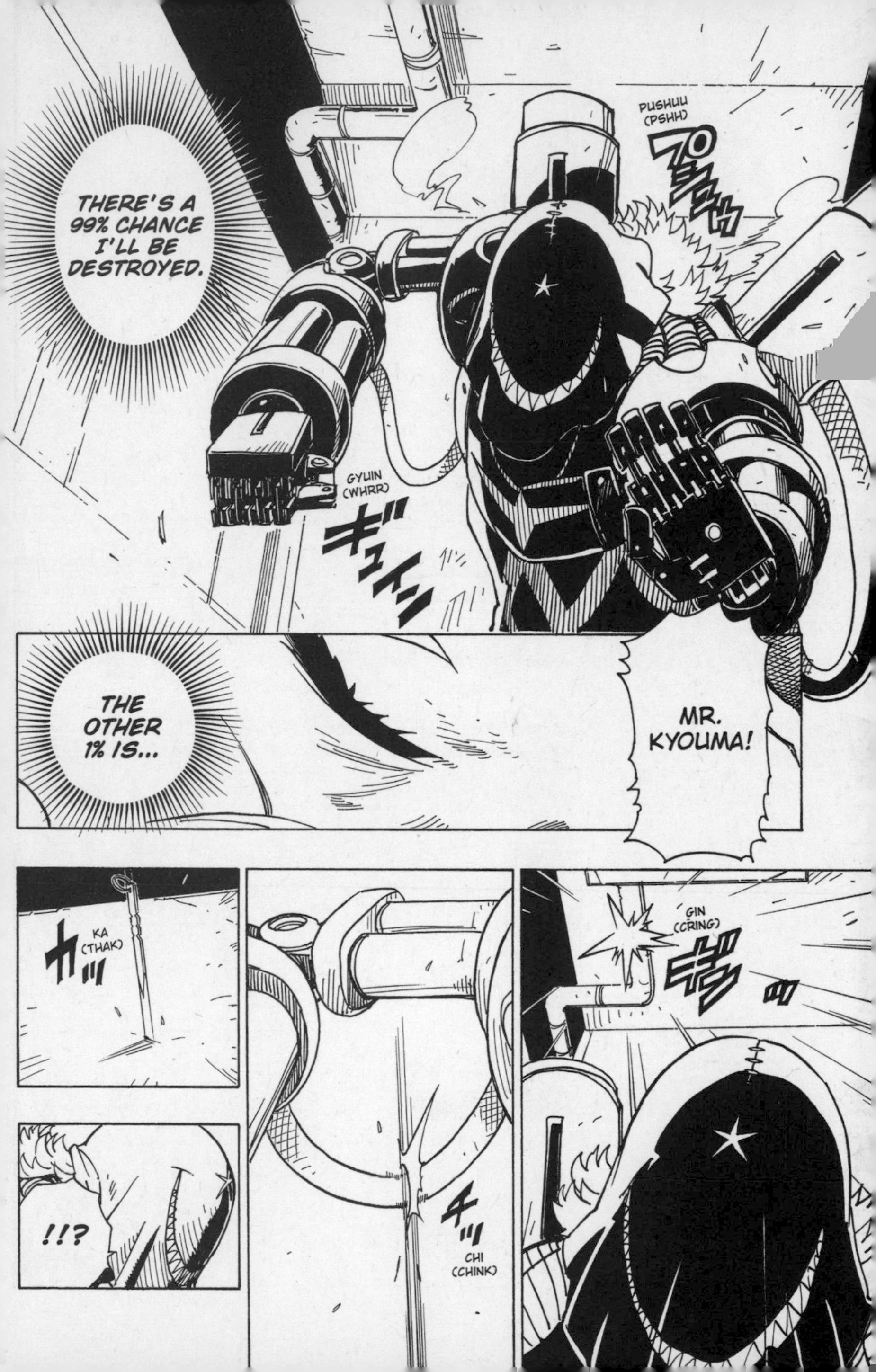
PUSHUU (PSHH)
THERE'S A 99% CHANCE I'LL BE DESTROYED.
GYUIN (WHRR)
MR. KYOUMA!
THE OTHER 1% IS...
GIN (CRING)
CHI (CHINK)
KA (THAK)
!!?

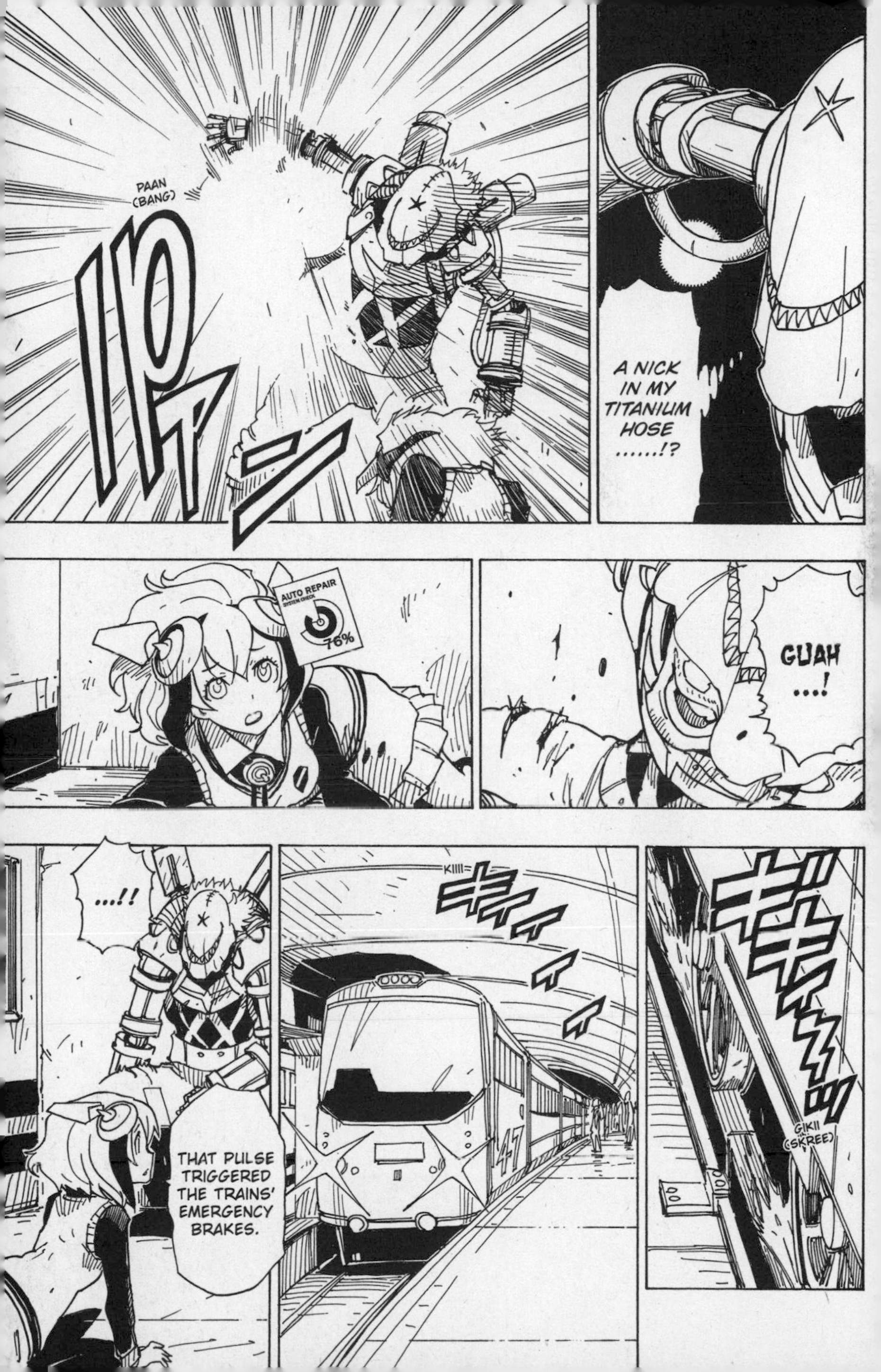
A NICK IN MY TITANIUM HOSE ......!?
PAAN (BANG)
GUAH ...!
AUTO REPAIR
SYSTEM CHECK
76%
GIKII (SKREE)
KIIII
...!!
THAT PULSE TRIGGERED THE TRAINS' EMERGENCY BRAKES.

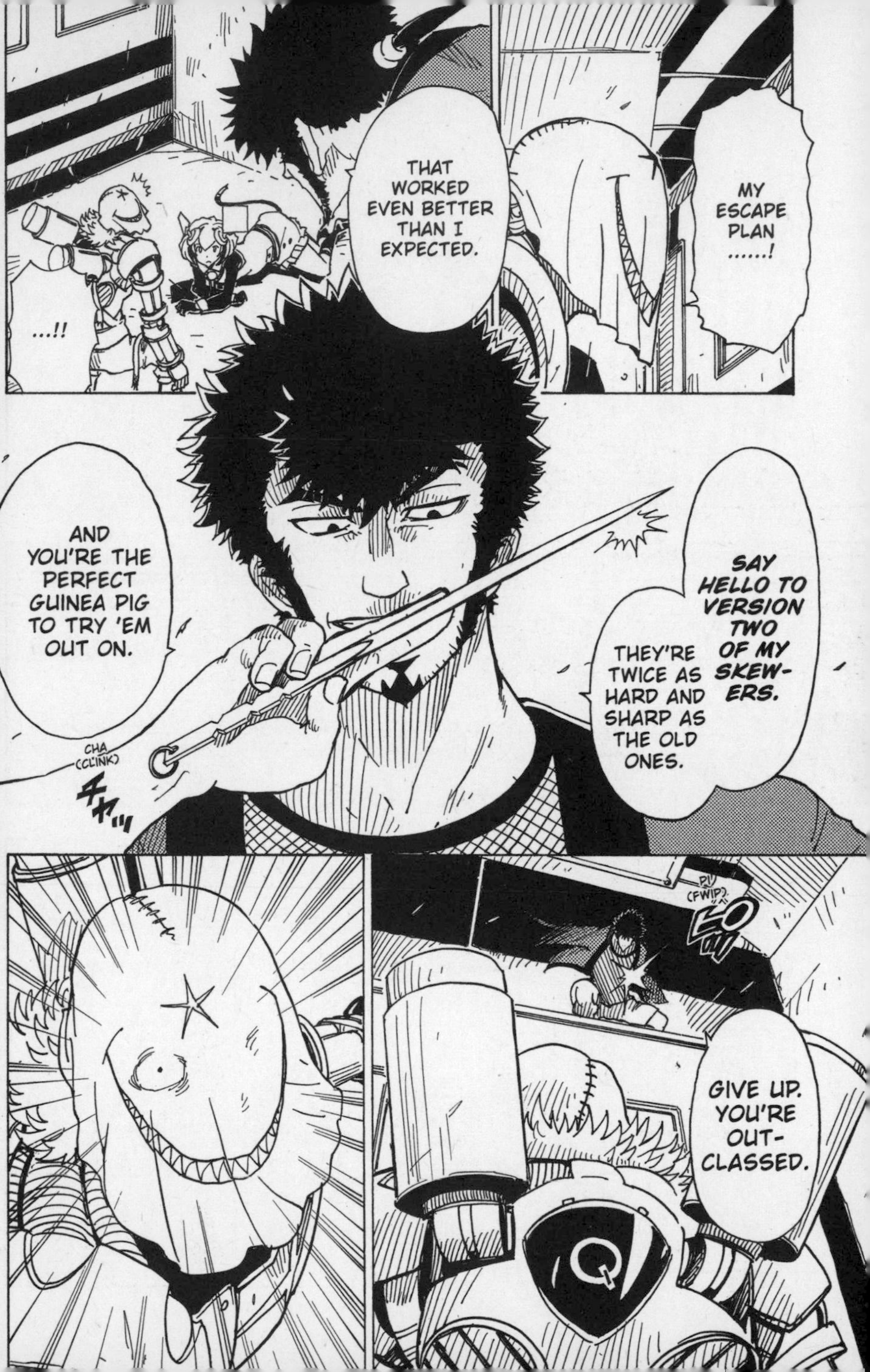
MY ESCAPE PLAN ......!
THAT WORKED EVEN BETTER THAN I EXPECTED.
...!!
SAY HELLO TO VERSION TWO OF MY SKEW-ERS.
THEY'RE TWICE AS HARD AND SHARP AS THE OLD ONES.
AND YOU'RE THE PERFECT GUINEA PIG TO TRY 'EM OUT ON.
CHA (CLINK)
PI (FWIP)
GIVE UP. YOU'RE OUT-CLASSED.

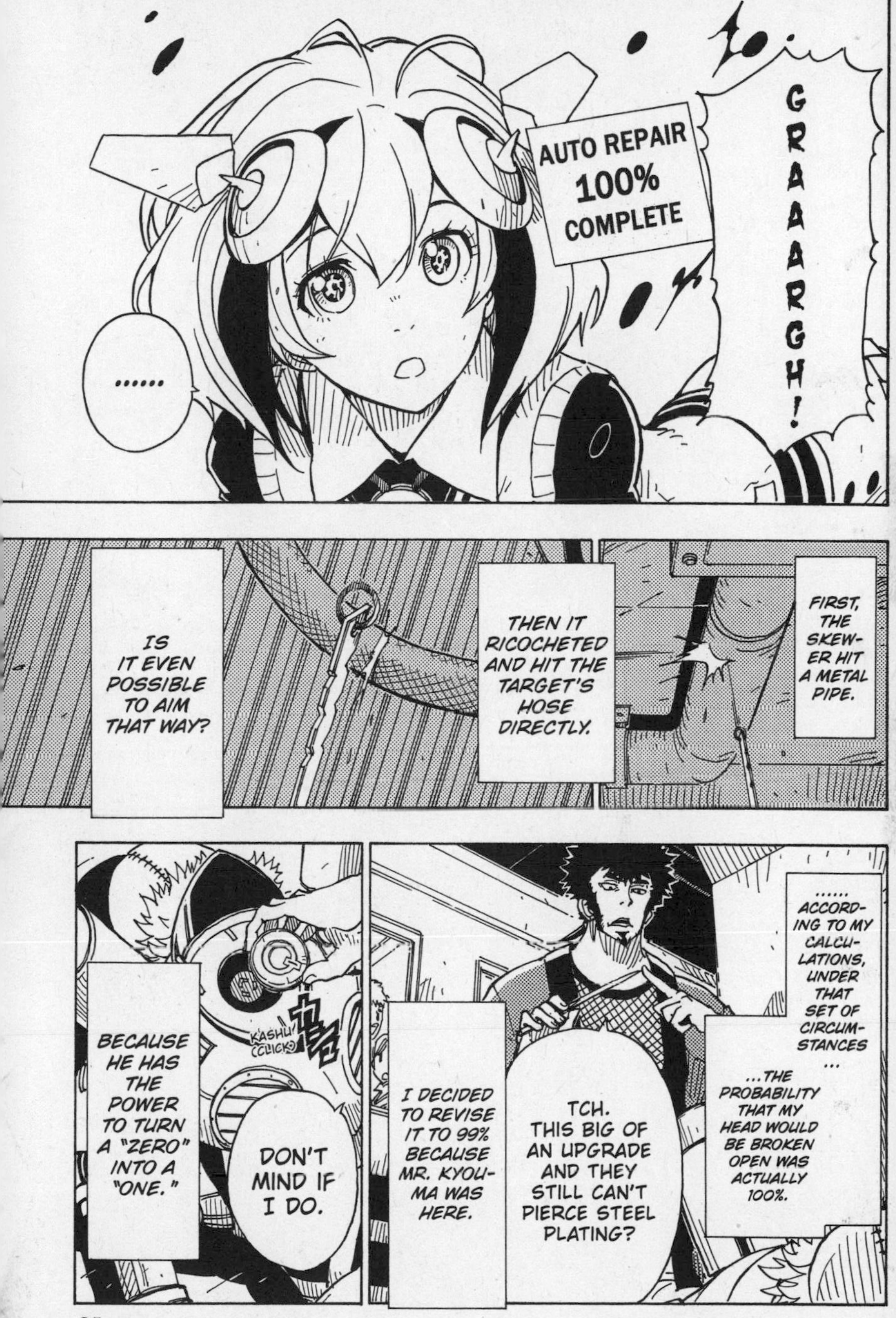
GRAAARGH!
AUTO REPAIR 100% COMPLETE
......
FIRST, THE SKEWER HIT A METAL PIPE.
THEN IT RICOCHETED AND HIT THE TARGET'S HOSE DIRECTLY.
IS IT EVEN POSSIBLE TO AIM THAT WAY?
......ACCORDING TO MY CALCULATIONS, UNDER THAT SET OF CIRCUMSTANCES...
...THE PROBABILITY THAT MY HEAD WOULD BE BROKEN OPEN WAS ACTUALLY 100%.
TCH. THIS BIG OF AN UPGRADE AND THEY STILL CAN'T PIERCE STEEL PLATING?
I DECIDED TO REVISE IT TO 99% BECAUSE MR. KYOUMA WAS HERE.
KASHU (CLICK)
DON'T MIND IF I DO.
BECAUSE HE HAS THE POWER TO TURN A "ZERO" INTO A "ONE."

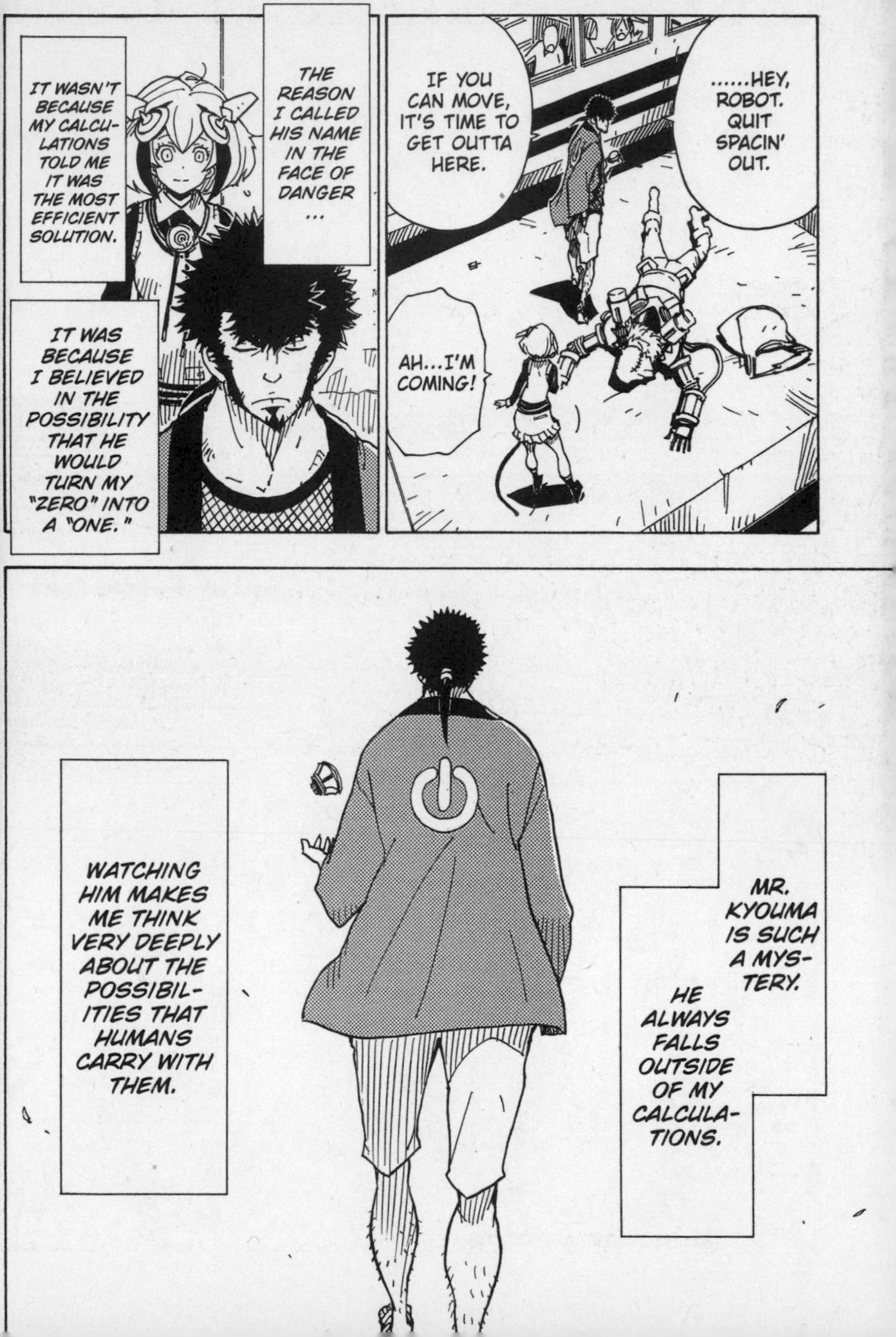
......HEY, ROBOT. QUIT SPACIN' OUT.
IF YOU CAN MOVE, IT'S TIME TO GET OUTTA HERE.
AH...I'M COMING!
THE REASON I CALLED HIS NAME IN THE FACE OF DANGER ...
IT WASN'T BECAUSE MY CALCULATIONS TOLD ME IT WAS THE MOST EFFICIENT SOLUTION.
IT WAS BECAUSE I BELIEVED IN THE POSSIBILITY THAT HE WOULD TURN MY "ZERO" INTO A "ONE."
MR. KYOUMA IS SUCH A MYSTERY.
HE ALWAYS FALLS OUTSIDE OF MY CALCULATIONS.
WATCHING HIM MAKES ME THINK VERY DEEPLY ABOUT THE POSSIBILITIES THAT HUMANS CARRY WITH THEM.

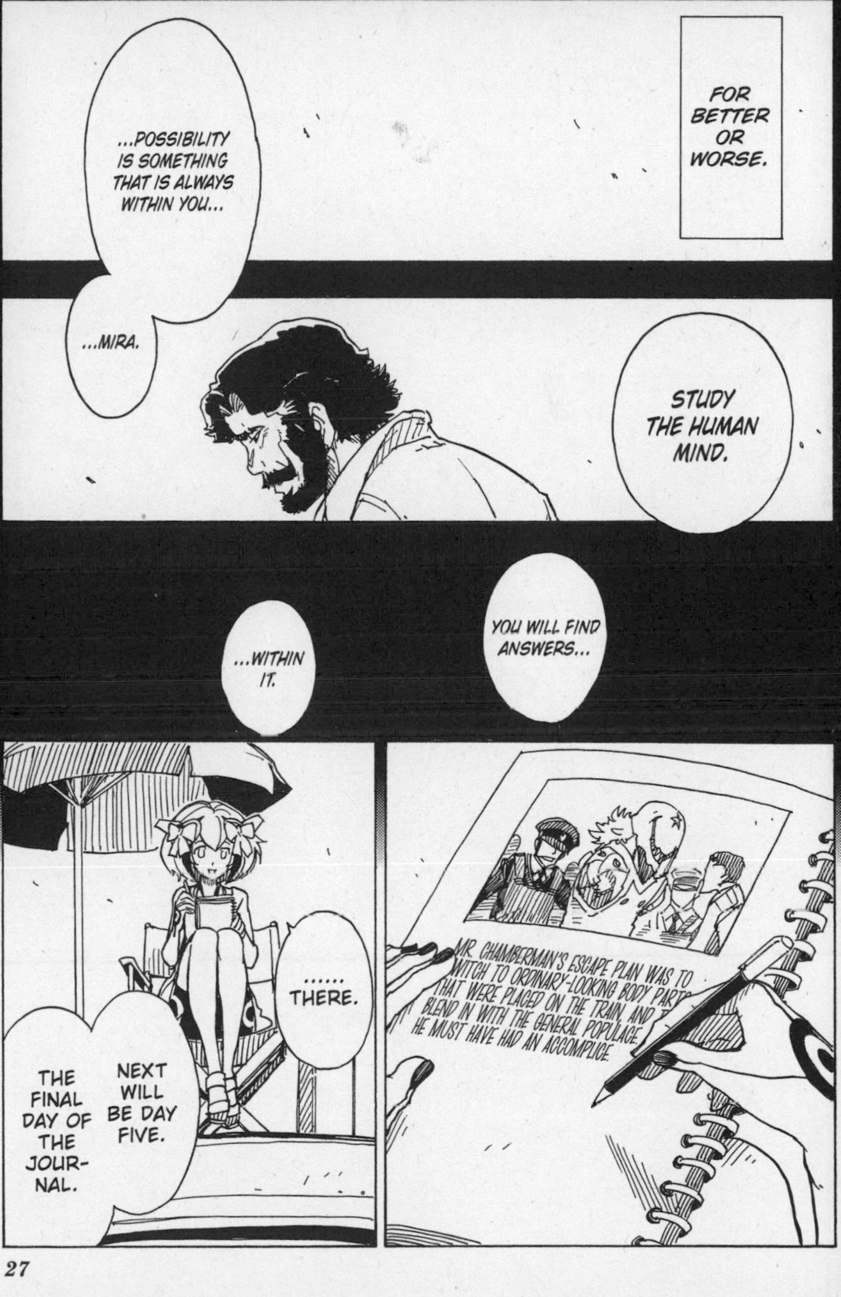
FOR BETTER OR WORSE.
...POSSIBILITY IS SOMETHING THAT IS ALWAYS WITHIN YOU...
...MIRA.
STUDY THE HUMAN MIND.
YOU WILL FIND ANSWERS...
...WITHIN IT.
MR. CHAMBERMAN'S ESCAPE PLAN WAS TO
WITCH TO ORDINARY-LOOKING BODY PARTS
THAT WERE PLACED ON THE TRAIN, AND T
BLEND IN WITH THE GENERAL POPULACE.
HE MUST HAVE HAD AN ACCOMPLICE.
......THERE.
NEXT WILL BE DAY FIVE.
THE FINAL DAY OF THE JOURNAL.

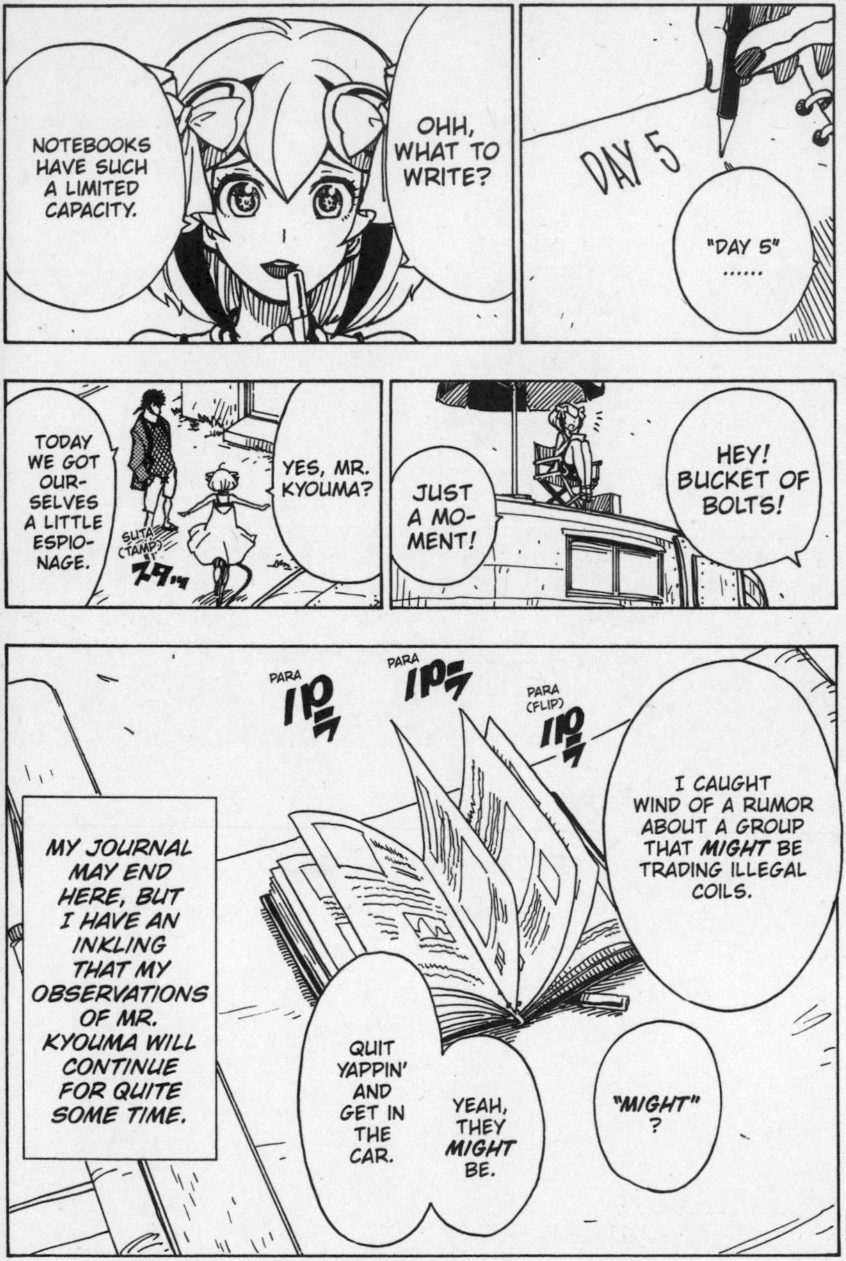
DAY 5
"DAY 5" ......
OHH, WHAT TO WRITE?
NOTEBOOKS HAVE SUCH A LIMITED CAPACITY.
HEY! BUCKET OF BOLTS!
JUST A MO-MENT!
YES, MR. KYOUMA?
TODAY WE GOT OUR-SELVES A LITTLE ESPIO-NAGE.
SUTA (TAMP)
PARA
PARA
PARA (FLIP)
I CAUGHT WIND OF A RUMOR ABOUT A GROUP THAT *MIGHT* BE TRADING ILLEGAL COILS.
"MIGHT" ?
YEAH, THEY *MIGHT* BE.
QUIT YAPPIN' AND GET IN THE CAR.
MY JOURNAL MAY END HERE, BUT I HAVE AN INKLING THAT MY OBSERVATIONS OF MR. KYOUMA WILL CONTINUE FOR QUITE SOME TIME.

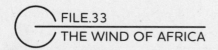
FILE.33
THE WIND OF AFRICA

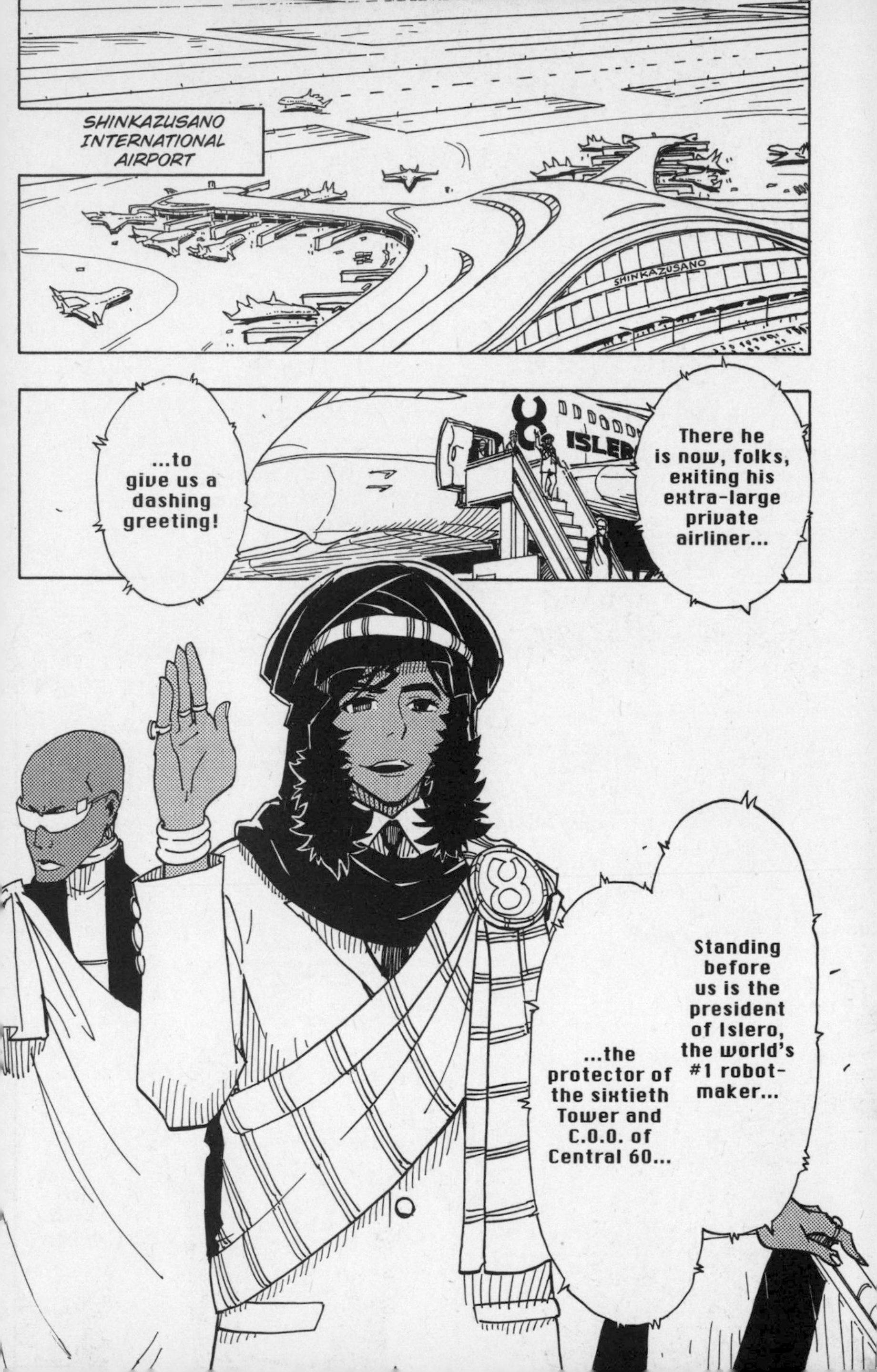
SHINKAZUSANO INTERNATIONAL AIRPORT
SHINKAZUSANO
There he is now, folks, exiting his extra-large private airliner...
...to give us a dashing greeting!
Standing before us is the president of Islero, the world's #1 robot-maker...
...the protector of the sixtieth Tower and C.O.O. of Central 60...

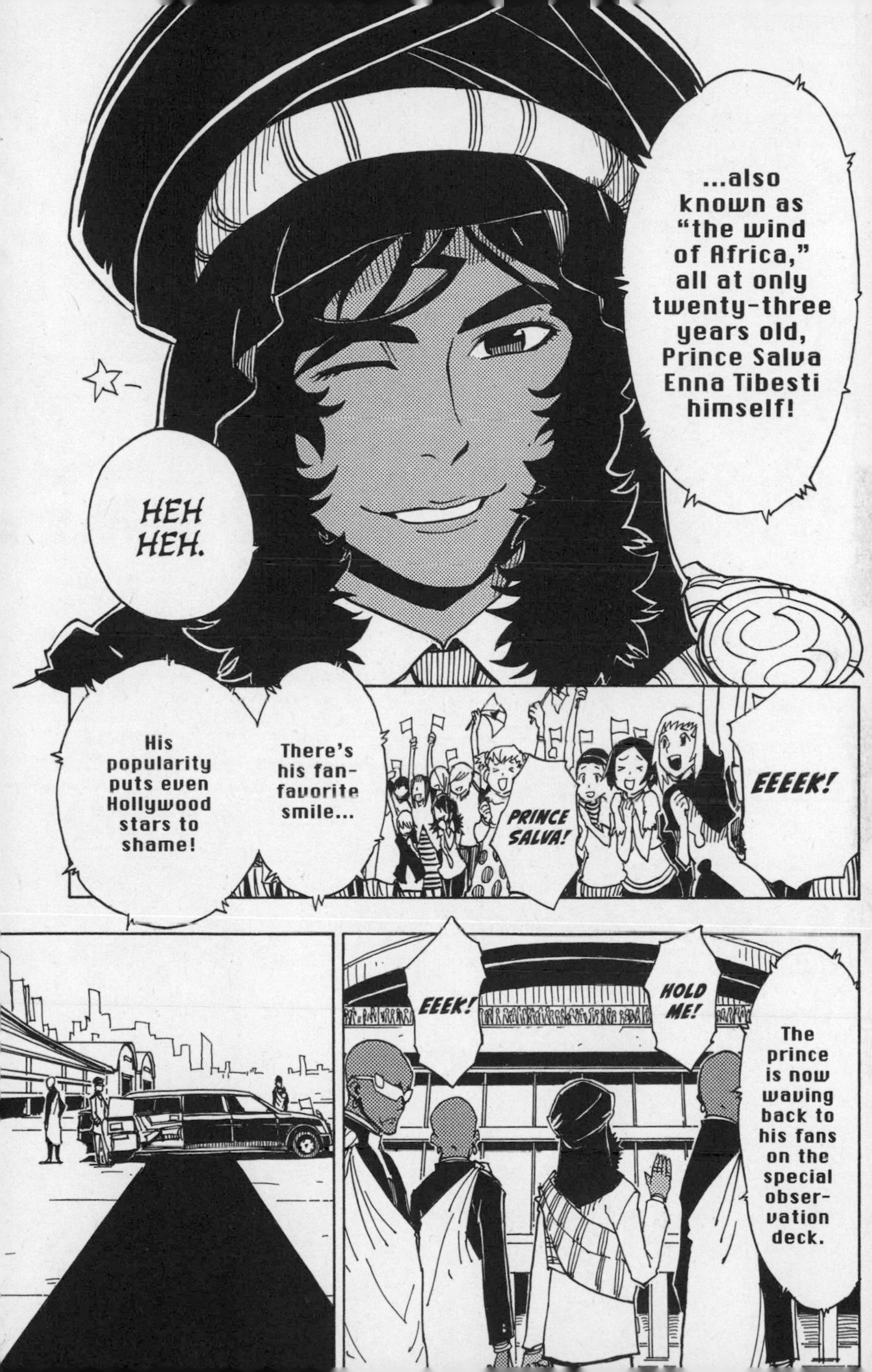
...also known as "the wind of Africa," all at only twenty-three years old, Prince Salva Enna Tibesti himself!
HEH HEH.
EEEEK!
PRINCE SALVA!
There's his fan-favorite smile...
His popularity puts even Hollywood stars to shame!
The prince is now waving back to his fans on the special observation deck.
HOLD ME!
EEEK!

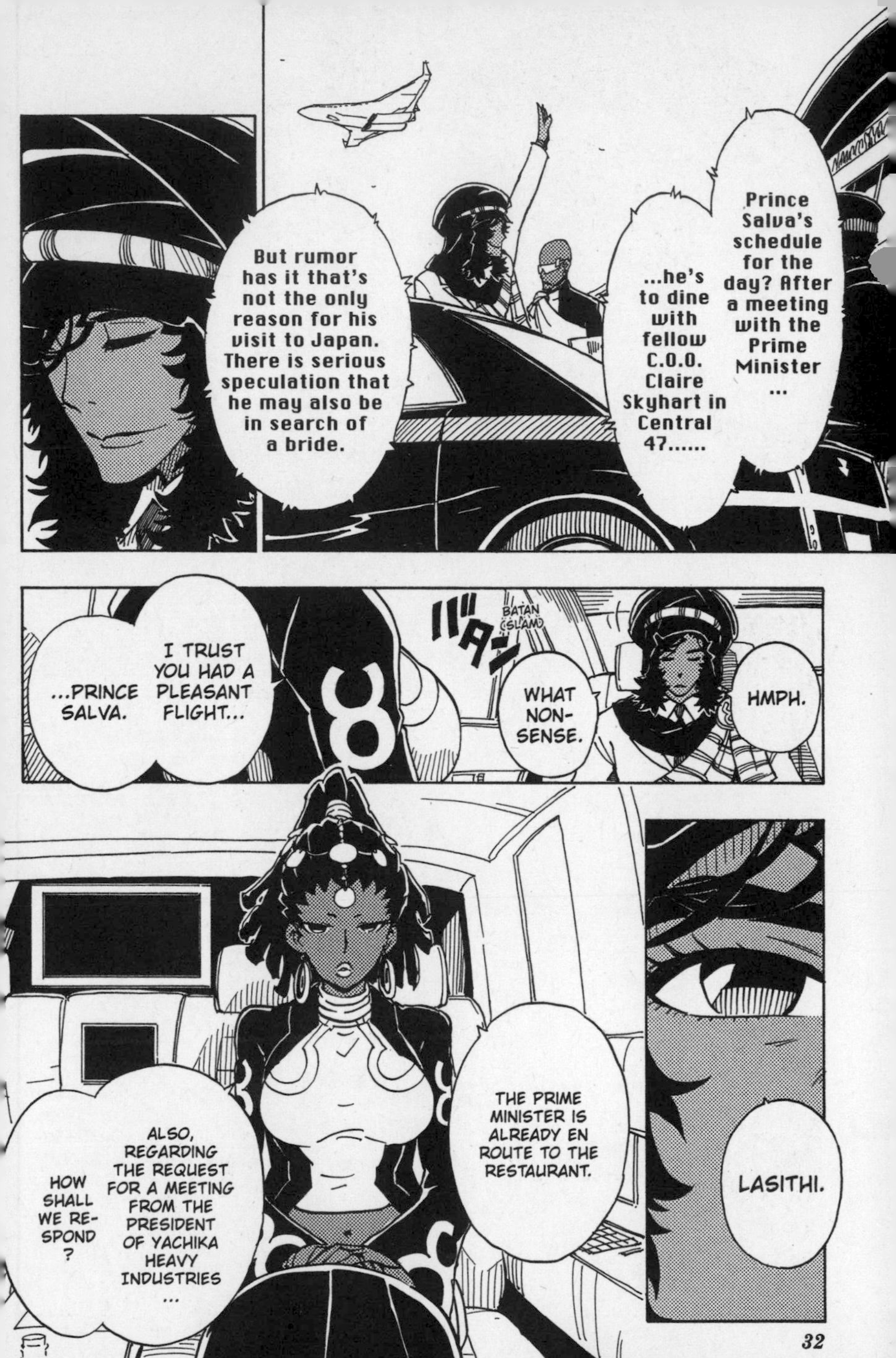
Prince Salva's schedule for the day? After a meeting with the Prime Minister ...
...he's to dine with fellow C.O.O. Claire Skyhart in Central 47......
But rumor has it that's not the only reason for his visit to Japan. There is serious speculation that he may also be in search of a bride.
HMPH.
BATAN (SLAM)
WHAT NONSENSE.
I TRUST YOU HAD A PLEASANT FLIGHT...
...PRINCE SALVA.
LASITHI.
THE PRIME MINISTER IS ALREADY EN ROUTE TO THE RESTAURANT.
ALSO, REGARDING THE REQUEST FOR A MEETING FROM THE PRESIDENT OF YACHIKA HEAVY INDUSTRIES ...
HOW SHALL WE RESPOND?

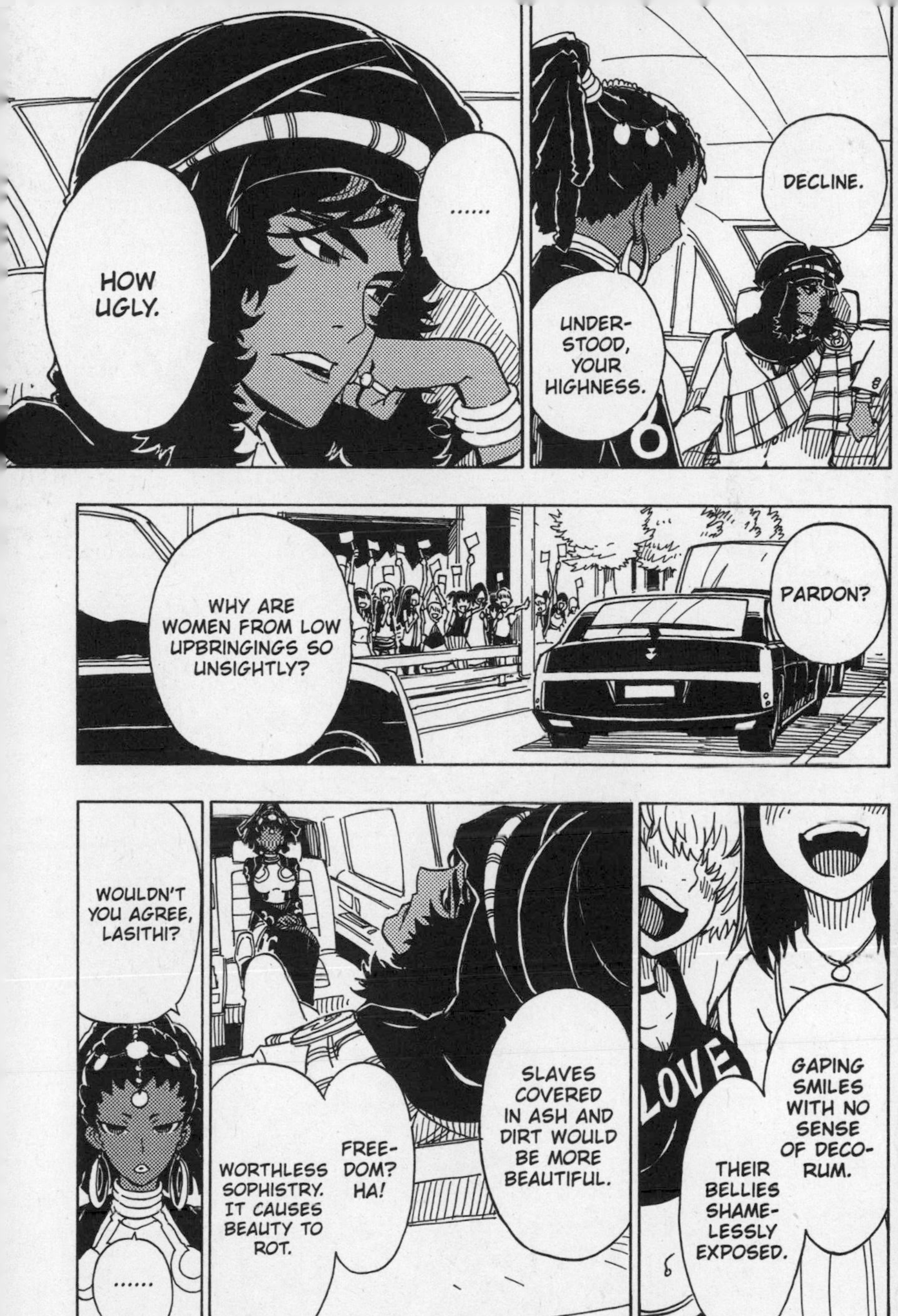
DECLINE.
UNDER-STOOD, YOUR HIGHNESS.
......
HOW UGLY.
PARDON?
WHY ARE WOMEN FROM LOW UPBRINGINGS SO UNSIGHTLY?
GAPING SMILES WITH NO SENSE OF DECO-RUM.
THEIR BELLIES SHAME-LESSLY EXPOSED.
SLAVES COVERED IN ASH AND DIRT WOULD BE MORE BEAUTIFUL.
FREE-DOM? HA!
WORTHLESS SOPHISTRY. IT CAUSES BEAUTY TO ROT.
WOULDN'T YOU AGREE, LASITHI?
......

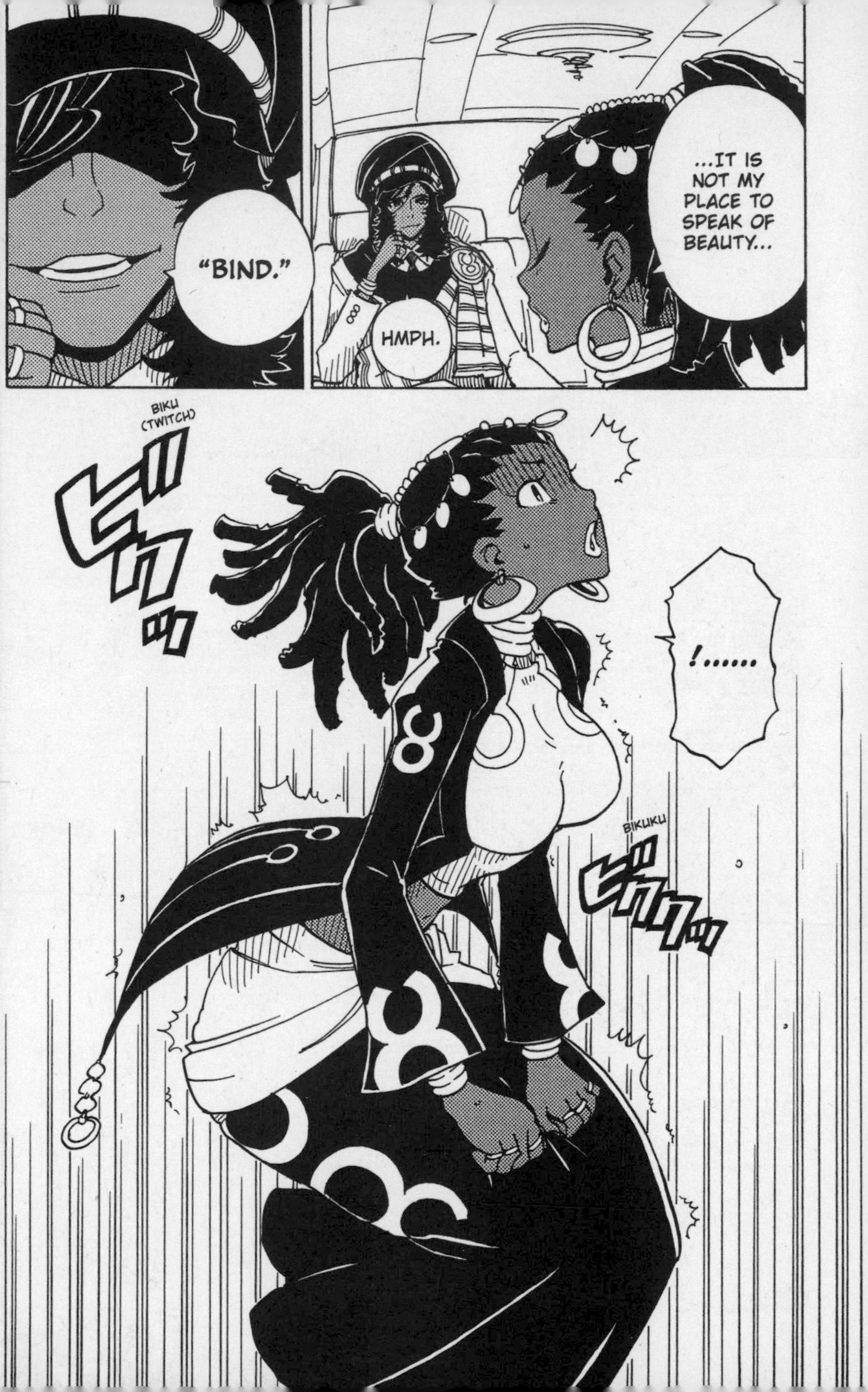
...IT IS NOT MY PLACE TO SPEAK OF BEAUTY...
HMPH.
"BIND."
!......
BIKU (TWITCH)
BIKUKU

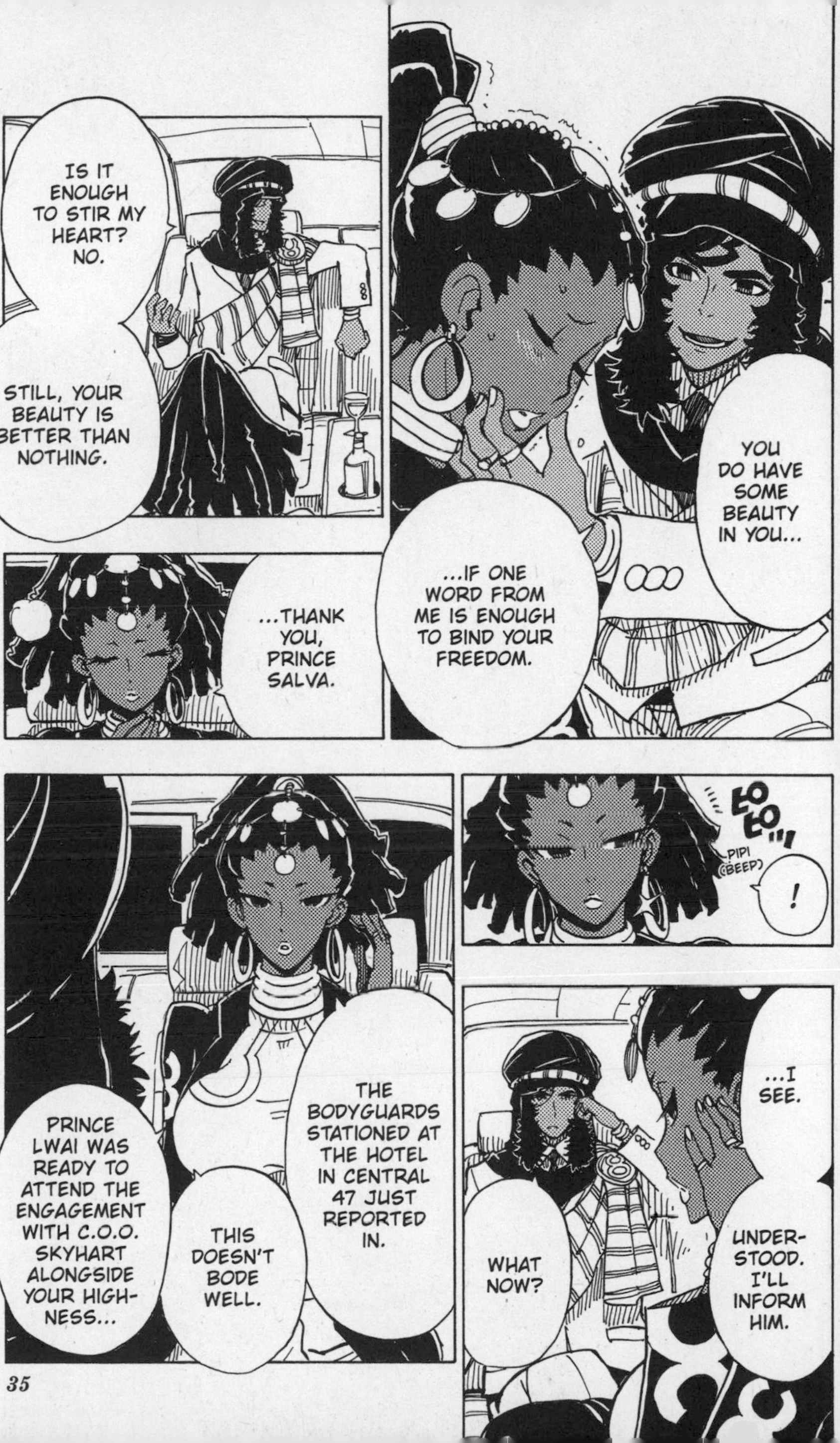
YOU DO HAVE SOME BEAUTY IN YOU...
...IF ONE WORD FROM ME IS ENOUGH TO BIND YOUR FREEDOM.
IS IT ENOUGH TO STIR MY HEART? NO.
STILL, YOUR BEAUTY IS BETTER THAN NOTHING.
...THANK YOU, PRINCE SALVA.
PIPI (BEEP)
!
...I SEE.
UNDER-STOOD. I'LL INFORM HIM.
WHAT NOW?
THE BODYGUARDS STATIONED AT THE HOTEL IN CENTRAL 47 JUST REPORTED IN.
PRINCE LWAI WAS READY TO ATTEND THE ENGAGEMENT WITH C.O.O. SKYHART ALONGSIDE YOUR HIGH-NESS...
THIS DOESN'T BODE WELL.

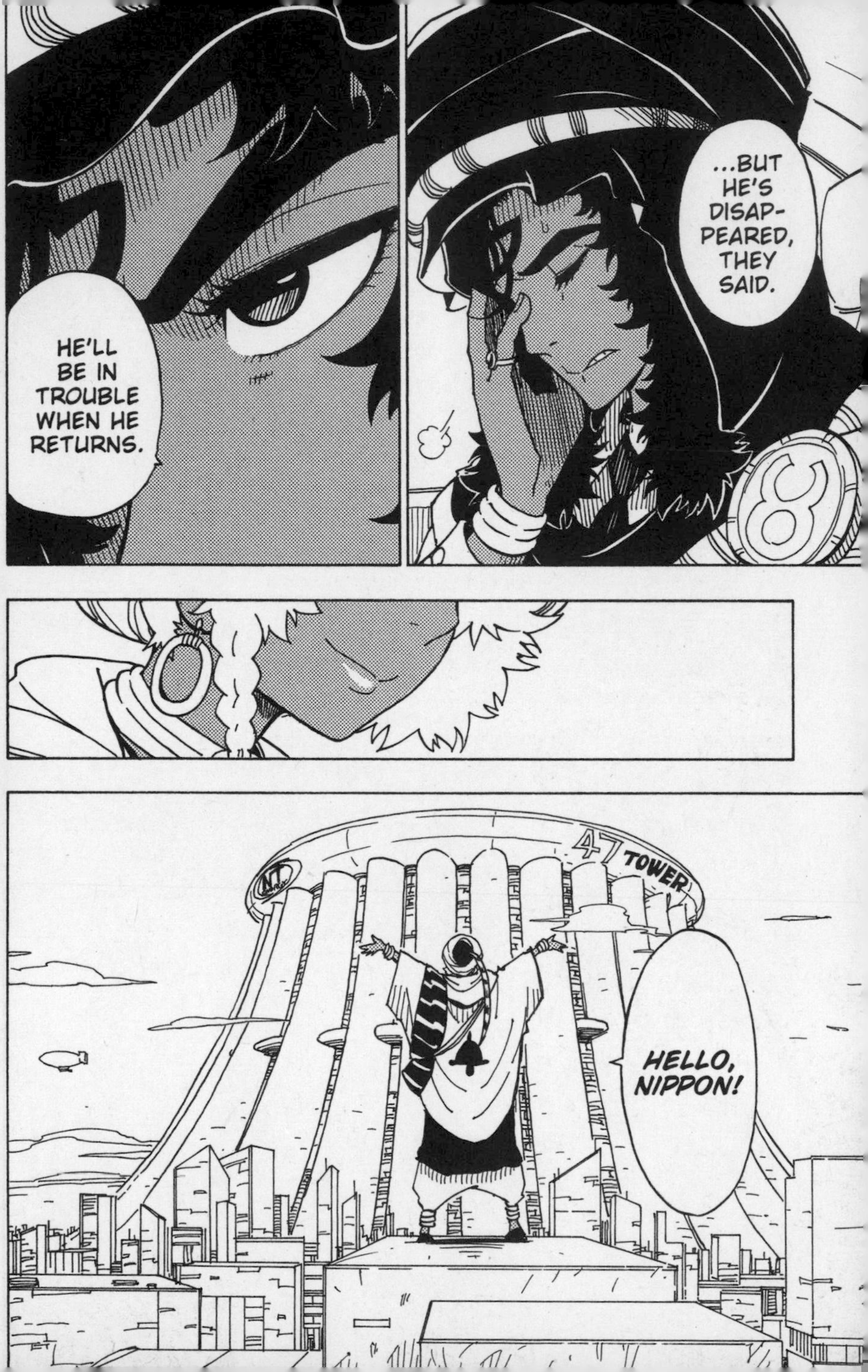

...BUT HE'S DISAP-PEARED, THEY SAID.
HE'LL BE IN TROUBLE WHEN HE RETURNS.
47 TOWER
HELLO, NIPPON!

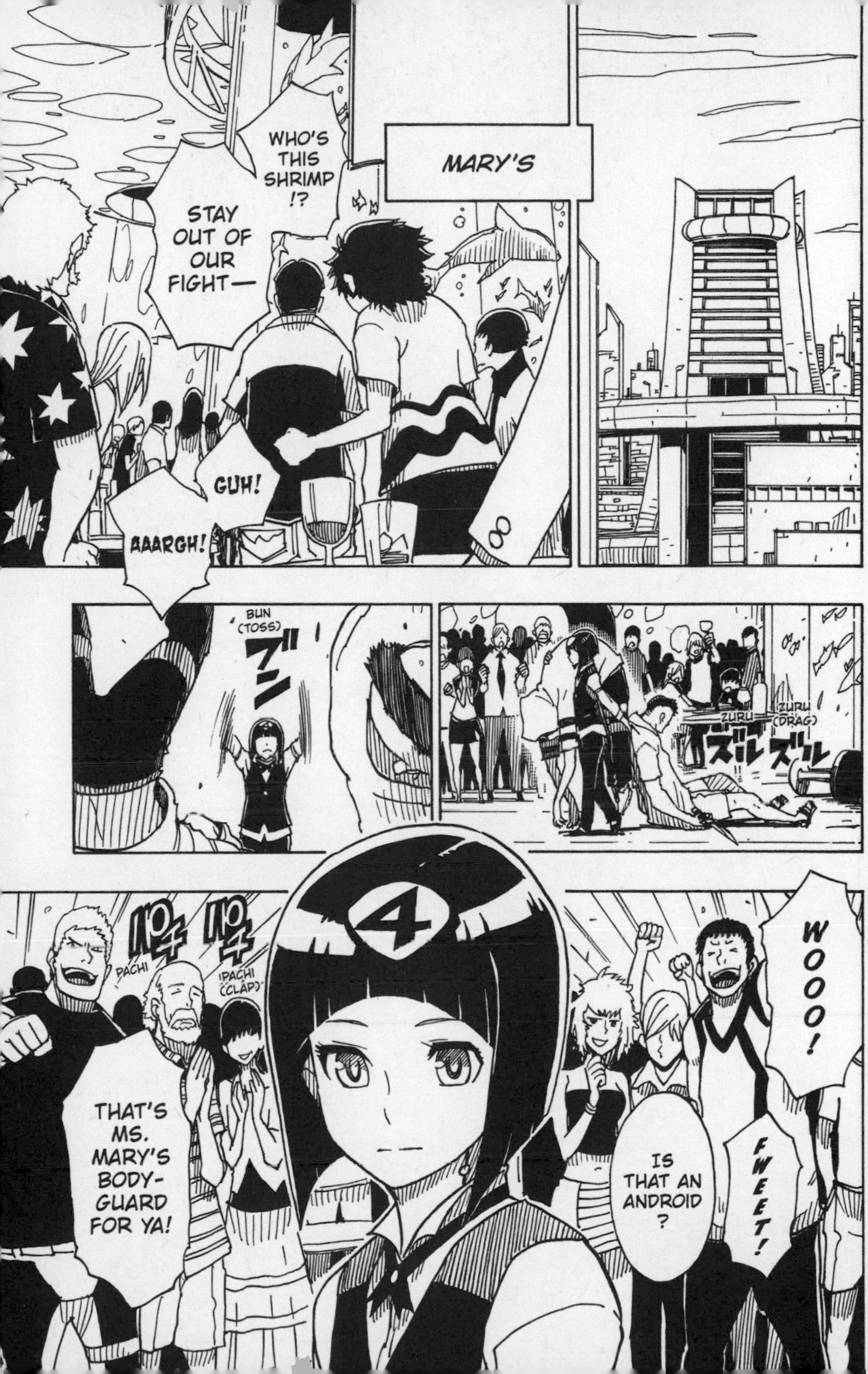
MARY'S
WHO'S THIS SHRIMP !?
STAY OUT OF OUR FIGHT—
GUH!
AAARGH!
ZURU ZURU (DRAG)
ズルズル
BUN (TOSS)
ブン
WOOOO!
FWEET!
IS THAT AN ANDROID ?
PACHI PACHI (CLAP)
パチパチ
THAT'S MS. MARY'S BODY-GUARD FOR YA!

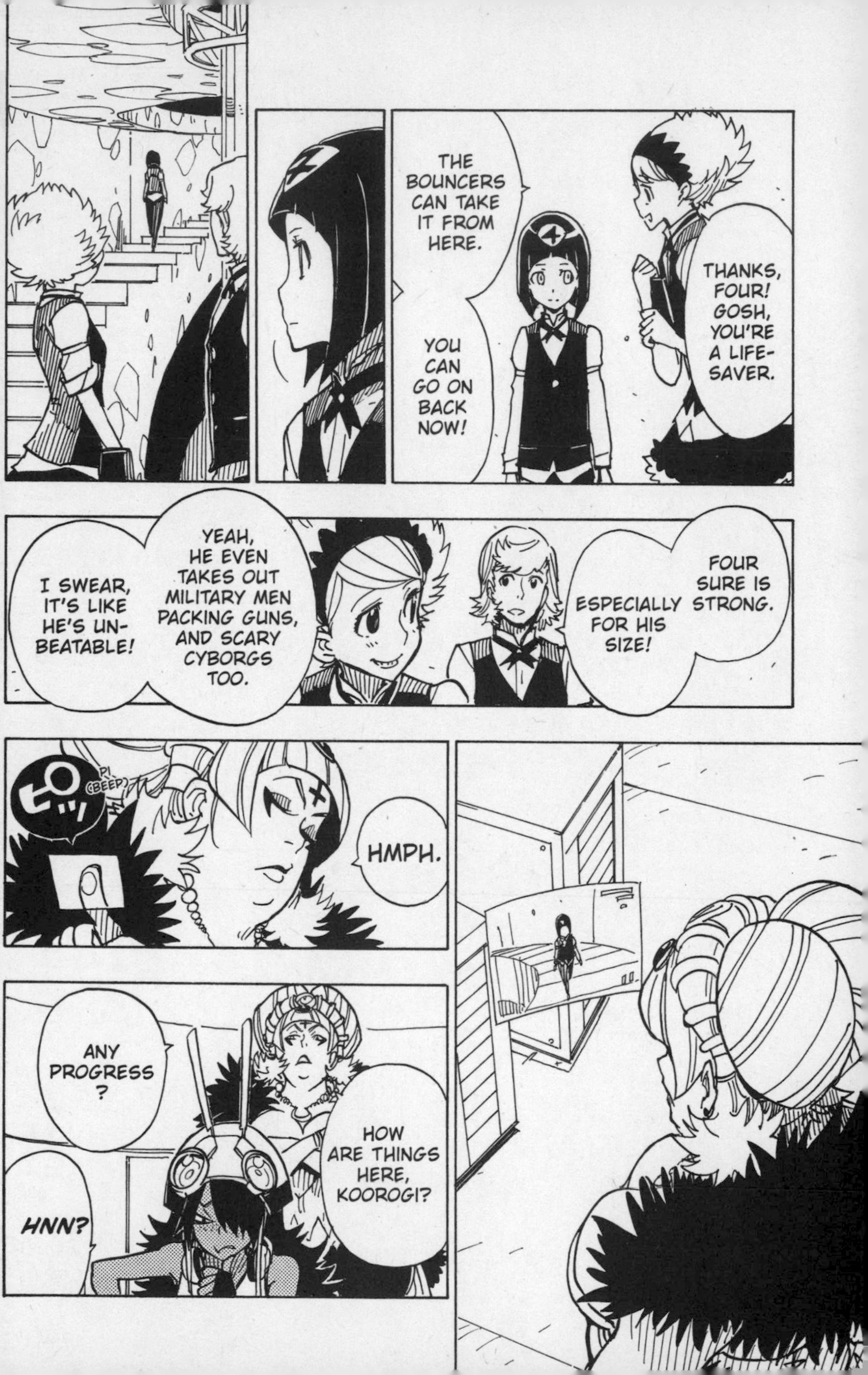
THANKS, FOUR! GOSH, YOU'RE A LIFE-SAVER.
THE BOUNCERS CAN TAKE IT FROM HERE.
YOU CAN GO ON BACK NOW!
FOUR SURE IS STRONG.
ESPECIALLY FOR HIS SIZE!
YEAH, HE EVEN TAKES OUT MILITARY MEN PACKING GUNS, AND SCARY CYBORGS TOO.
I SWEAR, IT'S LIKE HE'S UN-BEATABLE!
HMPH.
ピッ
PI (BEEP)
HOW ARE THINGS HERE, KOOROGI?
ANY PROGRESS?
HNN?

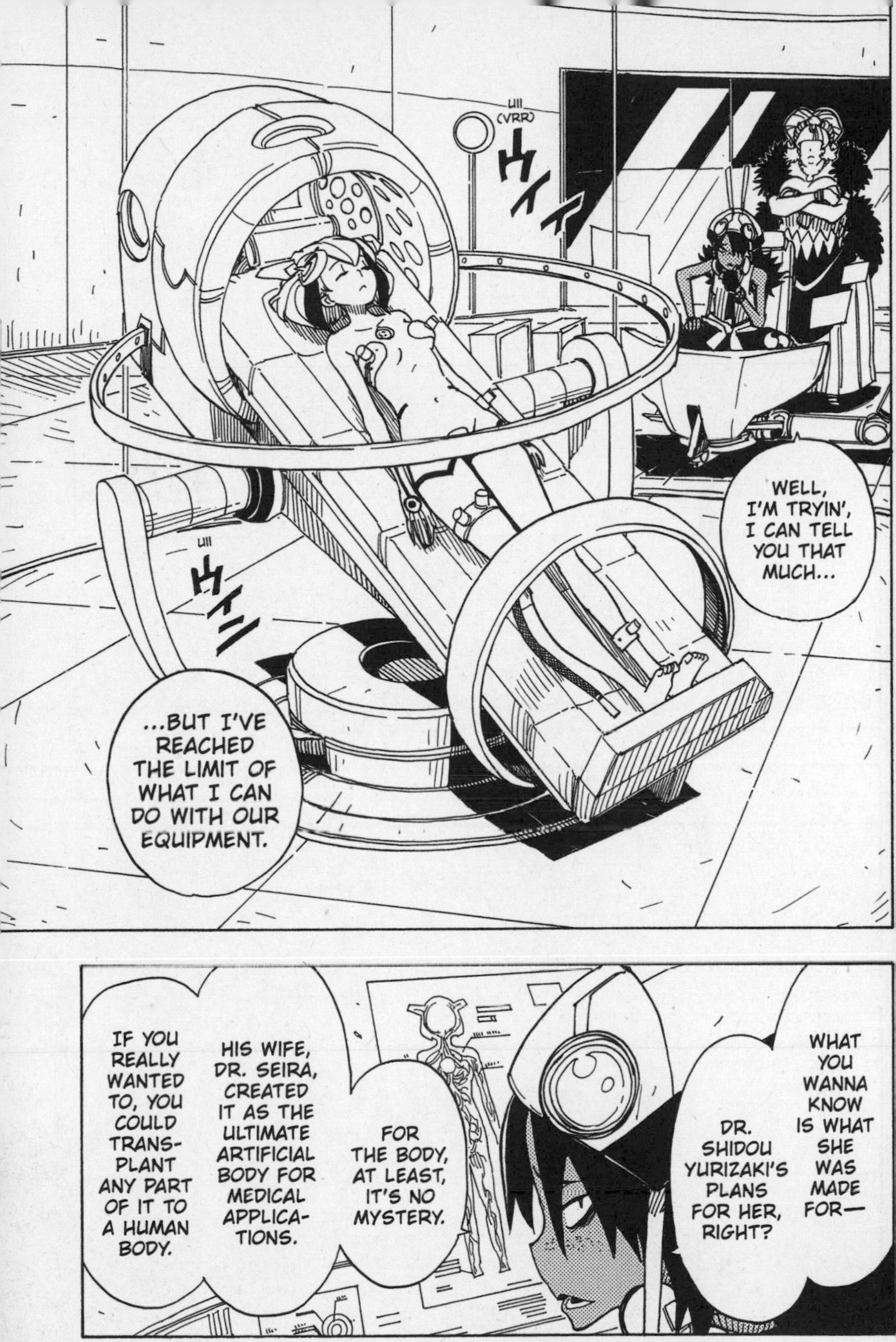
UII (VRR)
WELL, I'M TRYIN', I CAN TELL YOU THAT MUCH...
UII
...BUT I'VE REACHED THE LIMIT OF WHAT I CAN DO WITH OUR EQUIPMENT.
WHAT YOU WANNA KNOW IS WHAT SHE WAS MADE FOR—
DR. SHIDOU YURIZAKI'S PLANS FOR HER, RIGHT?
FOR THE BODY, AT LEAST, IT'S NO MYSTERY.
HIS WIFE, DR. SEIRA, CREATED IT AS THE ULTIMATE ARTIFICIAL BODY FOR MEDICAL APPLICATIONS.
IF YOU REALLY WANTED TO, YOU COULD TRANSPLANT ANY PART OF IT TO A HUMAN BODY.

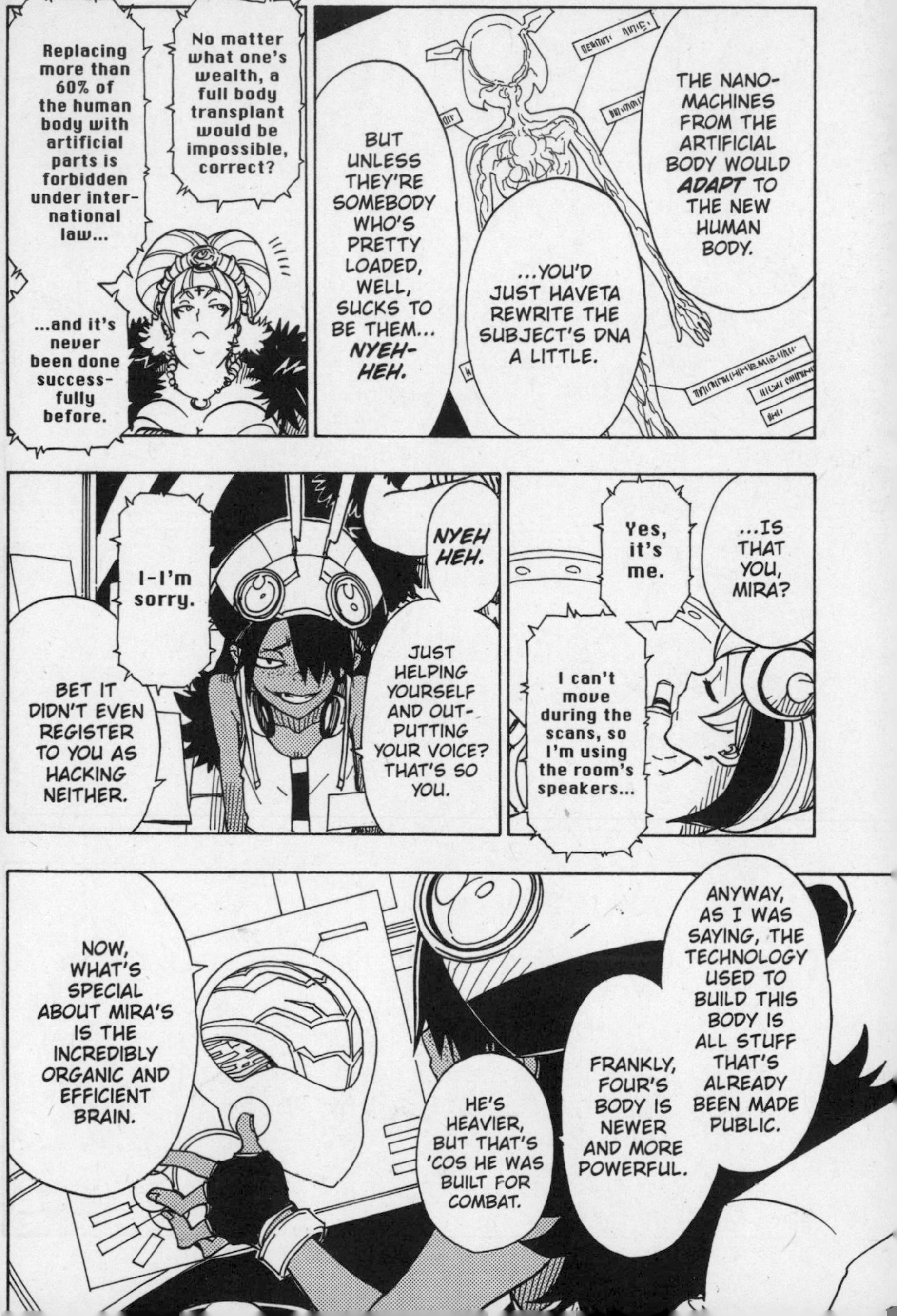
THE NANO-MACHINES FROM THE ARTIFICIAL BODY WOULD *ADAPT* TO THE NEW HUMAN BODY.
...YOU'D JUST HAVETA REWRITE THE SUBJECT'S DNA A LITTLE.
BUT UNLESS THEY'RE SOMEBODY WHO'S PRETTY LOADED, WELL, SUCKS TO BE THEM... *NYEH-HEH.*
No matter what one's wealth, a full body transplant would be impossible, correct?
Replacing more than 60% of the human body with artificial parts is forbidden under inter-national law...
...and it's never been done success-fully before.
...IS THAT YOU, MIRA?
Yes, it's me.
I can't move during the scans, so I'm using the room's speakers...
NYEH HEH.
JUST HELPING YOURSELF AND OUT-PUTTING YOUR VOICE? THAT'S SO YOU.
I-I'm sorry.
BET IT DIDN'T EVEN REGISTER TO YOU AS HACKING NEITHER.
ANYWAY, AS I WAS SAYING, THE TECHNOLOGY USED TO BUILD THIS BODY IS ALL STUFF THAT'S ALREADY BEEN MADE PUBLIC.
FRANKLY, FOUR'S BODY IS NEWER AND MORE POWERFUL.
HE'S HEAVIER, BUT THAT'S 'COS HE WAS BUILT FOR COMBAT.
NOW, WHAT'S SPECIAL ABOUT MIRA'S IS THE INCREDIBLY ORGANIC AND EFFICIENT BRAIN.

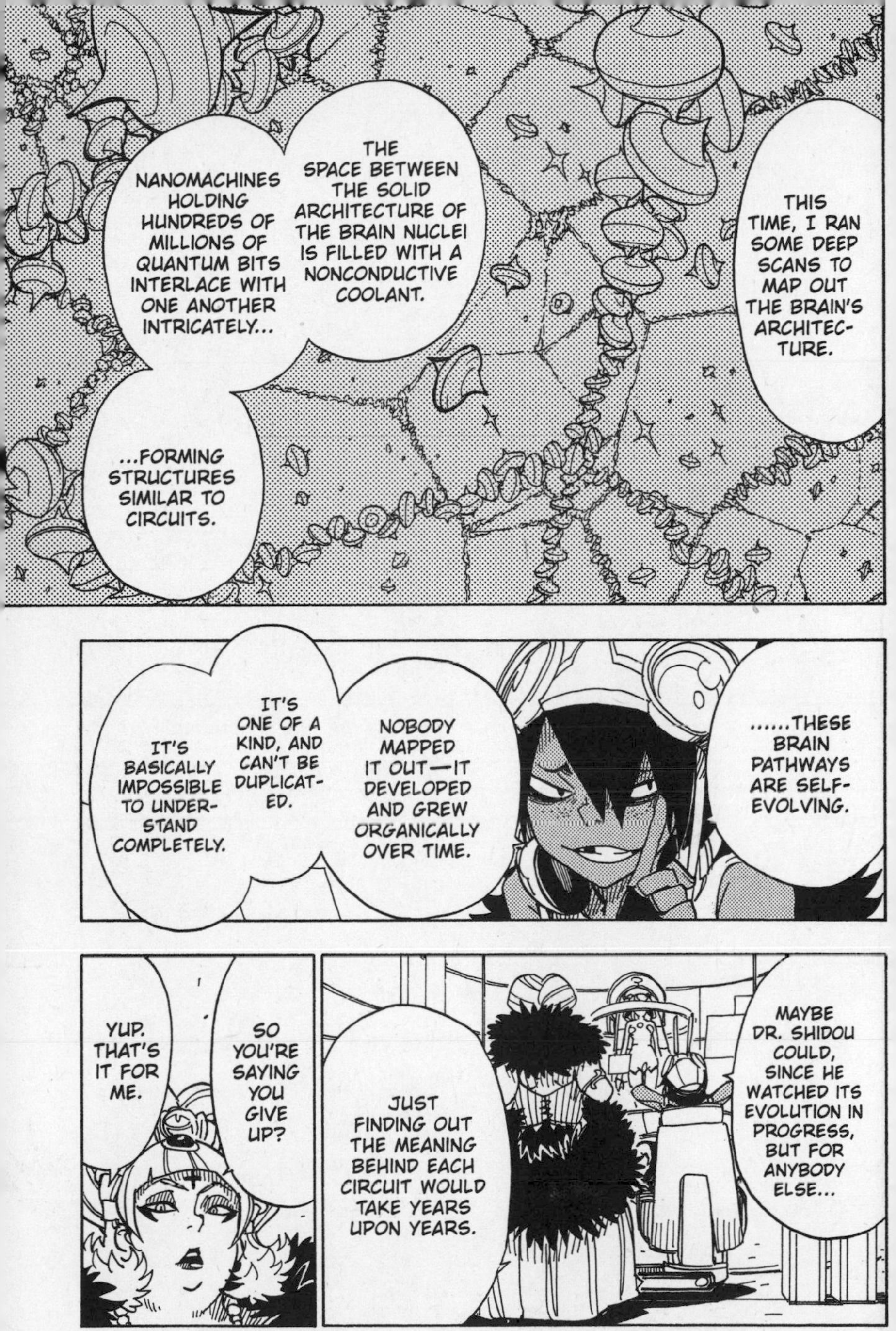
THIS TIME, I RAN SOME DEEP SCANS TO MAP OUT THE BRAIN'S ARCHITEC-TURE.
THE SPACE BETWEEN THE SOLID ARCHITECTURE OF THE BRAIN NUCLEI IS FILLED WITH A NONCONDUCTIVE COOLANT.
NANOMACHINES HOLDING HUNDREDS OF MILLIONS OF QUANTUM BITS INTERLACE WITH ONE ANOTHER INTRICATELY...
...FORMING STRUCTURES SIMILAR TO CIRCUITS.
......THESE BRAIN PATHWAYS ARE SELF-EVOLVING.
NOBODY MAPPED IT OUT—IT DEVELOPED AND GREW ORGANICALLY OVER TIME.
IT'S ONE OF A KIND, AND CAN'T BE DUPLICAT-ED.
IT'S BASICALLY IMPOSSIBLE TO UNDER-STAND COMPLETELY.
MAYBE DR. SHIDOU COULD, SINCE HE WATCHED ITS EVOLUTION IN PROGRESS, BUT FOR ANYBODY ELSE...
JUST FINDING OUT THE MEANING BEHIND EACH CIRCUIT WOULD TAKE YEARS UPON YEARS.
SO YOU'RE SAYING YOU GIVE UP?
YUP. THAT'S IT FOR ME.

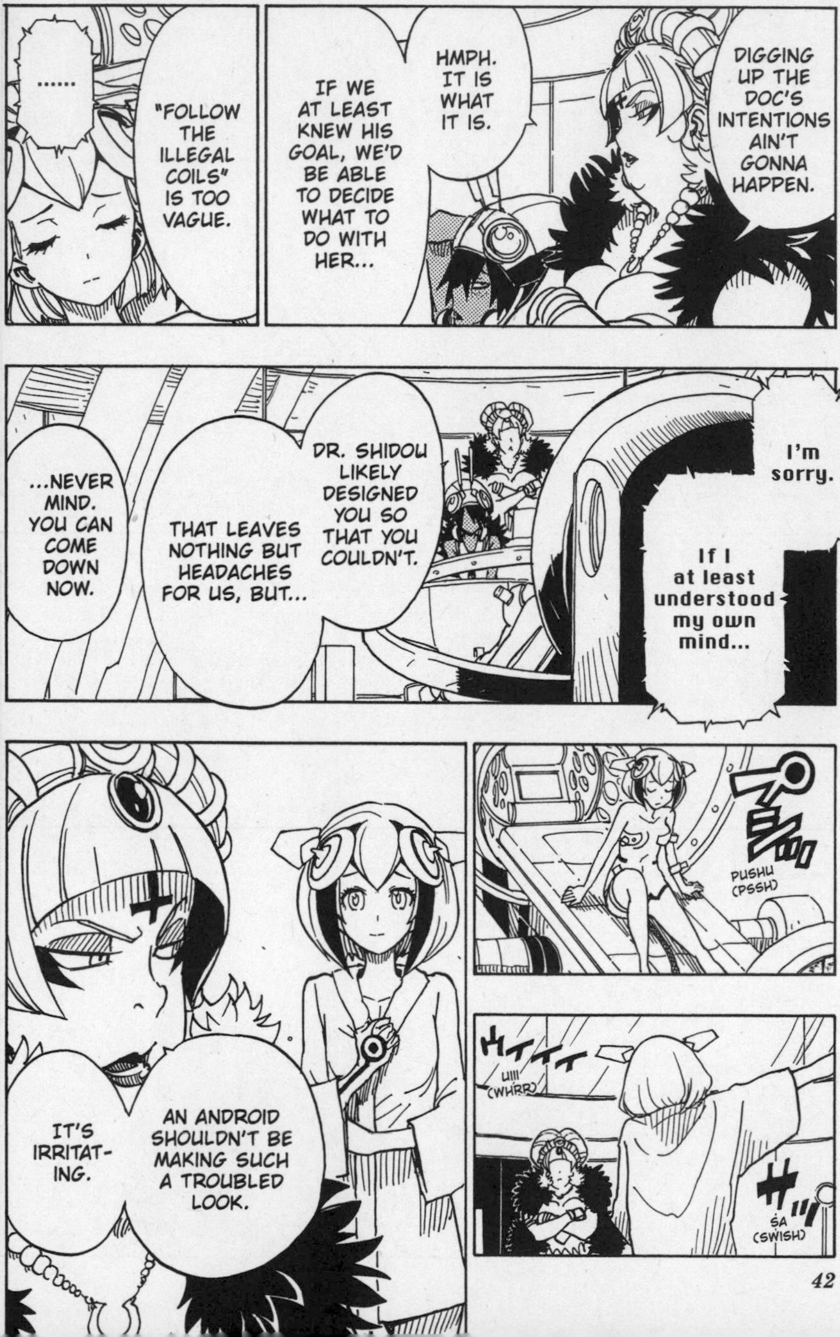
DIGGING UP THE DOC'S INTENTIONS AIN'T GONNA HAPPEN.
HMPH. IT IS WHAT IT IS.
IF WE AT LEAST KNEW HIS GOAL, WE'D BE ABLE TO DECIDE WHAT TO DO WITH HER...
"FOLLOW THE ILLEGAL COILS" IS TOO VAGUE.
......
I'm sorry.
If I at least understood my own mind...
DR. SHIDOU LIKELY DESIGNED YOU SO THAT YOU COULDN'T.
THAT LEAVES NOTHING BUT HEADACHES FOR US, BUT...
...NEVER MIND. YOU CAN COME DOWN NOW.
PUSHU (PSSH)
UIII (WHRR)
SA (SWISH)
AN ANDROID SHOULDN'T BE MAKING SUCH A TROUBLED LOOK.
IT'S IRRITATING.

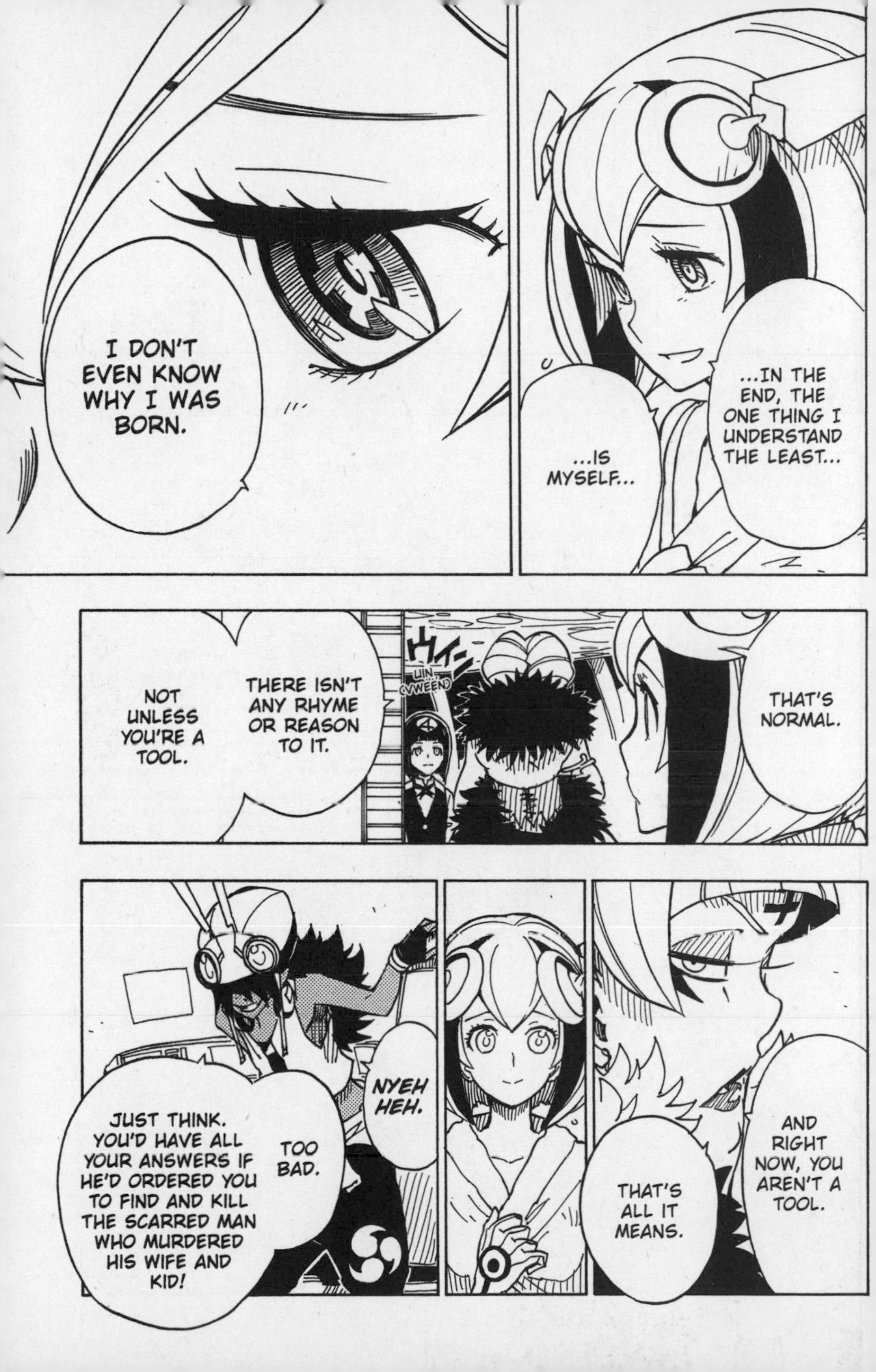
...IN THE END, THE ONE THING I UNDERSTAND THE LEAST...
...IS MYSELF...
I DON'T EVEN KNOW WHY I WAS BORN.
THAT'S NORMAL.
ウィーン
UIN (VWEEN)
THERE ISN'T ANY RHYME OR REASON TO IT.
NOT UNLESS YOU'RE A TOOL.
AND RIGHT NOW, YOU AREN'T A TOOL.
THAT'S ALL IT MEANS.
NYEH HEH.
TOO BAD.
JUST THINK. YOU'D HAVE ALL YOUR ANSWERS IF HE'D ORDERED YOU TO FIND AND KILL THE SCARRED MAN WHO MURDERED HIS WIFE AND KID!

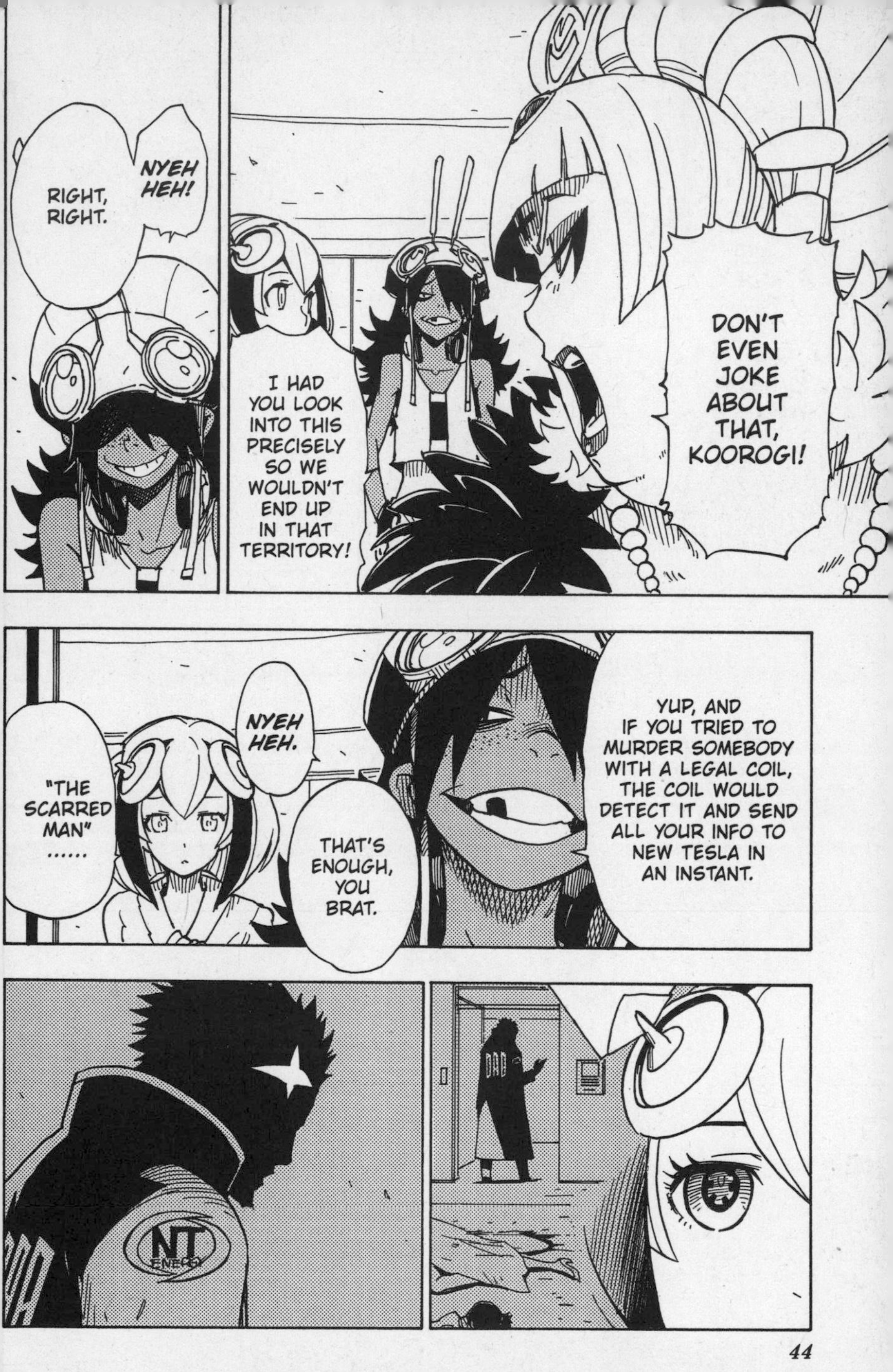
DON'T EVEN JOKE ABOUT THAT, KOOROGI!
I HAD YOU LOOK INTO THIS PRECISELY SO WE WOULDN'T END UP IN THAT TERRITORY!
NYEH HEH!
RIGHT, RIGHT.
YUP, AND IF YOU TRIED TO MURDER SOMEBODY WITH A LEGAL COIL, THE COIL WOULD DETECT IT AND SEND ALL YOUR INFO TO NEW TESLA IN AN INSTANT.
NYEH HEH.
THAT'S ENOUGH, YOU BRAT.
"THE SCARRED MAN" ......
NT ENERGY

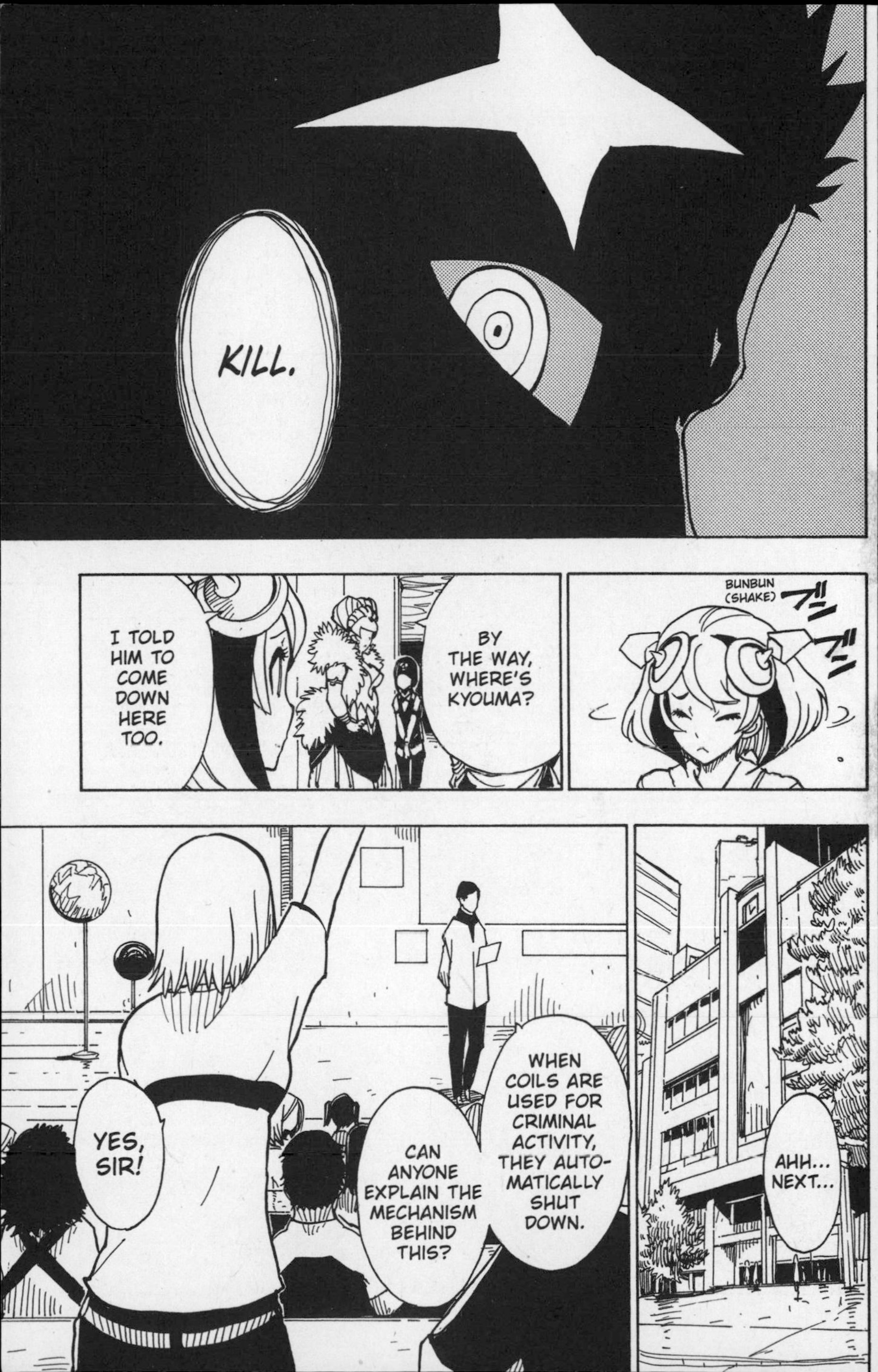
KILL.
BUNBUN (SHAKE)
BY THE WAY, WHERE'S KYOUMA?
I TOLD HIM TO COME DOWN HERE TOO.
AHH... NEXT...
WHEN COILS ARE USED FOR CRIMINAL ACTIVITY, THEY AUTO-MATICALLY SHUT DOWN.
CAN ANYONE EXPLAIN THE MECHANISM BEHIND THIS?
YES, SIR!

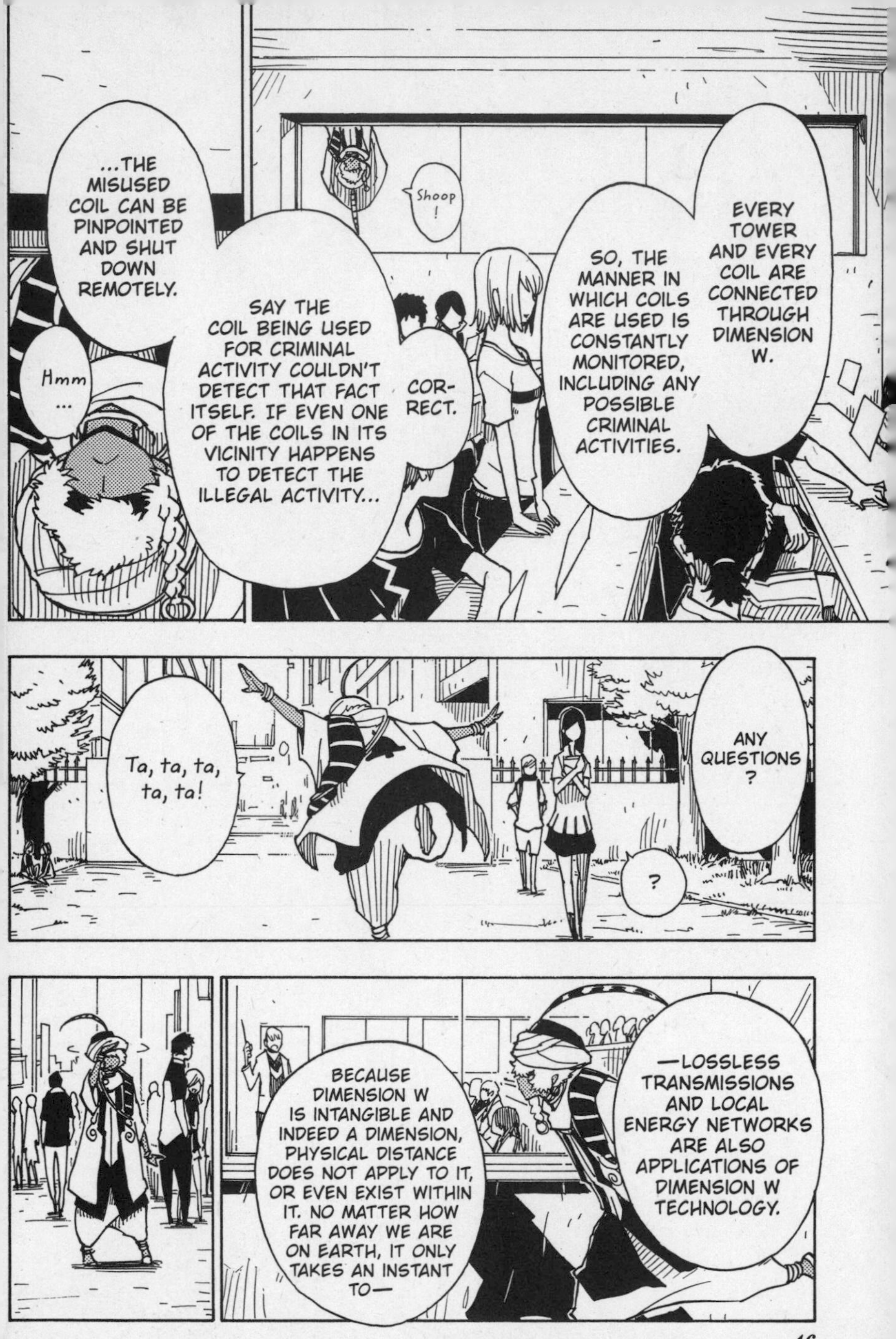
EVERY TOWER AND EVERY COIL ARE CONNECTED THROUGH DIMENSION W.
SO, THE MANNER IN WHICH COILS ARE USED IS CONSTANTLY MONITORED, INCLUDING ANY POSSIBLE CRIMINAL ACTIVITIES.
Shoop!
COR-RECT.
SAY THE COIL BEING USED FOR CRIMINAL ACTIVITY COULDN'T DETECT THAT FACT ITSELF. IF EVEN ONE OF THE COILS IN ITS VICINITY HAPPENS TO DETECT THE ILLEGAL ACTIVITY...
...THE MISUSED COIL CAN BE PINPOINTED AND SHUT DOWN REMOTELY.
Hmm ...
ANY QUESTIONS?
?
Ta, ta, ta, ta, ta!
—LOSSLESS TRANSMISSIONS AND LOCAL ENERGY NETWORKS ARE ALSO APPLICATIONS OF DIMENSION W TECHNOLOGY.
BECAUSE DIMENSION W IS INTANGIBLE AND INDEED A DIMENSION, PHYSICAL DISTANCE DOES NOT APPLY TO IT, OR EVEN EXIST WITHIN IT. NO MATTER HOW FAR AWAY WE ARE ON EARTH, IT ONLY TAKES AN INSTANT TO—

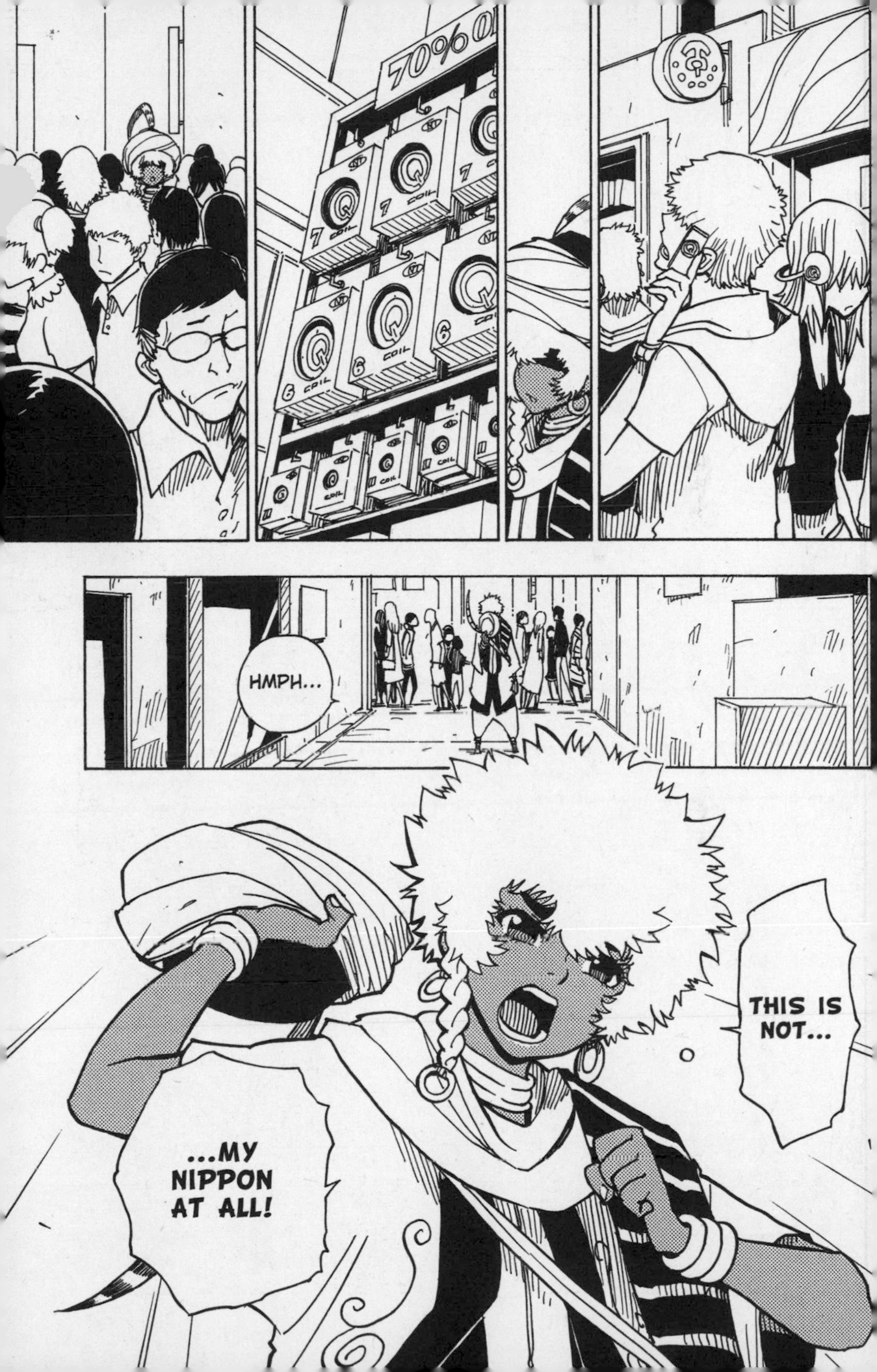
HMPH...
THIS IS NOT...
...MY NIPPON AT ALL!

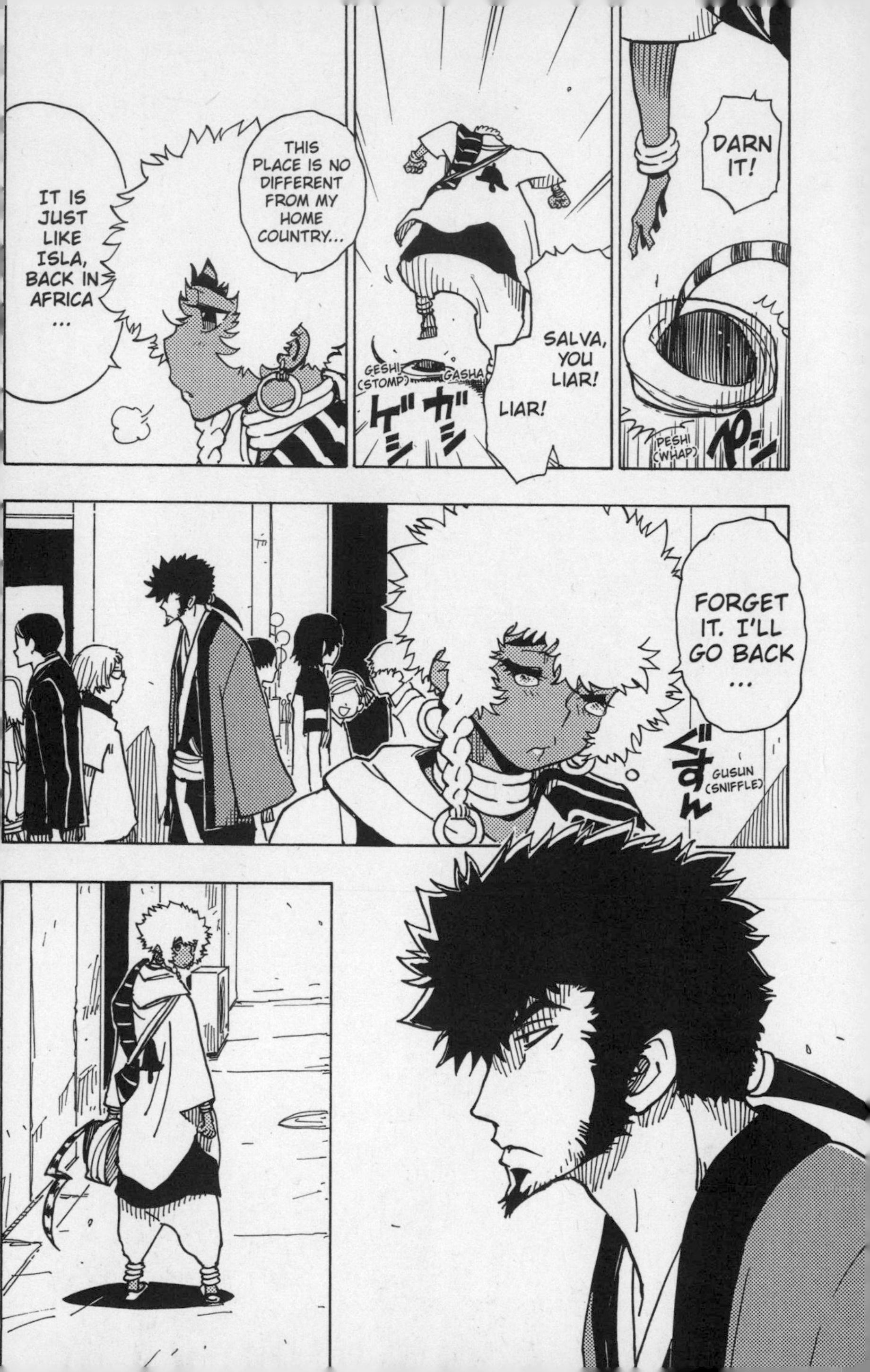
DARN IT!
PESHI (WHAP)
ペシ
SALVA, YOU LIAR!
LIAR!
GESHI (STOMP)
GASHA
ゲシ ガシ
THIS PLACE IS NO DIFFERENT FROM MY HOME COUNTRY...
IT IS JUST LIKE ISLA, BACK IN AFRICA...
FORGET IT. I'LL GO BACK...
ぐずん
GUSUN (SNIFFLE)

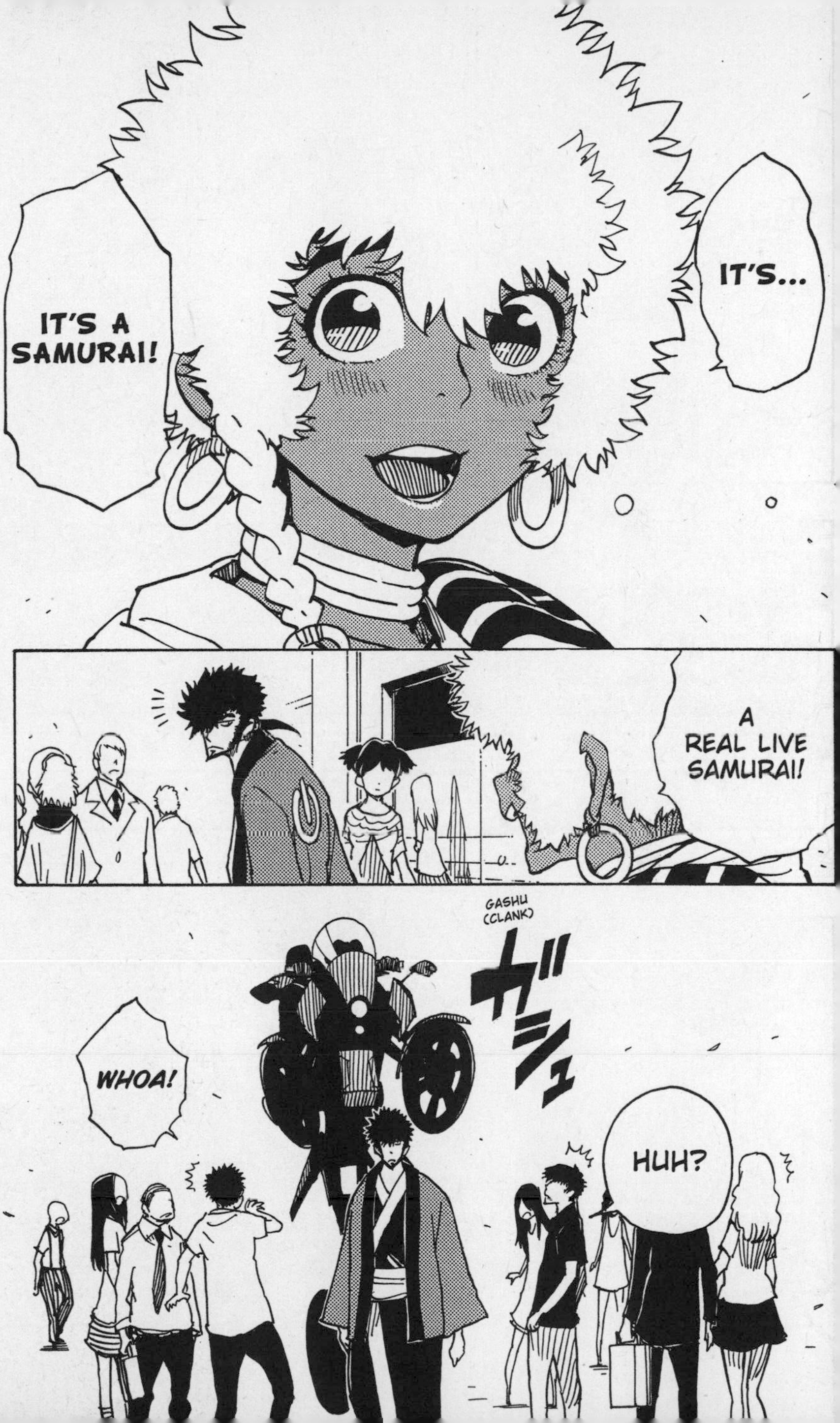
IT'S...
IT'S A SAMURAI!
A REAL LIVE SAMURAI!
GASHU (CLANK)
ガシュ
WHOA!
HUH?

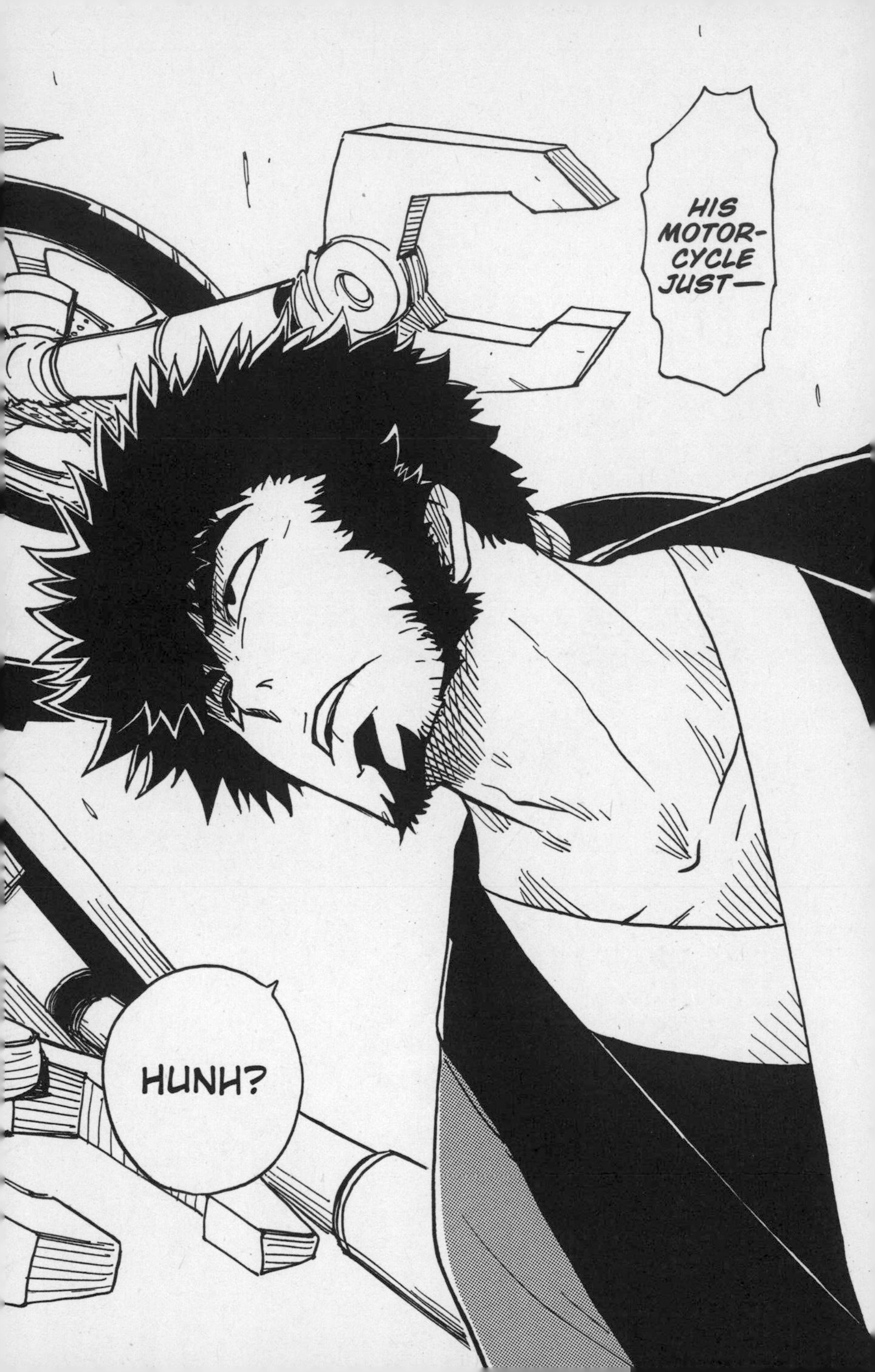
HIS MOTOR-CYCLE JUST—
HUNH?

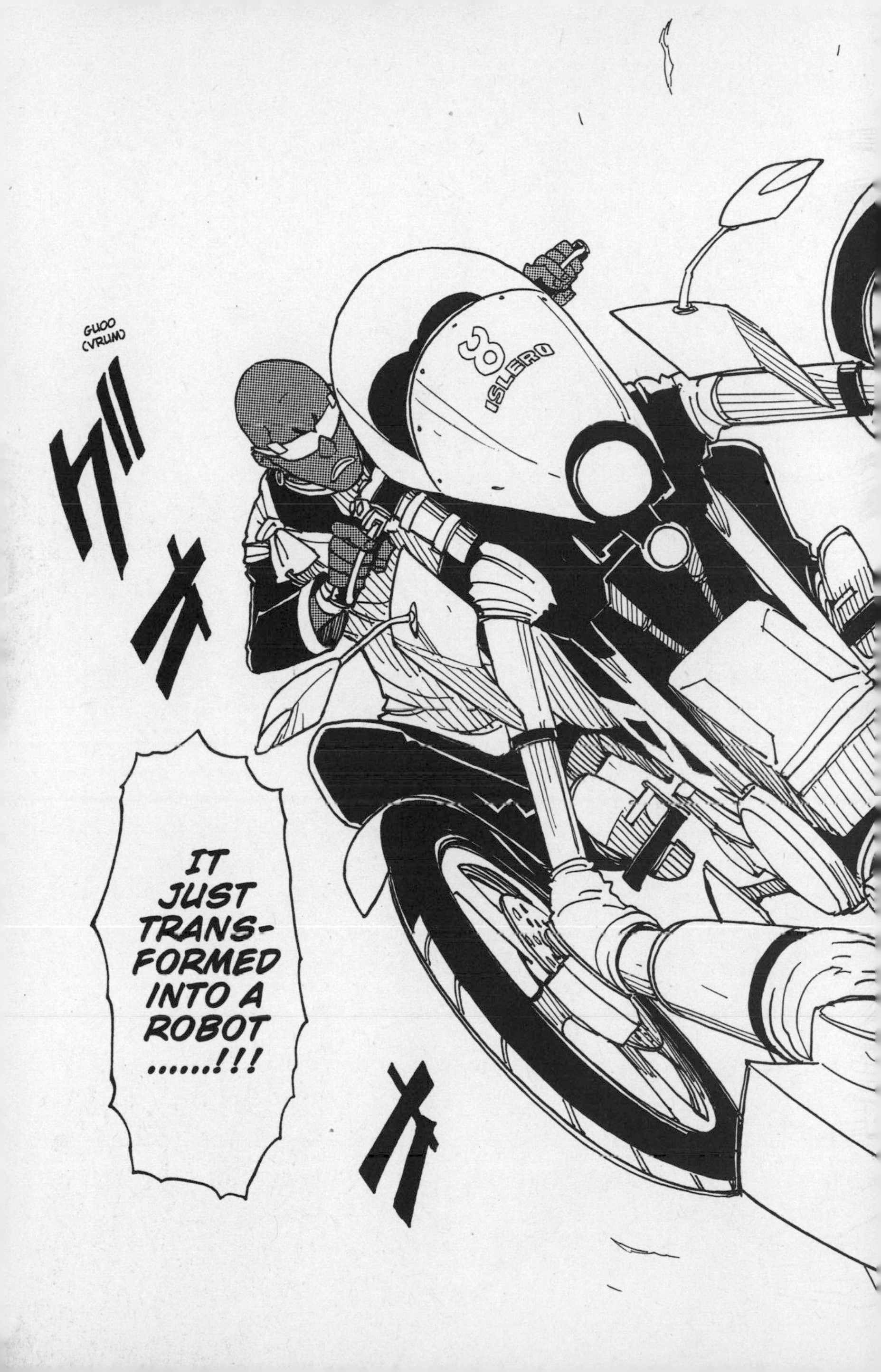
GUOO (VRUM)
IT JUST TRANS-FORMED INTO A ROBOT ......!!!

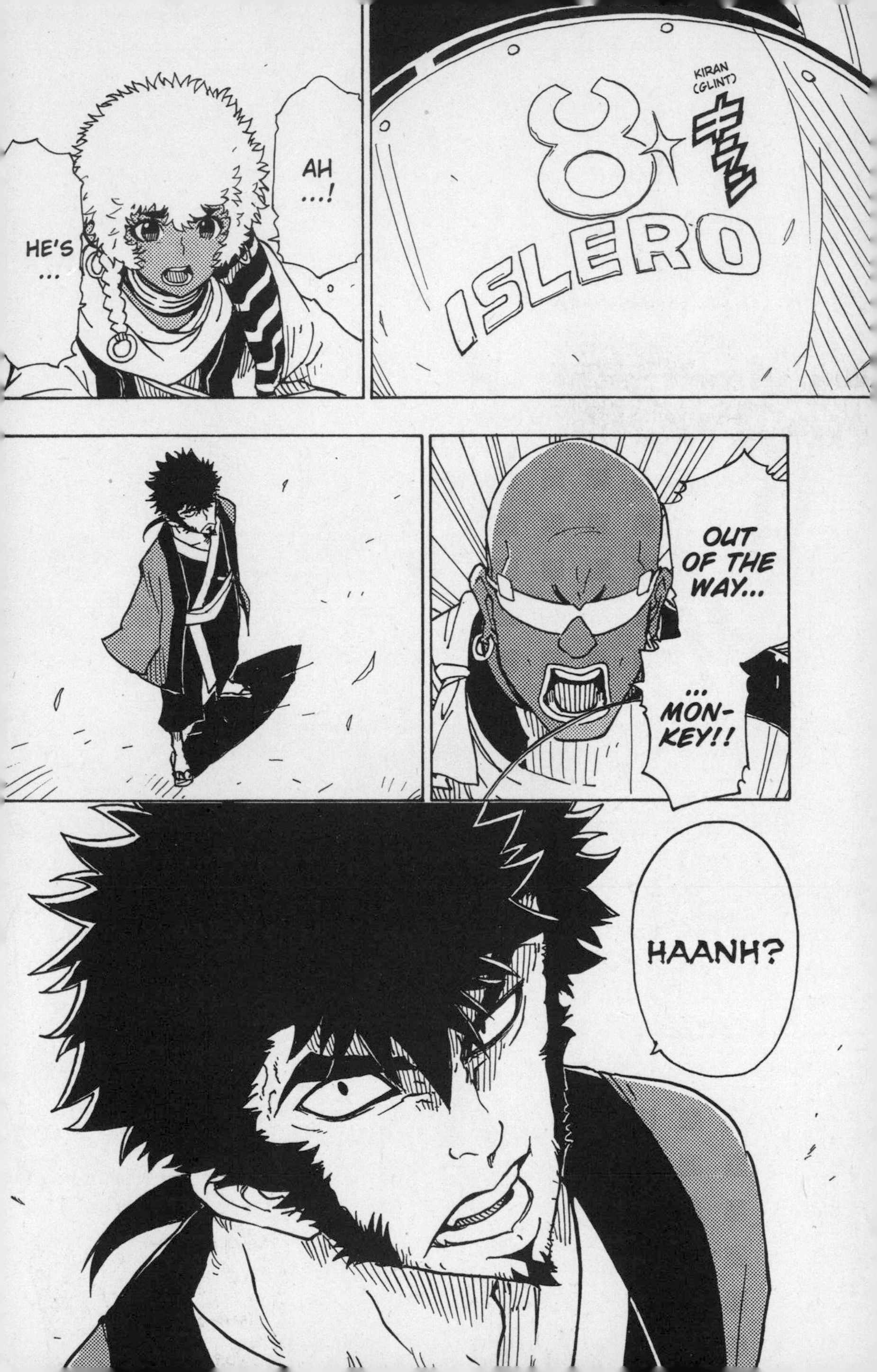
KIRAN (GLINT)
ISLERO
AH ...!
HE'S ...
OUT OF THE WAY...
... MON-KEY!!
HAANH?

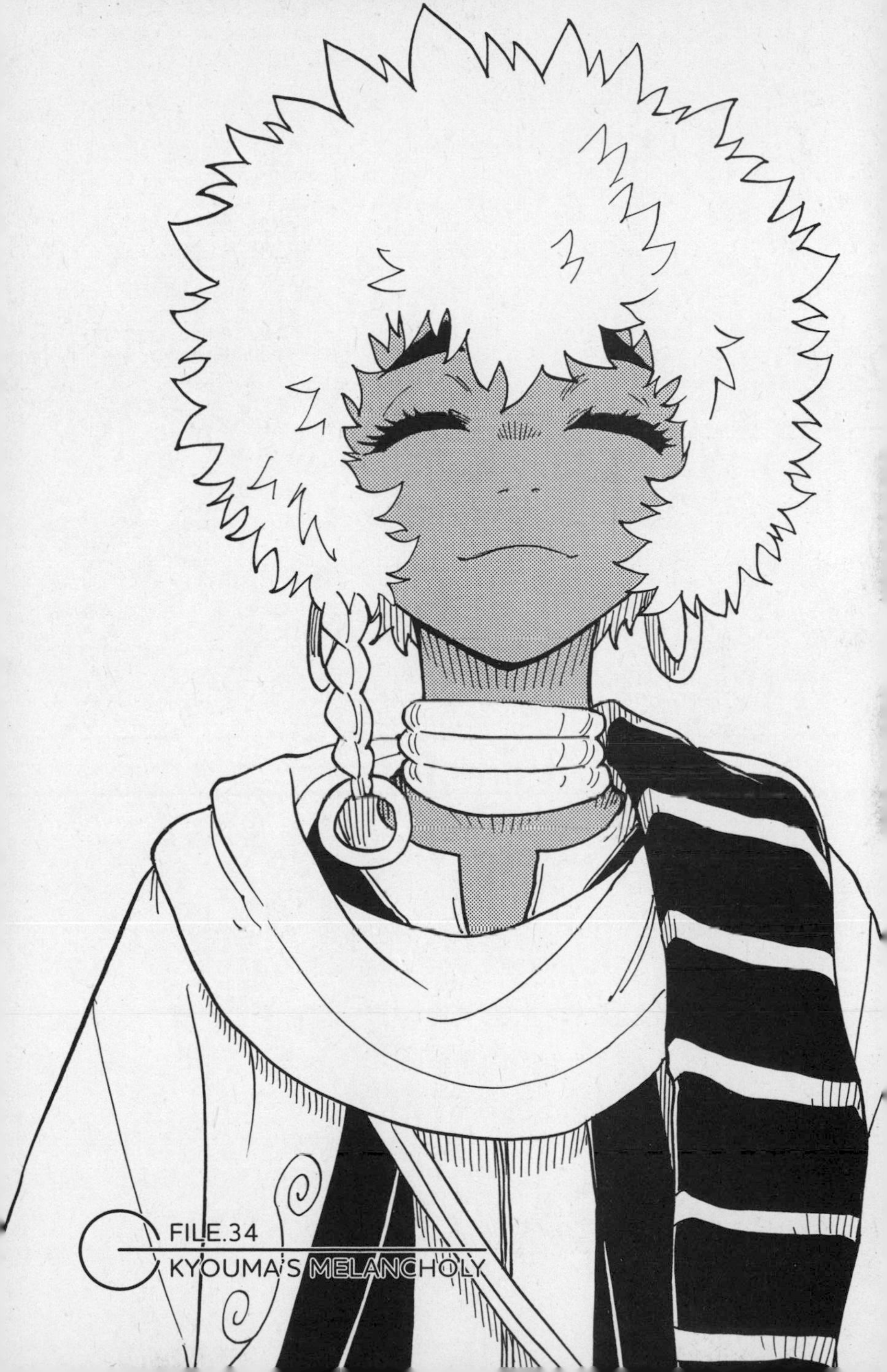
FILE.34
KYOUMA'S MELANCHOLY

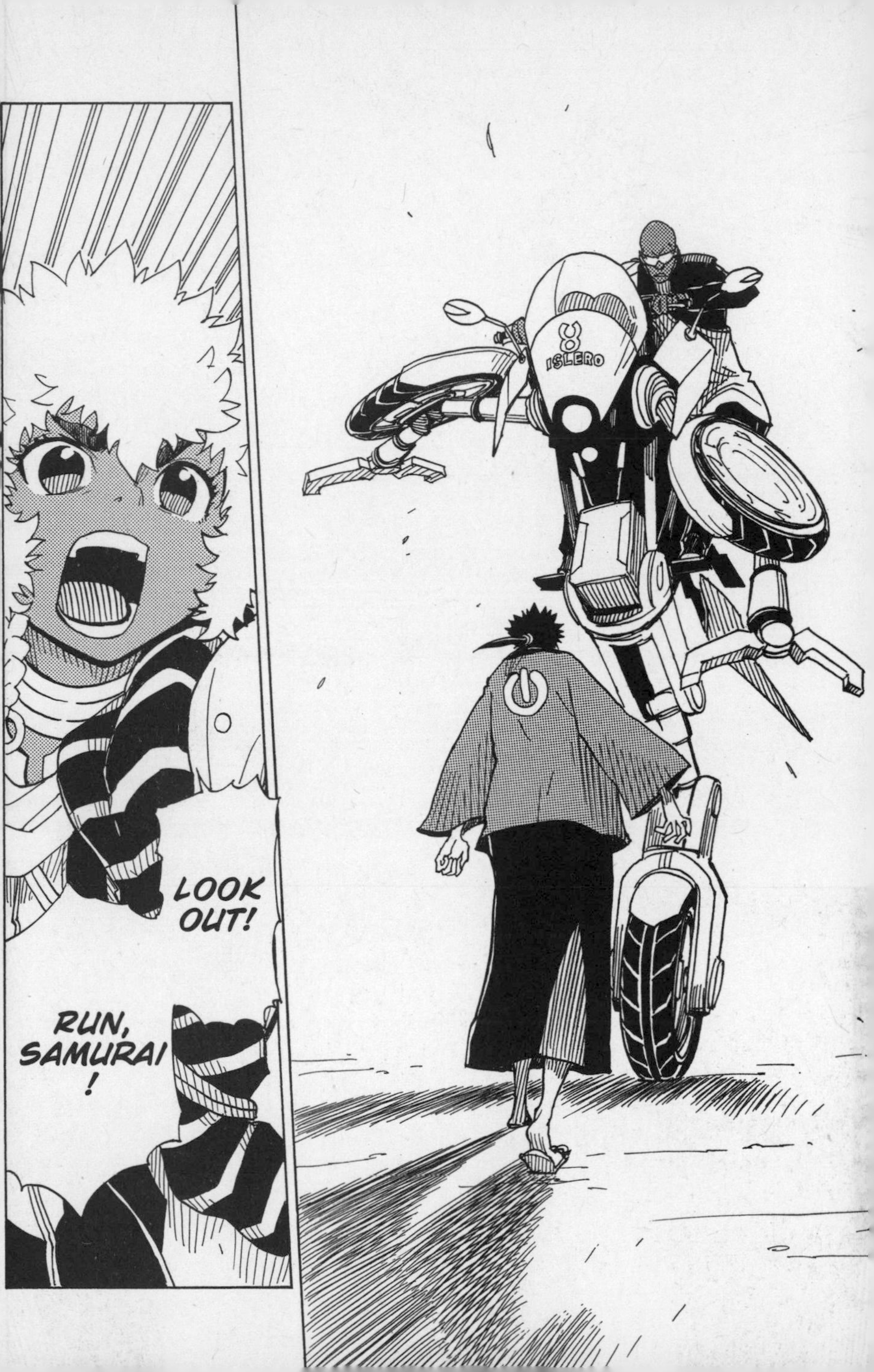
ISLERO
LOOK OUT!
RUN, SAMURAI!

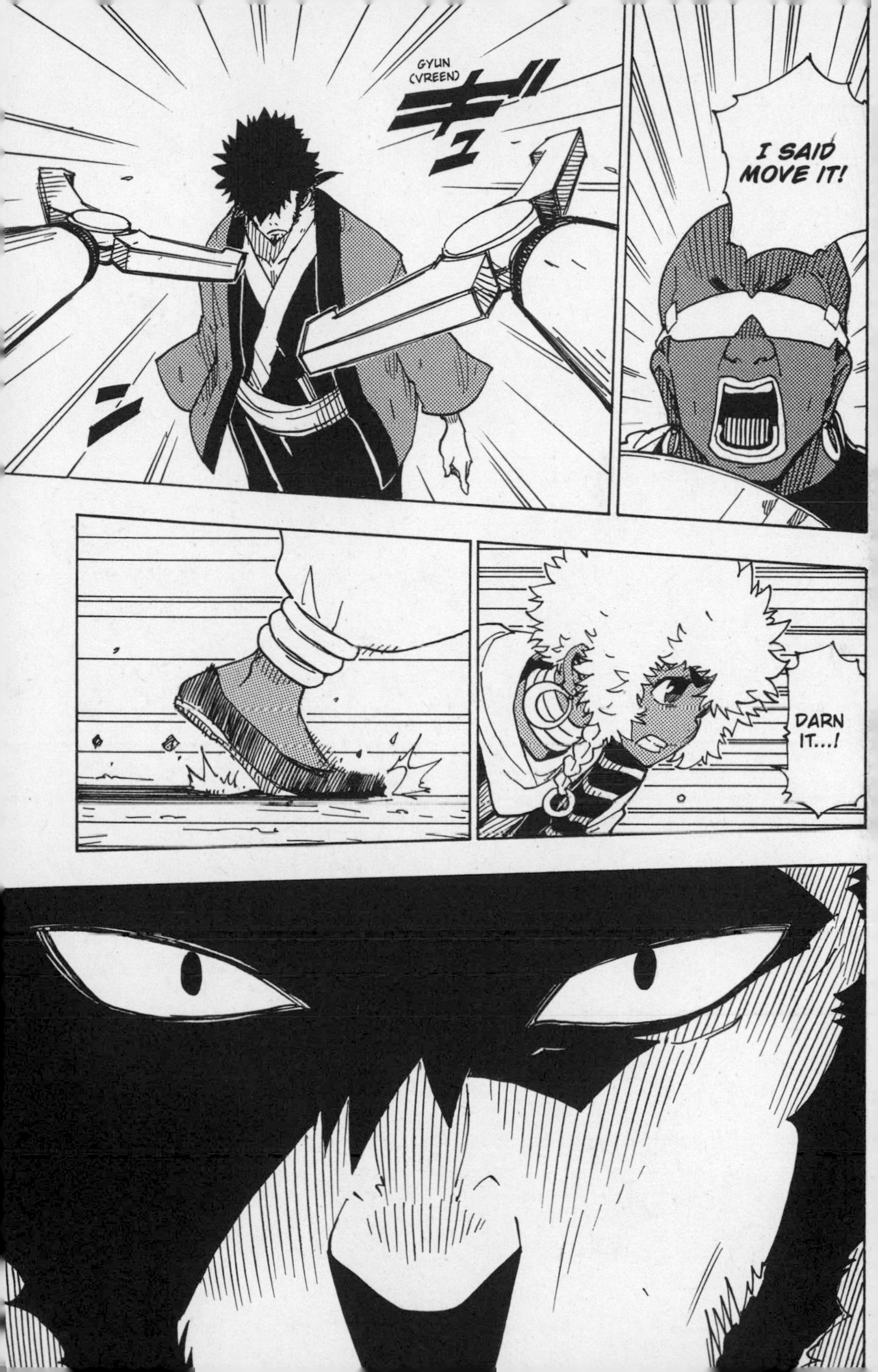
I SAID MOVE IT!
GYUN (VREEN)
DARN IT...!

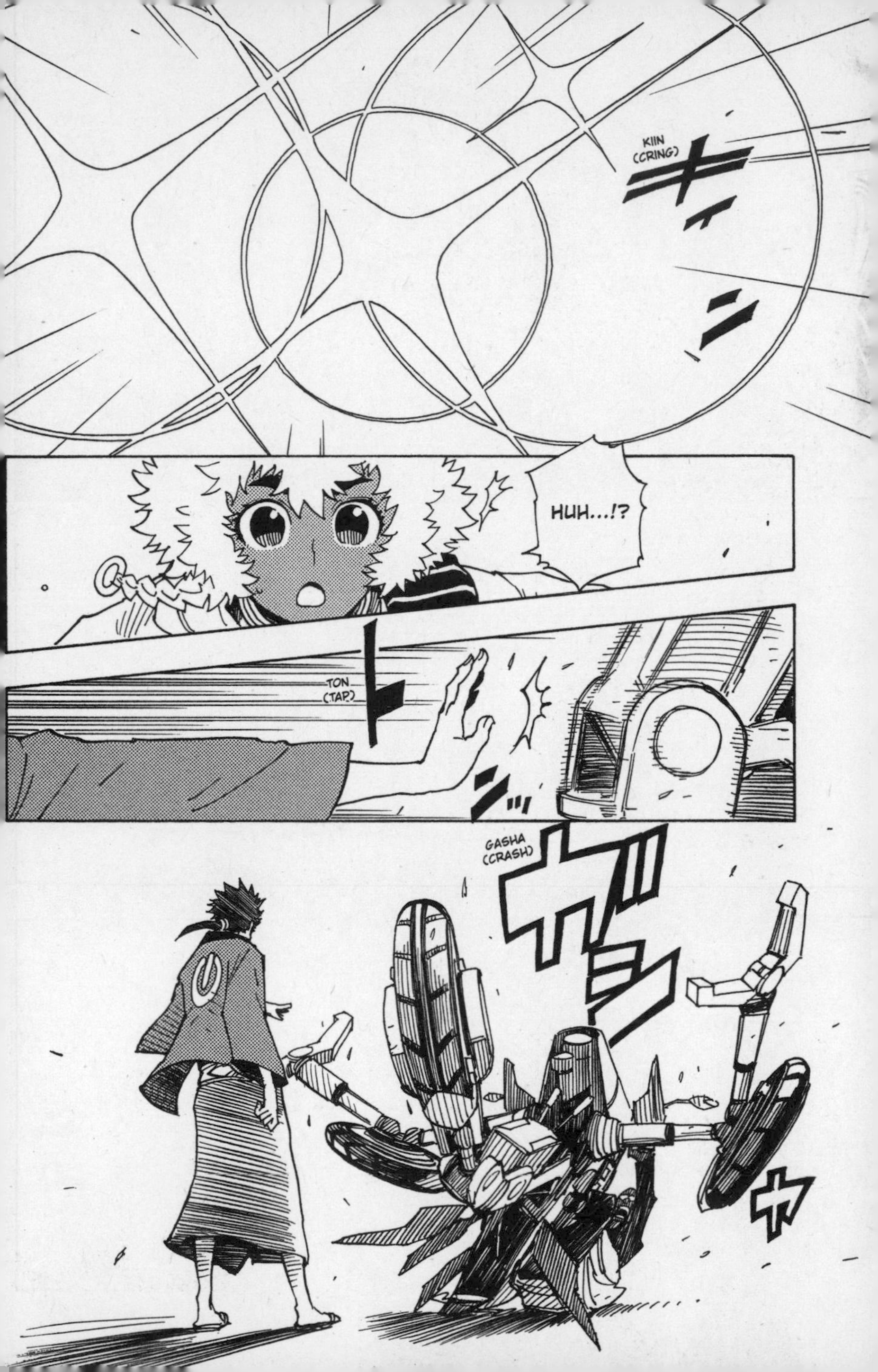
KIIN (CRING)
HUH...!?
TON (TAP)
GASHA (CRASH)

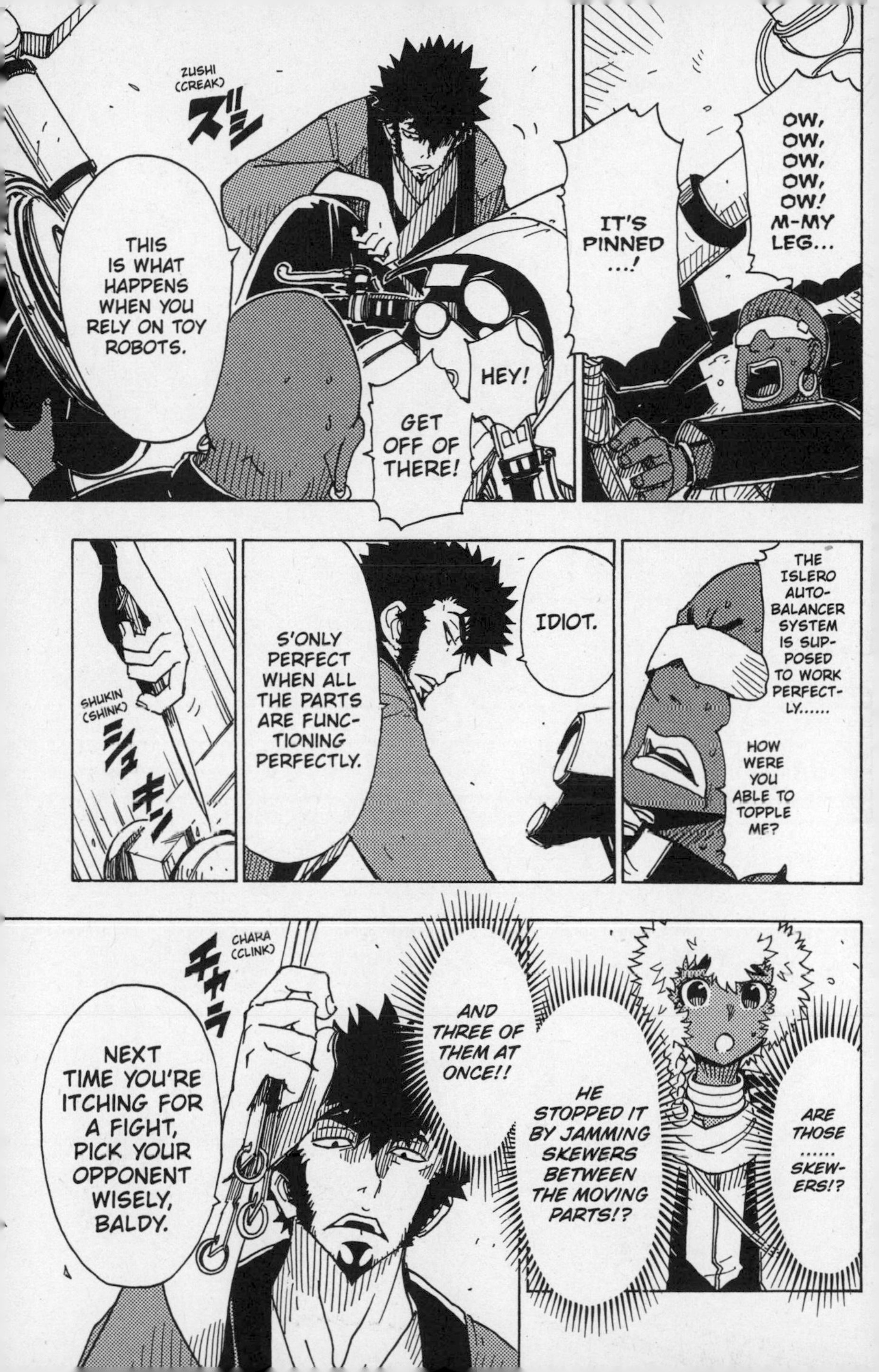
OW, OW, OW, OW, OW! M-MY LEG...
IT'S PINNED ....!
ZUSHI (CREAK)
ズシ
HEY!
GET OFF OF THERE!
THIS IS WHAT HAPPENS WHEN YOU RELY ON TOY ROBOTS.
THE ISLERO AUTO-BALANCER SYSTEM IS SUPPOSED TO WORK PERFECTLY......
HOW WERE YOU ABLE TO TOPPLE ME?
IDIOT.
S'ONLY PERFECT WHEN ALL THE PARTS ARE FUNCTIONING PERFECTLY.
SHUKIN (SHINK)
シュキン
ARE THOSE ...... SKEWERS!?
HE STOPPED IT BY JAMMING SKEWERS BETWEEN THE MOVING PARTS!?
AND THREE OF THEM AT ONCE!!
CHARA (CLINK)
チャラ
NEXT TIME YOU'RE ITCHING FOR A FIGHT, PICK YOUR OPPONENT WISELY, BALDY.

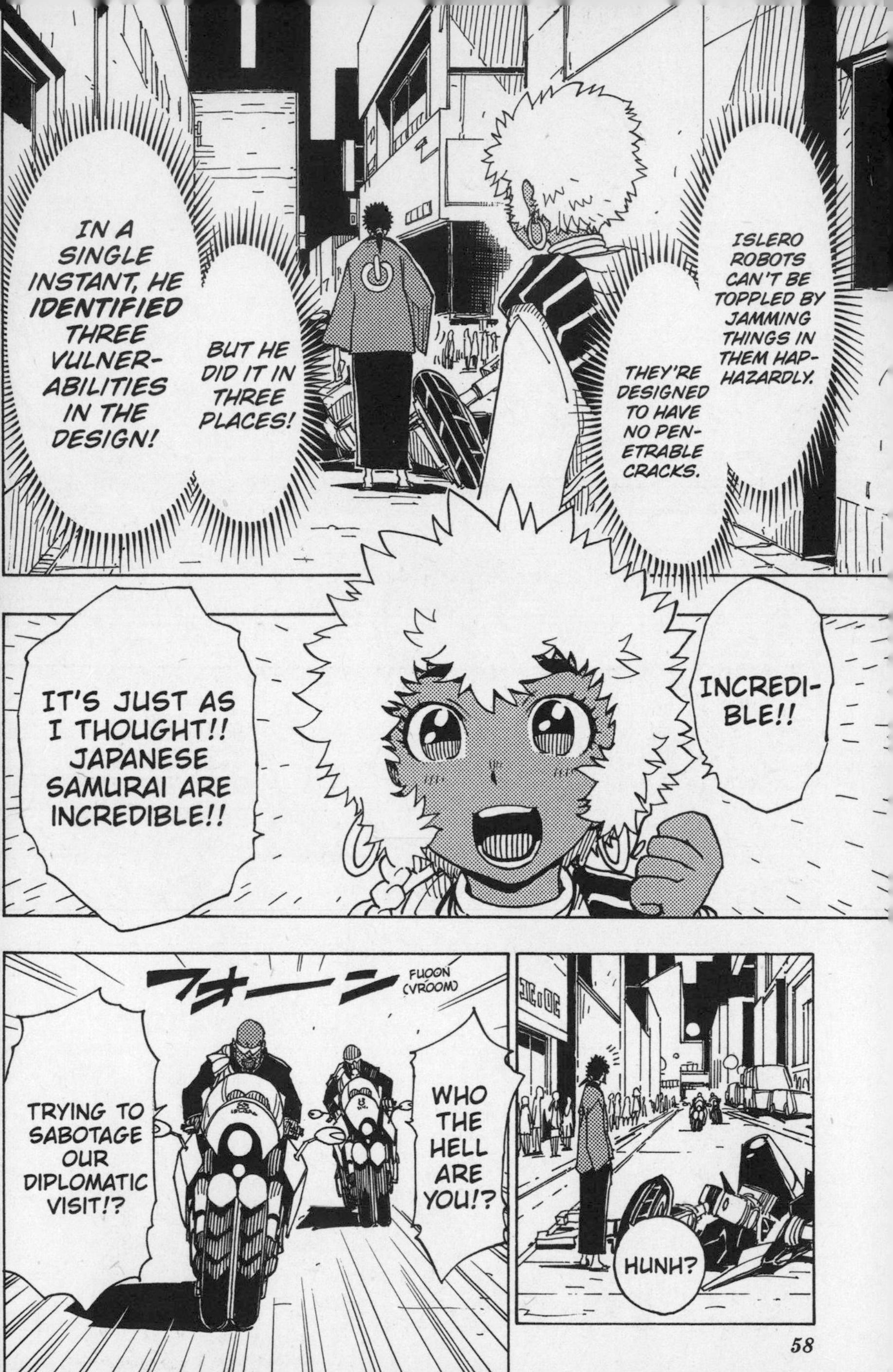
ISLERO ROBOTS CAN'T BE TOPPLED BY JAMMING THINGS IN THEM HAP-HAZARDLY.
THEY'RE DESIGNED TO HAVE NO PEN-ETRABLE CRACKS.
BUT HE DID IT IN THREE PLACES!
IN A SINGLE INSTANT, HE IDENTIFIED THREE VULNER-ABILITIES IN THE DESIGN!
INCREDI-BLE!!
IT'S JUST AS I THOUGHT!! JAPANESE SAMURAI ARE INCREDIBLE!!
HUNH?
フォーーン
FUOON (VROOM)
WHO THE HELL ARE YOU!?
TRYING TO SABOTAGE OUR DIPLOMATIC VISIT!?

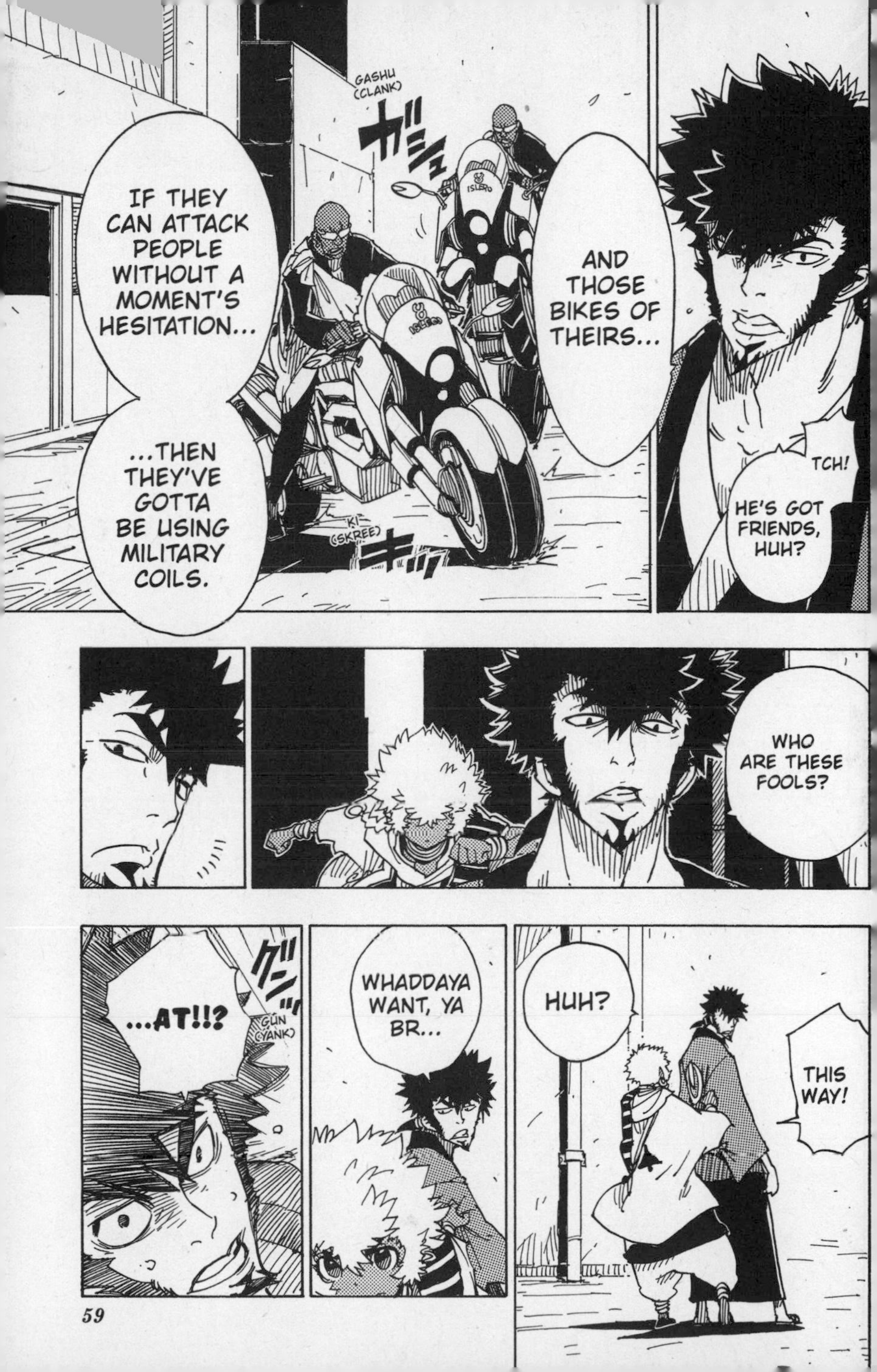
TCH!
HE'S GOT FRIENDS, HUH?
AND THOSE BIKES OF THEIRS...
GASHU (CLANK)
IF THEY CAN ATTACK PEOPLE WITHOUT A MOMENT'S HESITATION...
...THEN THEY'VE GOTTA BE USING MILITARY COILS.
KI (SKREE)
WHO ARE THESE FOOLS?
THIS WAY!
HUH?
WHADDAYA WANT, YA BR...
GUN (YANK)
...AT!!?

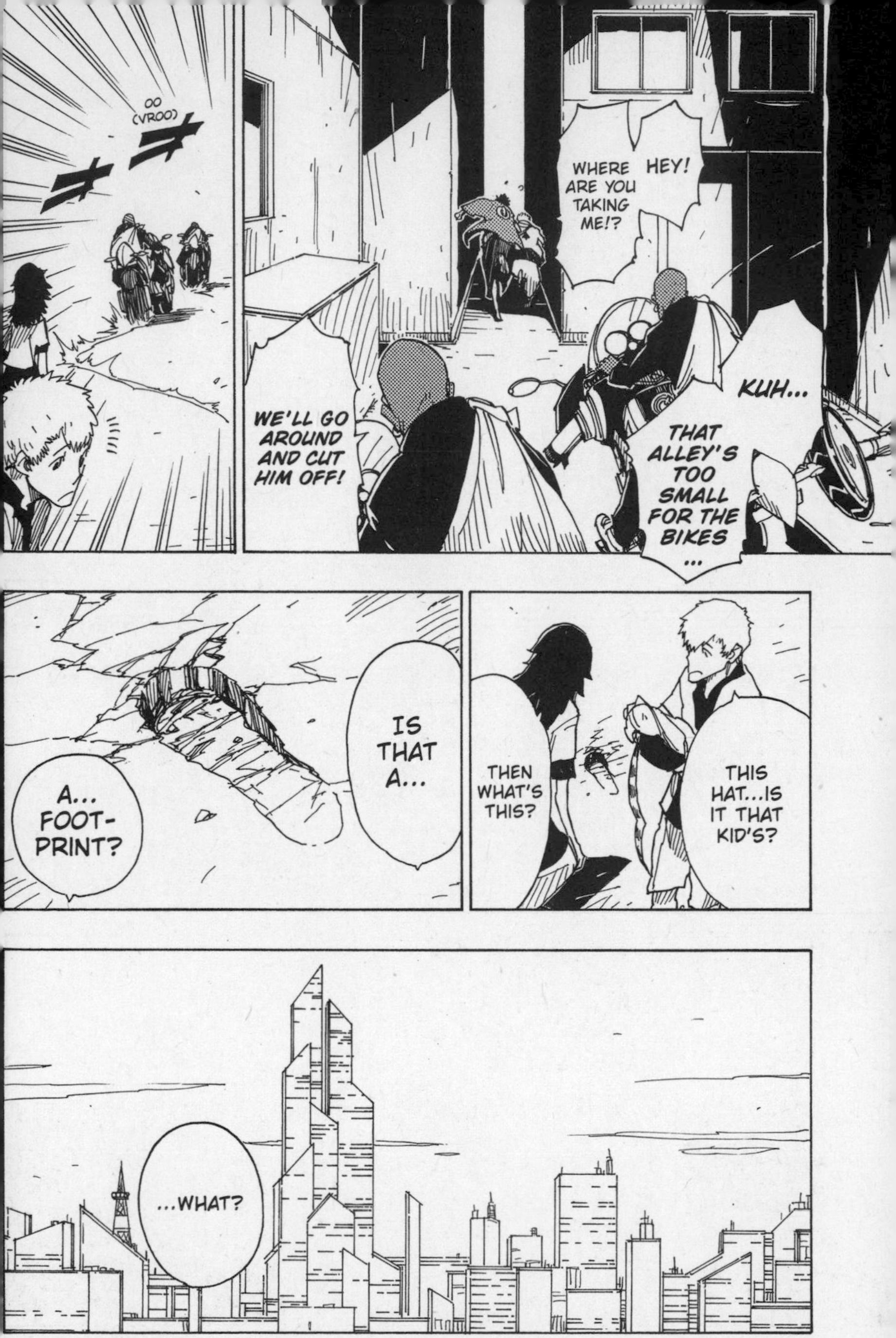
HEY!
WHERE ARE YOU TAKING ME!?
KUH...
THAT ALLEY'S TOO SMALL FOR THE BIKES ...
WE'LL GO AROUND AND CUT HIM OFF!
OO (VROO)
THIS HAT...IS IT THAT KID'S?
THEN WHAT'S THIS?
IS THAT A...
A... FOOT-PRINT?
...WHAT?

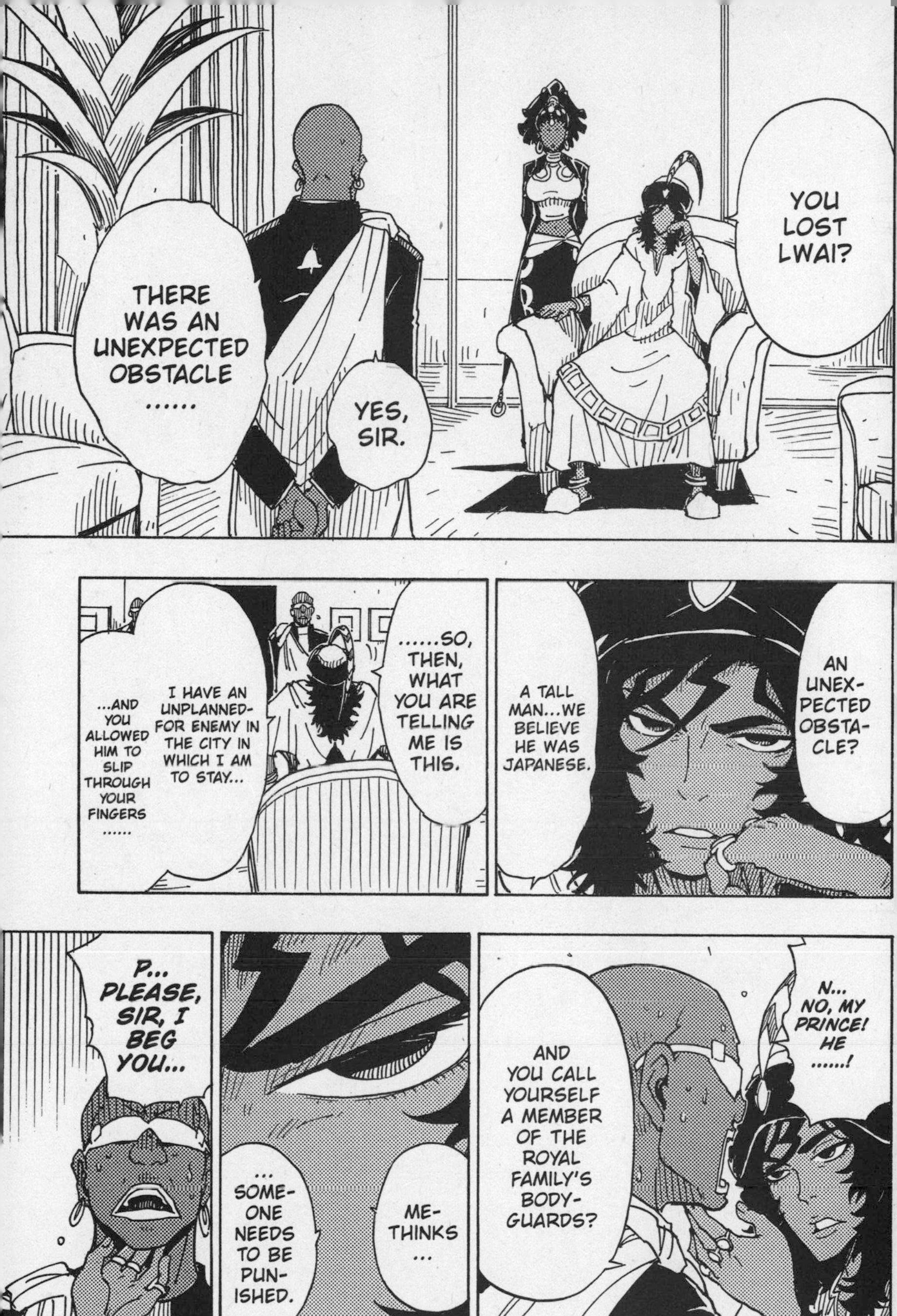
YOU LOST LWAI?
YES, SIR.
THERE WAS AN UNEXPECTED OBSTACLE ......
AN UNEXPECTED OBSTACLE?
A TALL MAN...WE BELIEVE HE WAS JAPANESE.
......SO, THEN, WHAT YOU ARE TELLING ME IS THIS.
I HAVE AN UNPLANNED-FOR ENEMY IN THE CITY IN WHICH I AM TO STAY...
...AND YOU ALLOWED HIM TO SLIP THROUGH YOUR FINGERS ......
N... NO, MY PRINCE! HE ......!
AND YOU CALL YOURSELF A MEMBER OF THE ROYAL FAMILY'S BODYGUARDS?
METHINKS ...
...SOMEONE NEEDS TO BE PUNISHED.
P... PLEASE, SIR, I BEG YOU...

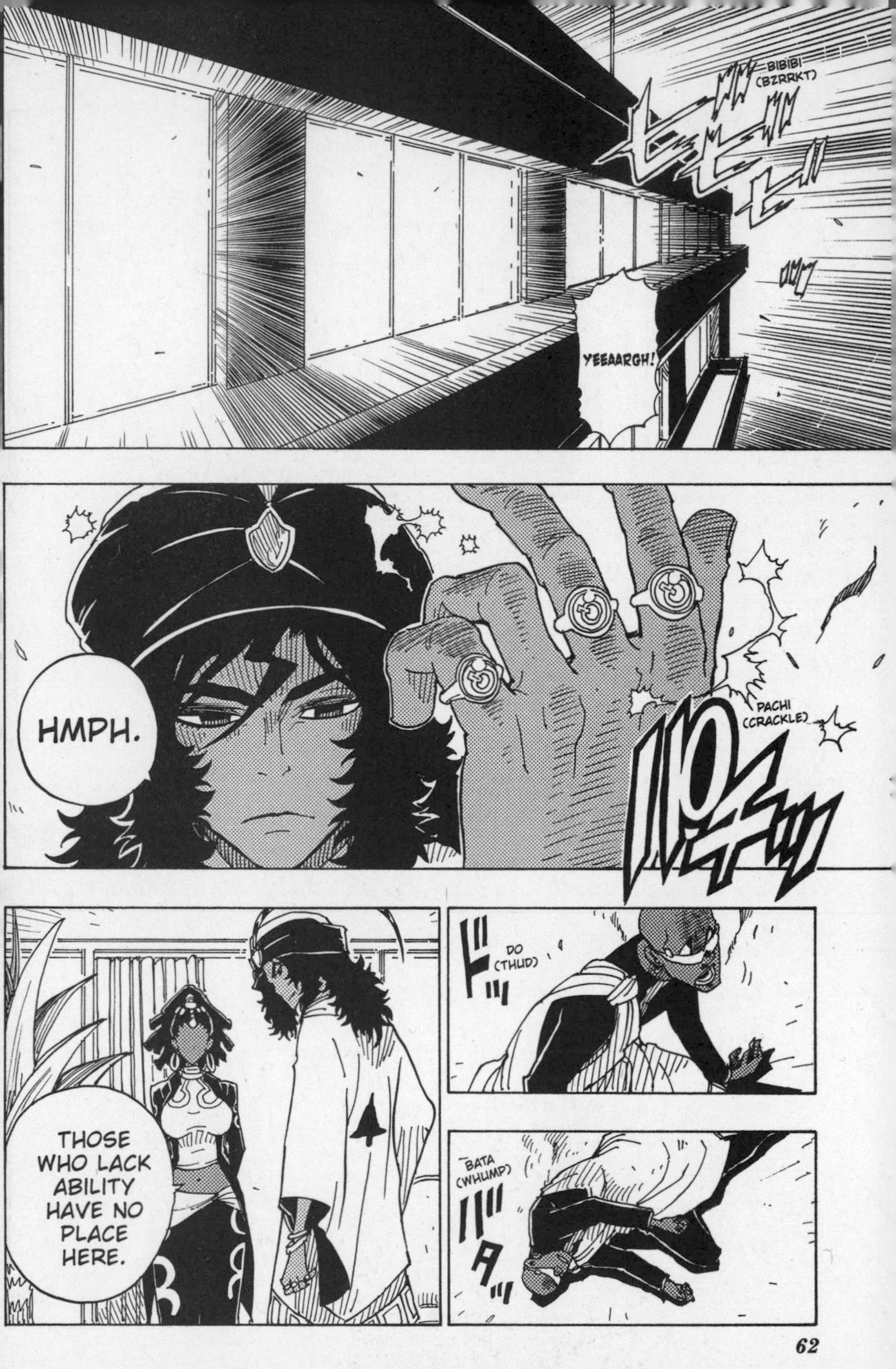
BIBIBI (BZRRKT)
YEEAARGH!
PACHI (CRACKLE)
HMPH.
DO (THUD)
BATA (WHUMP)
THOSE WHO LACK ABILITY HAVE NO PLACE HERE.

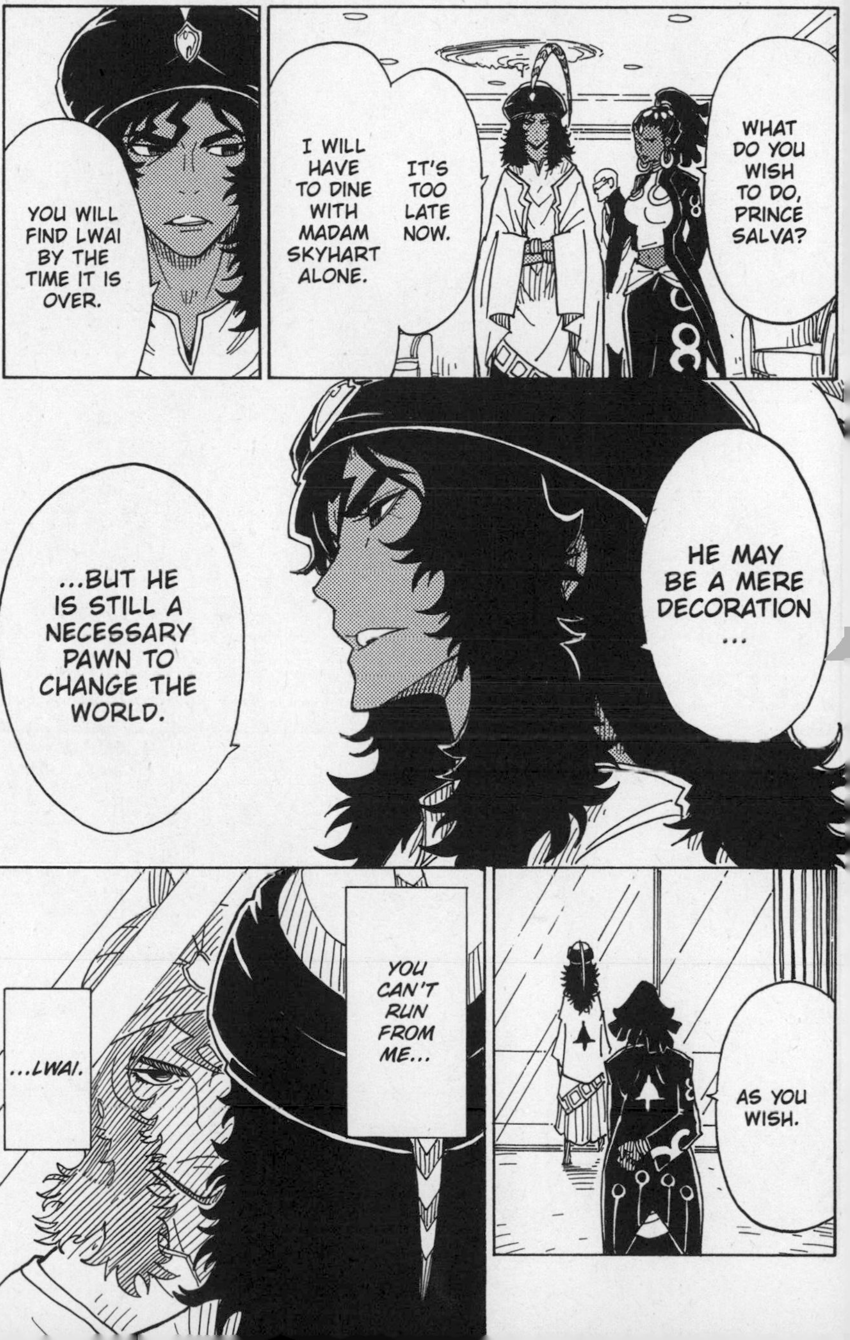
WHAT DO YOU WISH TO DO, PRINCE SALVA?
IT'S TOO LATE NOW.
I WILL HAVE TO DINE WITH MADAM SKYHART ALONE.
YOU WILL FIND LWAI BY THE TIME IT IS OVER.
HE MAY BE A MERE DECORATION ...
...BUT HE IS STILL A NECESSARY PAWN TO CHANGE THE WORLD.
AS YOU WISH.
YOU CAN'T RUN FROM ME...
...LWAI.

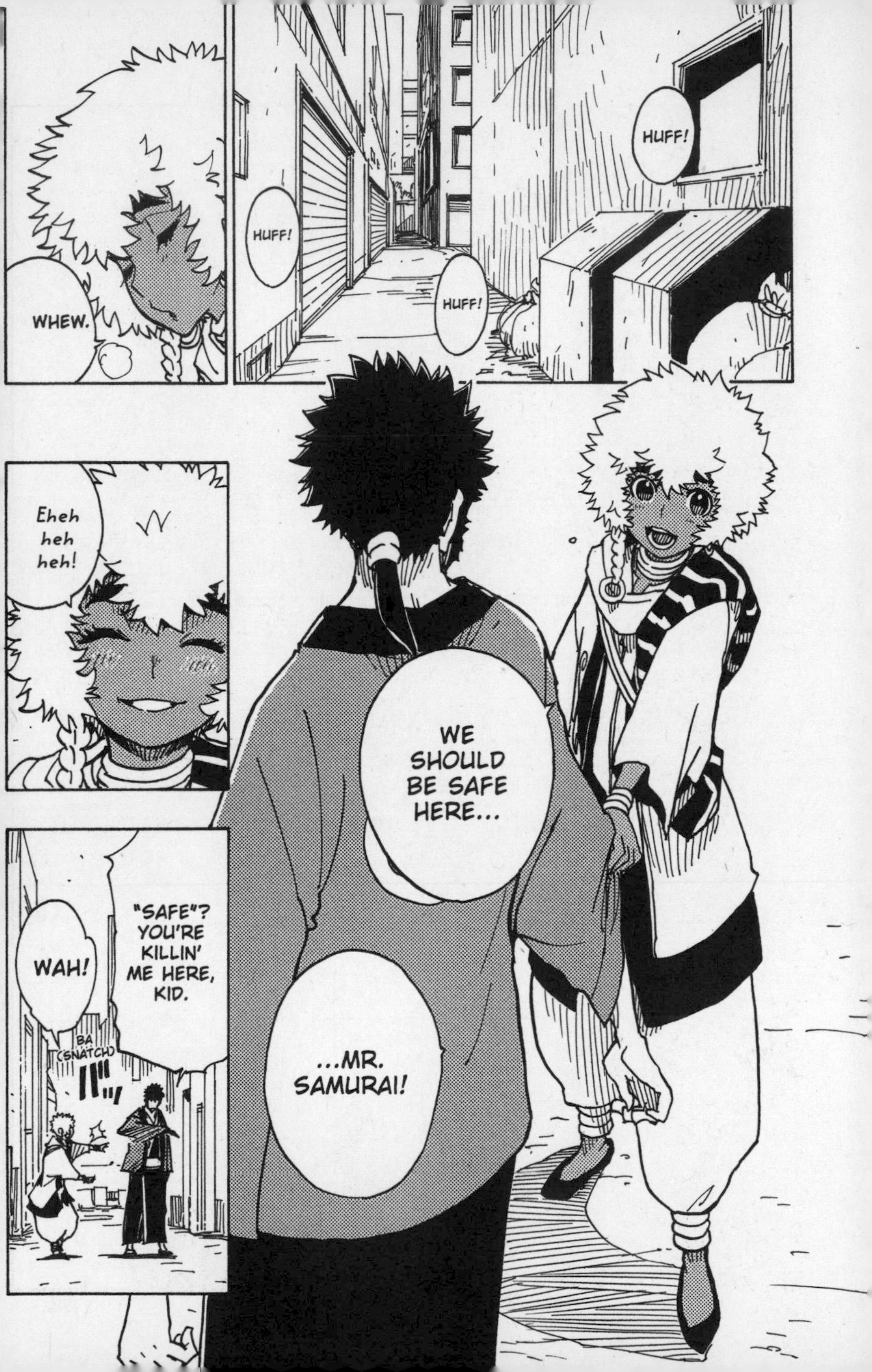
HUFF!
HUFF!
HUFF!
WHEW.
WE SHOULD BE SAFE HERE...
...MR. SAMURAI!
Eheh heh heh!
"SAFE"? YOU'RE KILLIN' ME HERE, KID.
WAH!
BA (SNATCH)

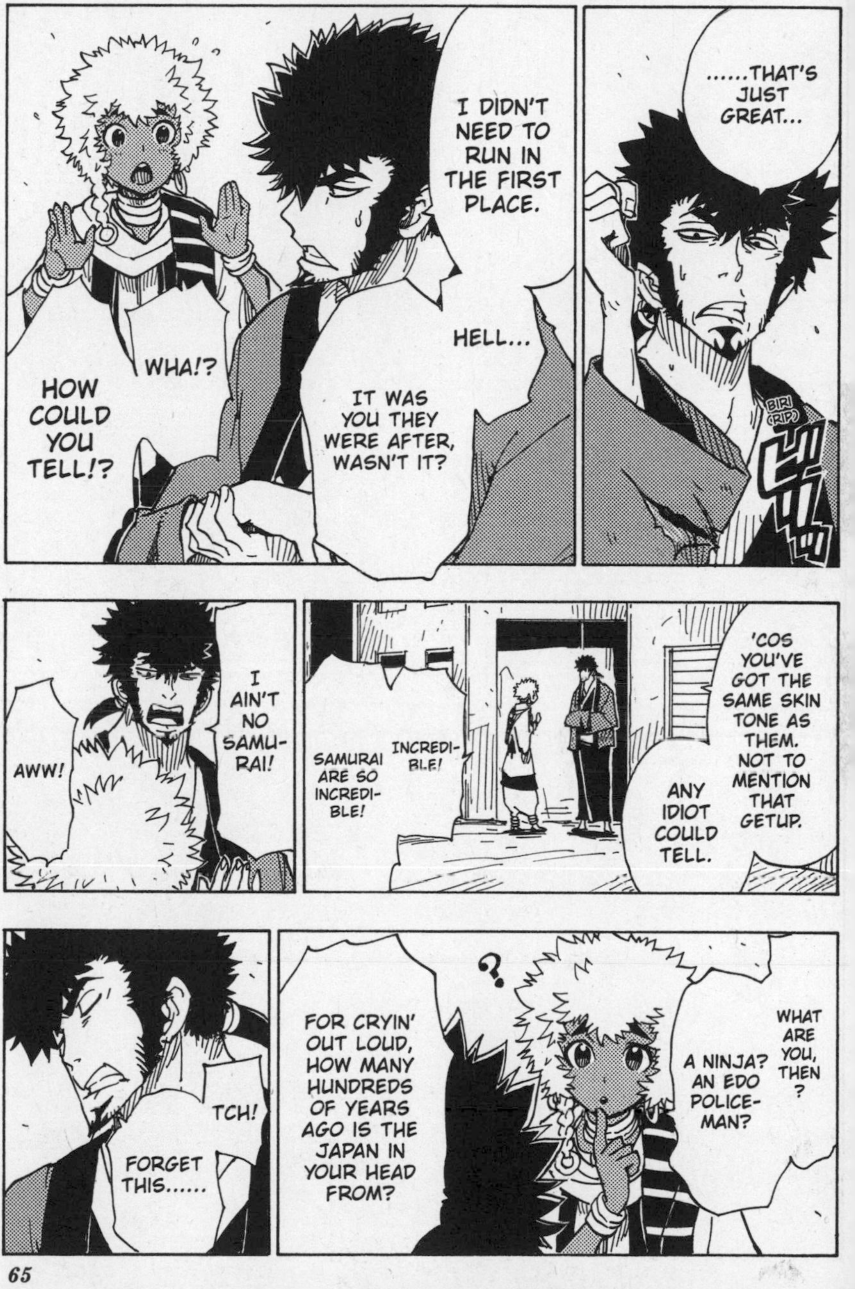
......THAT'S JUST GREAT...
BIRI (RIP)
I DIDN'T NEED TO RUN IN THE FIRST PLACE.
HELL...
IT WAS YOU THEY WERE AFTER, WASN'T IT?
WHA!?
HOW COULD YOU TELL!?
'COS YOU'VE GOT THE SAME SKIN TONE AS THEM. NOT TO MENTION THAT GETUP.
ANY IDIOT COULD TELL.
INCREDI-BLE!
SAMURAI ARE SO INCREDI-BLE!
I AIN'T NO SAMU-RAI!
AWW!
WHAT ARE YOU, THEN ?
A NINJA? AN EDO POLICE-MAN?
FOR CRYIN' OUT LOUD, HOW MANY HUNDREDS OF YEARS AGO IS THE JAPAN IN YOUR HEAD FROM?
TCH!
FORGET THIS......

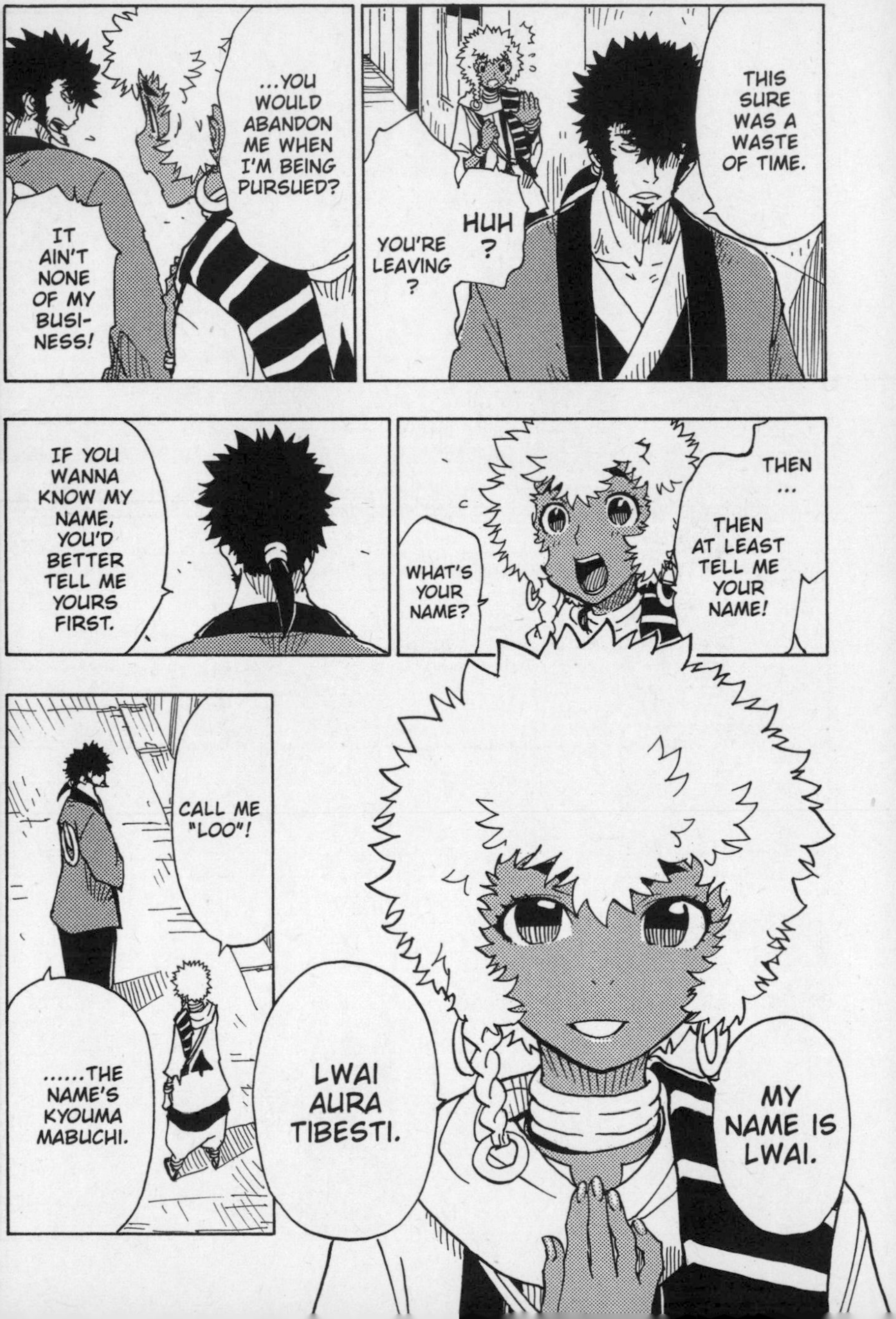
THIS SURE WAS A WASTE OF TIME.
HUH?
YOU'RE LEAVING?
...YOU WOULD ABANDON ME WHEN I'M BEING PURSUED?
IT AIN'T NONE OF MY BUSINESS!
THEN...
THEN AT LEAST TELL ME YOUR NAME!
WHAT'S YOUR NAME?
IF YOU WANNA KNOW MY NAME, YOU'D BETTER TELL ME YOURS FIRST.
MY NAME IS LWAI.
LWAI AURA TIBESTI.
CALL ME "LOO"!
......THE NAME'S KYOUMA MABUCHI.

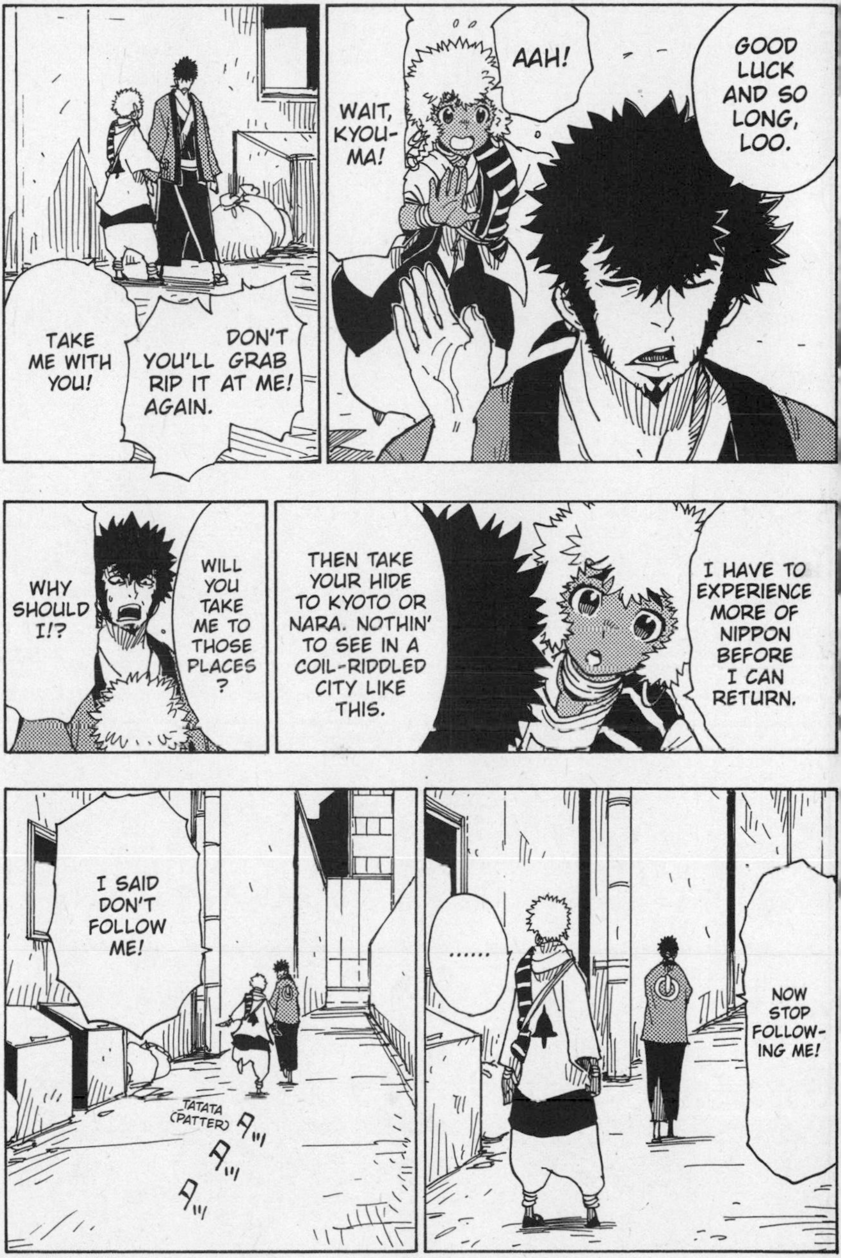
GOOD LUCK AND SO LONG, LOO.
AAH!
WAIT, KYOU-MA!
DON'T GRAB AT ME!
YOU'LL RIP IT AGAIN.
TAKE ME WITH YOU!
I HAVE TO EXPERIENCE MORE OF NIPPON BEFORE I CAN RETURN.
THEN TAKE YOUR HIDE TO KYOTO OR NARA. NOTHIN' TO SEE IN A COIL-RIDDLED CITY LIKE THIS.
WILL YOU TAKE ME TO THOSE PLACES?
WHY SHOULD I!?
NOW STOP FOLLOWING ME!
......
I SAID DON'T FOLLOW ME!
TATATA (PATTER)

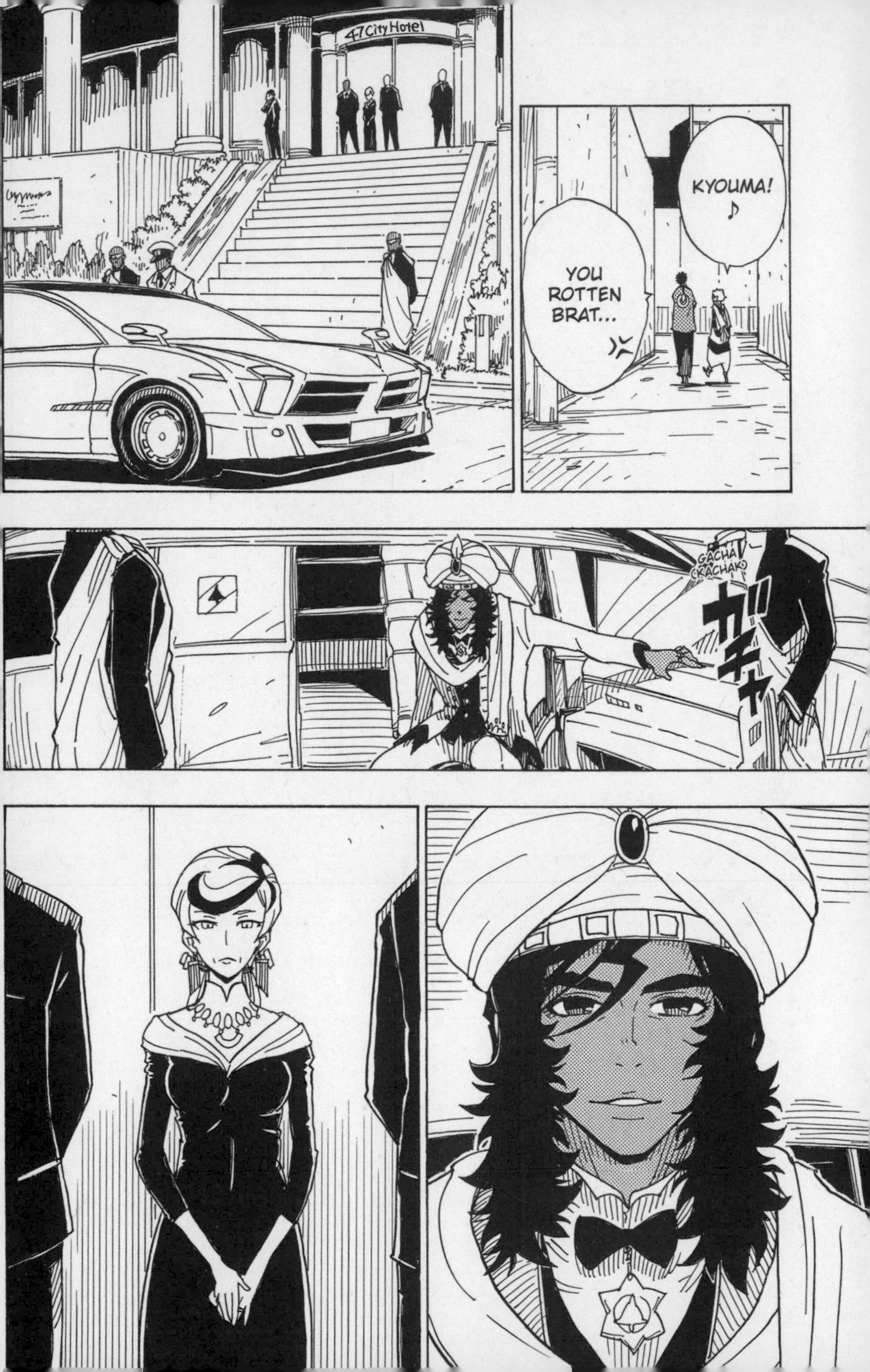
KYOUMA! ♪
YOU ROTTEN BRAT...
47 City Hotel
GACHA (KACHAK)
ガチャ

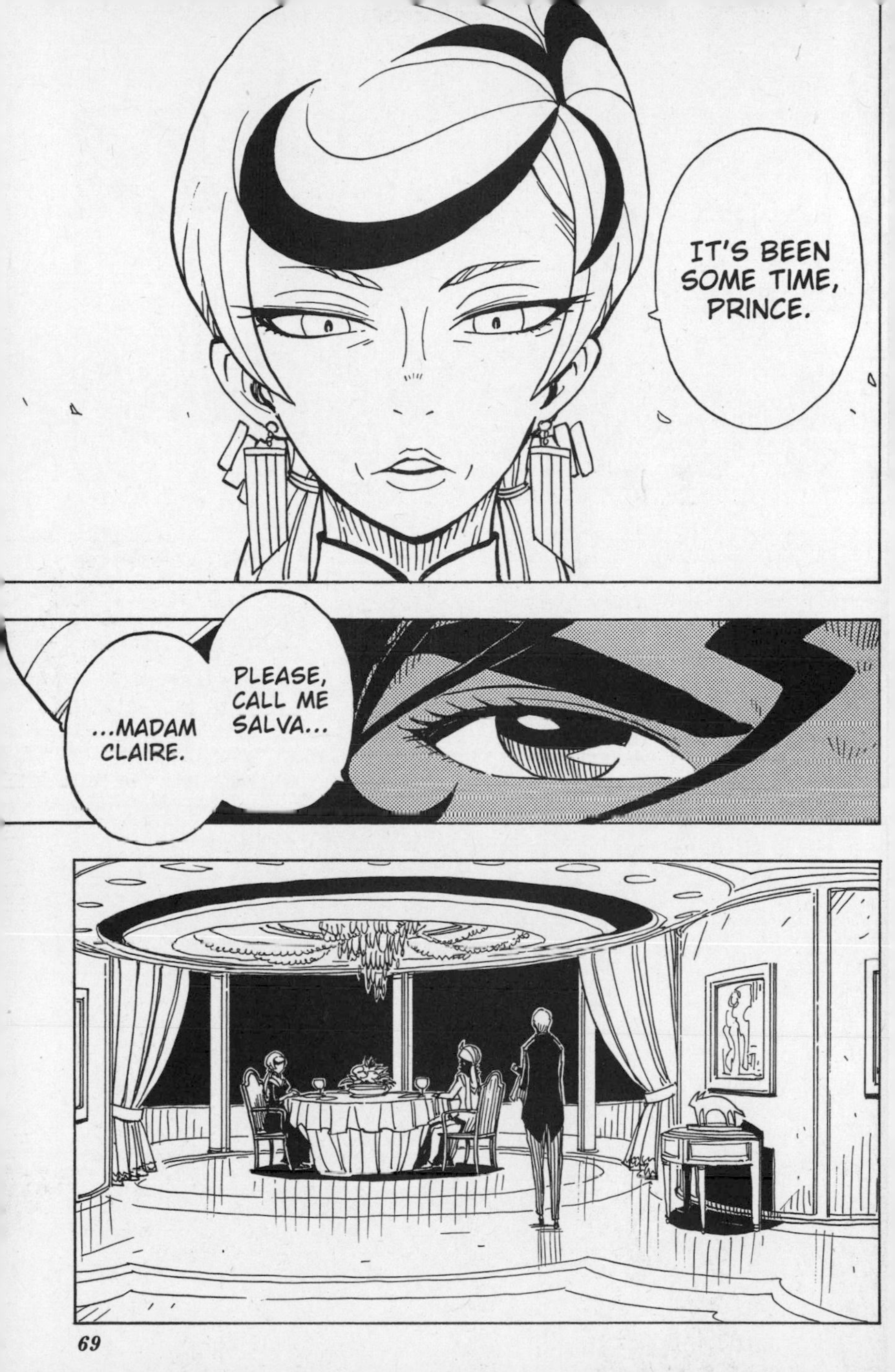
IT'S BEEN SOME TIME, PRINCE.
PLEASE, CALL ME SALVA...
...MADAM CLAIRE.

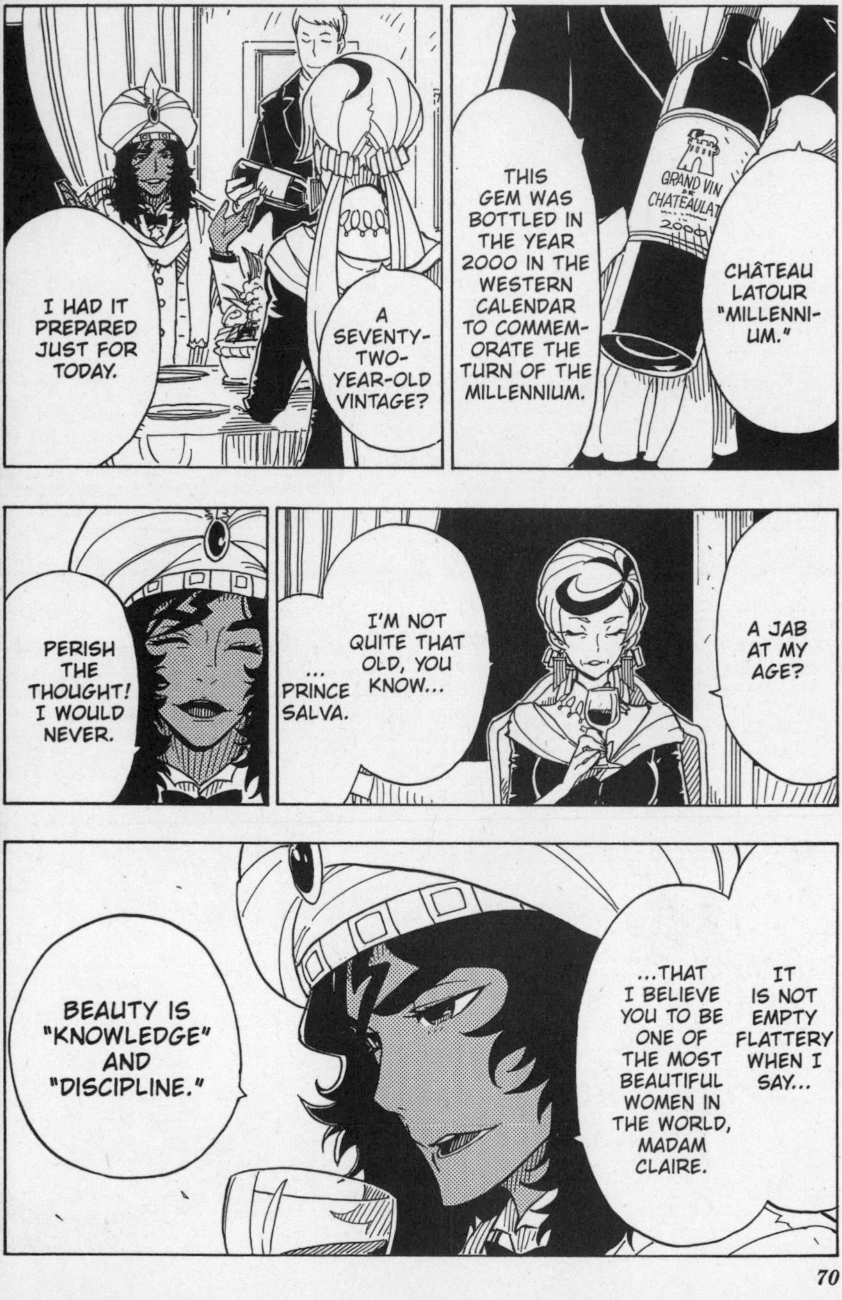

CHÂTEAU LATOUR "MILLENNIUM."
GRAND VIN DE CHÂTEAULAT 2000
THIS GEM WAS BOTTLED IN THE YEAR 2000 IN THE WESTERN CALENDAR TO COMMEMORATE THE TURN OF THE MILLENNIUM.
A SEVENTY-TWO-YEAR-OLD VINTAGE?
I HAD IT PREPARED JUST FOR TODAY.
A JAB AT MY AGE?
I'M NOT QUITE THAT OLD, YOU KNOW...
...PRINCE SALVA.
PERISH THE THOUGHT! I WOULD NEVER.
IT IS NOT EMPTY FLATTERY WHEN I SAY...
...THAT I BELIEVE YOU TO BE ONE OF THE MOST BEAUTIFUL WOMEN IN THE WORLD, MADAM CLAIRE.
BEAUTY IS "KNOWLEDGE" AND "DISCIPLINE."

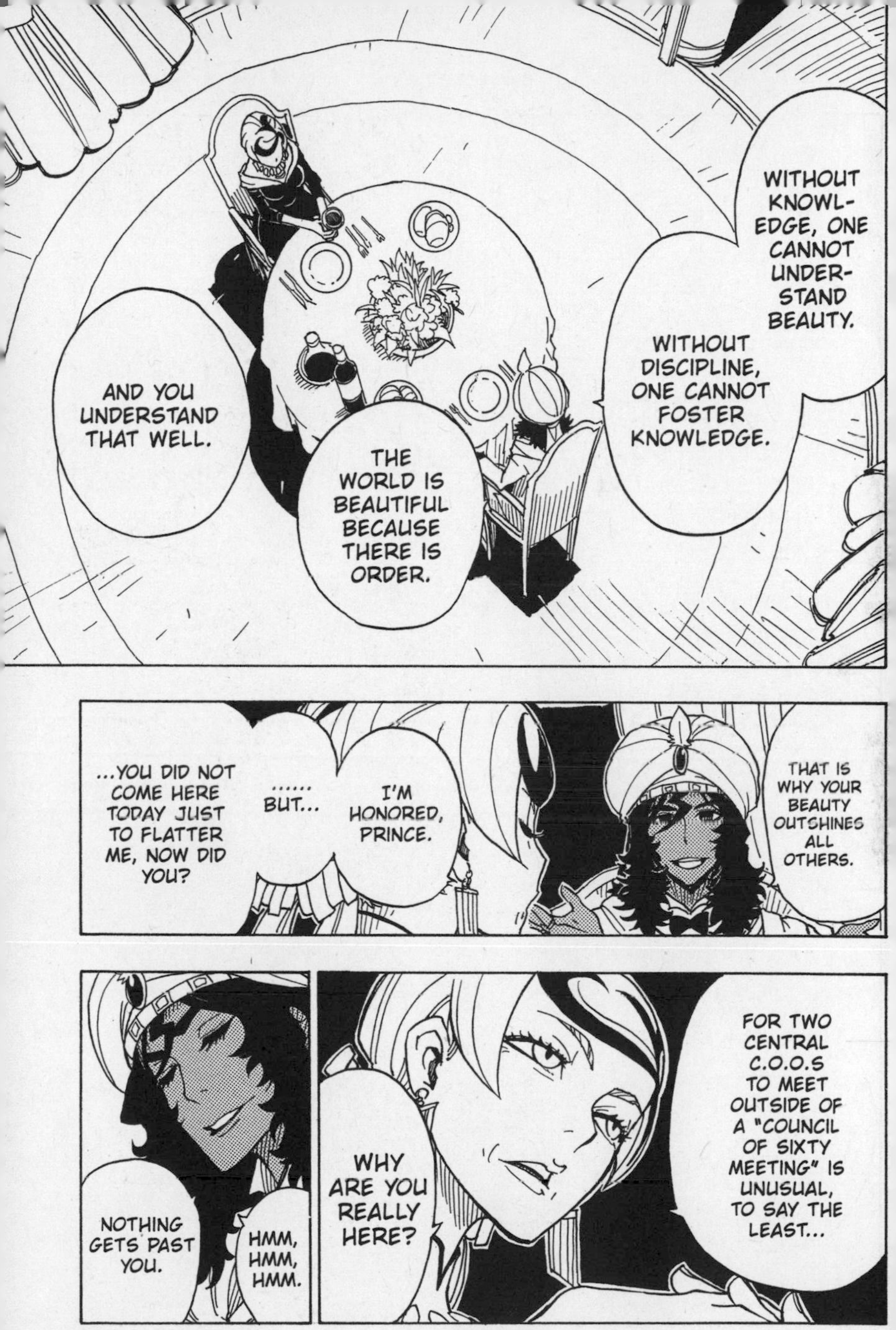
WITHOUT KNOWL-EDGE, ONE CANNOT UNDER-STAND BEAUTY.
WITHOUT DISCIPLINE, ONE CANNOT FOSTER KNOWLEDGE.
THE WORLD IS BEAUTIFUL BECAUSE THERE IS ORDER.
AND YOU UNDERSTAND THAT WELL.
THAT IS WHY YOUR BEAUTY OUTSHINES ALL OTHERS.
I'M HONORED, PRINCE.
...... BUT...
...YOU DID NOT COME HERE TODAY JUST TO FLATTER ME, NOW DID YOU?
FOR TWO CENTRAL C.O.O.S TO MEET OUTSIDE OF A "COUNCIL OF SIXTY MEETING" IS UNUSUAL, TO SAY THE LEAST...
WHY ARE YOU REALLY HERE?
HMM, HMM, HMM.
NOTHING GETS PAST YOU.

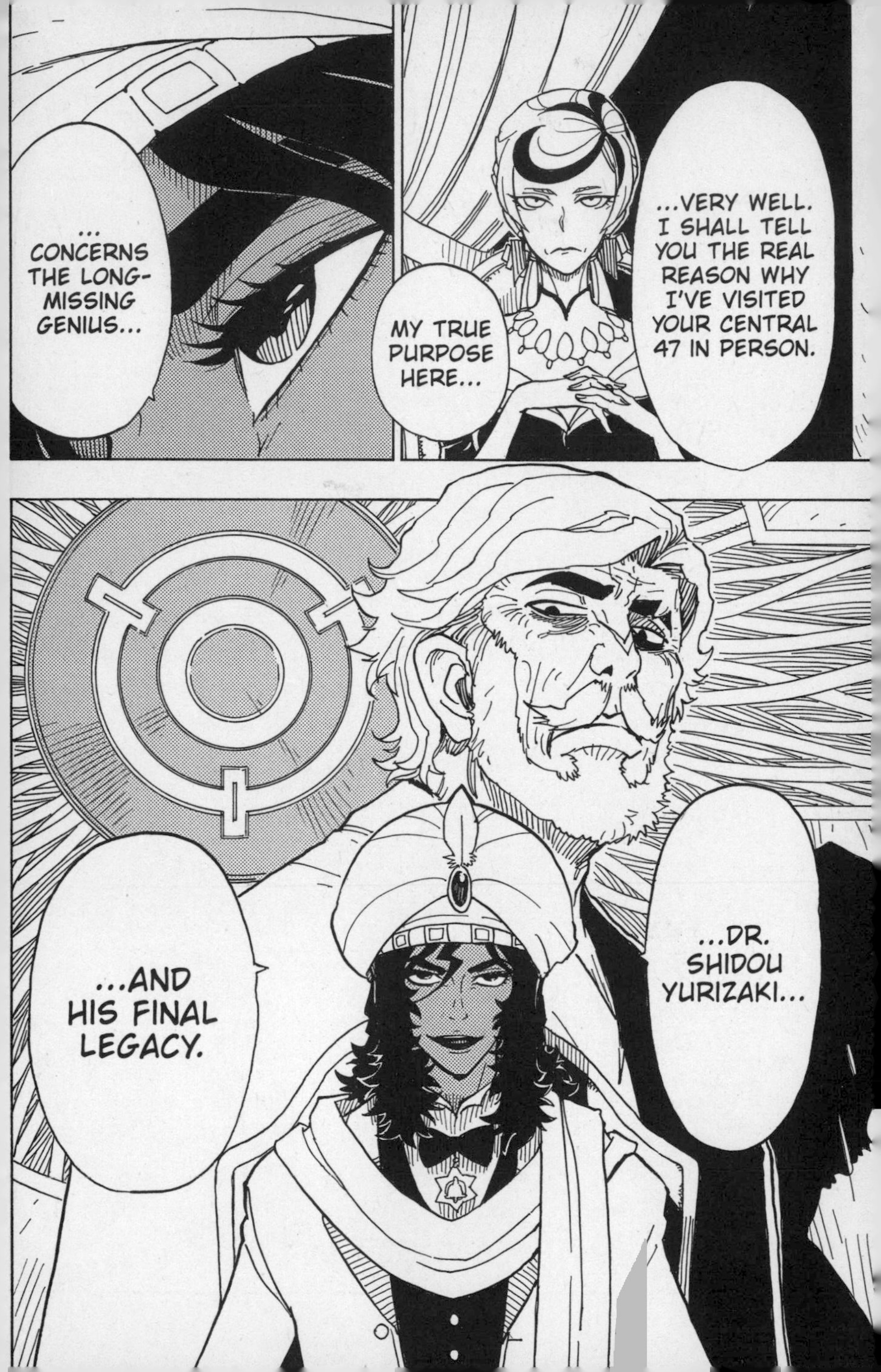
...VERY WELL. I SHALL TELL YOU THE REAL REASON WHY I'VE VISITED YOUR CENTRAL 47 IN PERSON.
MY TRUE PURPOSE HERE...
... CONCERNS THE LONG-MISSING GENIUS...
...DR. SHIDOU YURIZAKI...
...AND HIS FINAL LEGACY.

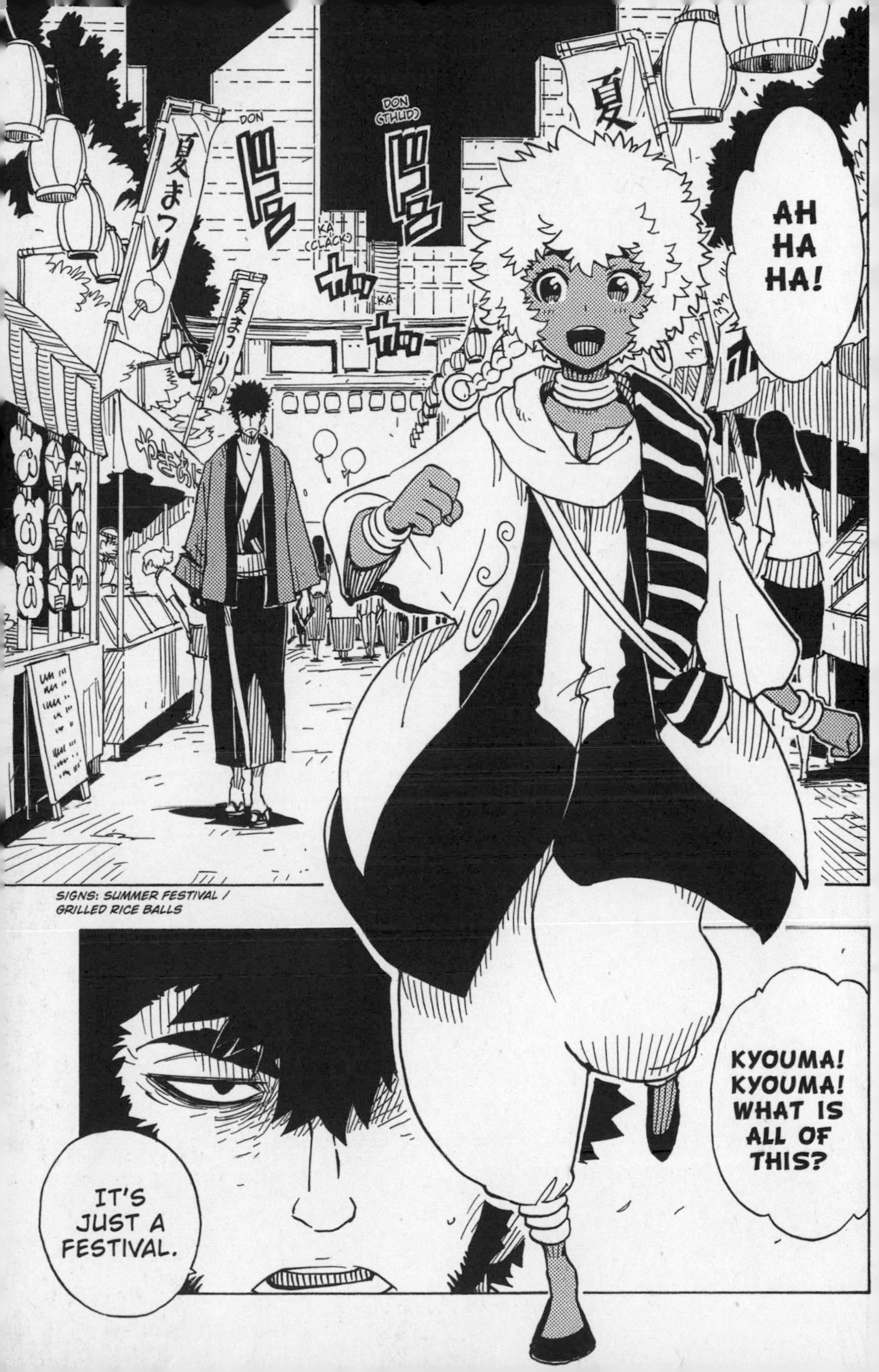
AH HA HA!
DON (THUD)
KA (CLACK)
KA
DON
SIGNS: SUMMER FESTIVAL / GRILLED RICE BALLS
KYOUMA! KYOUMA! WHAT IS ALL OF THIS?
IT'S JUST A FESTIVAL.

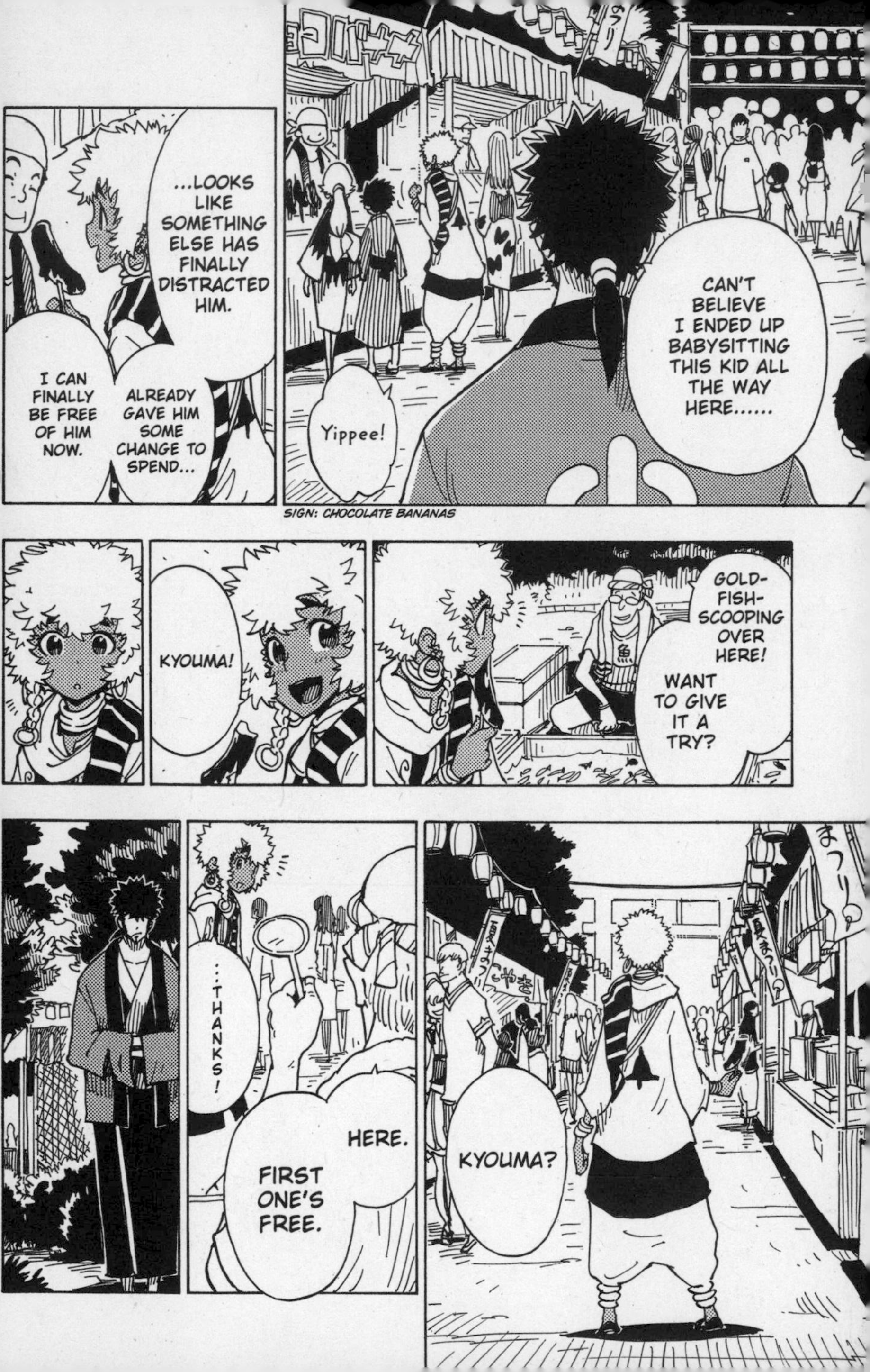
CAN'T BELIEVE I ENDED UP BABYSITTING THIS KID ALL THE WAY HERE......
Yippee!
...LOOKS LIKE SOMETHING ELSE HAS FINALLY DISTRACTED HIM.
ALREADY GAVE HIM SOME CHANGE TO SPEND...
I CAN FINALLY BE FREE OF HIM NOW.
GOLD-FISH-SCOOPING OVER HERE!
WANT TO GIVE IT A TRY?
KYOUMA!
KYOUMA?
HERE.
FIRST ONE'S FREE.
...THANKS!
SIGN: CHOCOLATE BANANAS

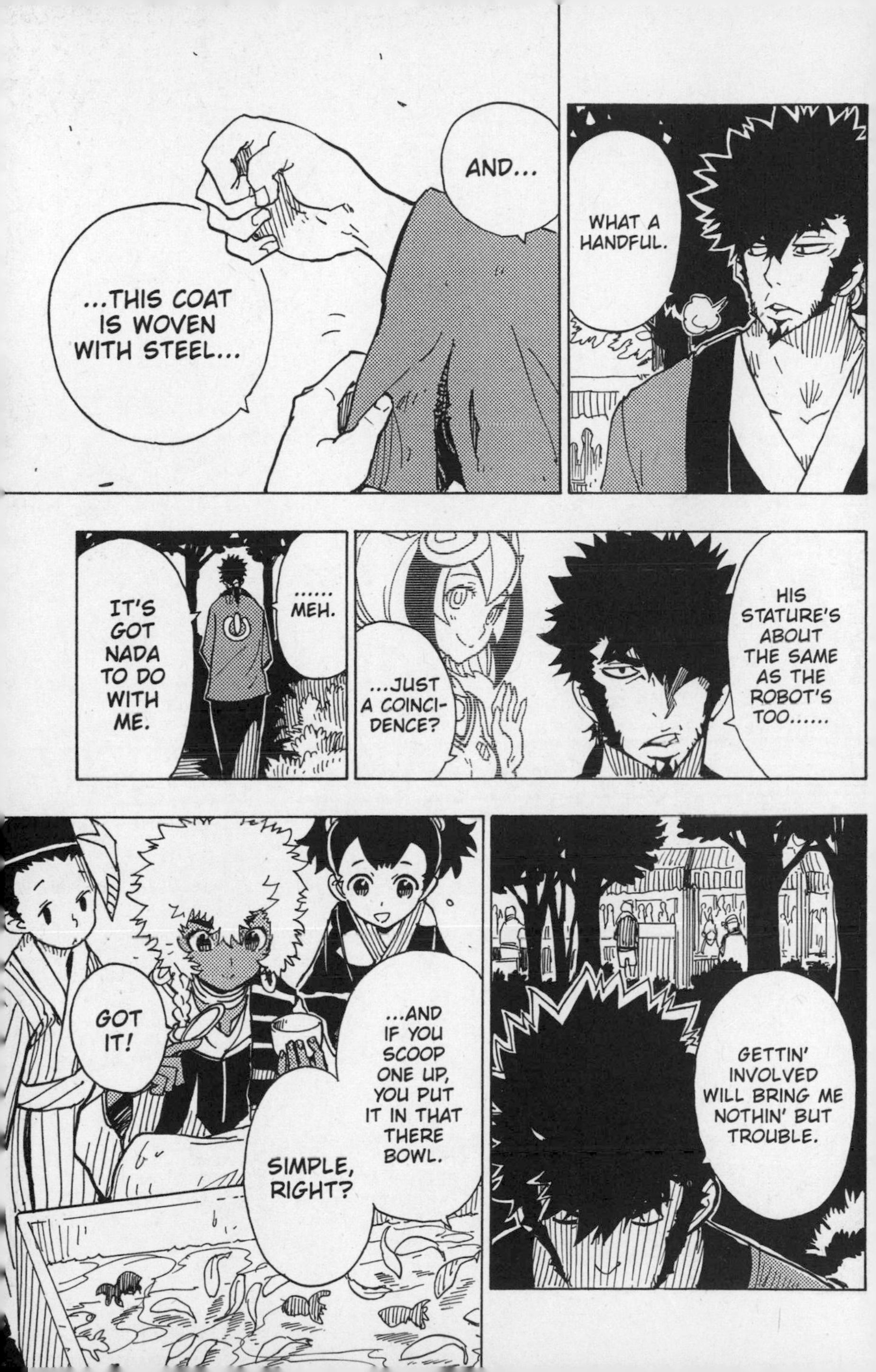
WHAT A HANDFUL.
AND...
...THIS COAT IS WOVEN WITH STEEL...
HIS STATURE'S ABOUT THE SAME AS THE ROBOT'S TOO......
...JUST A COINCIDENCE?
......MEH.
IT'S GOT NADA TO DO WITH ME.
GETTIN' INVOLVED WILL BRING ME NOTHIN' BUT TROUBLE.
...AND IF YOU SCOOP ONE UP, YOU PUT IT IN THAT THERE BOWL.
SIMPLE, RIGHT?
GOT IT!

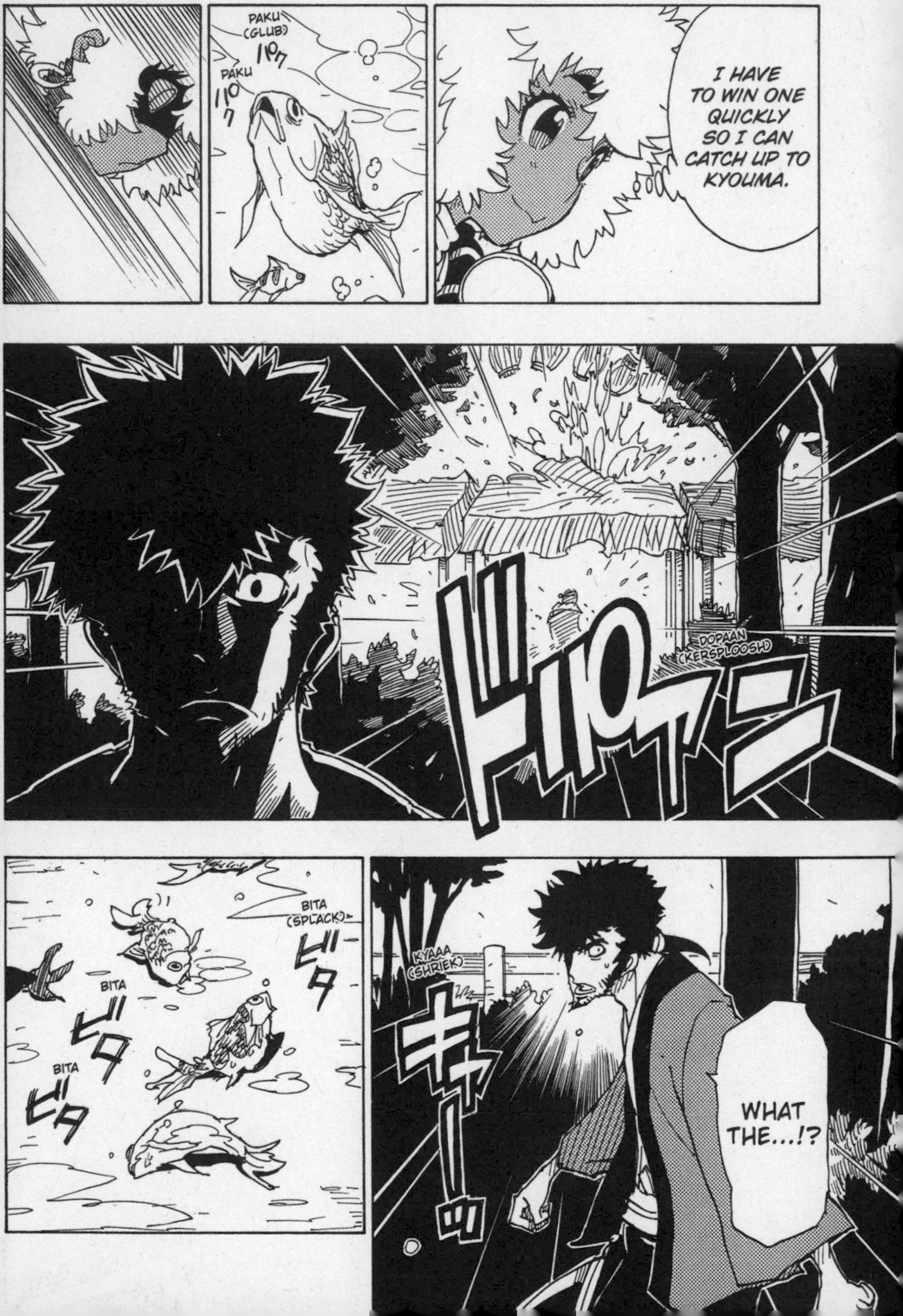
I HAVE TO WIN ONE QUICKLY SO I CAN CATCH UP TO KYOUMA.
PAKU (GLUB)
PAKU
DOPAAN (KERSPLOOSH)
KYAAA (SHRIEK)
WHAT THE...!?
BITA (SPLACK)
BITA
BITA

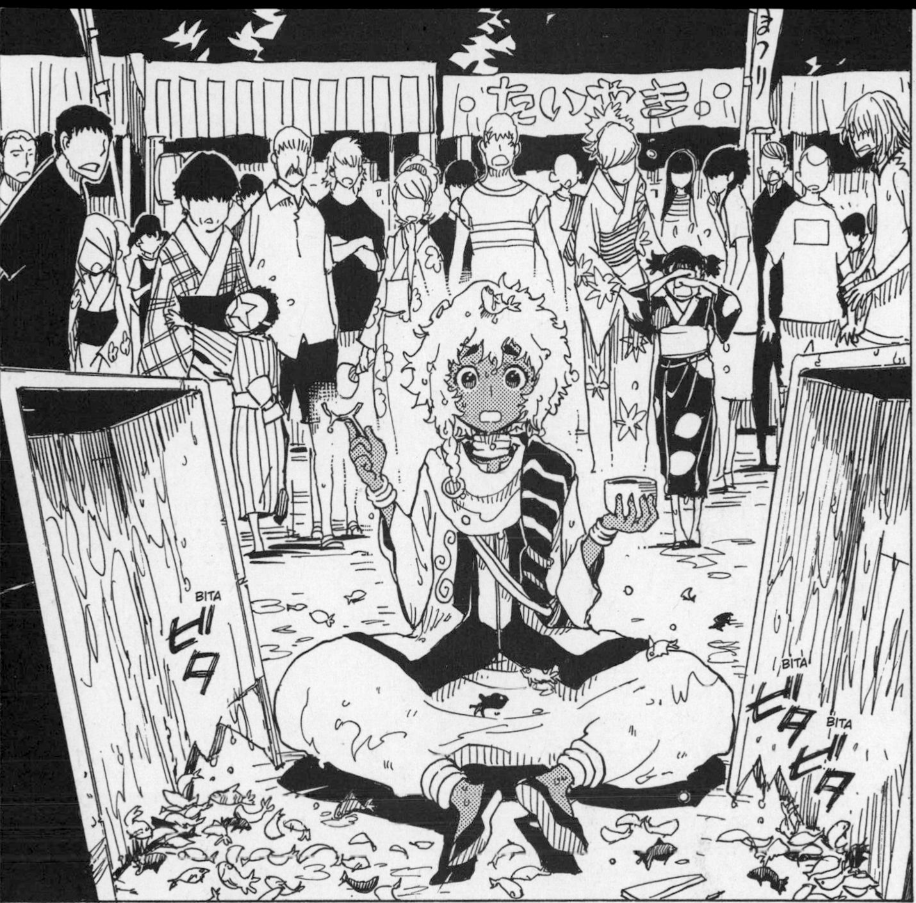
たいやき
BITA
ビタ
BITA
ビタ
BITA
ビタ
SIGN: TAIYAKI

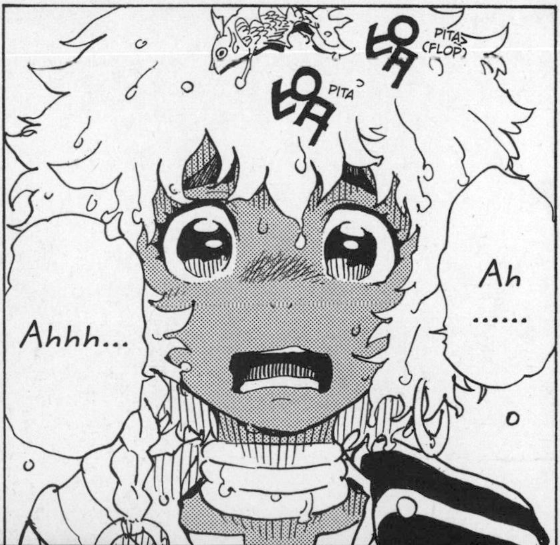
PITA (FLOP)
ピタ
PITA
ピタ
Ah ......
Ahhh...

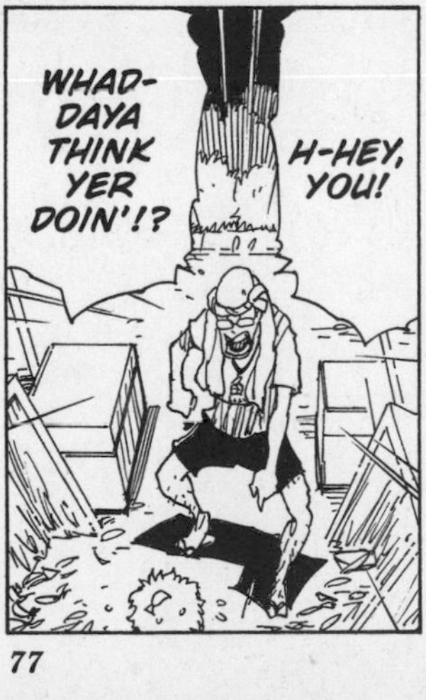
H-HEY, YOU!
WHAD-DAYA THINK YER DOIN'!?

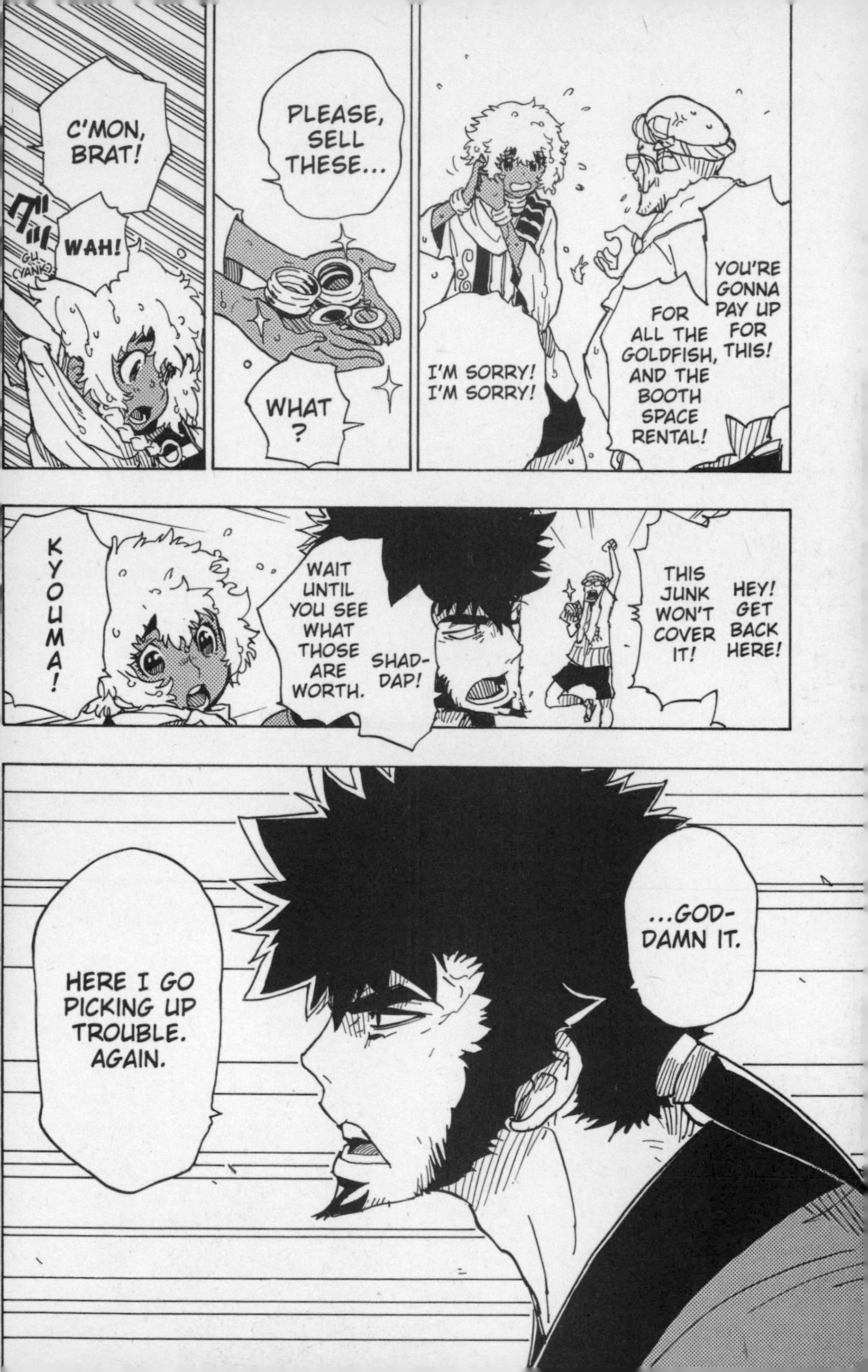
YOU'RE GONNA PAY UP FOR THIS!
FOR ALL THE GOLDFISH, AND THE BOOTH SPACE RENTAL!
I'M SORRY! I'M SORRY!
PLEASE, SELL THESE...
WHAT?
C'MON, BRAT!
WAH!
HEY! GET BACK HERE!
THIS JUNK WON'T COVER IT!
SHAD-DAP!
WAIT UNTIL YOU SEE WHAT THOSE ARE WORTH.
KYOUMA!
...GOD-DAMN IT.
HERE I GO PICKING UP TROUBLE. AGAIN.

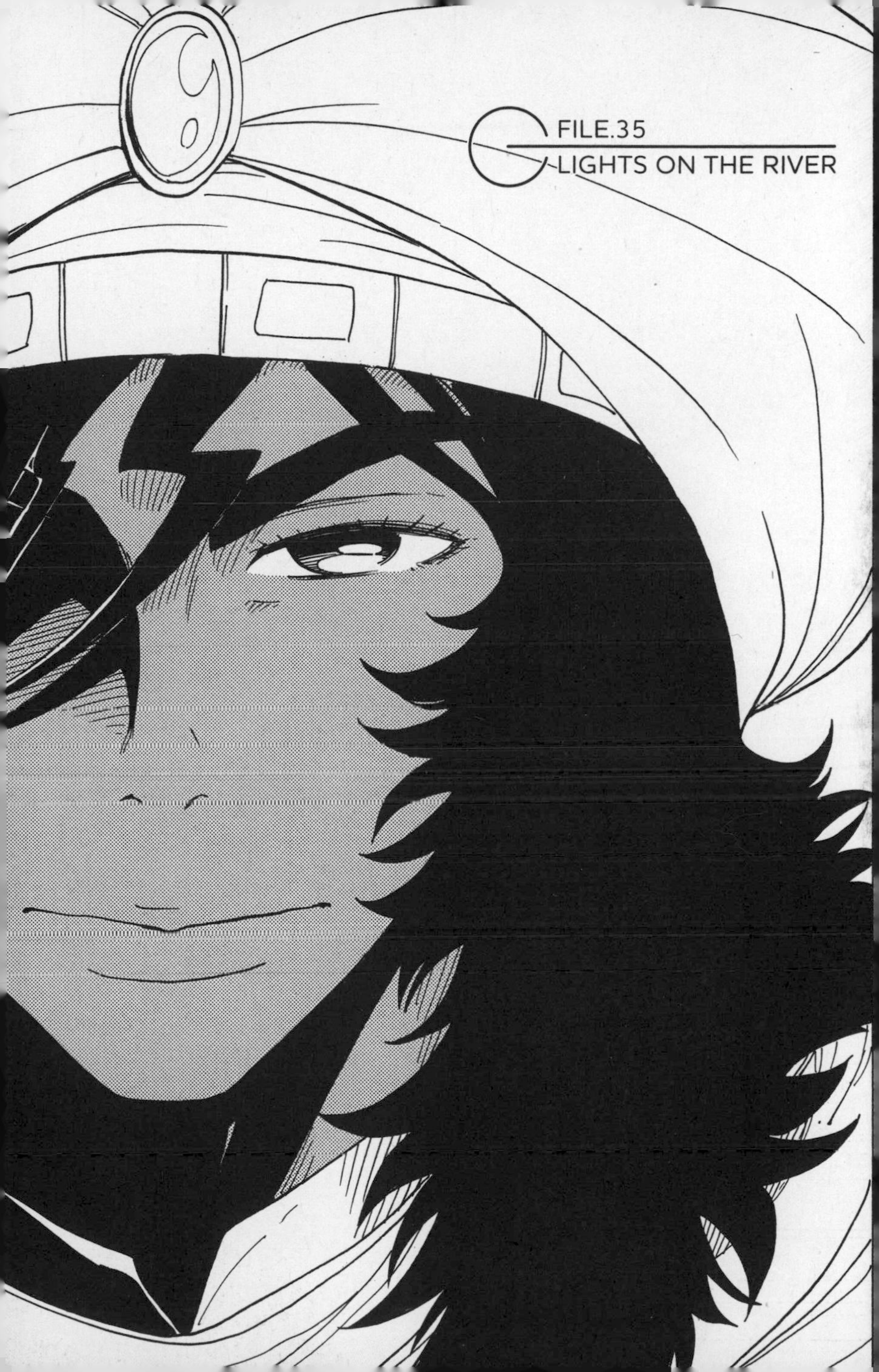
FILE.35
LIGHTS ON THE RIVER

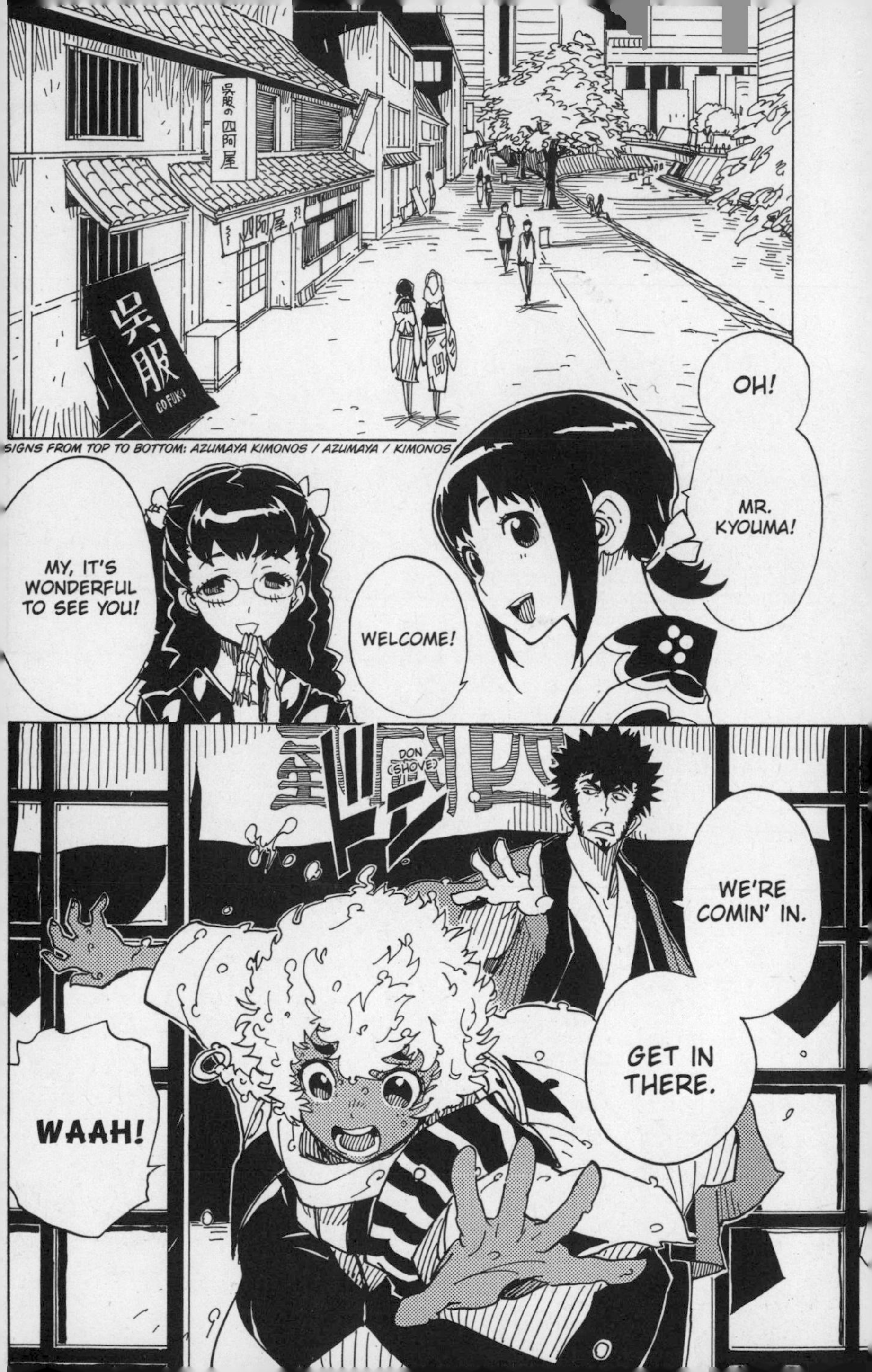
呉服の四阿屋
四阿屋
呉服
COFUKU
SIGNS FROM TOP TO BOTTOM: AZUMAYA KIMONOS / AZUMAYA / KIMONOS
OH!
MR. KYOUMA!
WELCOME!
MY, IT'S WONDERFUL TO SEE YOU!
DON (SHOVE)
WE'RE COMIN' IN.
GET IN THERE.
WAAH!

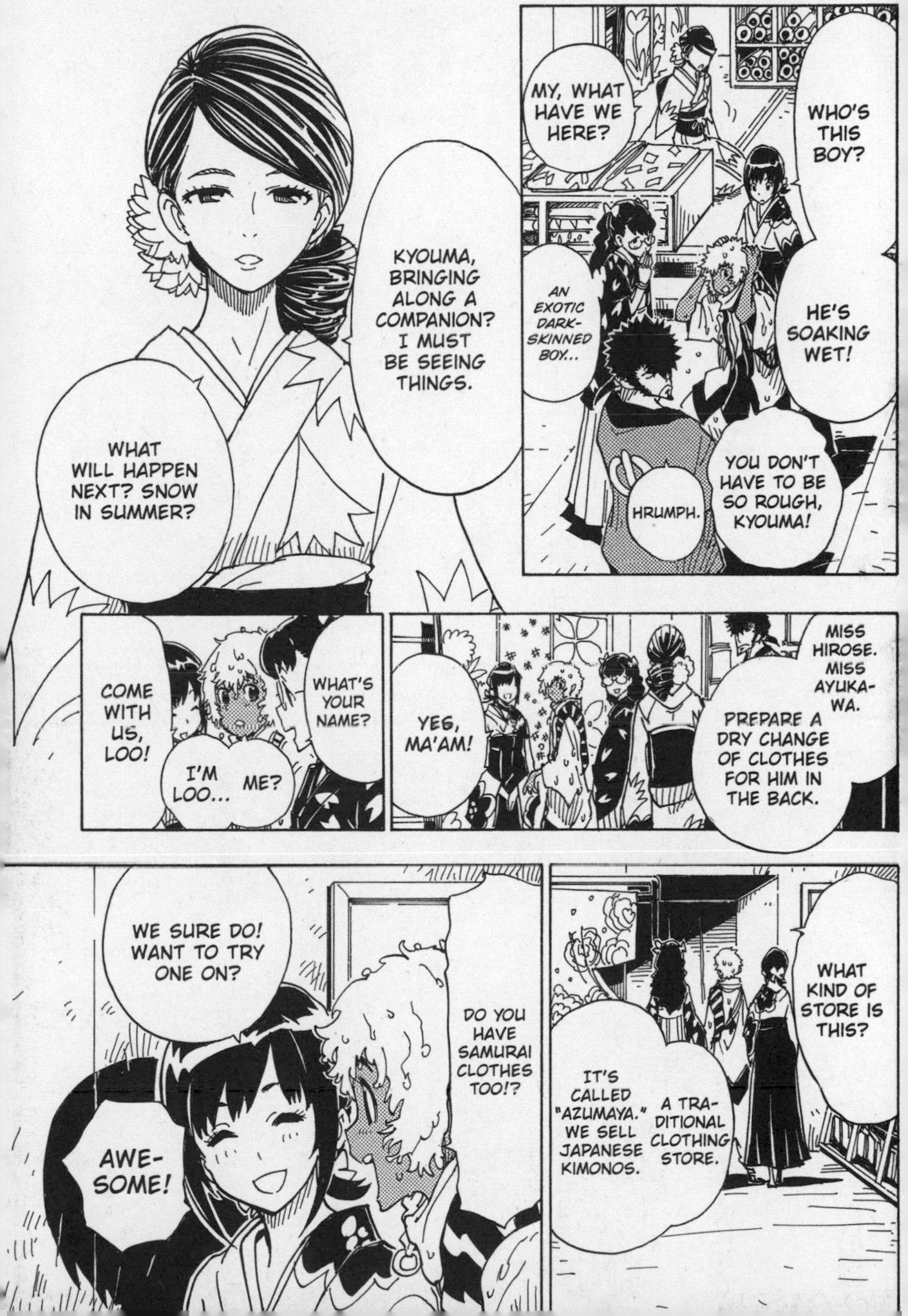
WHO'S THIS BOY?
MY, WHAT HAVE WE HERE?
HE'S SOAKING WET!
AN EXOTIC DARK-SKINNED BOY...
YOU DON'T HAVE TO BE SO ROUGH, KYOUMA!
HRUMPH.
KYOUMA, BRINGING ALONG A COMPANION? I MUST BE SEEING THINGS.
WHAT WILL HAPPEN NEXT? SNOW IN SUMMER?
MISS HIROSE. MISS AYUKAWA.
PREPARE A DRY CHANGE OF CLOTHES FOR HIM IN THE BACK.
YES, MA'AM!
WHAT'S YOUR NAME?
ME?
I'M LOO...
COME WITH US, LOO!
WHAT KIND OF STORE IS THIS?
A TRADITIONAL CLOTHING STORE.
IT'S CALLED "AZUMAYA." WE SELL JAPANESE KIMONOS.
DO YOU HAVE SAMURAI CLOTHES TOO!?
WE SURE DO! WANT TO TRY ONE ON?
AWESOME!

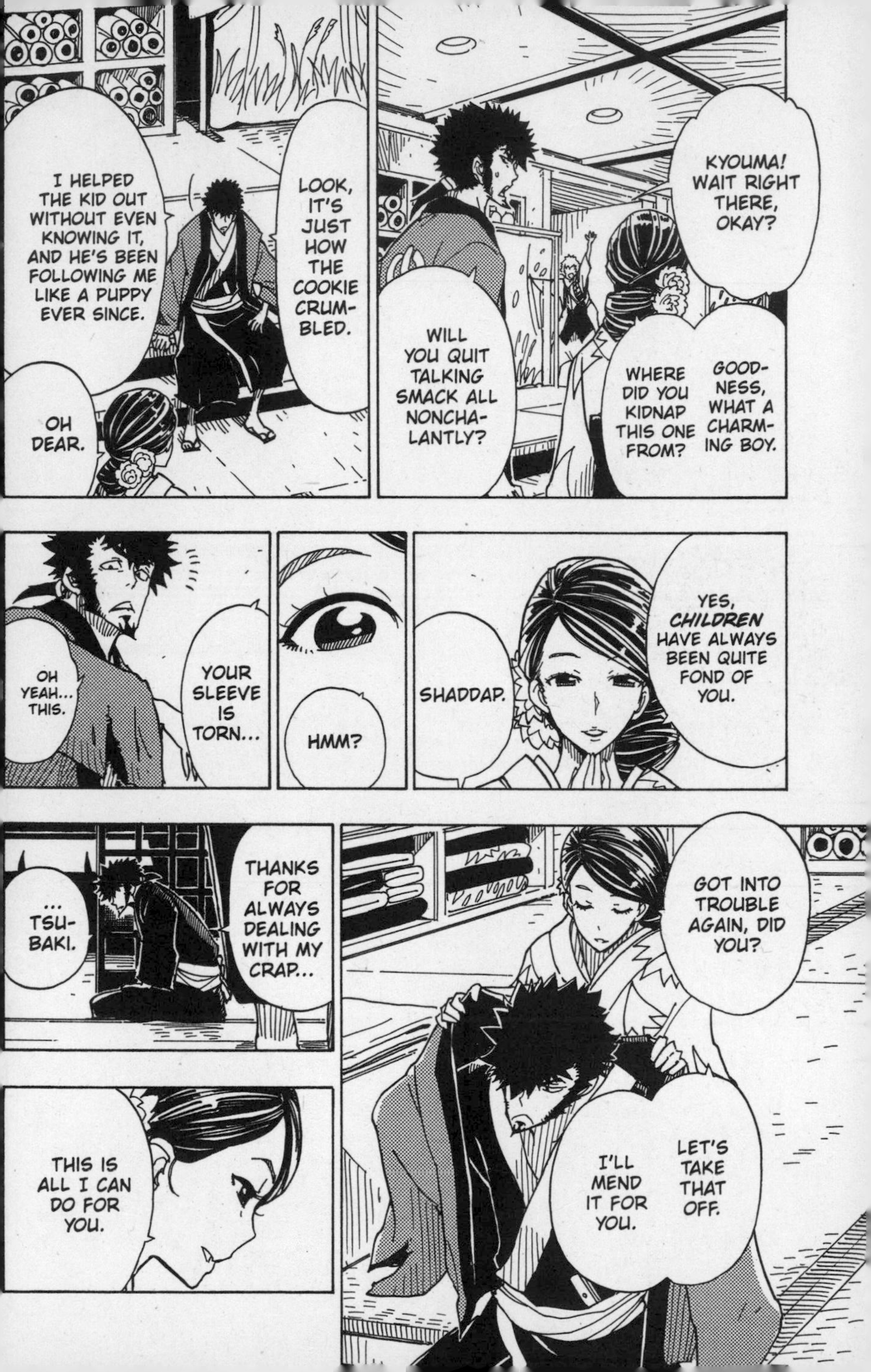
KYOUMA! WAIT RIGHT THERE, OKAY?
GOODNESS, WHAT A CHARMING BOY.
WHERE DID YOU KIDNAP THIS ONE FROM?
WILL YOU QUIT TALKING SMACK ALL NONCHALANTLY?
LOOK, IT'S JUST HOW THE COOKIE CRUMBLED.
I HELPED THE KID OUT WITHOUT EVEN KNOWING IT, AND HE'S BEEN FOLLOWING ME LIKE A PUPPY EVER SINCE.
OH DEAR.
YES, *CHILDREN* HAVE ALWAYS BEEN QUITE FOND OF YOU.
SHADDAP.
HMM?
YOUR SLEEVE IS TORN...
OH YEAH... THIS.
GOT INTO TROUBLE AGAIN, DID YOU?
LET'S TAKE THAT OFF.
I'LL MEND IT FOR YOU.
THANKS FOR ALWAYS DEALING WITH MY CRAP...
... TSUBAKI.
THIS IS ALL I CAN DO FOR YOU.

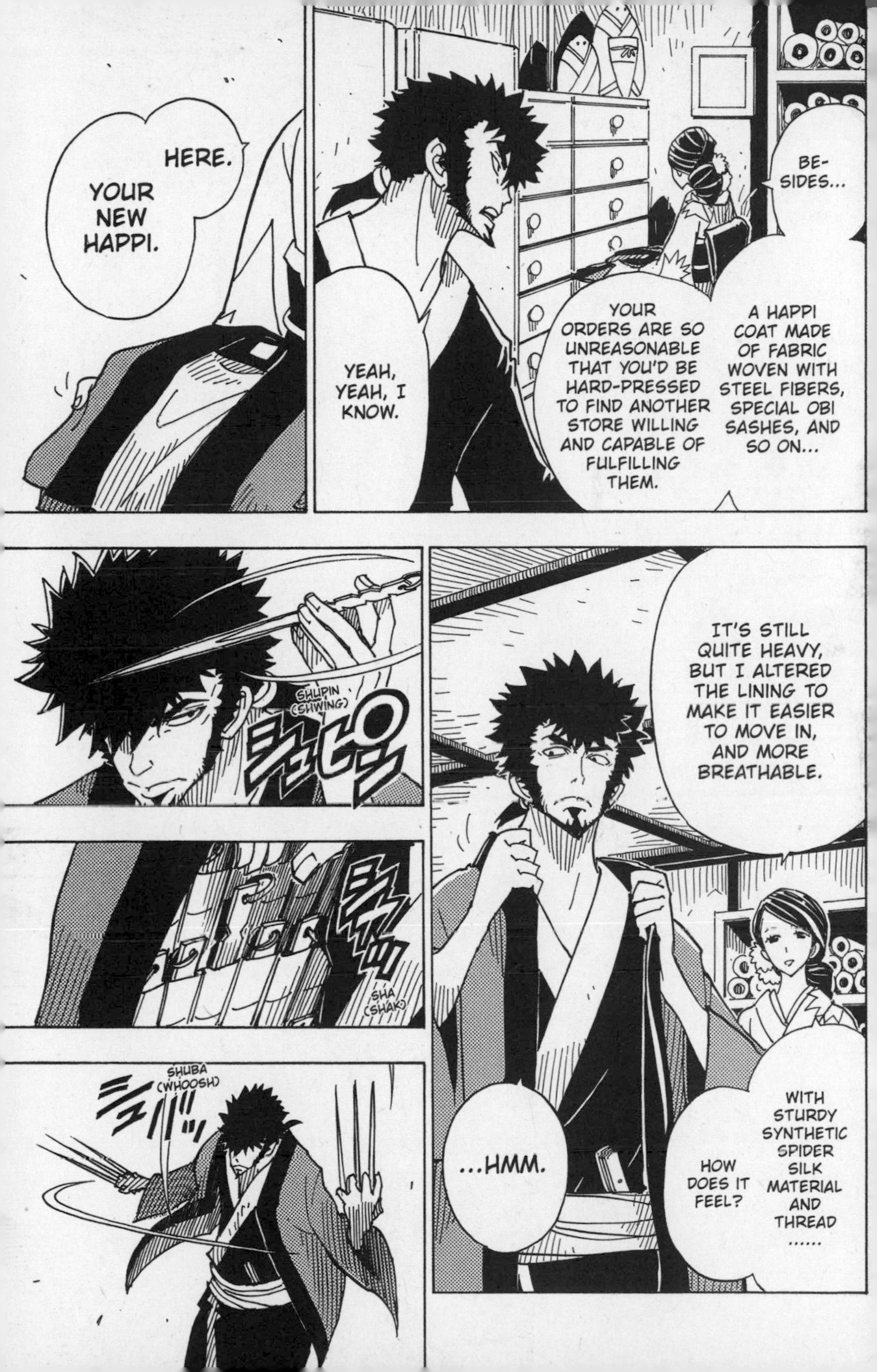

BE-SIDES...
A HAPPI COAT MADE OF FABRIC WOVEN WITH STEEL FIBERS, SPECIAL OBI SASHES, AND SO ON...
YOUR ORDERS ARE SO UNREASONABLE THAT YOU'D BE HARD-PRESSED TO FIND ANOTHER STORE WILLING AND CAPABLE OF FULFILLING THEM.
YEAH, YEAH, I KNOW.
HERE.
YOUR NEW HAPPI.
IT'S STILL QUITE HEAVY, BUT I ALTERED THE LINING TO MAKE IT EASIER TO MOVE IN, AND MORE BREATHABLE.
WITH STURDY SYNTHETIC SPIDER SILK MATERIAL AND THREAD ......
HOW DOES IT FEEL?
...HMM.
SHUPIN (SHWING)
SHA (SHAK)
SHUBA (WHOOSH)

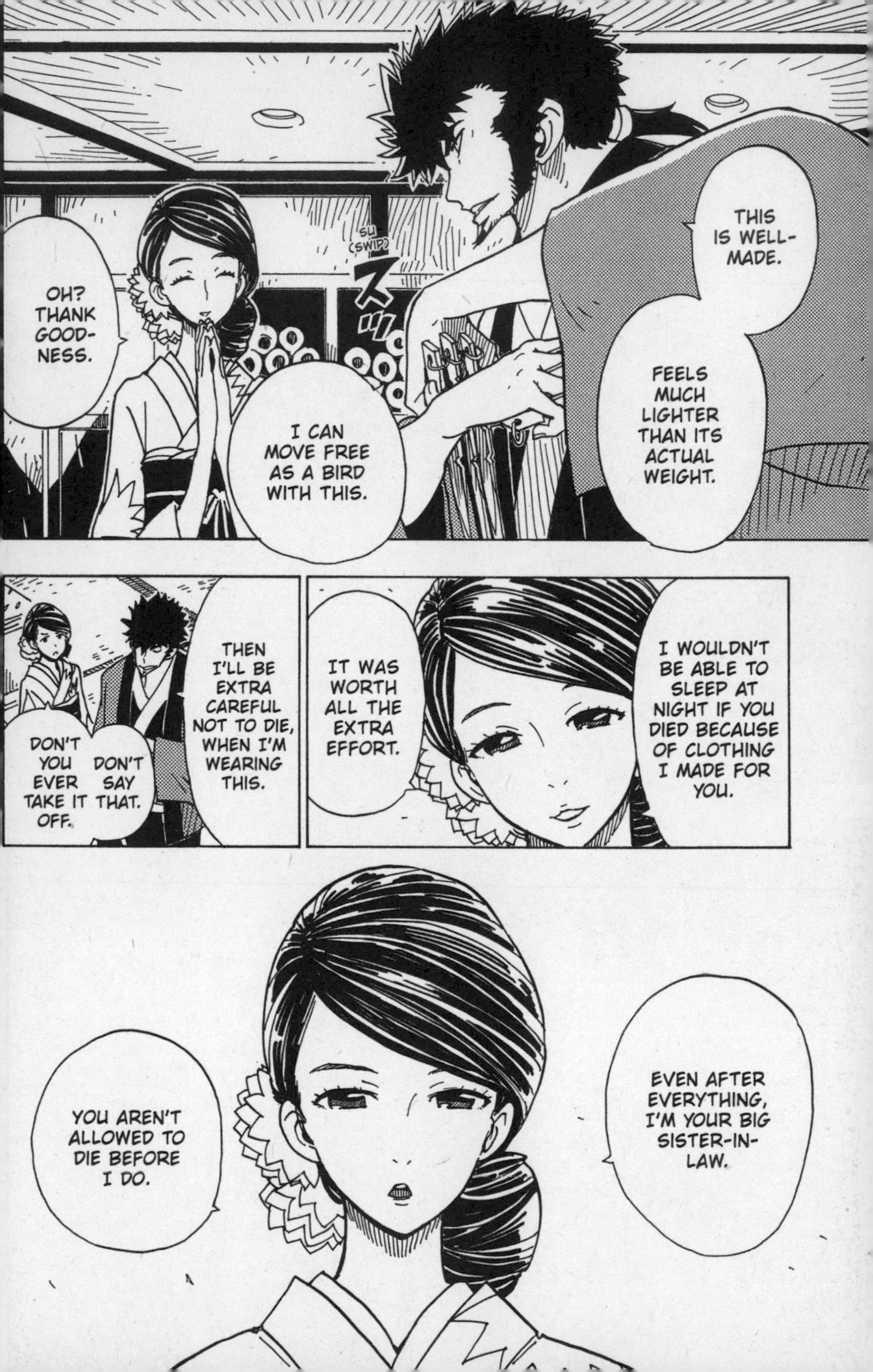
THIS IS WELL-MADE.
FEELS MUCH LIGHTER THAN ITS ACTUAL WEIGHT.
SU (SWIP)
I CAN MOVE FREE AS A BIRD WITH THIS.
OH? THANK GOODNESS.
I WOULDN'T BE ABLE TO SLEEP AT NIGHT IF YOU DIED BECAUSE OF CLOTHING I MADE FOR YOU.
IT WAS WORTH ALL THE EXTRA EFFORT.
THEN I'LL BE EXTRA CAREFUL NOT TO DIE, WHEN I'M WEARING THIS.
DON'T SAY THAT.
DON'T YOU EVER TAKE IT OFF.
EVEN AFTER EVERYTHING, I'M YOUR BIG SISTER-IN-LAW.
YOU AREN'T ALLOWED TO DIE BEFORE I DO.

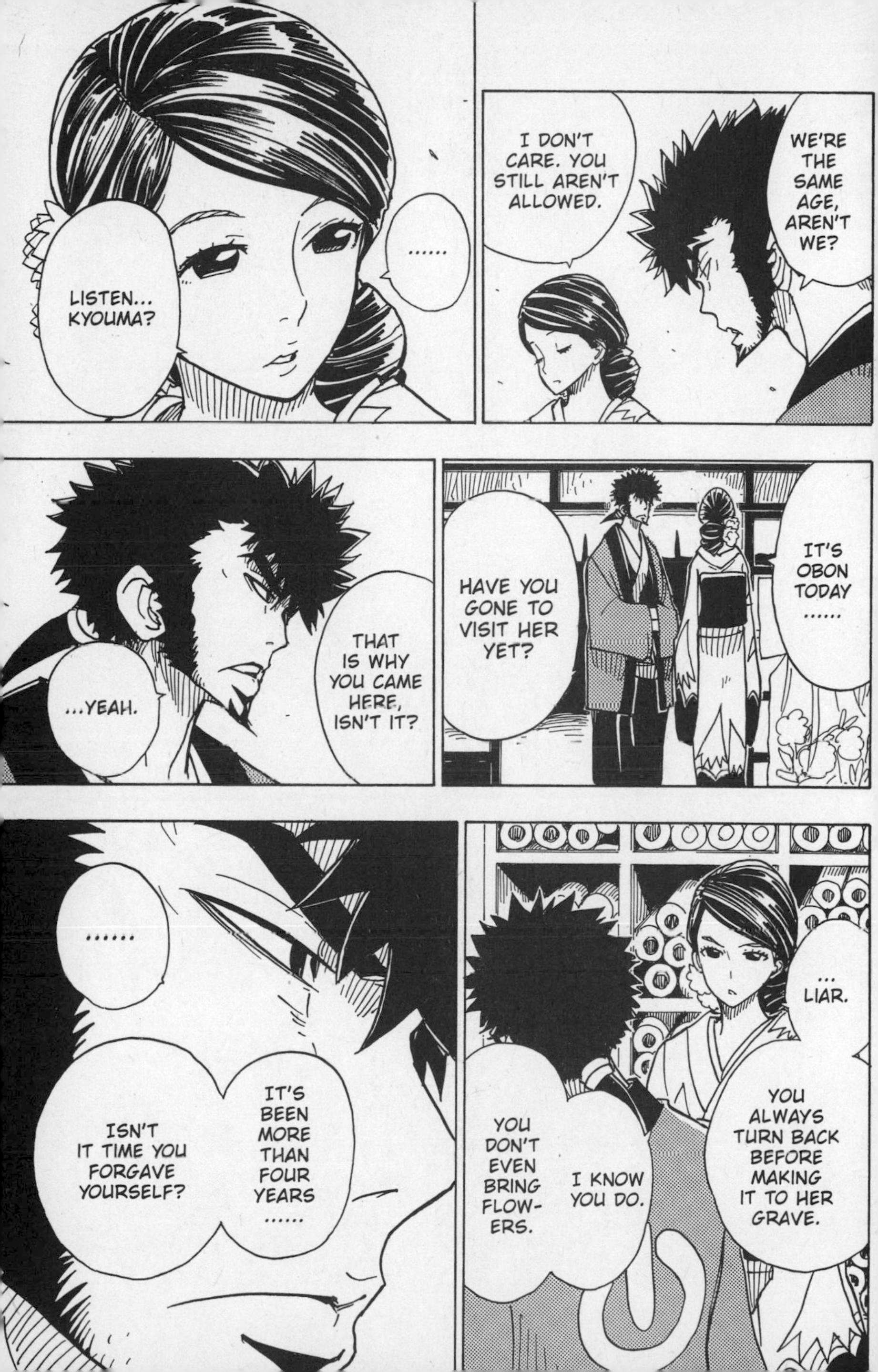
WE'RE THE SAME AGE, AREN'T WE?
I DON'T CARE. YOU STILL AREN'T ALLOWED.
......
LISTEN... KYOUMA?
IT'S OBON TODAY ......
HAVE YOU GONE TO VISIT HER YET?
THAT IS WHY YOU CAME HERE, ISN'T IT?
...YEAH.
... LIAR.
YOU ALWAYS TURN BACK BEFORE MAKING IT TO HER GRAVE.
I KNOW YOU DO.
YOU DON'T EVEN BRING FLOW-ERS.
......
IT'S BEEN MORE THAN FOUR YEARS ......
ISN'T IT TIME YOU FORGAVE YOURSELF?

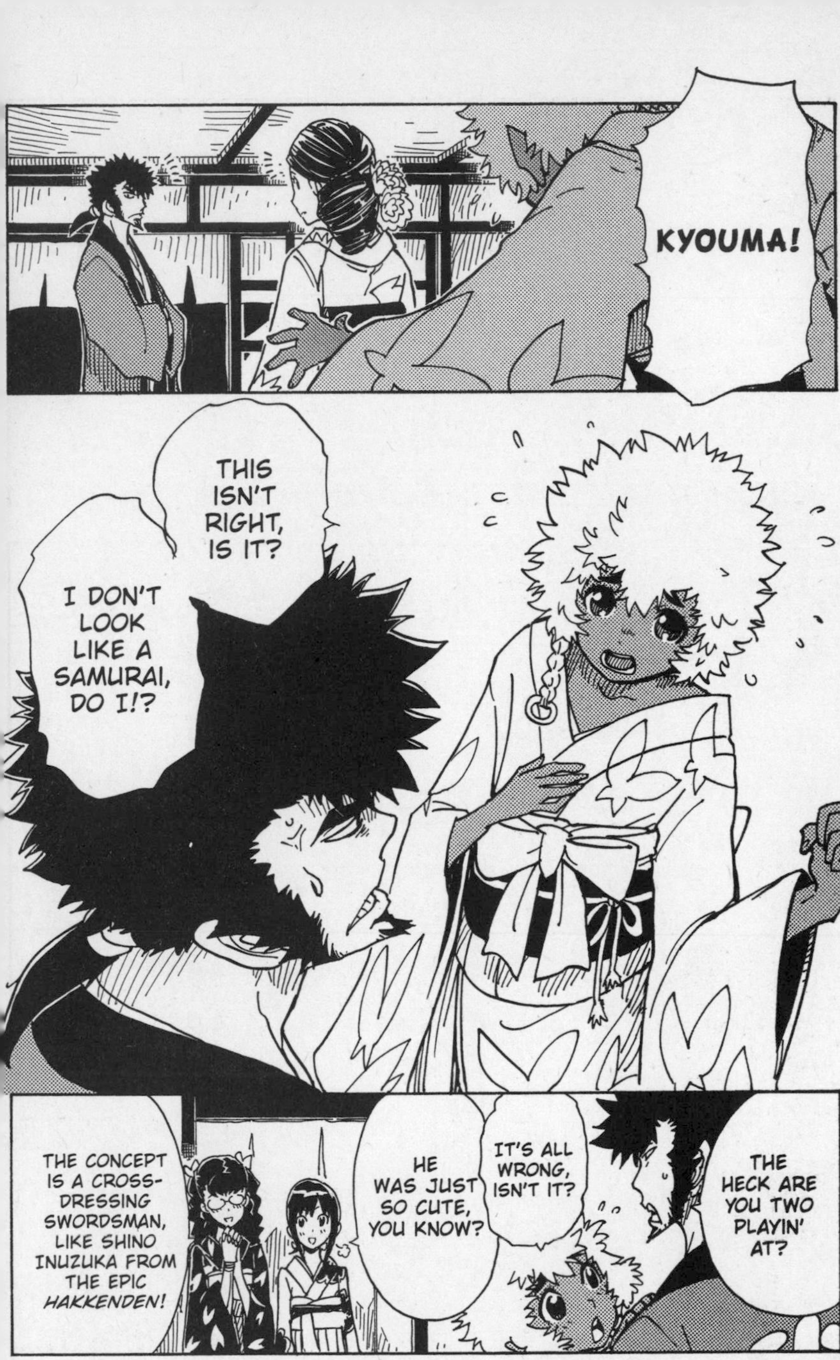
KYOUMA!
THIS ISN'T RIGHT, IS IT?
I DON'T LOOK LIKE A SAMURAI, DO I!?
THE HECK ARE YOU TWO PLAYIN' AT?
IT'S ALL WRONG, ISN'T IT?
HE WAS JUST SO CUTE, YOU KNOW?
THE CONCEPT IS A CROSS-DRESSING SWORDSMAN, LIKE SHINO INUZUKA FROM THE EPIC *HAKKENDEN*!

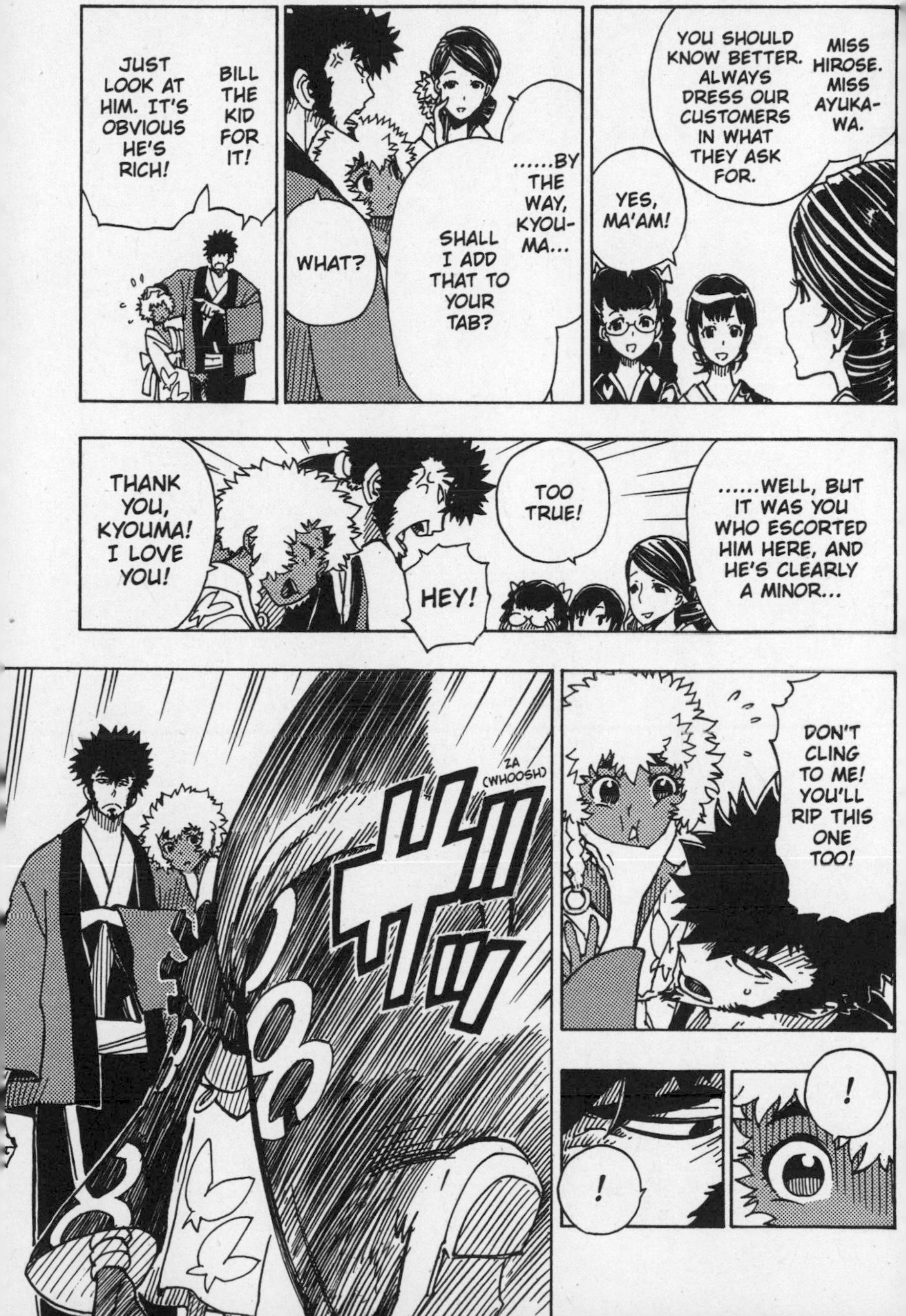
MISS HIROSE. MISS AYUKAWA.
YOU SHOULD KNOW BETTER. ALWAYS DRESS OUR CUSTOMERS IN WHAT THEY ASK FOR.
YES, MA'AM!
......BY THE WAY, KYOUMA...
SHALL I ADD THAT TO YOUR TAB?
WHAT?
BILL THE KID FOR IT!
JUST LOOK AT HIM. IT'S OBVIOUS HE'S RICH!
......WELL, BUT IT WAS YOU WHO ESCORTED HIM HERE, AND HE'S CLEARLY A MINOR...
TOO TRUE!
HEY!
THANK YOU, KYOUMA! I LOVE YOU!
DON'T CLING TO ME! YOU'LL RIP THIS ONE TOO!
!
!
ZA (WHOOSH)

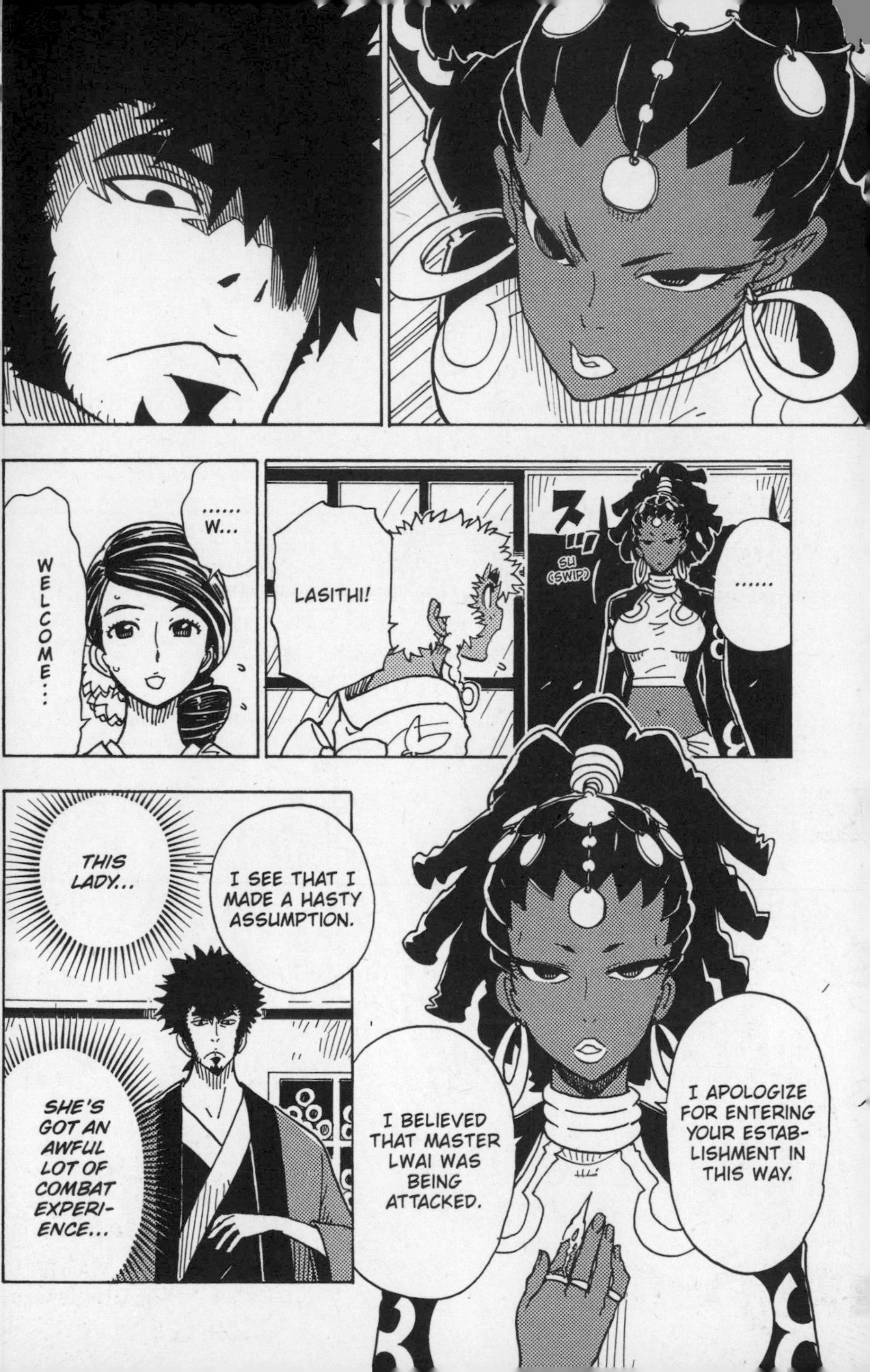
ス
SU (SWIP)
......
LASITHI!
...... W...
WELCOME...
I APOLOGIZE FOR ENTERING YOUR ESTABLISHMENT IN THIS WAY.
I BELIEVED THAT MASTER LWAI WAS BEING ATTACKED.
I SEE THAT I MADE A HASTY ASSUMPTION.
THIS LADY...
SHE'S GOT AN AWFUL LOT OF COMBAT EXPERIENCE...

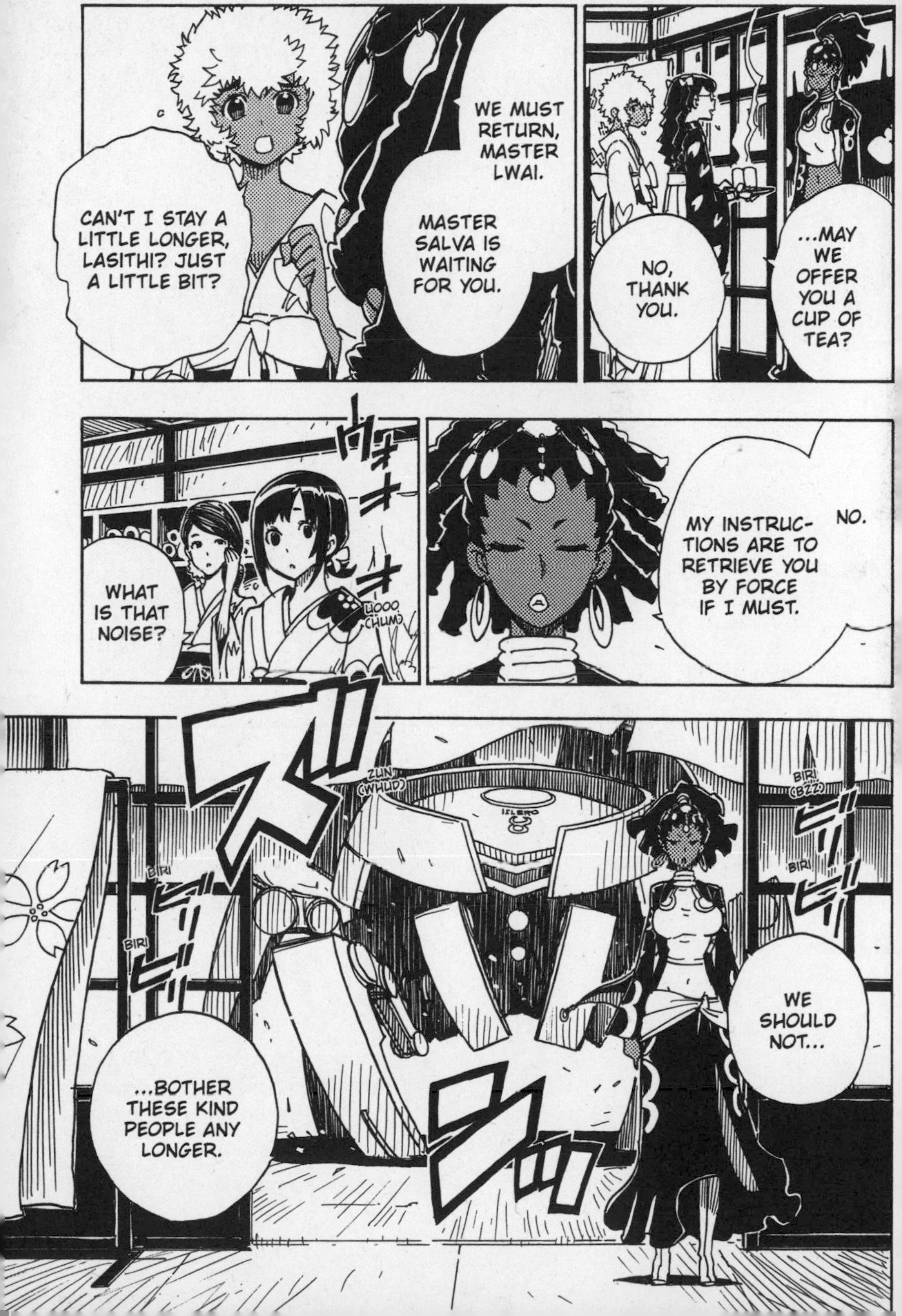
...MAY WE OFFER YOU A CUP OF TEA?
NO, THANK YOU.
WE MUST RETURN, MASTER LWAI.
MASTER SALVA IS WAITING FOR YOU.
CAN'T I STAY A LITTLE LONGER, LASITHI? JUST A LITTLE BIT?
NO.
MY INSTRUC-TIONS ARE TO RETRIEVE YOU BY FORCE IF I MUST.
UOOO (HUM)
WHAT IS THAT NOISE?
BIRI (BZZ)
BIRI
ZUN (WHUD)
ISLERO
BIRI
BIRI
WE SHOULD NOT...
...BOTHER THESE KIND PEOPLE ANY LONGER.

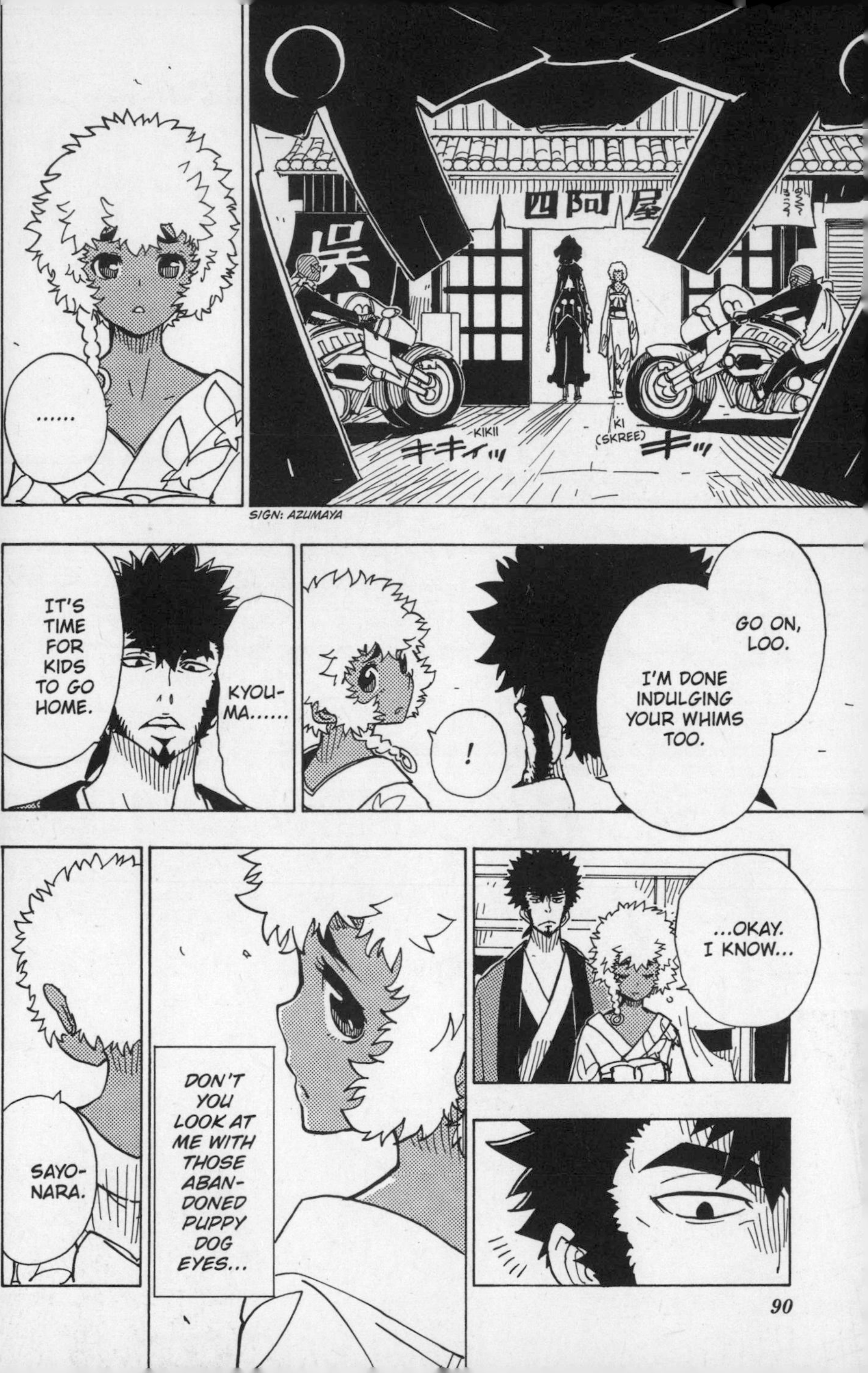
四阿屋
KIKII
キキィッ
KI (SKREE)
ギッ
SIGN: AZUMAYA
......
GO ON, LOO.
I'M DONE INDULGING YOUR WHIMS TOO.
!
IT'S TIME FOR KIDS TO GO HOME.
KYOU-MA......
...OKAY. I KNOW...
DON'T YOU LOOK AT ME WITH THOSE ABAN-DONED PUPPY DOG EYES...
SAYO-NARA.

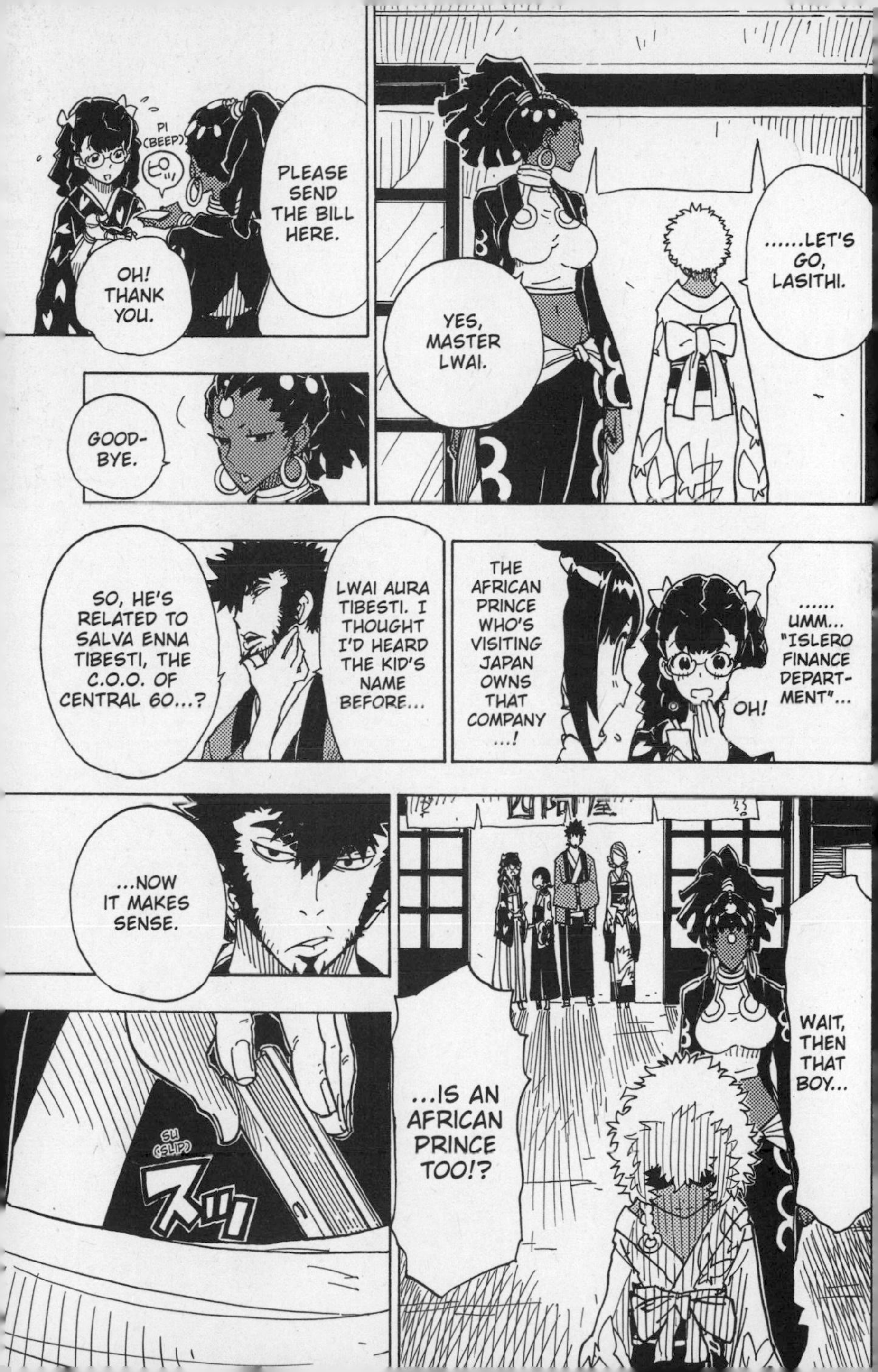
......LET'S GO, LASITHI.
YES, MASTER LWAI.
PLEASE SEND THE BILL HERE.
PI (BEEP)
OH! THANK YOU.
GOOD-BYE.
...... UMM... "ISLERO FINANCE DEPARTMENT"...
OH!
THE AFRICAN PRINCE WHO'S VISITING JAPAN OWNS THAT COMPANY ...!
LWAI AURA TIBESTI. I THOUGHT I'D HEARD THE KID'S NAME BEFORE...
SO, HE'S RELATED TO SALVA ENNA TIBESTI, THE C.O.O. OF CENTRAL 60...?
WAIT, THEN THAT BOY...
...IS AN AFRICAN PRINCE TOO!?
...NOW IT MAKES SENSE.
SU (SLIP)

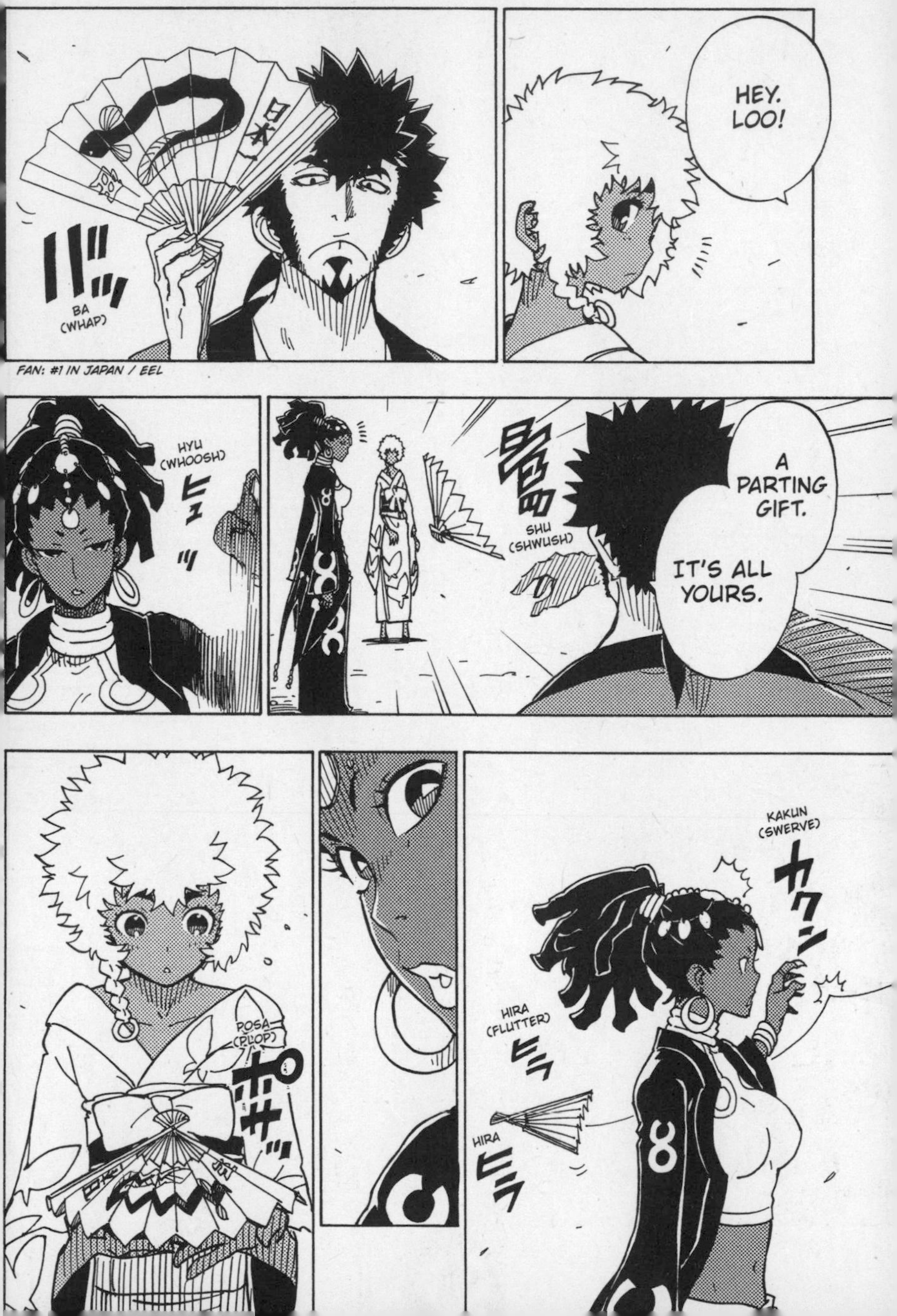
HEY. LOO!
BA (WHAP)
バッ
FAN: #1 IN JAPAN / EEL
A PARTING GIFT.
IT'S ALL YOURS.
SHU (SHWUSH)
HYU (WHOOSH)
ヒュッ
KAKUN (SWERVE)
カクン
HIRA (FLUTTER)
ヒラ
HIRA
ヒラ
POSA (PLOP)
ポサッ

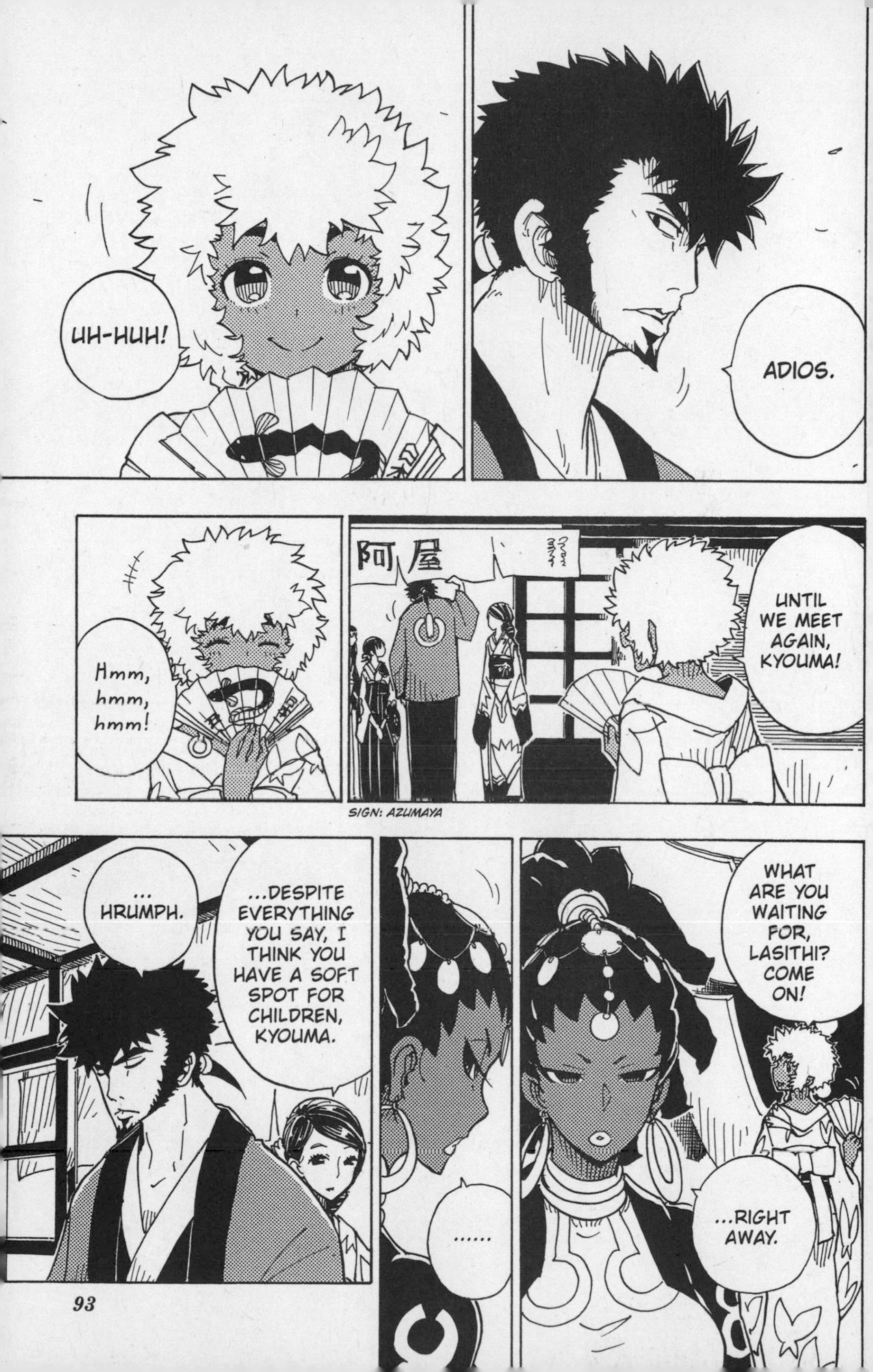
ADIOS.
UH-HUH!
UNTIL WE MEET AGAIN, KYOUMA!
阿 屋
Hmm, hmm, hmm!
SIGN: AZUMAYA
WHAT ARE YOU WAITING FOR, LASITHI? COME ON!
...RIGHT AWAY.
......
...DESPITE EVERYTHING YOU SAY, I THINK YOU HAVE A SOFT SPOT FOR CHILDREN, KYOUMA.
... HRUMPH.

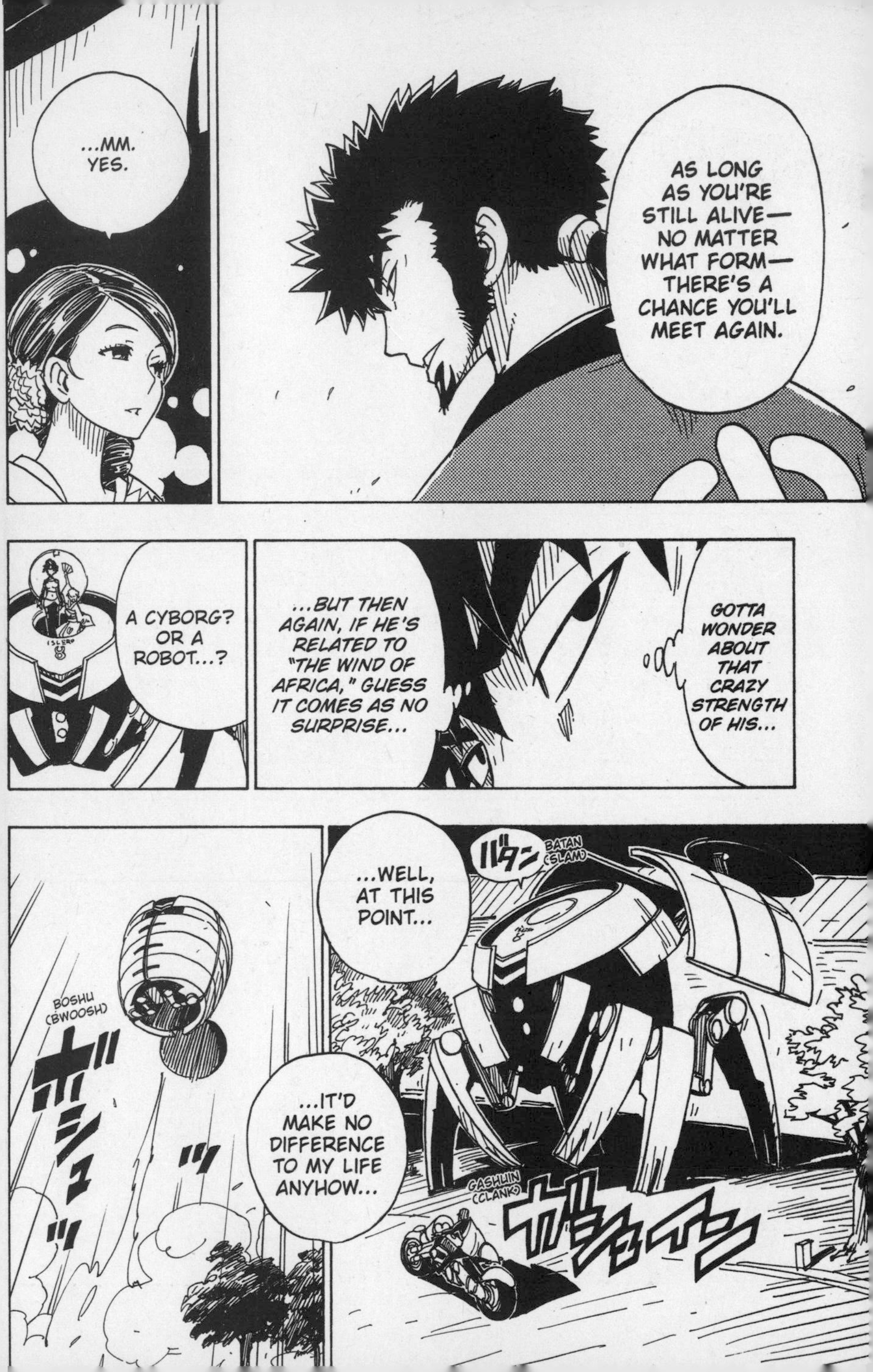
AS LONG AS YOU'RE STILL ALIVE— NO MATTER WHAT FORM— THERE'S A CHANCE YOU'LL MEET AGAIN.
...MM. YES.
GOTTA WONDER ABOUT THAT CRAZY STRENGTH OF HIS...
...BUT THEN AGAIN, IF HE'S RELATED TO "THE WIND OF AFRICA," GUESS IT COMES AS NO SURPRISE...
A CYBORG? OR A ROBOT...?
バタン
BATAN (SLAM)
...WELL, AT THIS POINT...
...IT'D MAKE NO DIFFERENCE TO MY LIFE ANYHOW...
GASHUIN (CLANK)
BOSHU (BWOOSH)

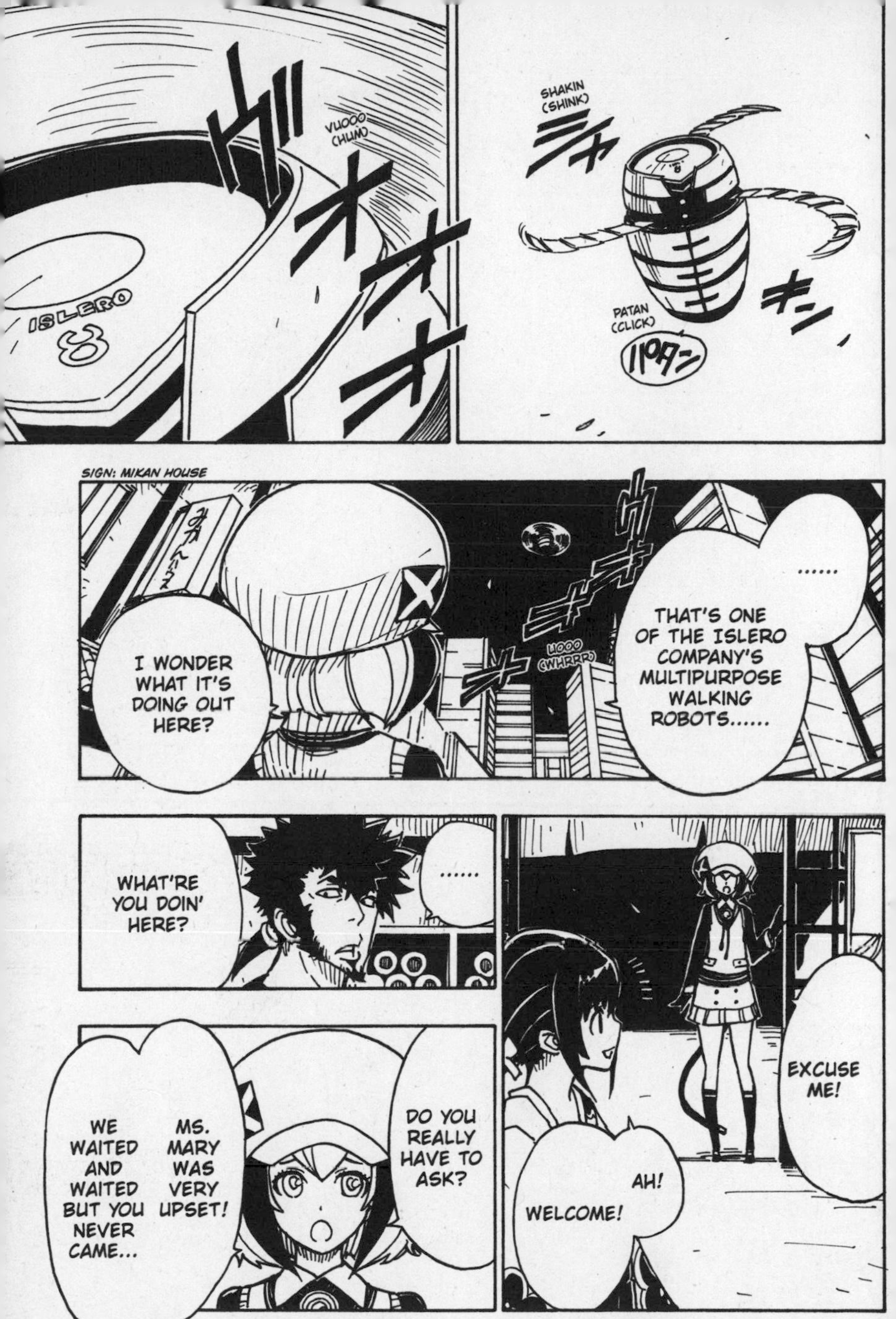
SHAKIN (SHINK)
PATAN (CLICK)
VUOOO (HUM)
ISLERO 8
SIGN: MIKAN HOUSE
......
THAT'S ONE OF THE ISLERO COMPANY'S MULTIPURPOSE WALKING ROBOTS......
WOOO (WHRRR)
I WONDER WHAT IT'S DOING OUT HERE?
EXCUSE ME!
AH! WELCOME!
......
WHAT'RE YOU DOIN' HERE?
DO YOU REALLY HAVE TO ASK?
MS. MARY WAS VERY UPSET!
WE WAITED AND WAITED BUT YOU NEVER CAME...

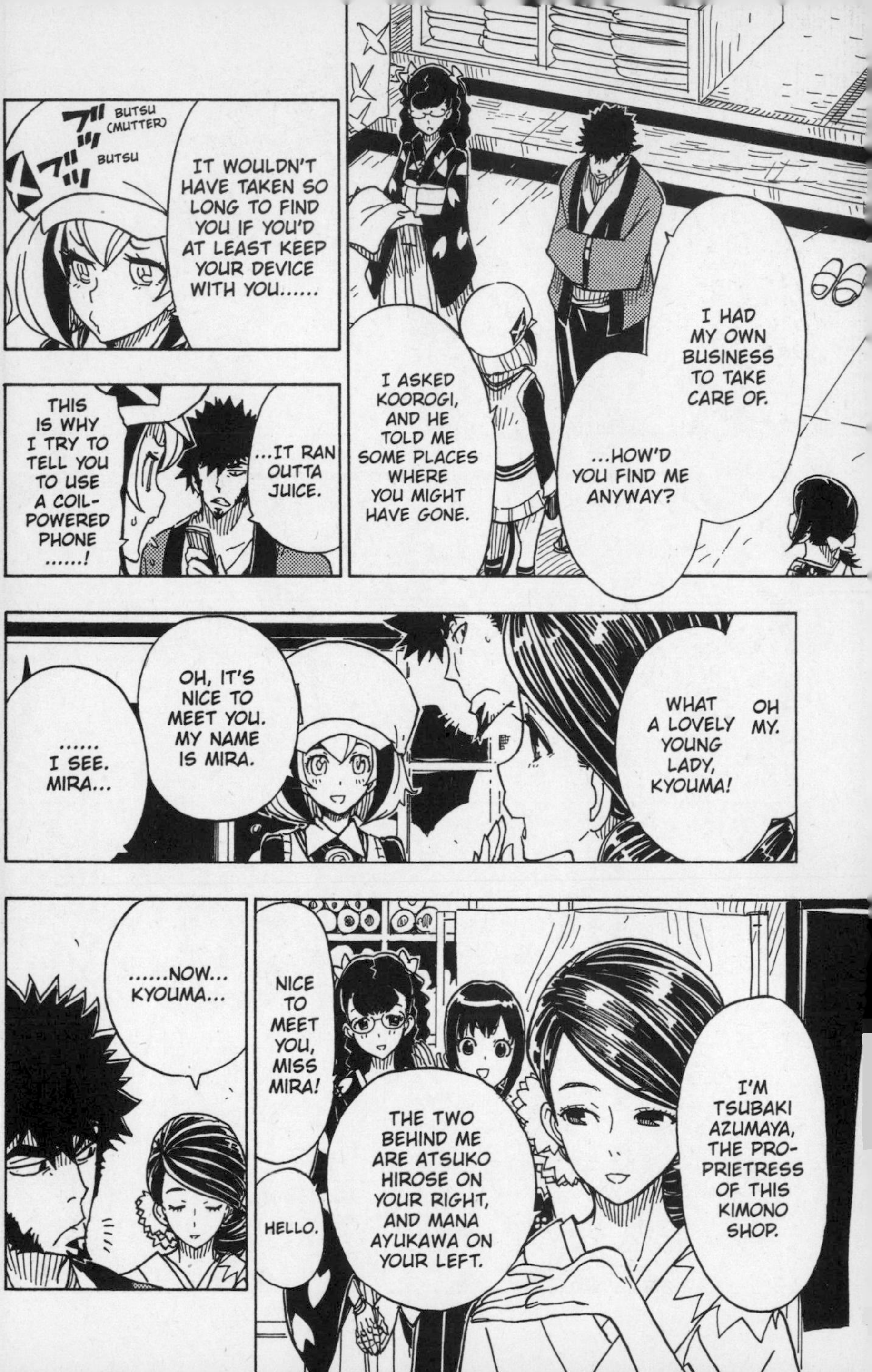
I HAD MY OWN BUSINESS TO TAKE CARE OF.
...HOW'D YOU FIND ME ANYWAY?
I ASKED KOOROGI, AND HE TOLD ME SOME PLACES WHERE YOU MIGHT HAVE GONE.
ブツ ブツ
BUTSU (MUTTER) BUTSU
IT WOULDN'T HAVE TAKEN SO LONG TO FIND YOU IF YOU'D AT LEAST KEEP YOUR DEVICE WITH YOU......
...IT RAN OUTTA JUICE.
THIS IS WHY I TRY TO TELL YOU TO USE A COIL-POWERED PHONE......!
OH MY.
WHAT A LOVELY YOUNG LADY, KYOUMA!
OH, IT'S NICE TO MEET YOU. MY NAME IS MIRA.
...... I SEE. MIRA...
I'M TSUBAKI AZUMAYA, THE PRO-PRIETRESS OF THIS KIMONO SHOP.
THE TWO BEHIND ME ARE ATSUKO HIROSE ON YOUR RIGHT, AND MANA AYUKAWA ON YOUR LEFT.
NICE TO MEET YOU, MISS MIRA!
HELLO.
......NOW... KYOUMA...

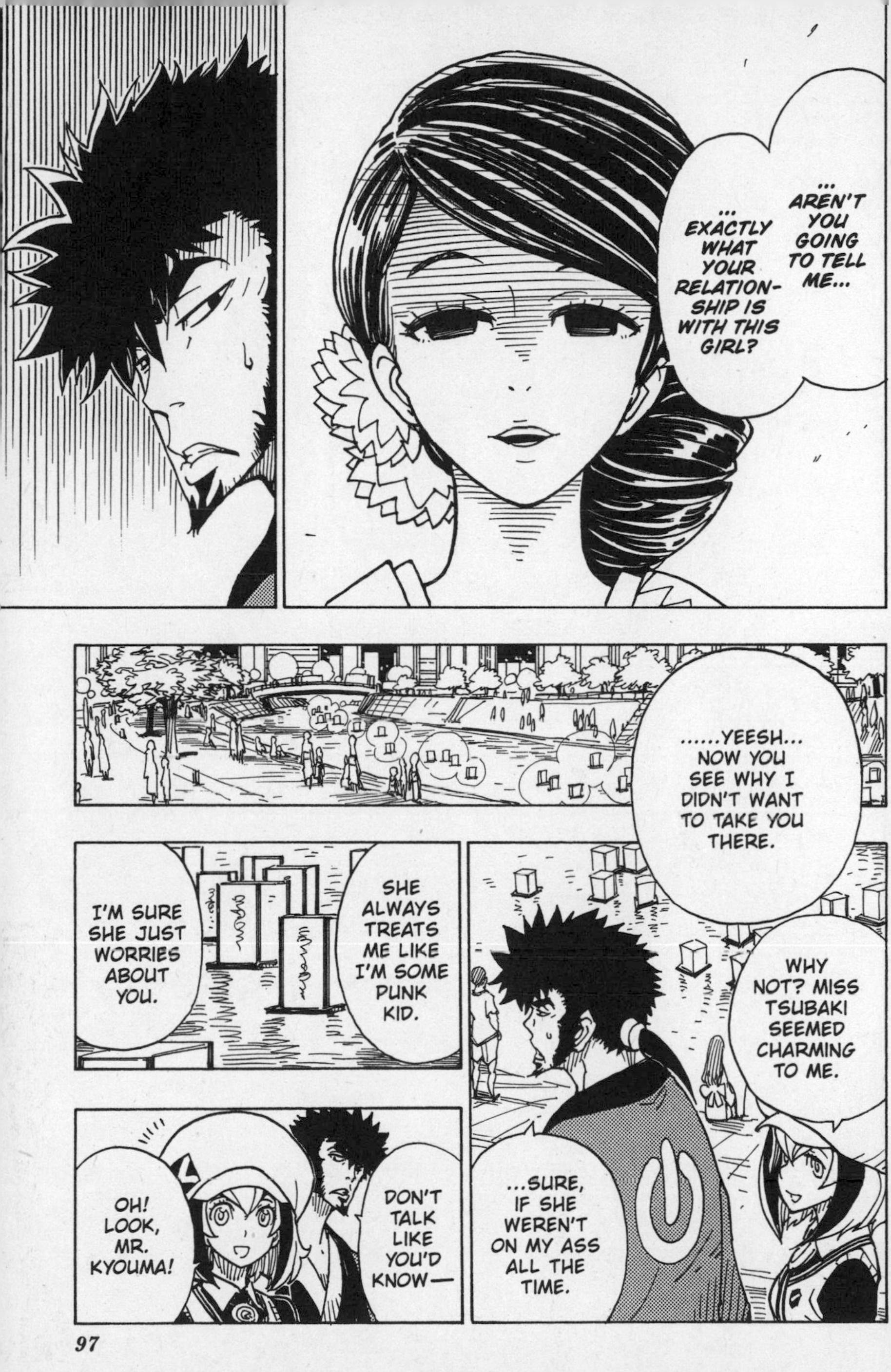
... AREN'T YOU GOING TO TELL ME...
... EXACTLY WHAT YOUR RELATIONSHIP IS WITH THIS GIRL?
......YEESH... NOW YOU SEE WHY I DIDN'T WANT TO TAKE YOU THERE.
WHY NOT? MISS TSUBAKI SEEMED CHARMING TO ME.
...SURE, IF SHE WEREN'T ON MY ASS ALL THE TIME.
SHE ALWAYS TREATS ME LIKE I'M SOME PUNK KID.
I'M SURE SHE JUST WORRIES ABOUT YOU.
DON'T TALK LIKE YOU'D KNOW—
OH! LOOK, MR. KYOUMA!

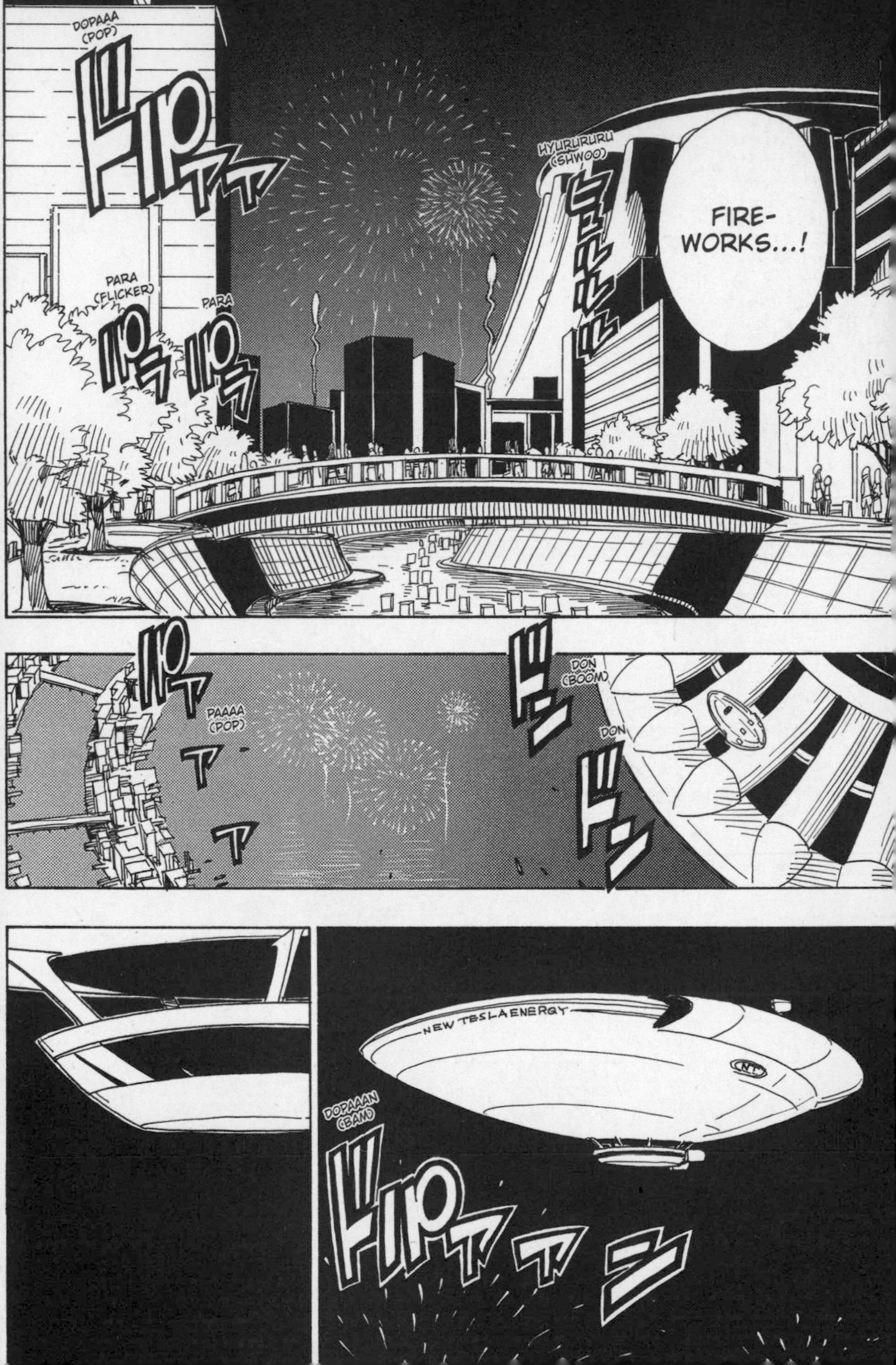
HYURURURU
(SHWOO)
FIRE-WORKS...!
DOPAAA
(POP)
PARA
PARA
(FLICKER)
DON
(BOOM)
DON
PAAAA
(POP)
NEW TESLA ENERGY
DOPAAAN
(BAM)

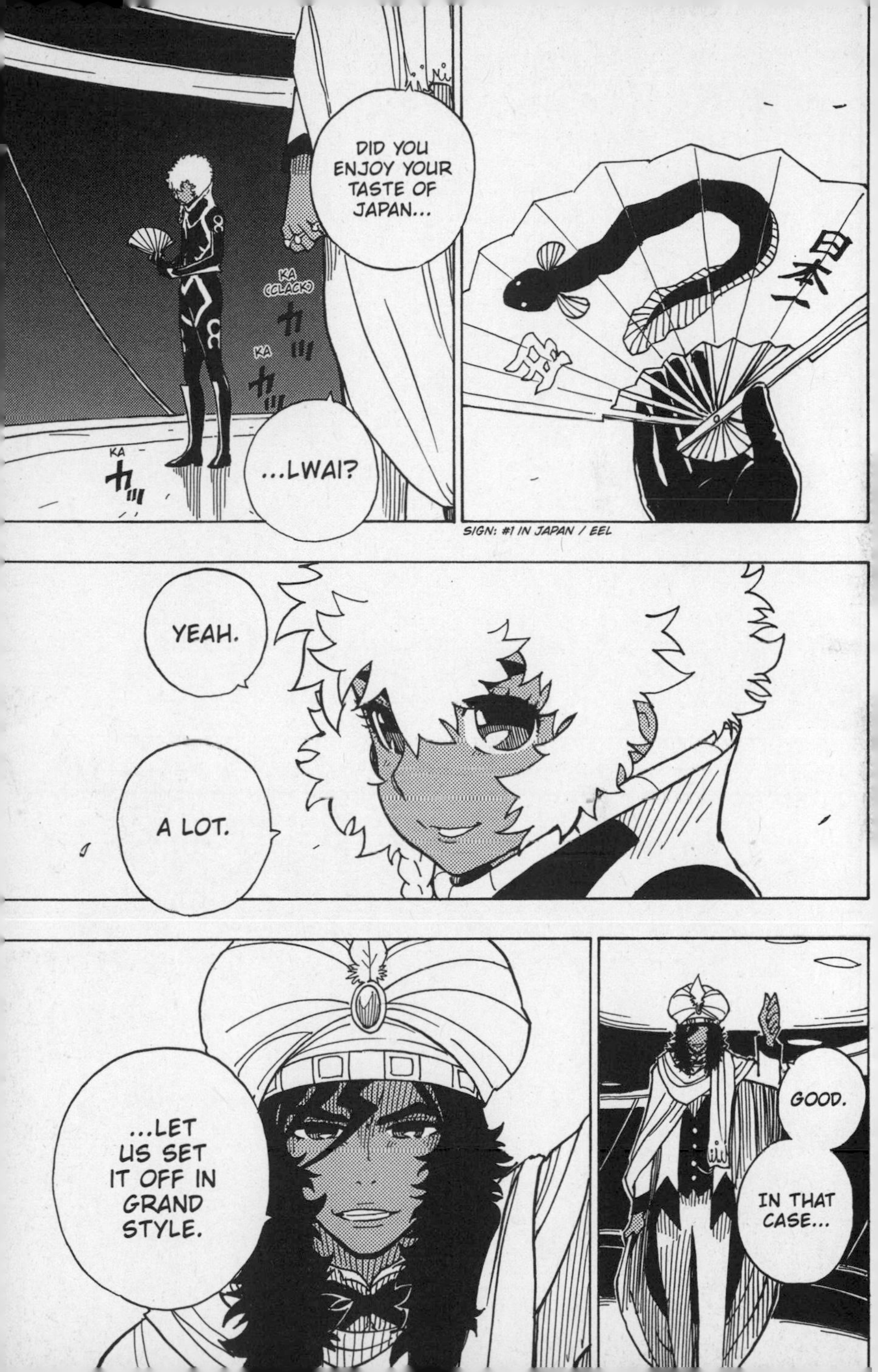
日本一
SIGN: #1 IN JAPAN / EEL
DID YOU ENJOY YOUR TASTE OF JAPAN...
KA (CLACK)
カッ
KA
カッ
KA
カッ
...LWAI?
YEAH.
A LOT.
GOOD.
IN THAT CASE...
...LET US SET IT OFF IN GRAND STYLE.

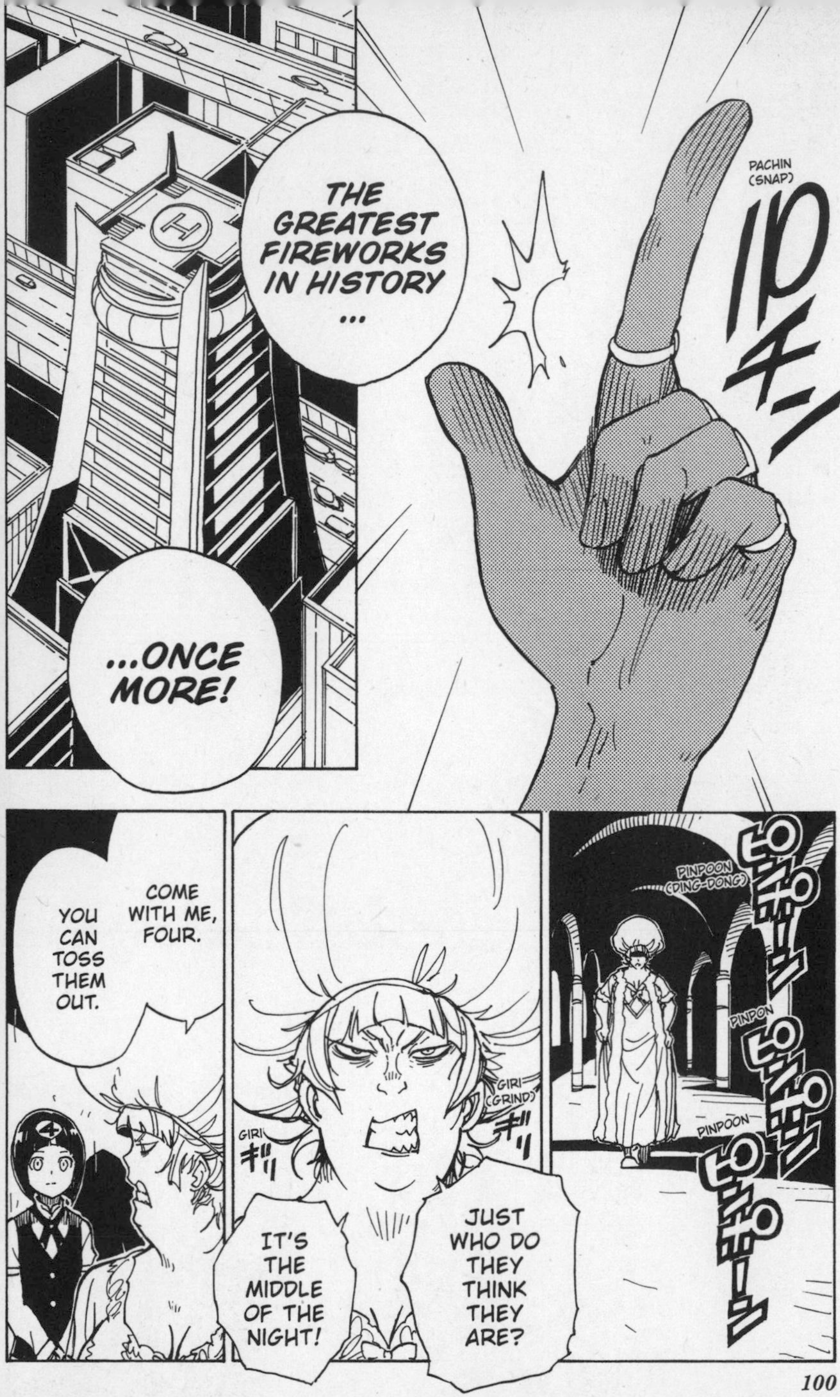
PACHIN (SNAP)
THE GREATEST FIREWORKS IN HISTORY ...
...ONCE MORE!
PINPOON (DING-DONG)
PINPON
PINPOON
GIRI (GRIND)
GIRI
JUST WHO DO THEY THINK THEY ARE?
IT'S THE MIDDLE OF THE NIGHT!
COME WITH ME, FOUR.
YOU CAN TOSS THEM OUT.

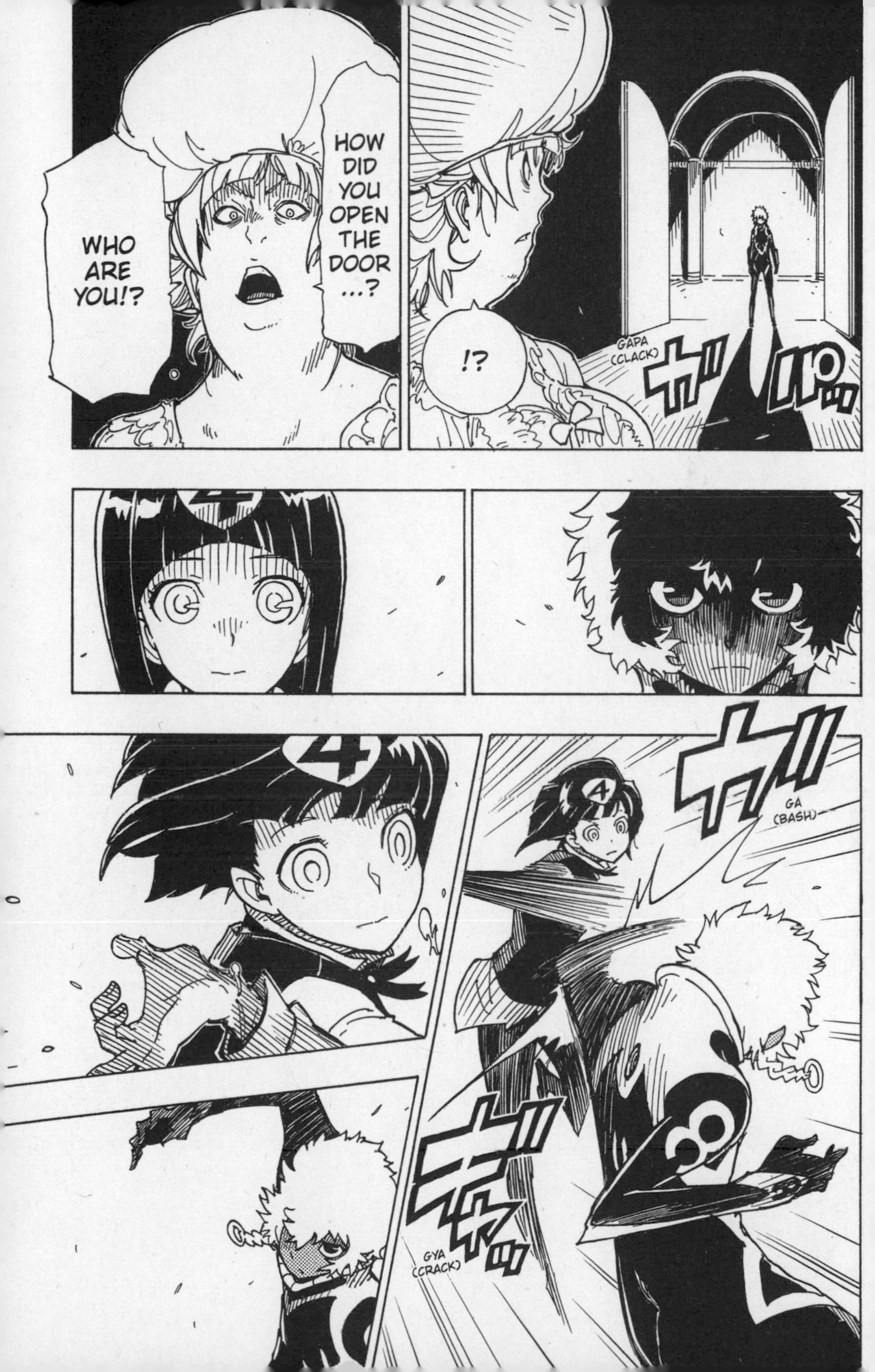
GAPA (CLACK)
!?
HOW DID YOU OPEN THE DOOR ...?
WHO ARE YOU!?
GA (BASH)
GYA (CRACK)

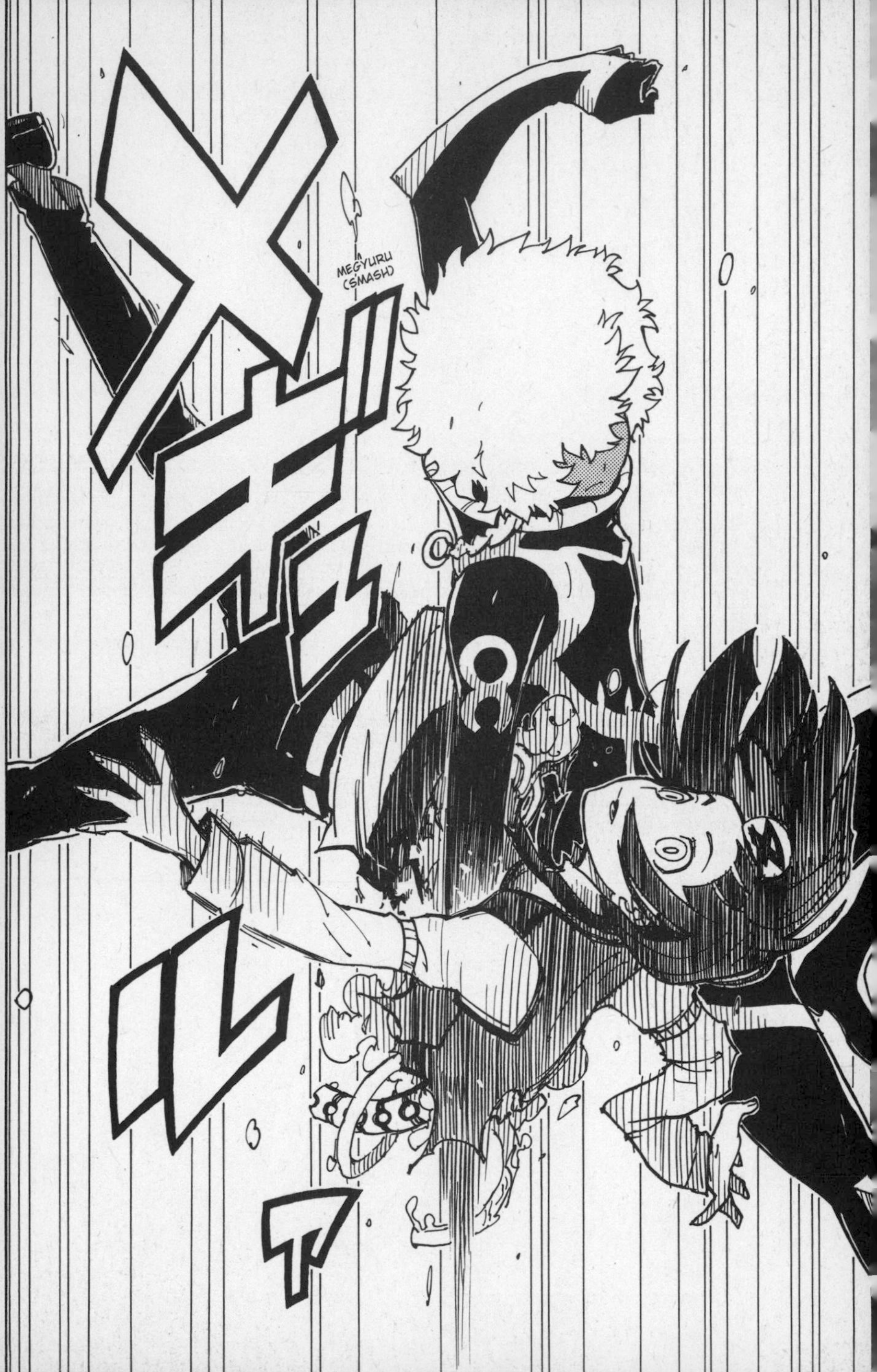
MEGYURU
(SMASH)

Dimension W

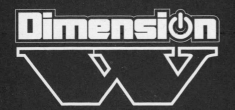

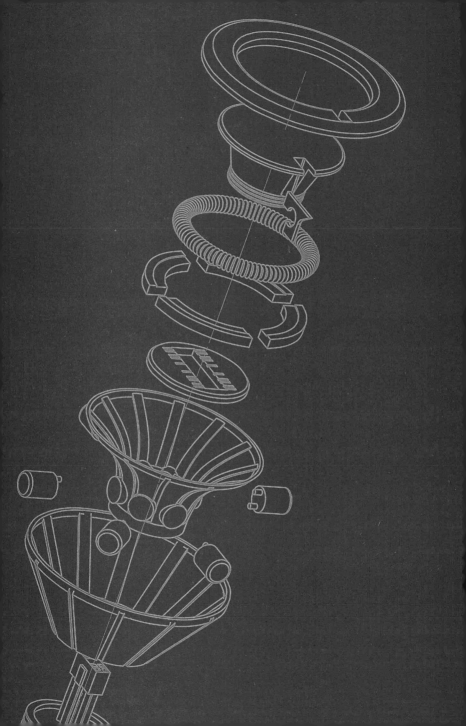

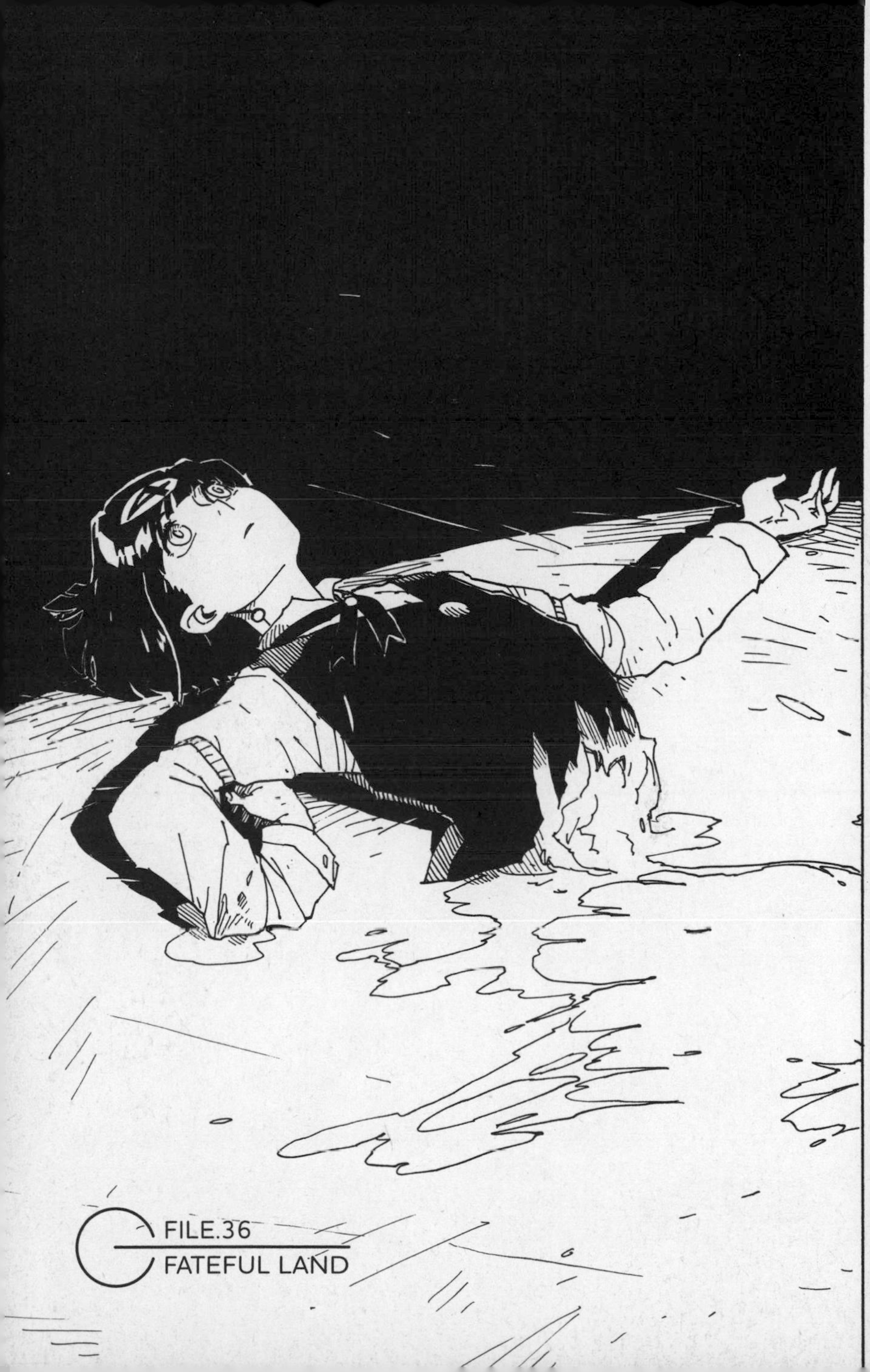
FILE.36
FATEFUL LAND

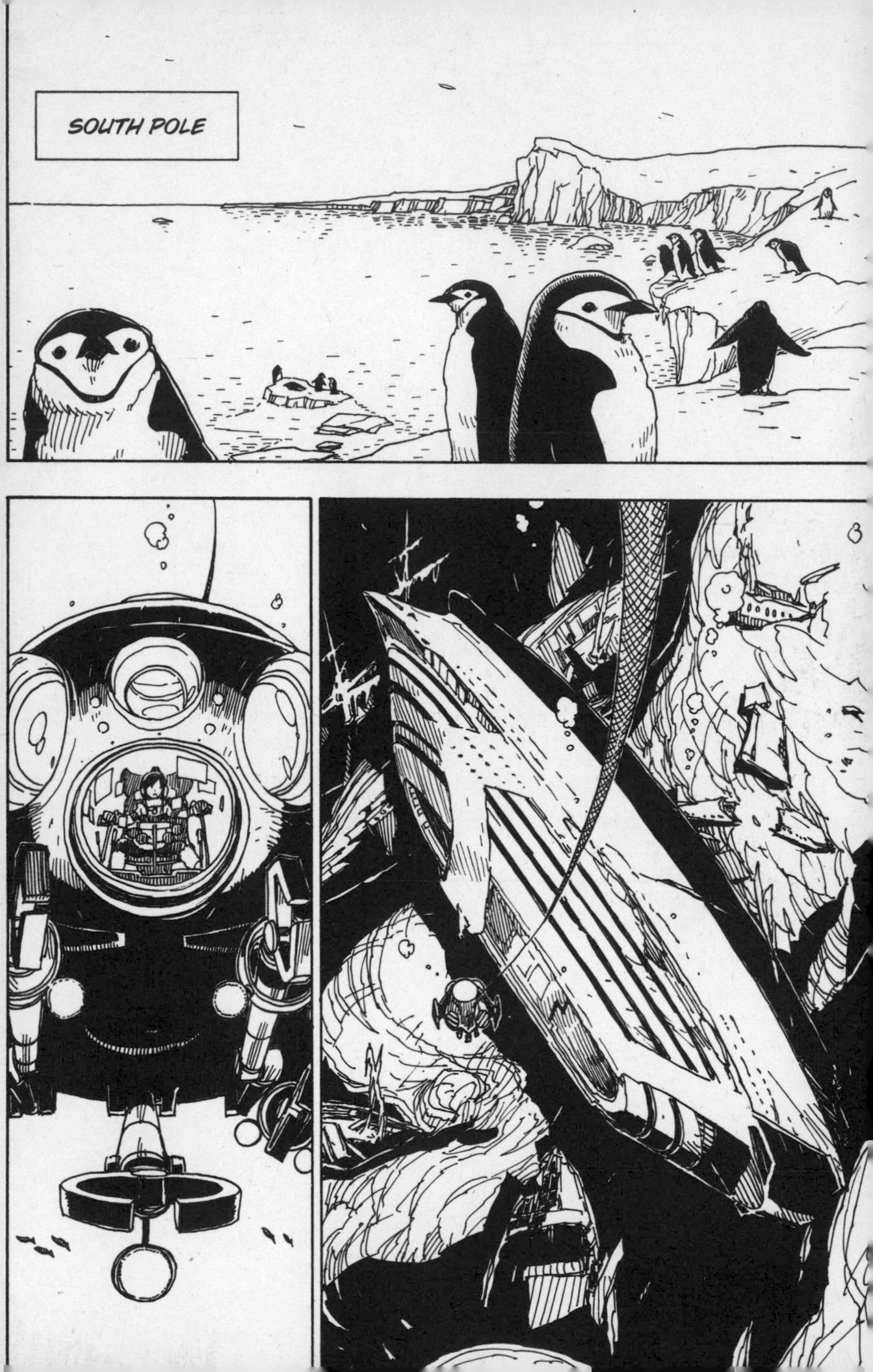
SOUTH POLE

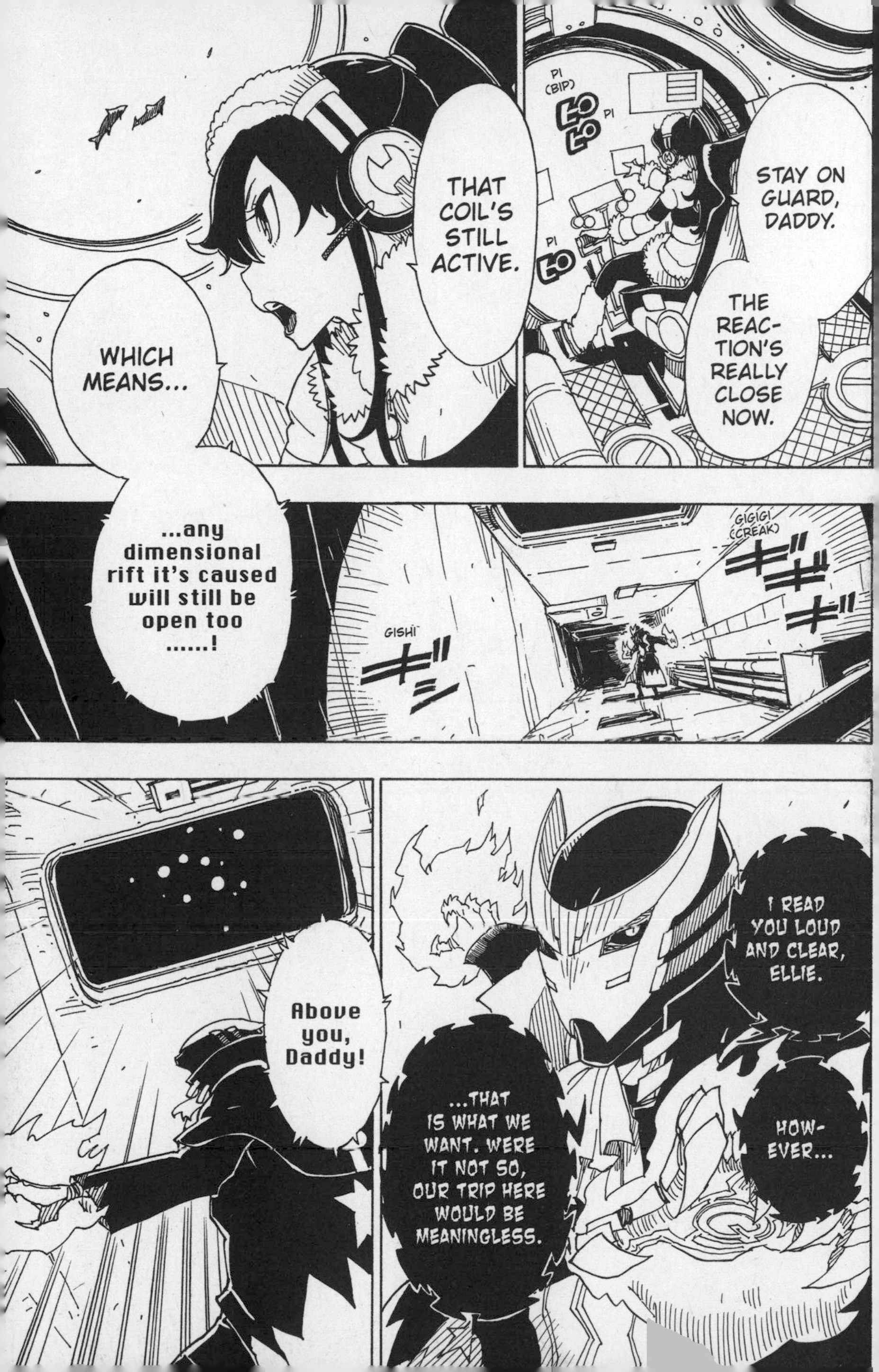

STAY ON GUARD, DADDY.
THE REAC-TION'S REALLY CLOSE NOW.
PI (BIP)
PI
PI
THAT COIL'S STILL ACTIVE.
WHICH MEANS...
GIGIGI (CREAK)
GISHI
...any dimensional rift it's caused will still be open too ......!
I READ YOU LOUD AND CLEAR, ELLIE.
...THAT IS WHAT WE WANT. WERE IT NOT SO, OUR TRIP HERE WOULD BE MEANINGLESS.
HOW-EVER...
Above you, Daddy!

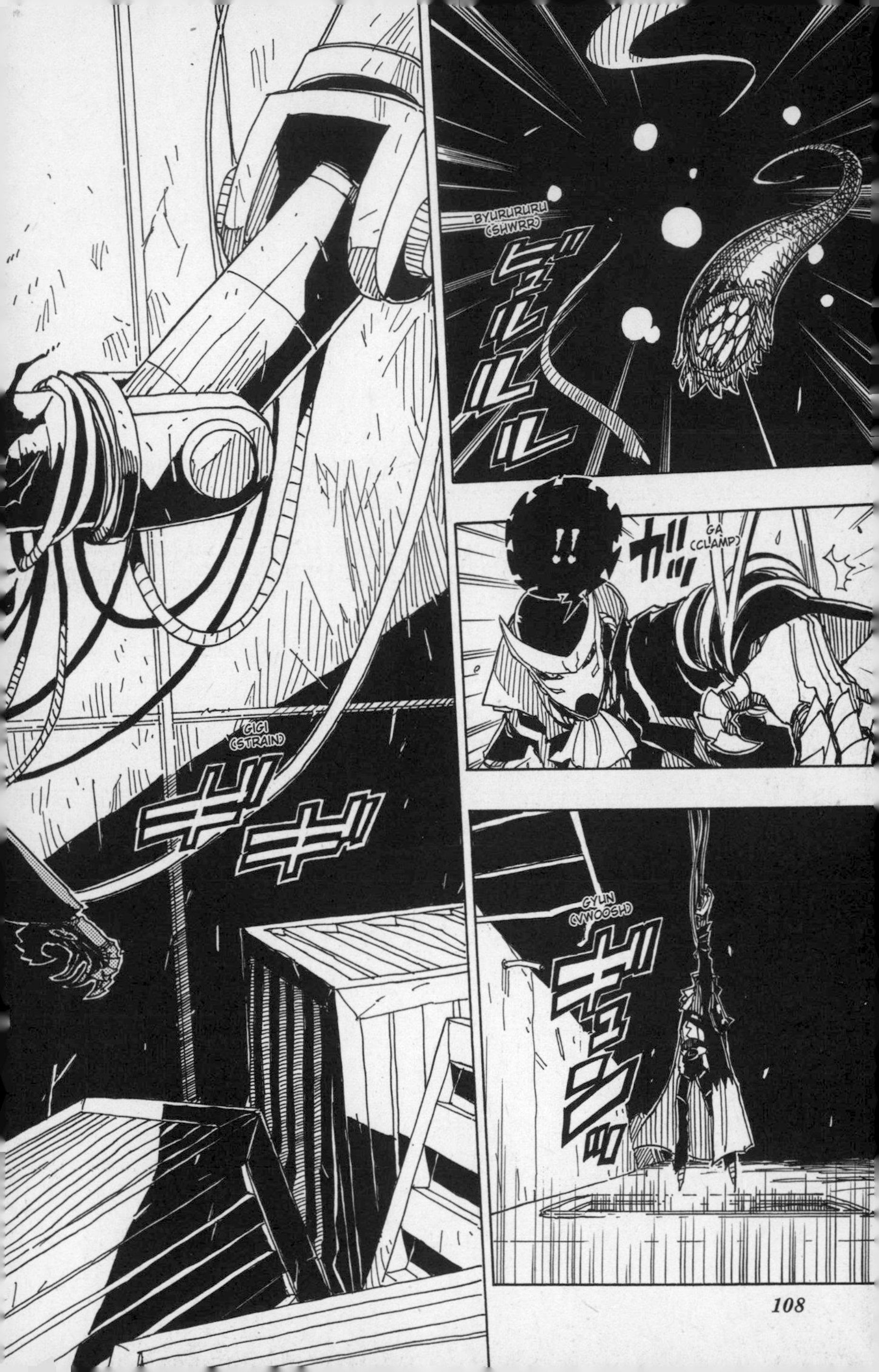
BYURURURU (SHWRR)
GA (CLAMP)
!!
GYUN (VWOOSH)
GIGI (STRAIN)

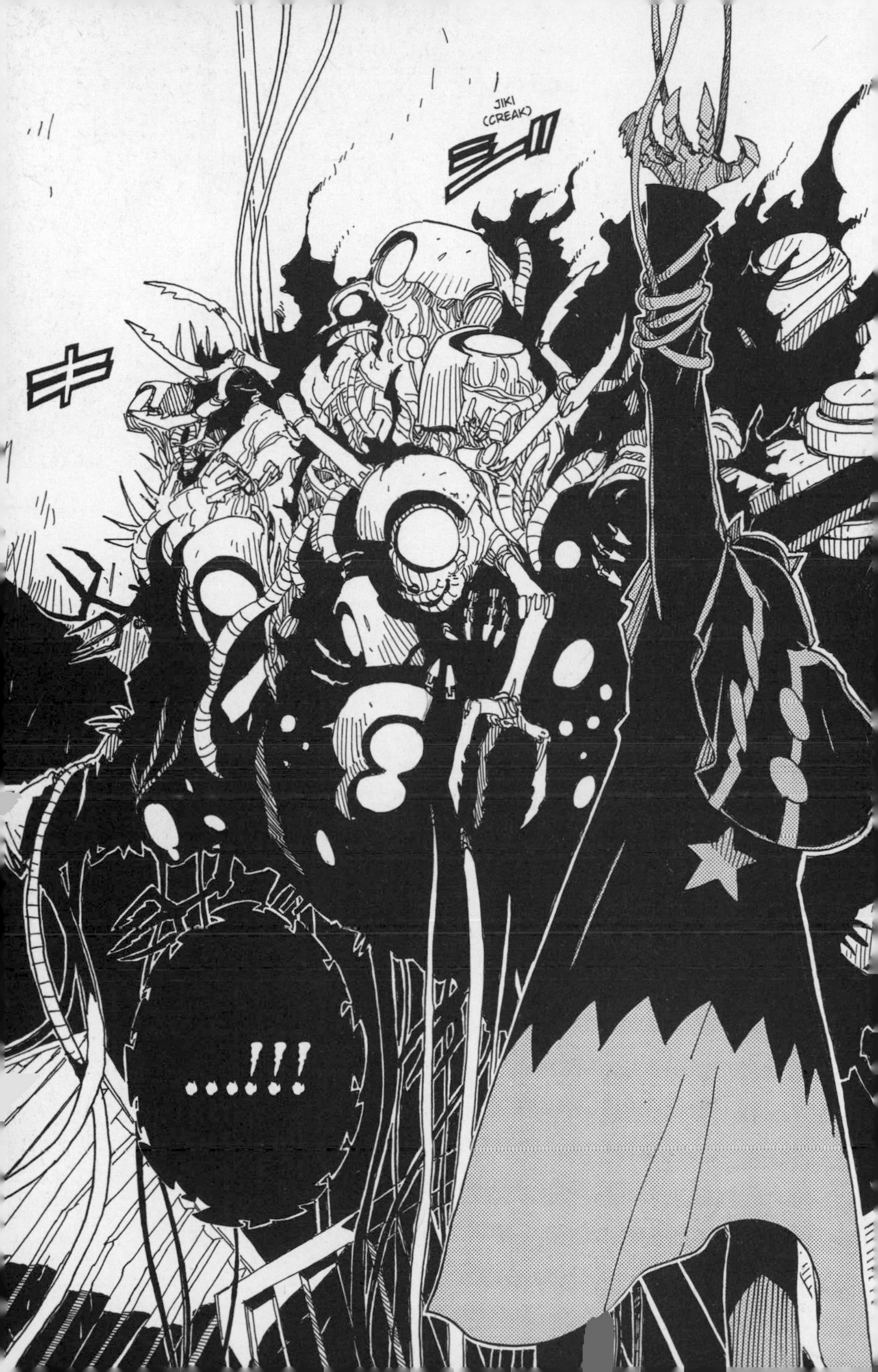
JIKI
(CREAK)
......!!!

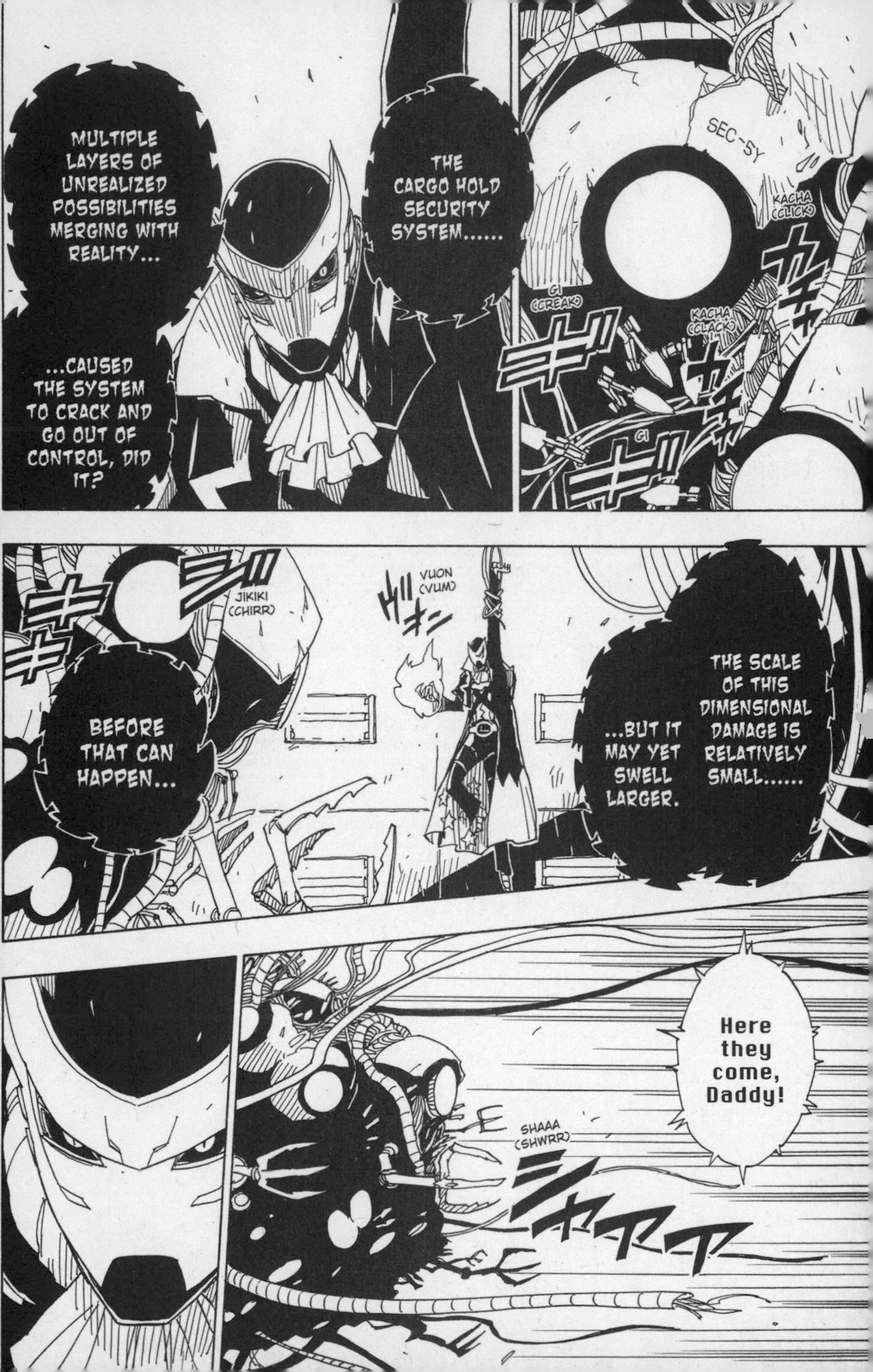
SEC-SY
KACHA (CLICK)
GI (CREAK)
KACHA (CLACK)
GI
THE CARGO HOLD SECURITY SYSTEM......
MULTIPLE LAYERS OF UNREALIZED POSSIBILITIES MERGING WITH REALITY...
...CAUSED THE SYSTEM TO CRACK AND GO OUT OF CONTROL, DID IT?
THE SCALE OF THIS DIMENSIONAL DAMAGE IS RELATIVELY SMALL......
...BUT IT MAY YET SWELL LARGER.
VUON (VUM)
JIKIKI (CHIRR)
BEFORE THAT CAN HAPPEN...
Here they come, Daddy!
SHAAA (SHWRR)

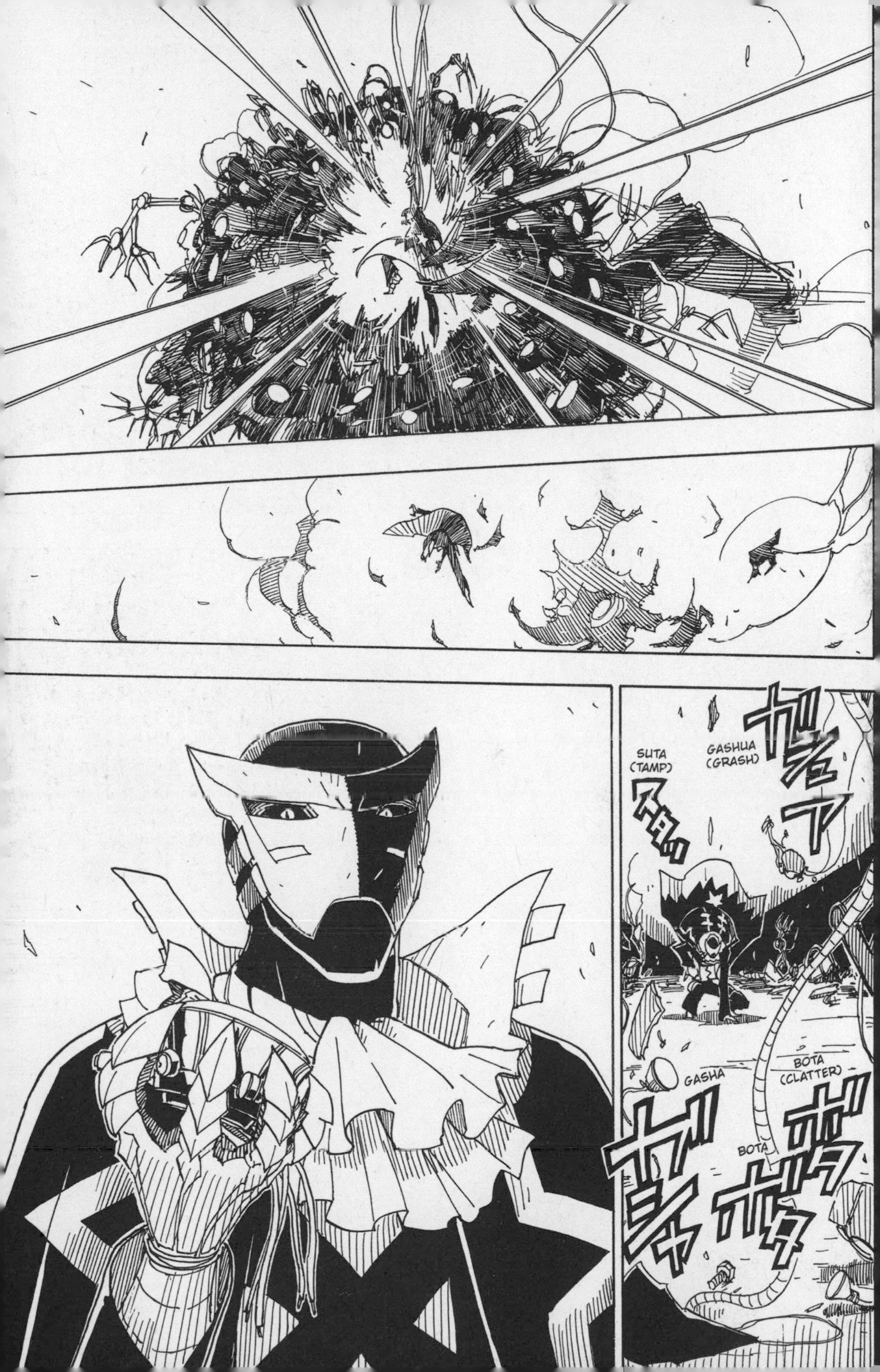
GASHUA
(GRASH)
SUTA
(TAMP)
BOTA
(CLATTER)
GASHA
BOTA

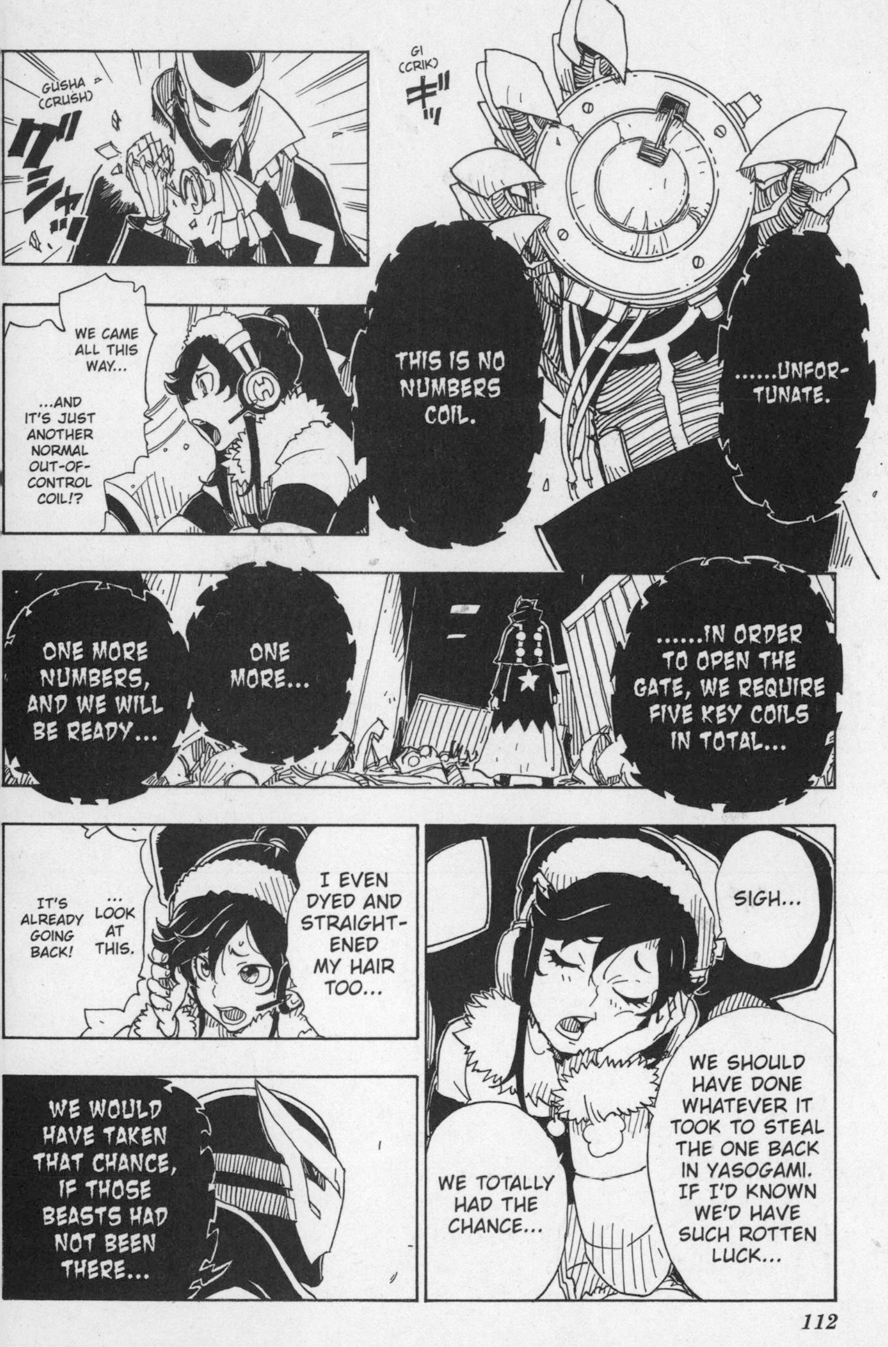
GI
(CRIK)
ギッ
......UNFOR-TUNATE.
THIS IS NO NUMBERS COIL.
GUSHA
(CRUSH)
グシャッ
WE CAME ALL THIS WAY...
...AND IT'S JUST ANOTHER NORMAL OUT-OF-CONTROL COIL!?
......IN ORDER TO OPEN THE GATE, WE REQUIRE FIVE KEY COILS IN TOTAL...
ONE MORE...
ONE MORE NUMBERS, AND WE WILL BE READY...
SIGH...
WE SHOULD HAVE DONE WHATEVER IT TOOK TO STEAL THE ONE BACK IN YASOGAMI. IF I'D KNOWN WE'D HAVE SUCH ROTTEN LUCK...
WE TOTALLY HAD THE CHANCE...
I EVEN DYED AND STRAIGHT-ENED MY HAIR TOO...
...LOOK AT THIS.
IT'S ALREADY GOING BACK!
WE WOULD HAVE TAKEN THAT CHANCE, IF THOSE BEASTS HAD NOT BEEN THERE...

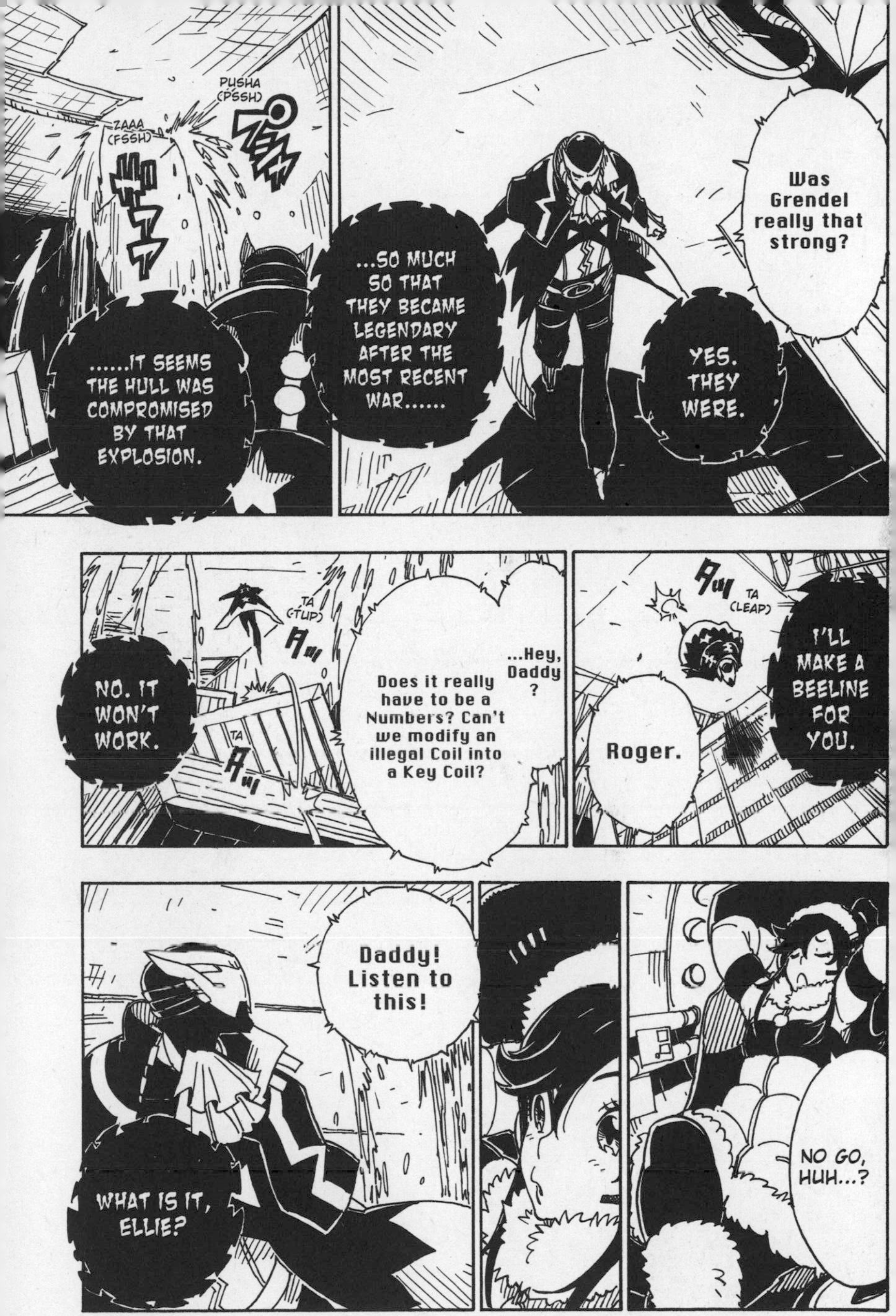
Was Grendel really that strong?
Yes. They were.
...So much so that they became legendary after the most recent war......
PUSHA (PSSSH)
ZAAA (FSSH)
......It seems the hull was compromised by that explosion.
TA (LEAP)
I'll make a beeline for you.
Roger.
...Hey, Daddy?
Does it really have to be a Numbers? Can't we modify an illegal Coil into a Key Coil?
TA (TUP)
TA
No. It won't work.
No go, huh...?
Daddy! Listen to this!
What is it, Ellie?

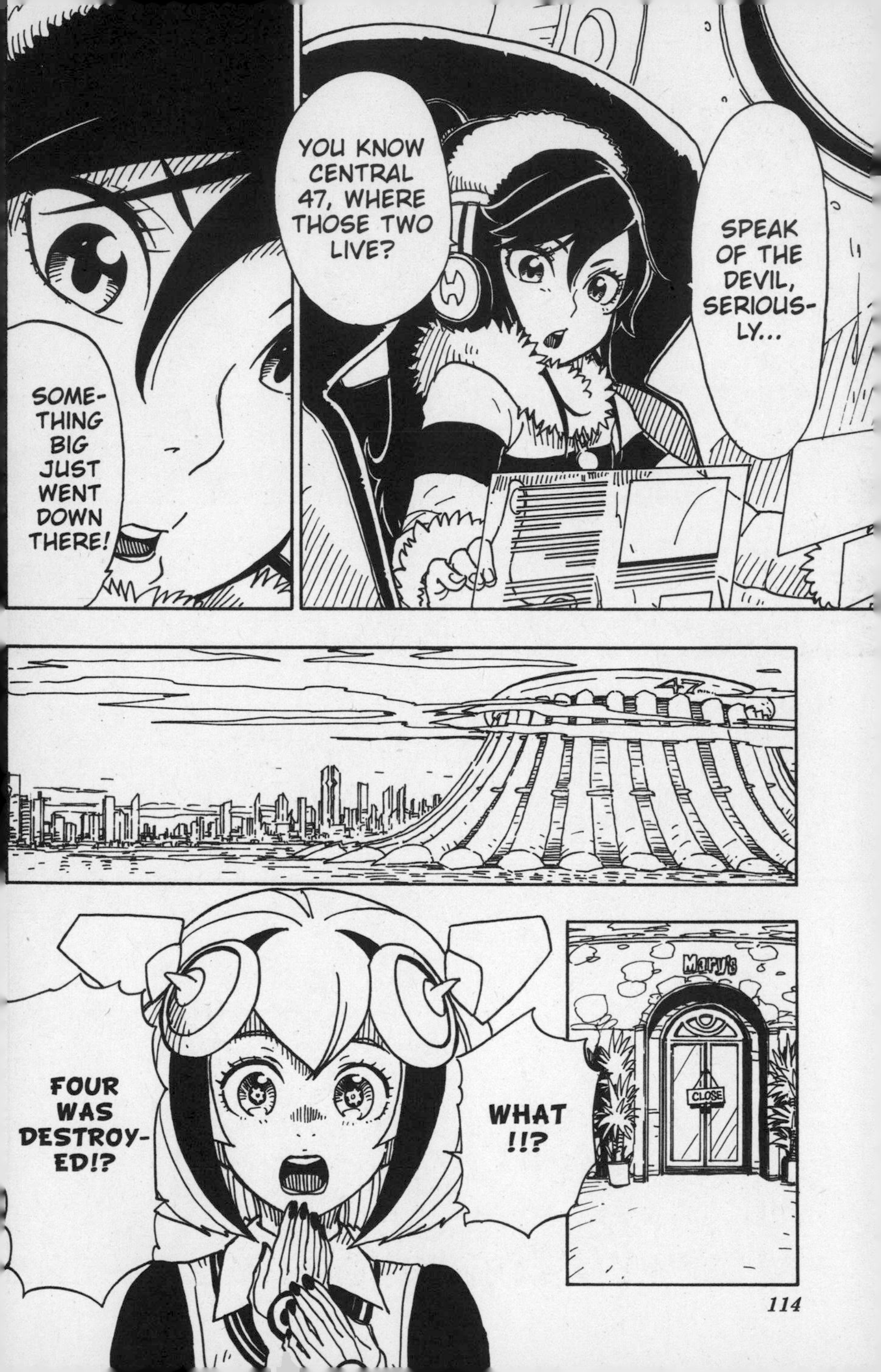
SPEAK OF THE DEVIL, SERIOUSLY...
YOU KNOW CENTRAL 47, WHERE THOSE TWO LIVE?
SOMETHING BIG JUST WENT DOWN THERE!
47
Mary's
CLOSE
WHAT!!?
FOUR WAS DESTROYED!?

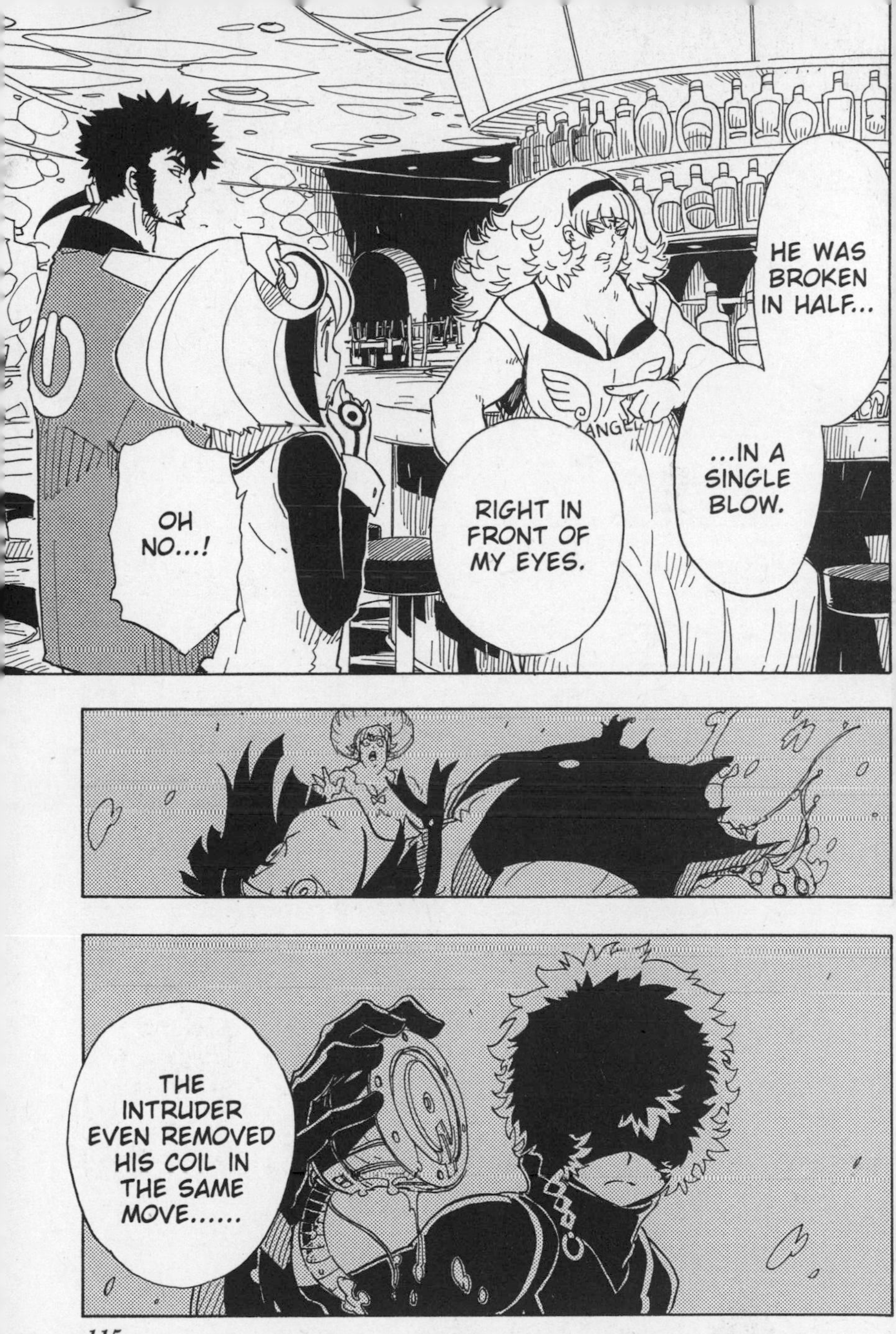
HE WAS BROKEN IN HALF...
...IN A SINGLE BLOW.
RIGHT IN FRONT OF MY EYES.
ANGEL
OH NO...!
THE INTRUDER EVEN REMOVED HIS COIL IN THE SAME MOVE......

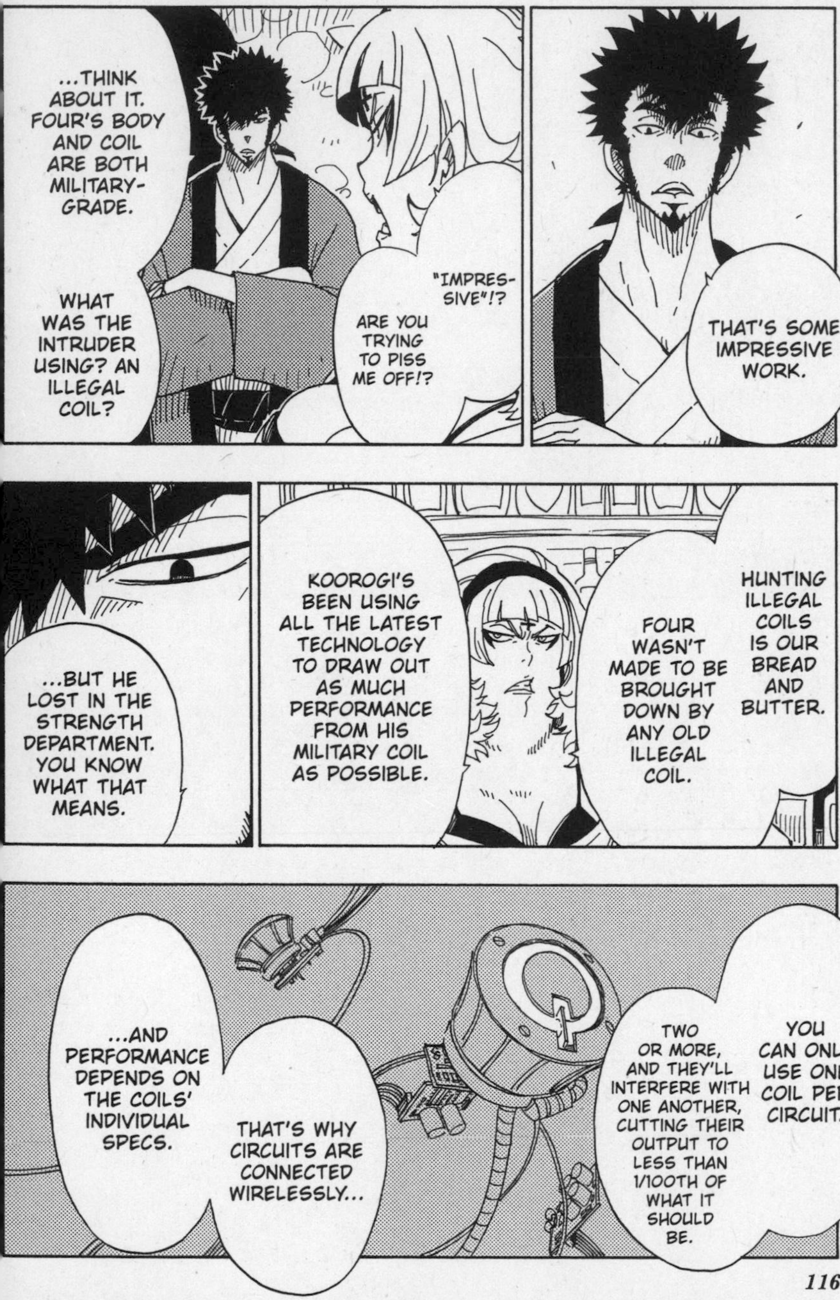
THAT'S SOME IMPRESSIVE WORK.
"IMPRESSIVE"!?
ARE YOU TRYING TO PISS ME OFF!?
...THINK ABOUT IT. FOUR'S BODY AND COIL ARE BOTH MILITARY-GRADE.
WHAT WAS THE INTRUDER USING? AN ILLEGAL COIL?
HUNTING ILLEGAL COILS IS OUR BREAD AND BUTTER.
FOUR WASN'T MADE TO BE BROUGHT DOWN BY ANY OLD ILLEGAL COIL.
KOOROGI'S BEEN USING ALL THE LATEST TECHNOLOGY TO DRAW OUT AS MUCH PERFORMANCE FROM HIS MILITARY COIL AS POSSIBLE.
...BUT HE LOST IN THE STRENGTH DEPARTMENT. YOU KNOW WHAT THAT MEANS.
YOU CAN ONLY USE ONE COIL PER CIRCUIT.
TWO OR MORE, AND THEY'LL INTERFERE WITH ONE ANOTHER, CUTTING THEIR OUTPUT TO LESS THAN 1/100TH OF WHAT IT SHOULD BE.
THAT'S WHY CIRCUITS ARE CONNECTED WIRELESSLY...
...AND PERFORMANCE DEPENDS ON THE COILS' INDIVIDUAL SPECS.

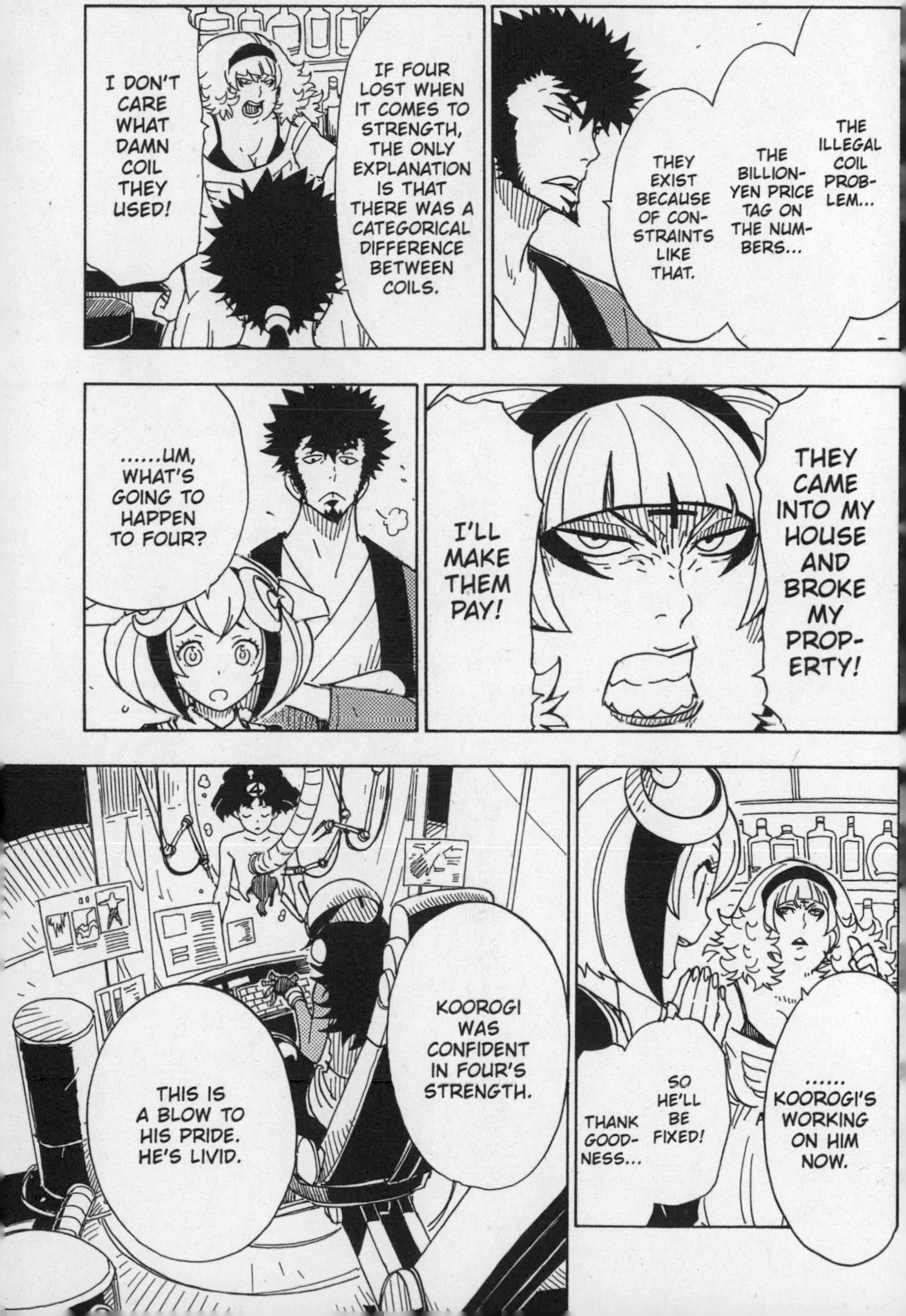
THE ILLEGAL COIL PROBLEM...
THE BILLION-YEN PRICE TAG ON THE NUMBERS...
THEY EXIST BECAUSE OF CONSTRAINTS LIKE THAT.
IF FOUR LOST WHEN IT COMES TO STRENGTH, THE ONLY EXPLANATION IS THAT THERE WAS A CATEGORICAL DIFFERENCE BETWEEN COILS.
I DON'T CARE WHAT DAMN COIL THEY USED!
THEY CAME INTO MY HOUSE AND BROKE MY PROPERTY!
I'LL MAKE THEM PAY!
......UM, WHAT'S GOING TO HAPPEN TO FOUR?
......KOOROGI'S WORKING ON HIM NOW.
SO HE'LL BE FIXED!
THANK GOODNESS...
KOOROGI WAS CONFIDENT IN FOUR'S STRENGTH.
THIS IS A BLOW TO HIS PRIDE. HE'S LIVID.

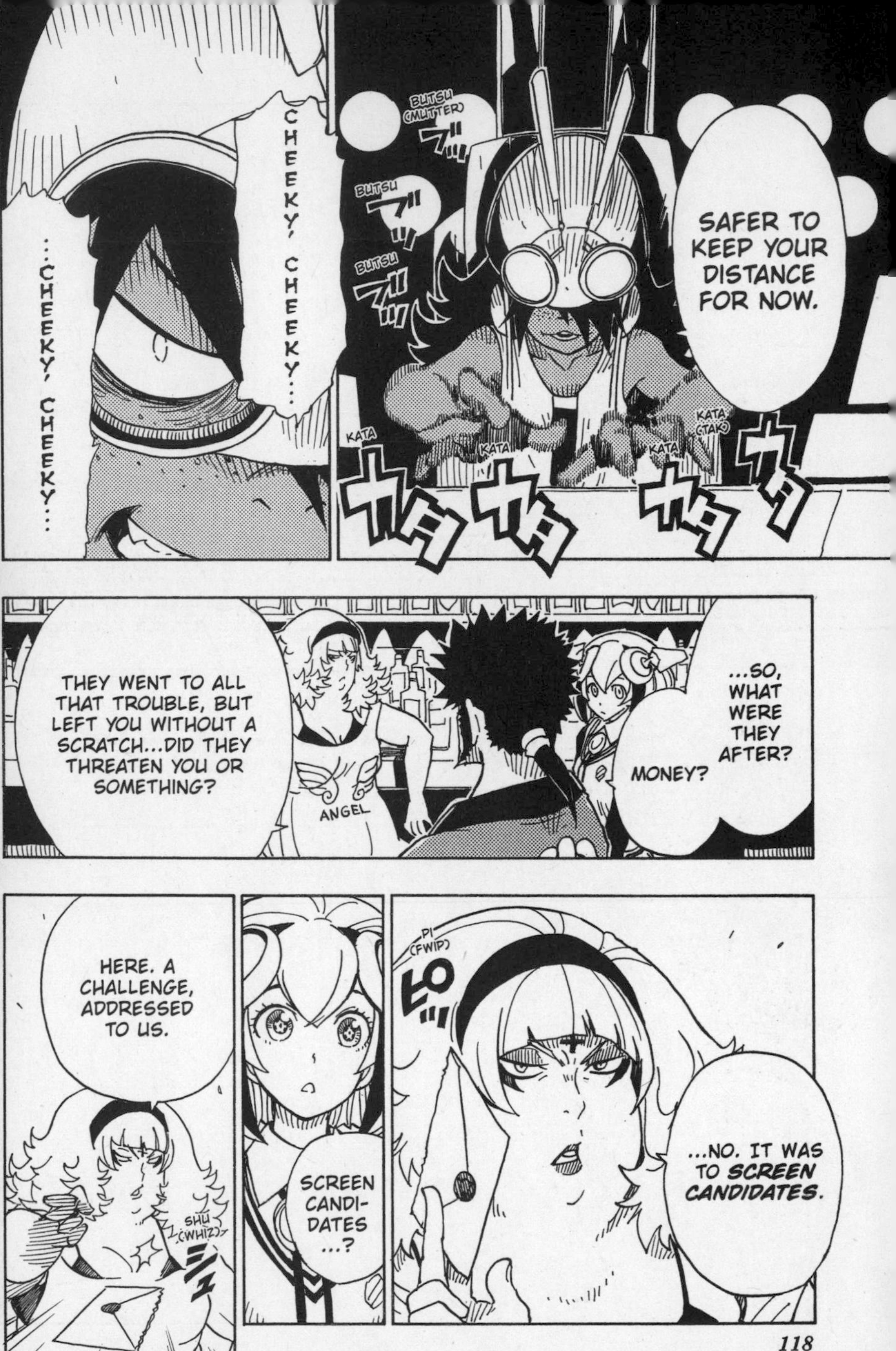
SAFER TO KEEP YOUR DISTANCE FOR NOW.
BUTSU (MUTTER)
BUTSU
BUTSU
KATA (TAK)
KATA
KATA
KATA
CHEEKY, CHEEKY, CHEEKY...
...CHEEKY, CHEEKY...
...SO, WHAT WERE THEY AFTER?
MONEY?
THEY WENT TO ALL THAT TROUBLE, BUT LEFT YOU WITHOUT A SCRATCH...DID THEY THREATEN YOU OR SOMETHING?
ANGEL
PI (FWIP)
...NO. IT WAS TO *SCREEN CANDIDATES*.
SCREEN CANDI-DATES ...?
HERE. A CHALLENGE, ADDRESSED TO US.
SHU (WHIZ)

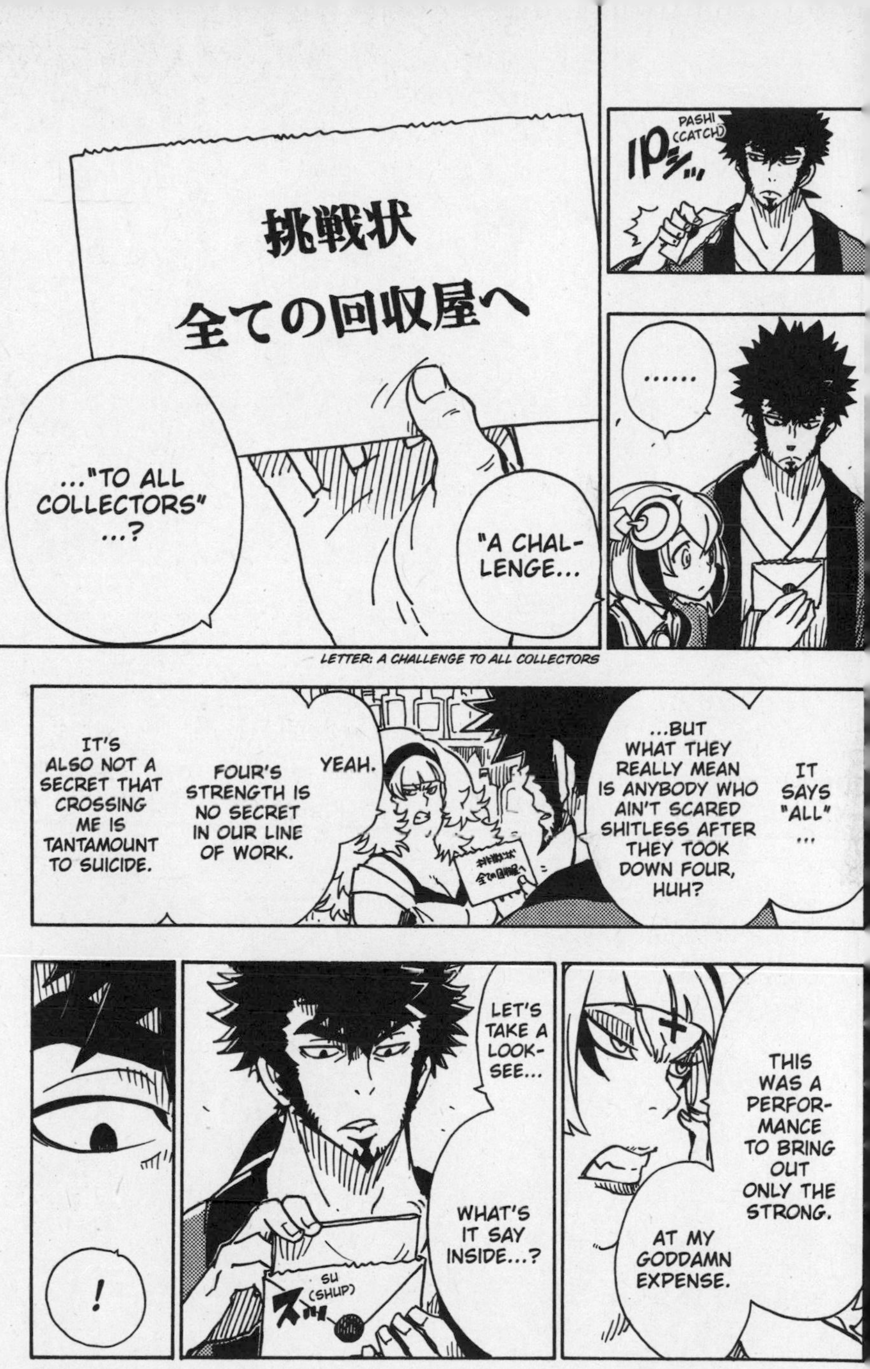
PASHI (CATCH)
......
挑戦状
全ての回収屋へ
"A CHAL-LENGE...
..."TO ALL COLLECTORS" ...?
LETTER: A CHALLENGE TO ALL COLLECTORS
IT SAYS "ALL" ...
...BUT WHAT THEY REALLY MEAN IS ANYBODY WHO AIN'T SCARED SHITLESS AFTER THEY TOOK DOWN FOUR, HUH?
YEAH.
FOUR'S STRENGTH IS NO SECRET IN OUR LINE OF WORK.
IT'S ALSO NOT A SECRET THAT CROSSING ME IS TANTAMOUNT TO SUICIDE.
THIS WAS A PERFOR-MANCE TO BRING OUT ONLY THE STRONG.
AT MY GODDAMN EXPENSE.
LET'S TAKE A LOOK-SEE...
WHAT'S IT SAY INSIDE...?
SU (SHUP)
!

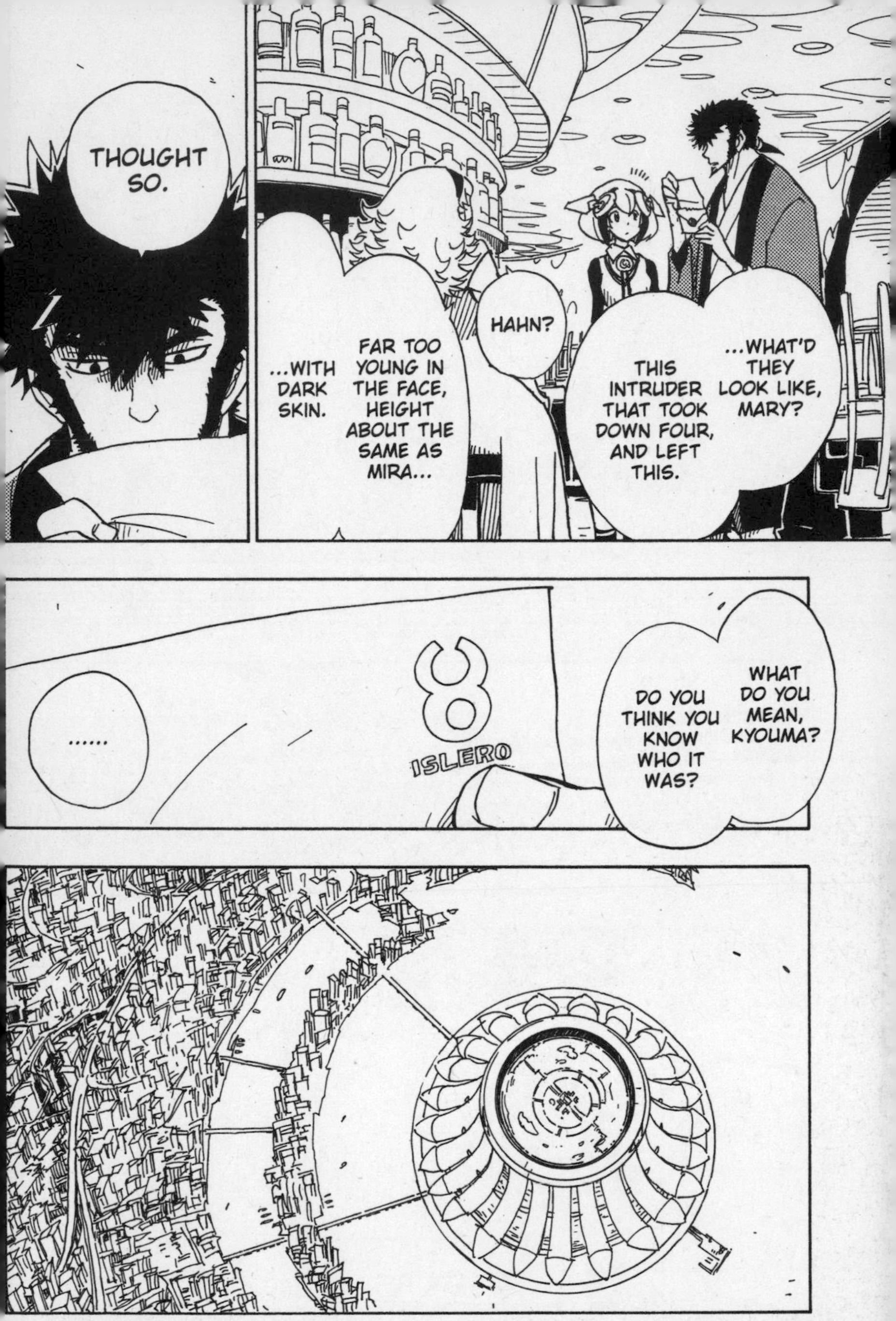
...WHAT'D THEY LOOK LIKE, MARY?
THIS INTRUDER THAT TOOK DOWN FOUR, AND LEFT THIS.
HAHN?
FAR TOO YOUNG IN THE FACE, HEIGHT ABOUT THE SAME AS MIRA...
...WITH DARK SKIN.
THOUGHT SO.
WHAT DO YOU MEAN, KYOUMA?
DO YOU THINK YOU KNOW WHO IT WAS?
ISLERO
......

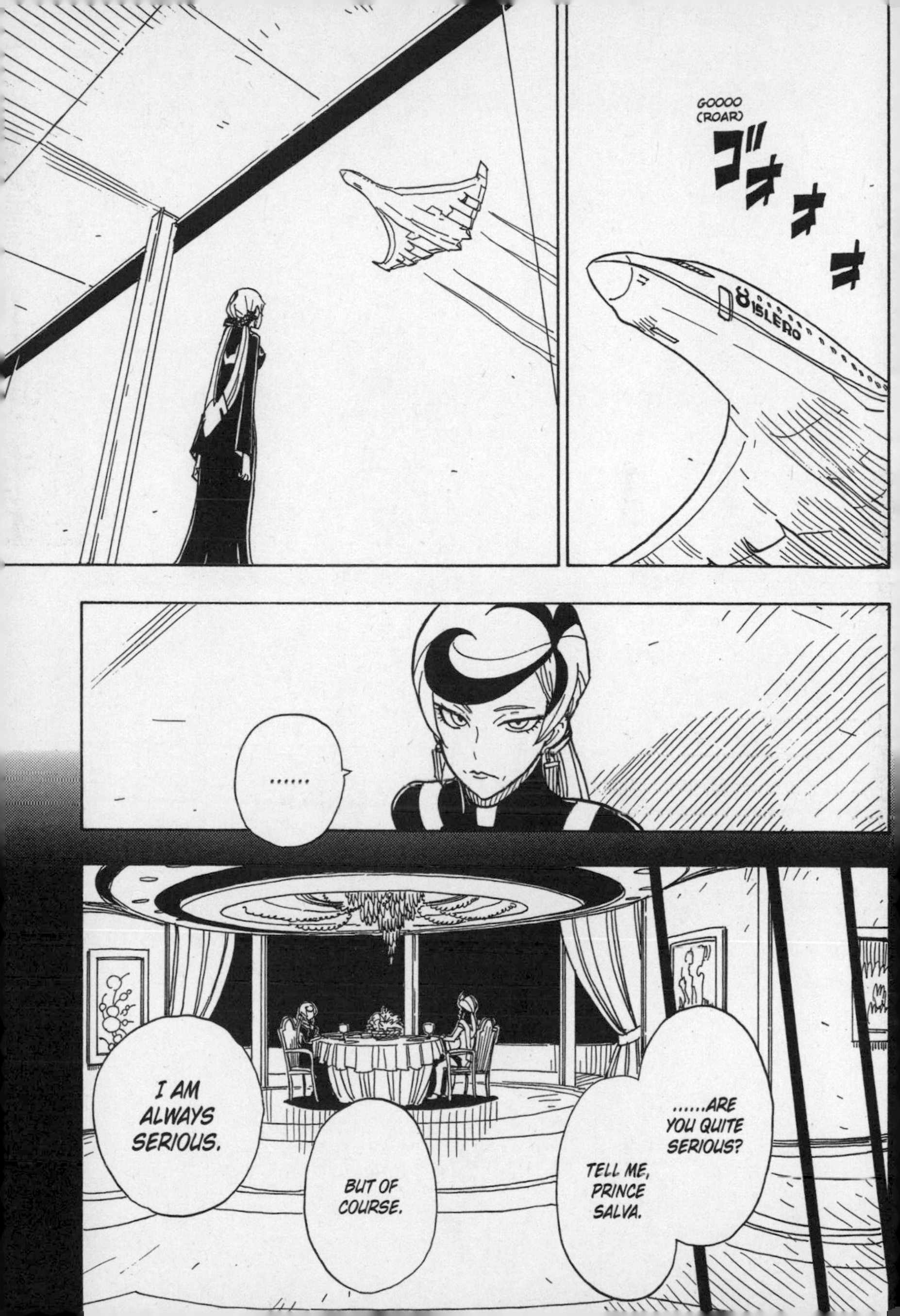
GOOOO (ROAR)
ゴオオオ
......
......ARE YOU QUITE SERIOUS?
TELL ME, PRINCE SALVA.
BUT OF COURSE.
I AM ALWAYS SERIOUS.

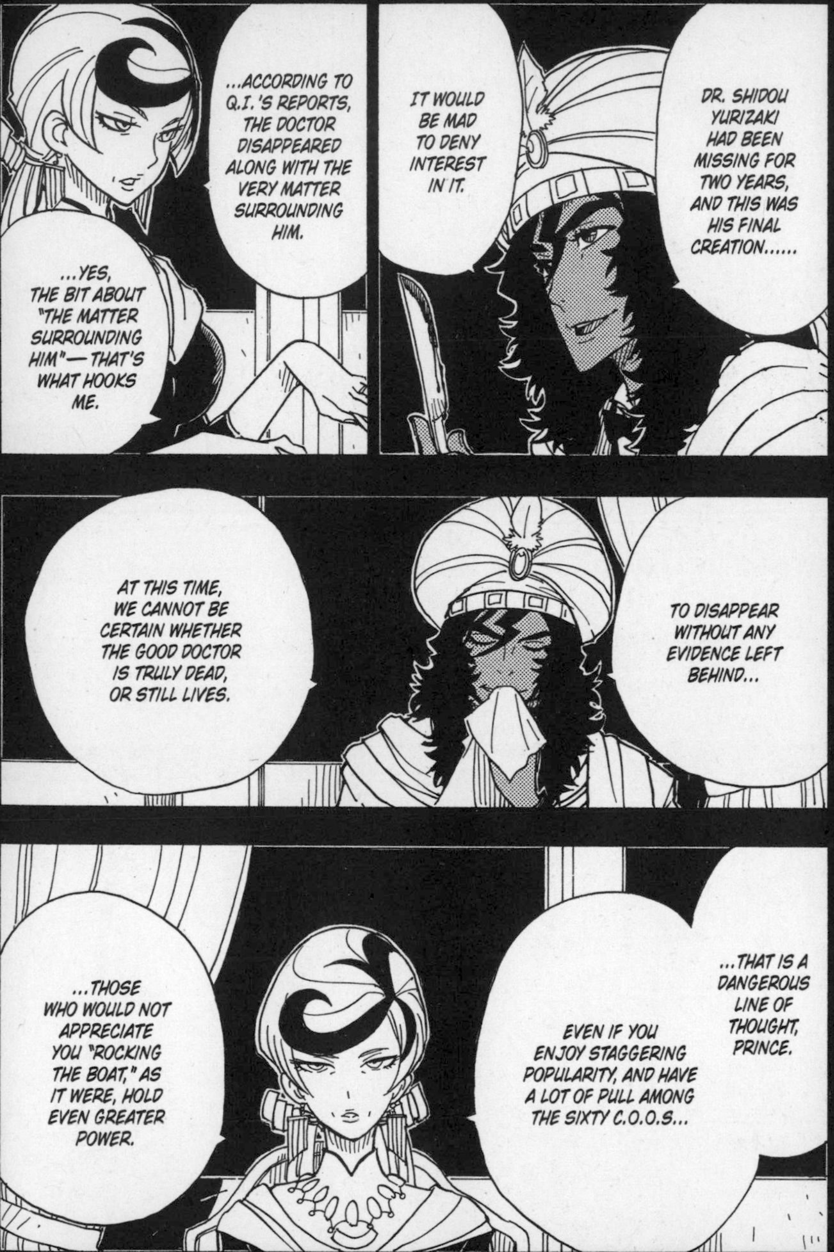
DR. SHIDOU YURIZAKI HAD BEEN MISSING FOR TWO YEARS, AND THIS WAS HIS FINAL CREATION......
IT WOULD BE MAD TO DENY INTEREST IN IT.
...ACCORDING TO Q.I.'S REPORTS, THE DOCTOR DISAPPEARED ALONG WITH THE VERY MATTER SURROUNDING HIM.
...YES, THE BIT ABOUT "THE MATTER SURROUNDING HIM"—THAT'S WHAT HOOKS ME.
TO DISAPPEAR WITHOUT ANY EVIDENCE LEFT BEHIND...
AT THIS TIME, WE CANNOT BE CERTAIN WHETHER THE GOOD DOCTOR IS TRULY DEAD, OR STILL LIVES.
...THAT IS A DANGEROUS LINE OF THOUGHT, PRINCE.
EVEN IF YOU ENJOY STAGGERING POPULARITY, AND HAVE A LOT OF PULL AMONG THE SIXTY C.O.O.S...
...THOSE WHO WOULD NOT APPRECIATE YOU "ROCKING THE BOAT," AS IT WERE, HOLD EVEN GREATER POWER.

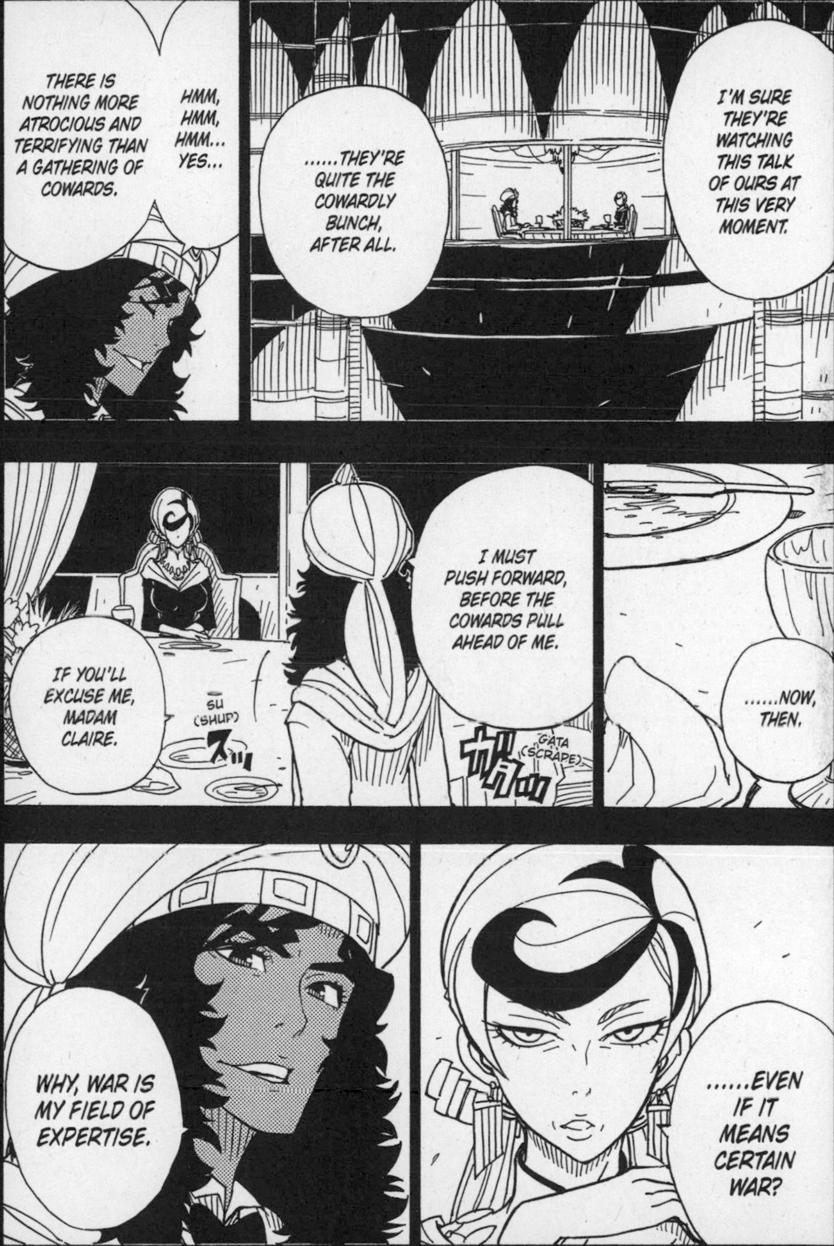
I'M SURE THEY'RE WATCHING THIS TALK OF OURS AT THIS VERY MOMENT.
......THEY'RE QUITE THE COWARDLY BUNCH, AFTER ALL.
HMM, HMM, HMM... YES...
THERE IS NOTHING MORE ATROCIOUS AND TERRIFYING THAN A GATHERING OF COWARDS.
......NOW, THEN.
I MUST PUSH FORWARD, BEFORE THE COWARDS PULL AHEAD OF ME.
GATA (SCRAPE)
ガタッ
SU (SHUP)
ズッ
IF YOU'LL EXCUSE ME, MADAM CLAIRE.
......EVEN IF IT MEANS CERTAIN WAR?
WHY, WAR IS MY FIELD OF EXPERTISE.

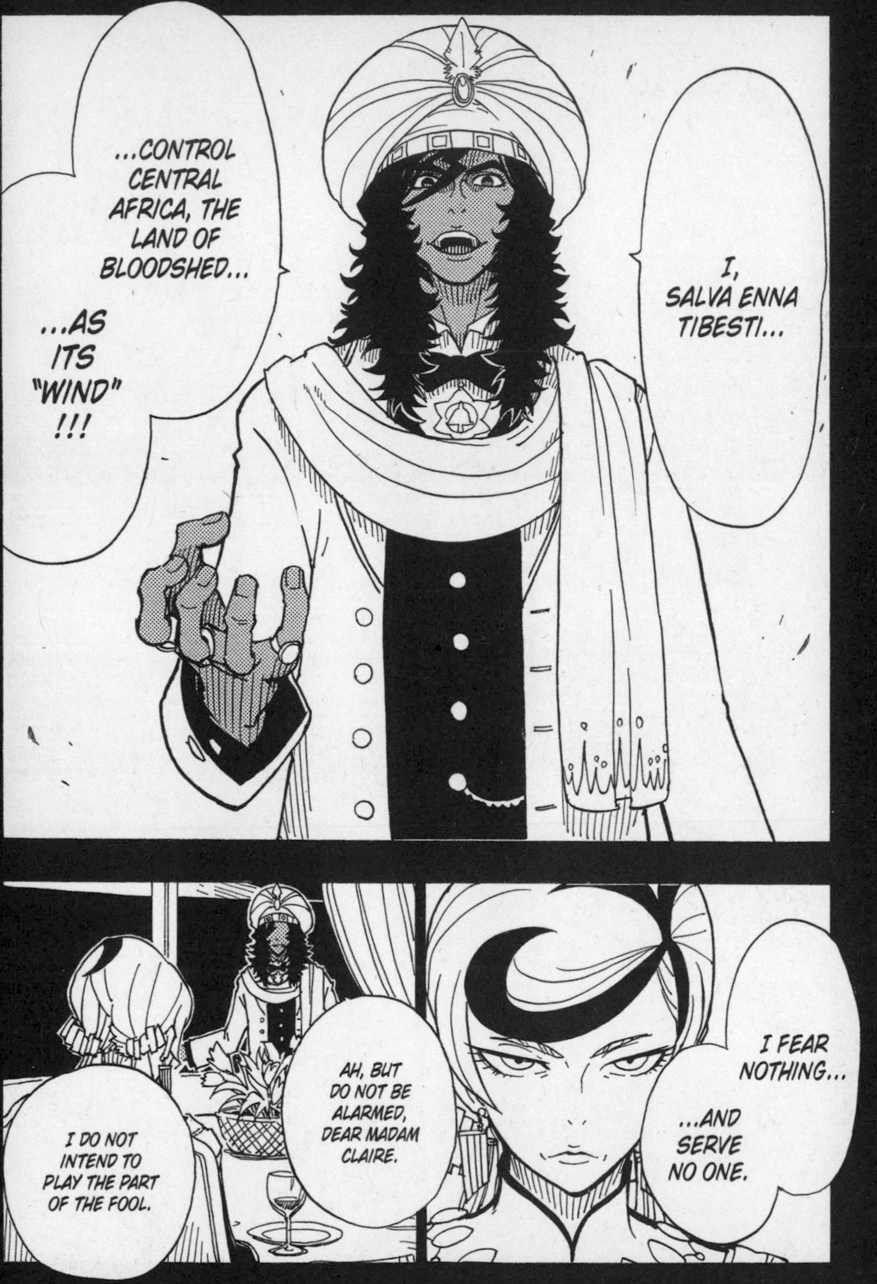
I, SALVA ENNA TIBESTI...
...CONTROL CENTRAL AFRICA, THE LAND OF BLOODSHED...
...AS ITS "WIND" !!!
I FEAR NOTHING...
...AND SERVE NO ONE.
AH, BUT DO NOT BE ALARMED, DEAR MADAM CLAIRE.
I DO NOT INTEND TO PLAY THE PART OF THE FOOL.

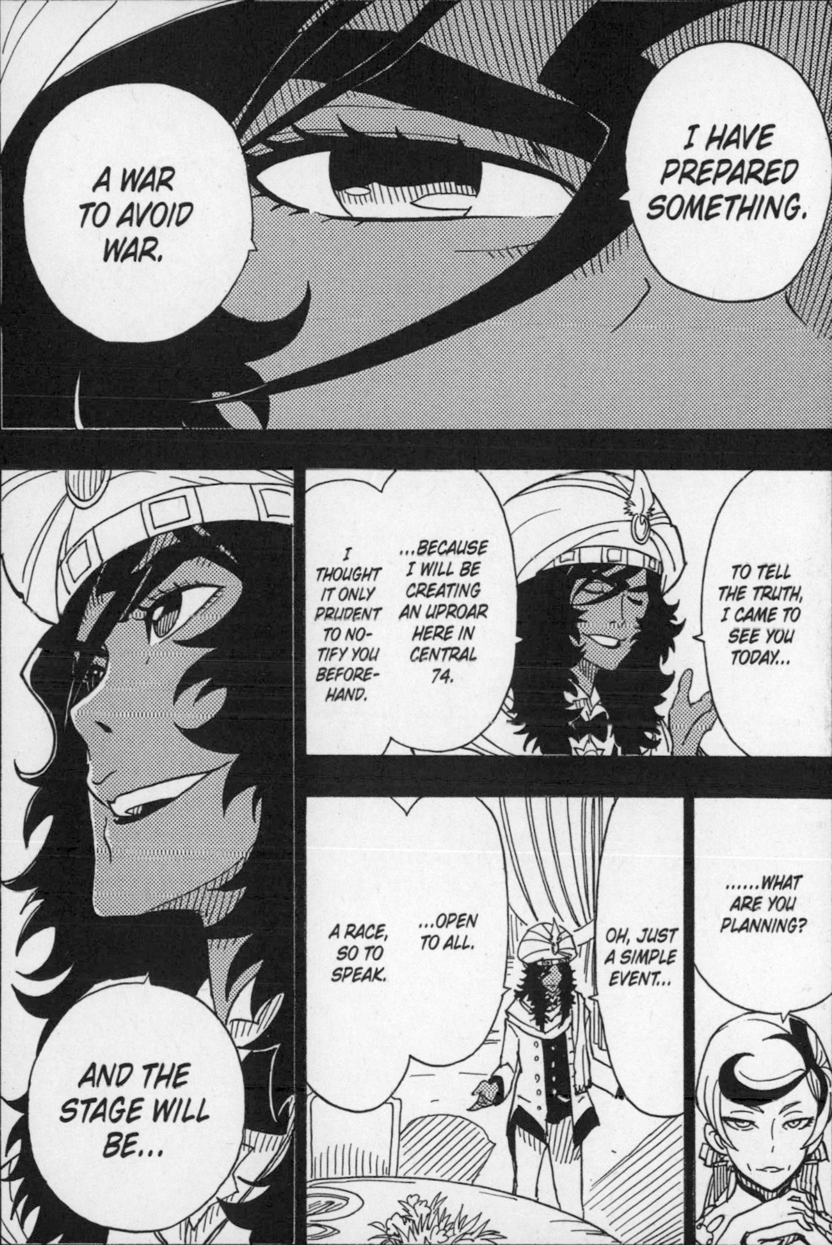
I HAVE PREPARED SOMETHING.
A WAR TO AVOID WAR.
TO TELL THE TRUTH, I CAME TO SEE YOU TODAY...
...BECAUSE I WILL BE CREATING AN UPROAR HERE IN CENTRAL 74.
I THOUGHT IT ONLY PRUDENT TO NOTIFY YOU BEFOREHAND.
......WHAT ARE YOU PLANNING?
OH, JUST A SIMPLE EVENT...
...OPEN TO ALL.
A RACE, SO TO SPEAK.
AND THE STAGE WILL BE...

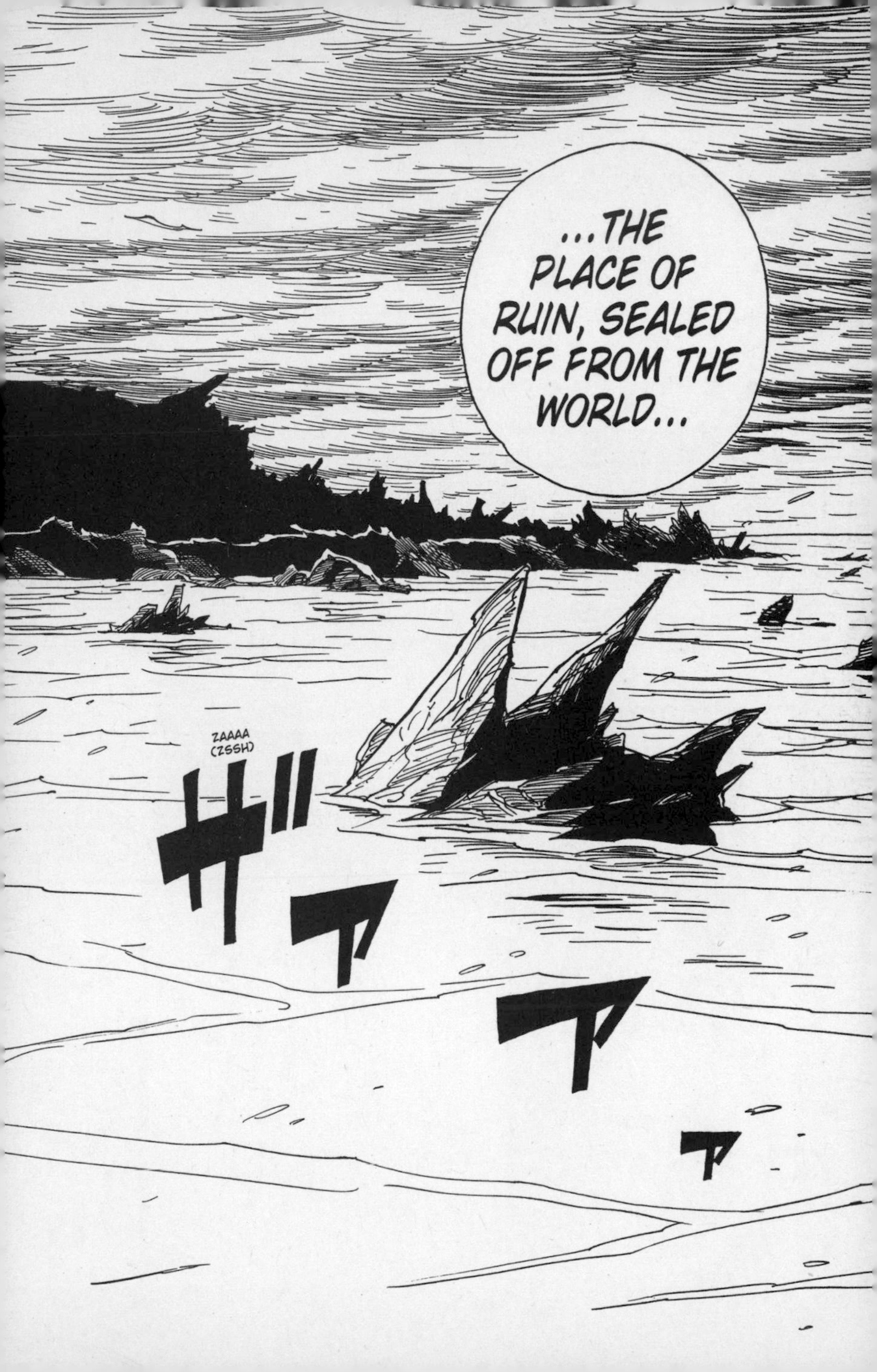
...THE PLACE OF RUIN, SEALED OFF FROM THE WORLD...
ZAAAA (ZSSH)
ザァァァ

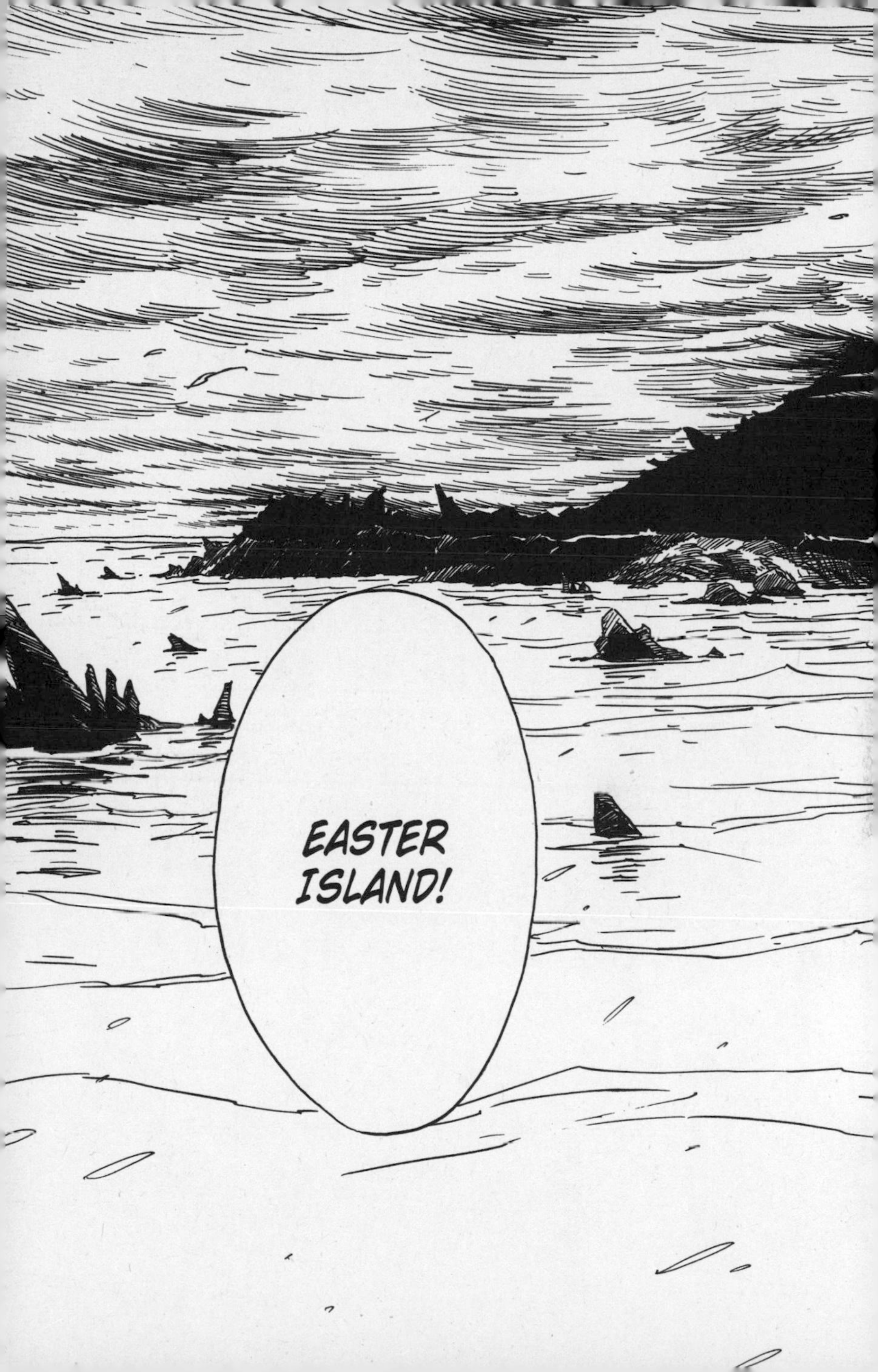
EASTER ISLAND!

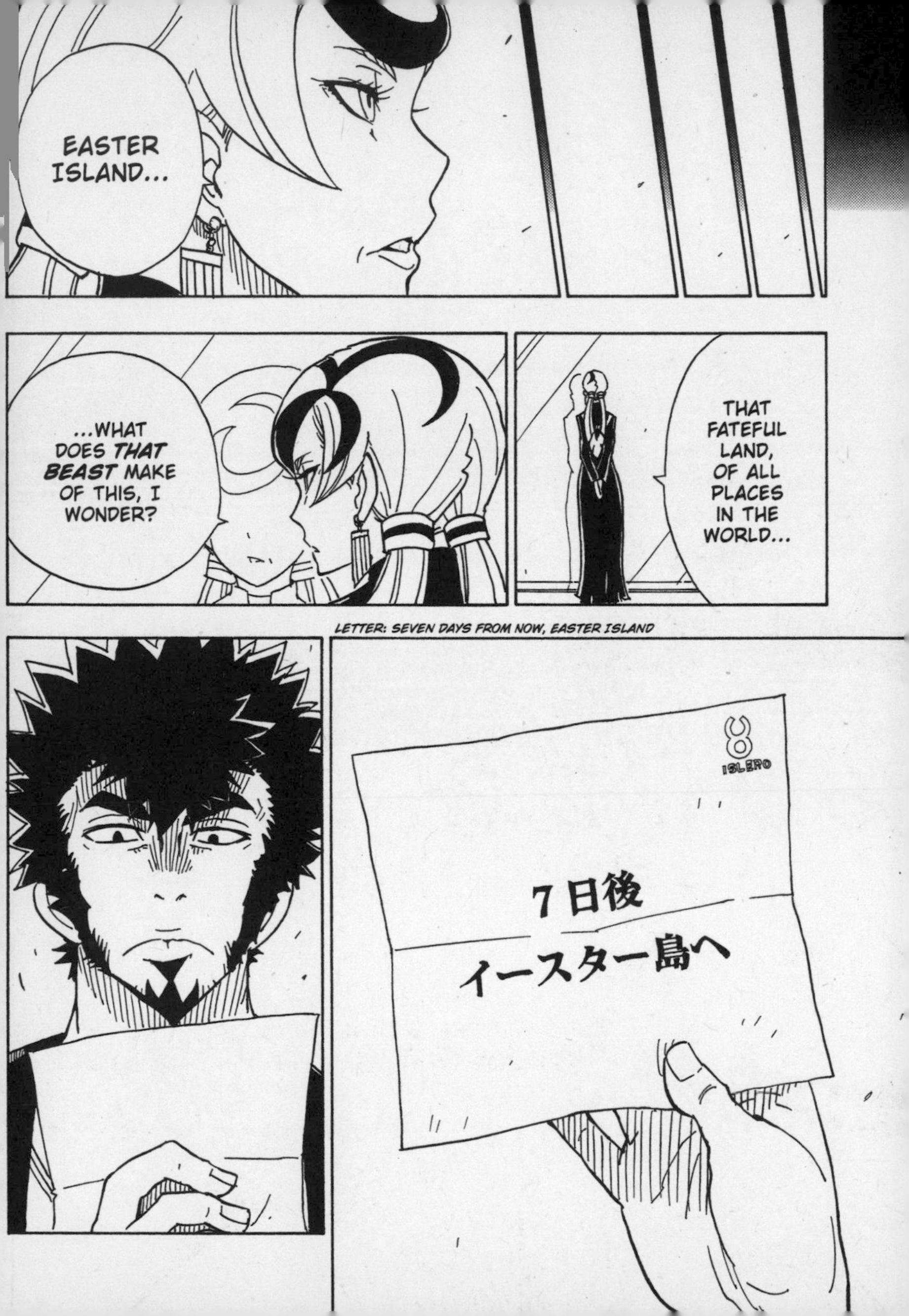
EASTER ISLAND...
THAT FATEFUL LAND, OF ALL PLACES IN THE WORLD...
...WHAT DOES *THAT BEAST* MAKE OF THIS, I WONDER?
LETTER: SEVEN DAYS FROM NOW, EASTER ISLAND
ISLERO
7日後
イースター島へ

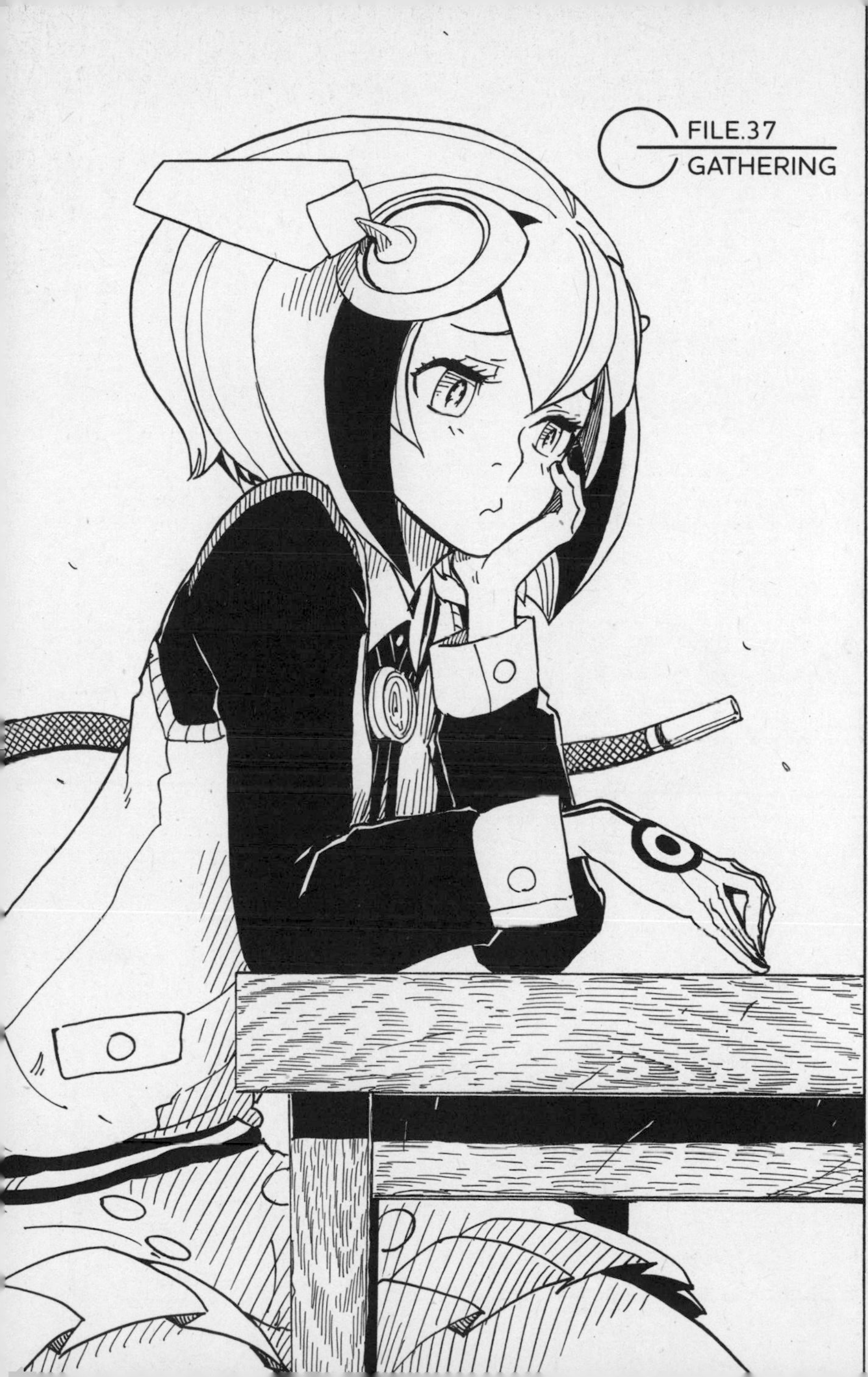
FILE.37
GATHERING

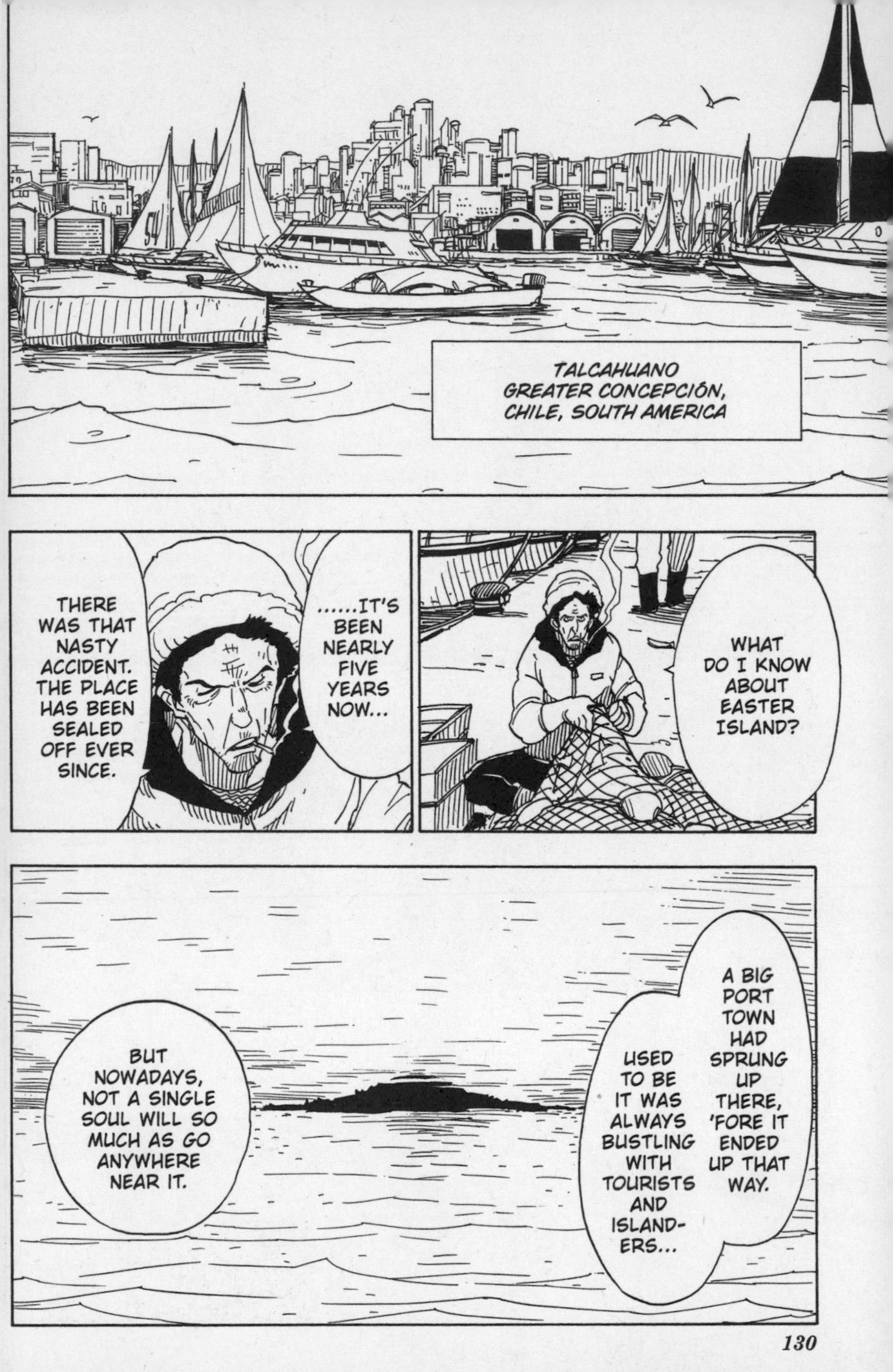
TALCAHUANO GREATER CONCEPCIÓN, CHILE, SOUTH AMERICA
WHAT DO I KNOW ABOUT EASTER ISLAND?
......IT'S BEEN NEARLY FIVE YEARS NOW...
THERE WAS THAT NASTY ACCIDENT. THE PLACE HAS BEEN SEALED OFF EVER SINCE.
A BIG PORT TOWN HAD SPRUNG UP THERE, 'FORE IT ENDED UP THAT WAY.
USED TO BE IT WAS ALWAYS BUSTLING WITH TOURISTS AND ISLAND-ERS...
BUT NOWADAYS, NOT A SINGLE SOUL WILL SO MUCH AS GO ANYWHERE NEAR IT.

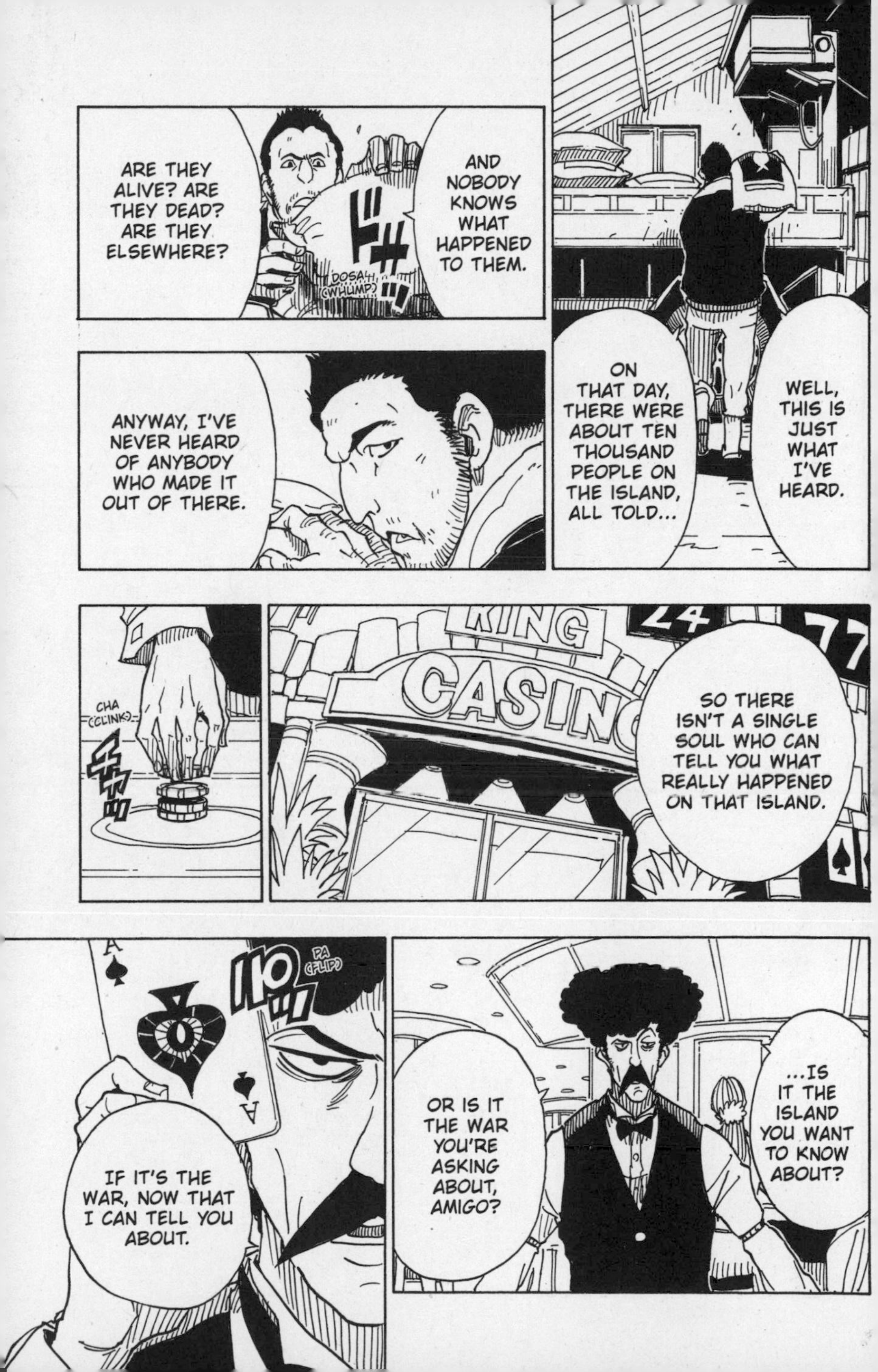
WELL, THIS IS JUST WHAT I'VE HEARD.
ON THAT DAY, THERE WERE ABOUT TEN THOUSAND PEOPLE ON THE ISLAND, ALL TOLD...
AND NOBODY KNOWS WHAT HAPPENED TO THEM.
DOSA (WHUMP)
ARE THEY ALIVE? ARE THEY DEAD? ARE THEY ELSEWHERE?
ANYWAY, I'VE NEVER HEARD OF ANYBODY WHO MADE IT OUT OF THERE.
KING
CASINO
SO THERE ISN'T A SINGLE SOUL WHO CAN TELL YOU WHAT REALLY HAPPENED ON THAT ISLAND.
CHA (CLINK)
...IS IT THE ISLAND YOU WANT TO KNOW ABOUT?
OR IS IT THE WAR YOU'RE ASKING ABOUT, AMIGO?
PA (FLIP)
IF IT'S THE WAR, NOW THAT I CAN TELL YOU ABOUT.

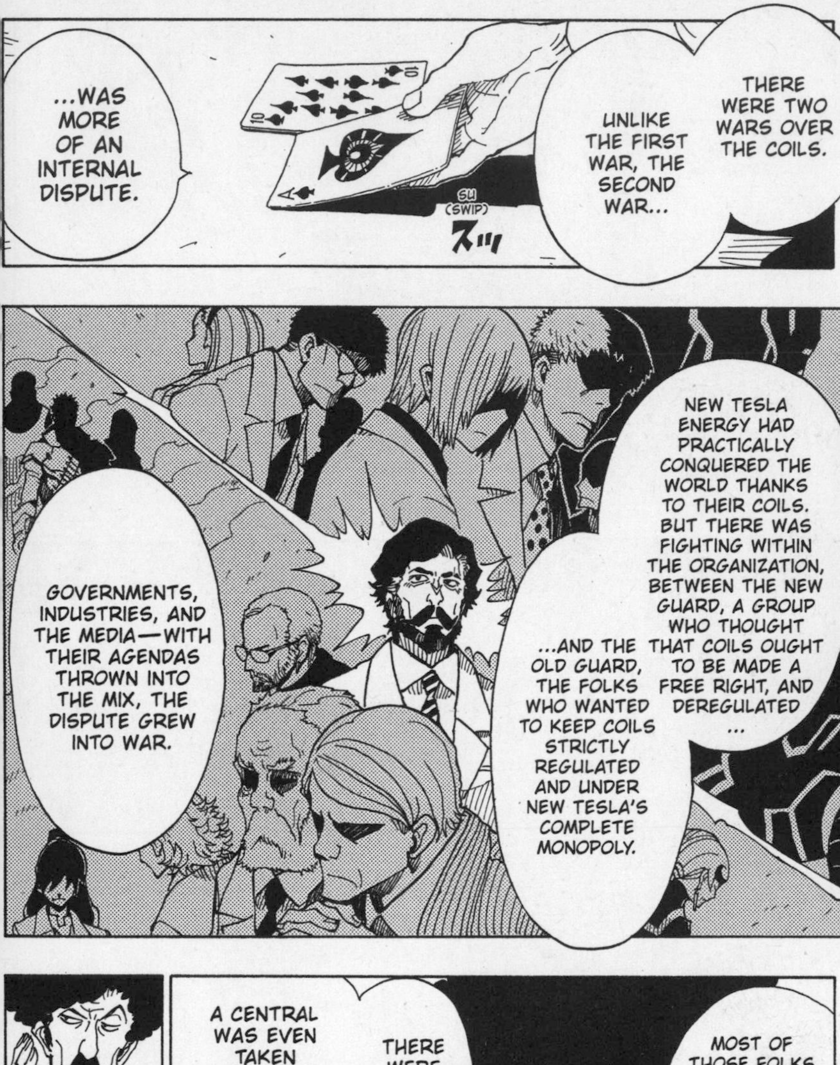
THERE WERE TWO WARS OVER THE COILS.
UNLIKE THE FIRST WAR, THE SECOND WAR...
SU (SWIP) スッ
...WAS MORE OF AN INTERNAL DISPUTE.
NEW TESLA ENERGY HAD PRACTICALLY CONQUERED THE WORLD THANKS TO THEIR COILS. BUT THERE WAS FIGHTING WITHIN THE ORGANIZATION, BETWEEN THE NEW GUARD, A GROUP WHO THOUGHT THAT COILS OUGHT TO BE MADE A FREE RIGHT, AND DEREGULATED...
...AND THE OLD GUARD, THE FOLKS WHO WANTED TO KEEP COILS STRICTLY REGULATED AND UNDER NEW TESLA'S COMPLETE MONOPOLY.
GOVERNMENTS, INDUSTRIES, AND THE MEDIA—WITH THEIR AGENDAS THROWN INTO THE MIX, THE DISPUTE GREW INTO WAR.
MOST OF THOSE FOLKS HAD A HAND IN RILING UP THE PUBLIC, BUT THAT WAS IT. THEY NEVER CAME OUT INTO THE FOREFRONT. BUT, AMIGO...
THERE WERE UNSTABLE COUNTRIES THAT TURNED INTO REAL WAR-ZONES.
A CENTRAL WAS EVEN TAKEN OVER, AND ITS TOWER ALMOST BROUGHT DOWN, ACCORDING TO THE STORIES.
AND THEN, AMIGO...

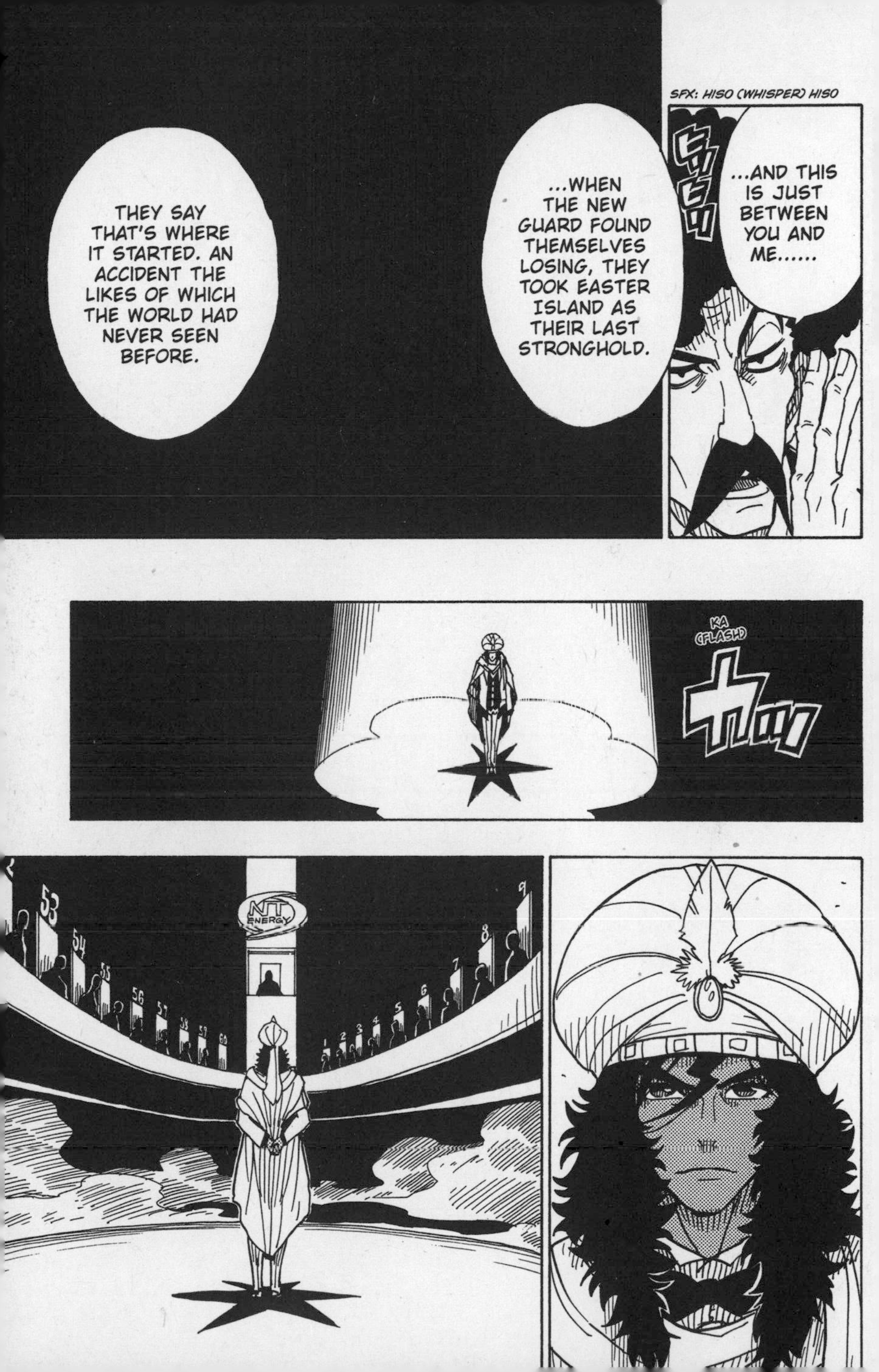
SFX: HISO (WHISPER) HISO
...AND THIS IS JUST BETWEEN YOU AND ME......
...WHEN THE NEW GUARD FOUND THEMSELVES LOSING, THEY TOOK EASTER ISLAND AS THEIR LAST STRONGHOLD.
THEY SAY THAT'S WHERE IT STARTED. AN ACCIDENT THE LIKES OF WHICH THE WORLD HAD NEVER SEEN BEFORE.
KA (FLASH)
NT ENERGY

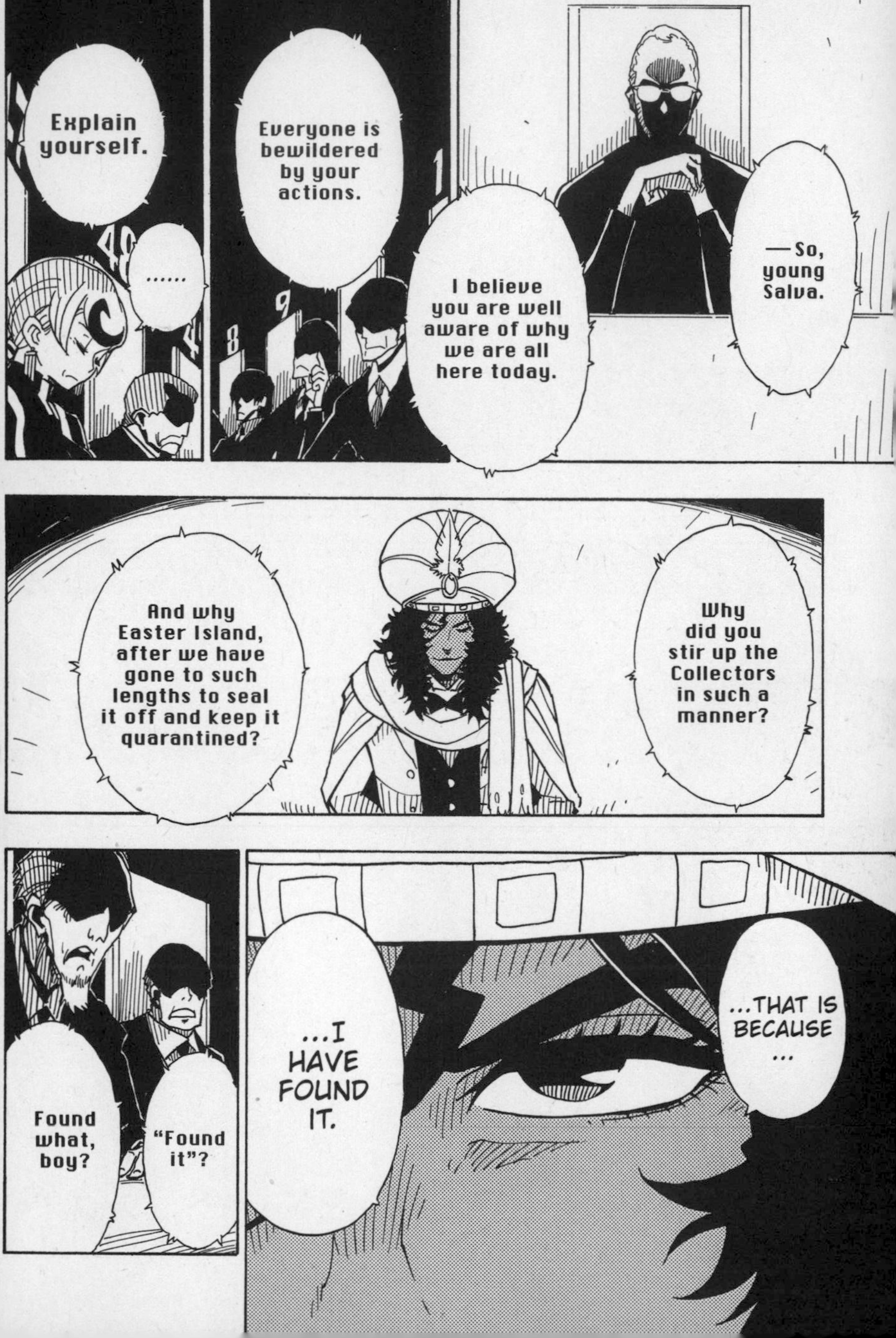
—So, young Salva.
I believe you are well aware of why we are all here today.
Everyone is bewildered by your actions.
Explain yourself.
......
Why did you stir up the Collectors in such a manner?
And why Easter Island, after we have gone to such lengths to seal it off and keep it quarantined?
...THAT IS BECAUSE ...
...I HAVE FOUND IT.
"Found it"?
Found what, boy?

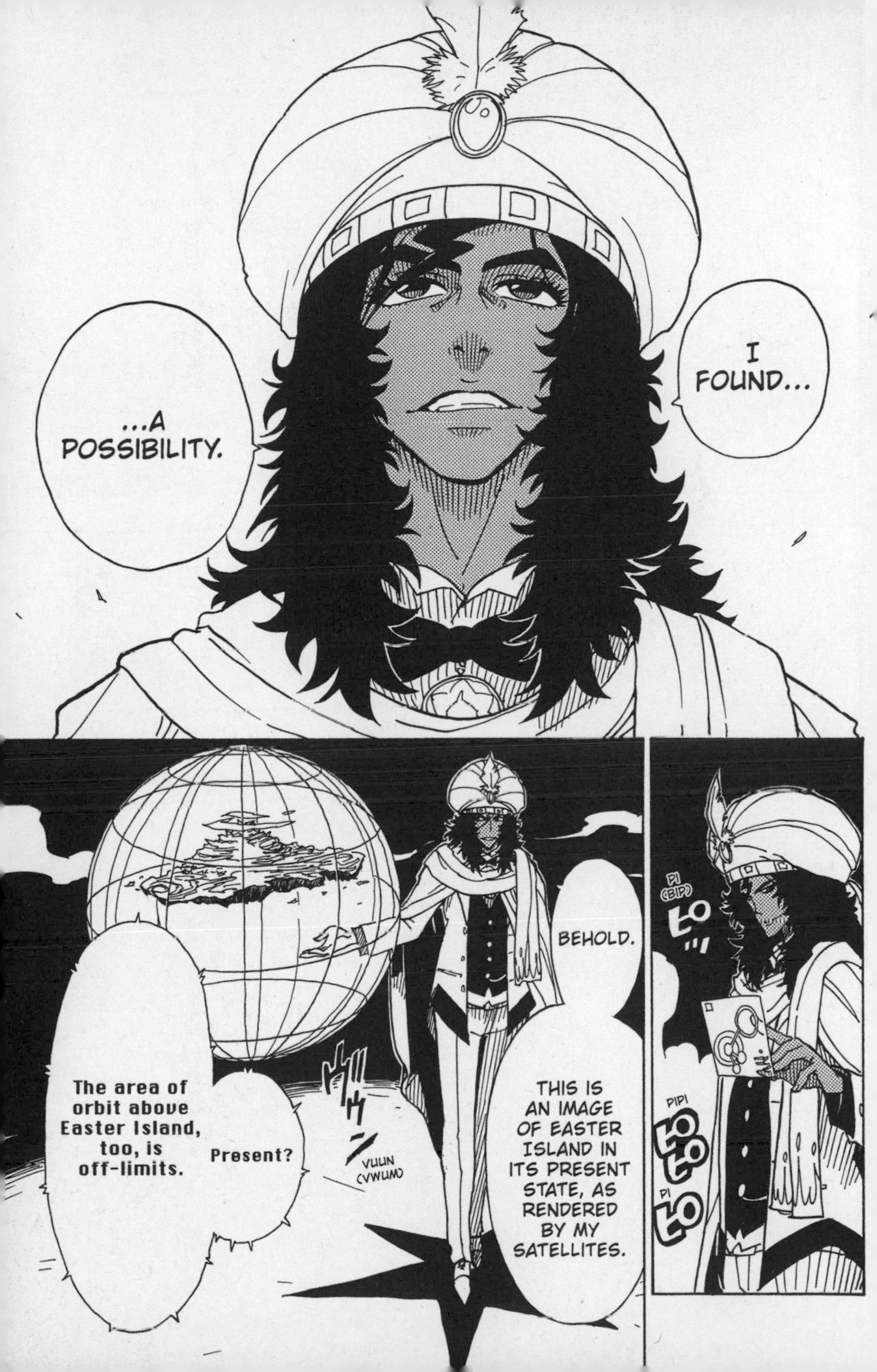
I FOUND...
...A POSSIBILITY.
PI (BIP)
PIPI
PI
BEHOLD.
THIS IS AN IMAGE OF EASTER ISLAND IN ITS PRESENT STATE, AS RENDERED BY MY SATELLITES.
VUUN (VWUM)
Present?
The area of orbit above Easter Island, too, is off-limits.

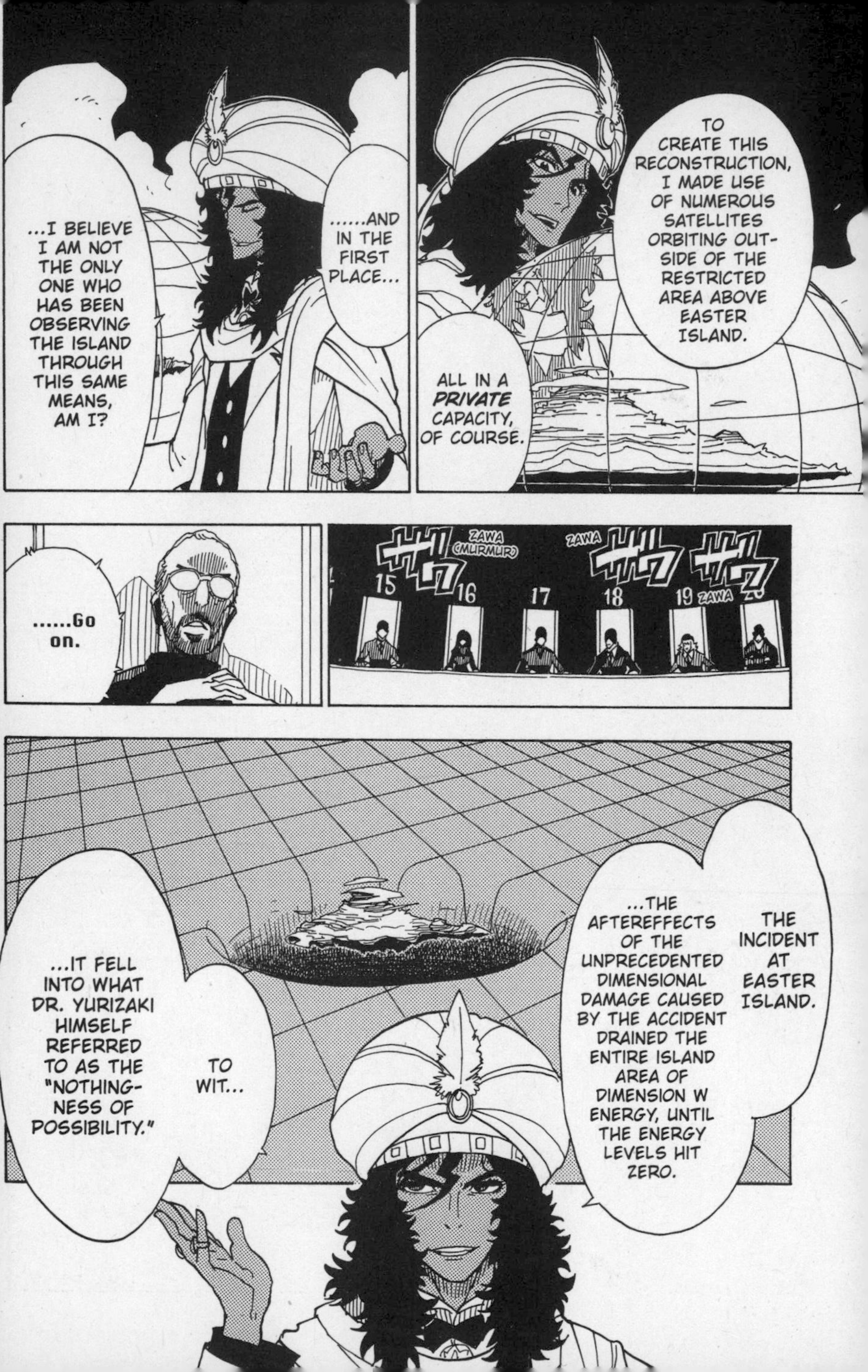
TO CREATE THIS RECONSTRUCTION, I MADE USE OF NUMEROUS SATELLITES ORBITING OUT-SIDE OF THE RESTRICTED AREA ABOVE EASTER ISLAND.
ALL IN A *PRIVATE* CAPACITY, OF COURSE.
......AND IN THE FIRST PLACE...
...I BELIEVE I AM NOT THE ONLY ONE WHO HAS BEEN OBSERVING THE ISLAND THROUGH THIS SAME MEANS, AM I?
ZAWA (MURMUR)
ZAWA
ZAWA
15
16
17
18
19
......Go on.
THE INCIDENT AT EASTER ISLAND.
...THE AFTEREFFECTS OF THE UNPRECEDENTED DIMENSIONAL DAMAGE CAUSED BY THE ACCIDENT DRAINED THE ENTIRE ISLAND AREA OF DIMENSION W ENERGY, UNTIL THE ENERGY LEVELS HIT ZERO.
TO WIT...
...IT FELL INTO WHAT DR. YURIZAKI HIMSELF REFERRED TO AS THE "NOTHING-NESS OF POSSIBILITY."

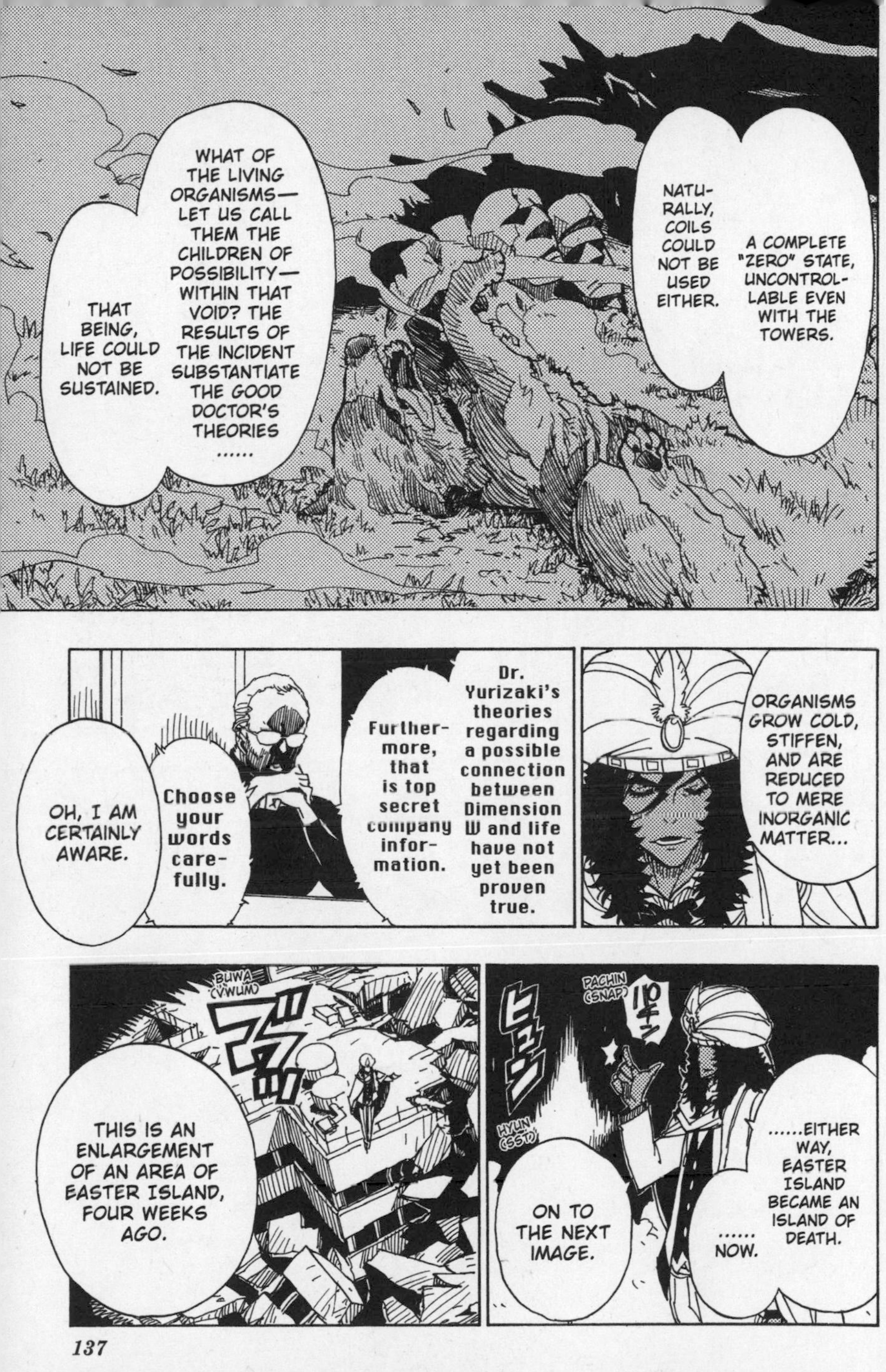
A COMPLETE "ZERO" STATE, UNCONTROLLABLE EVEN WITH THE TOWERS.
NATURALLY, COILS COULD NOT BE USED EITHER.
WHAT OF THE LIVING ORGANISMS—LET US CALL THEM THE CHILDREN OF POSSIBILITY—WITHIN THAT VOID? THE RESULTS OF THE INCIDENT SUBSTANTIATE THE GOOD DOCTOR'S THEORIES ......
THAT BEING, LIFE COULD NOT BE SUSTAINED.
ORGANISMS GROW COLD, STIFFEN, AND ARE REDUCED TO MERE INORGANIC MATTER...
Dr. Yurizaki's theories regarding a possible connection between Dimension W and life have not yet been proven true.
Furthermore, that is top secret company information.
Choose your words carefully.
OH, I AM CERTAINLY AWARE.
PACHIN (SNAP)
......EITHER WAY, EASTER ISLAND BECAME AN ISLAND OF DEATH.
......NOW.
ON TO THE NEXT IMAGE.
HYUN (SSST)
BUWA (VWUM)
THIS IS AN ENLARGEMENT OF AN AREA OF EASTER ISLAND, FOUR WEEKS AGO.

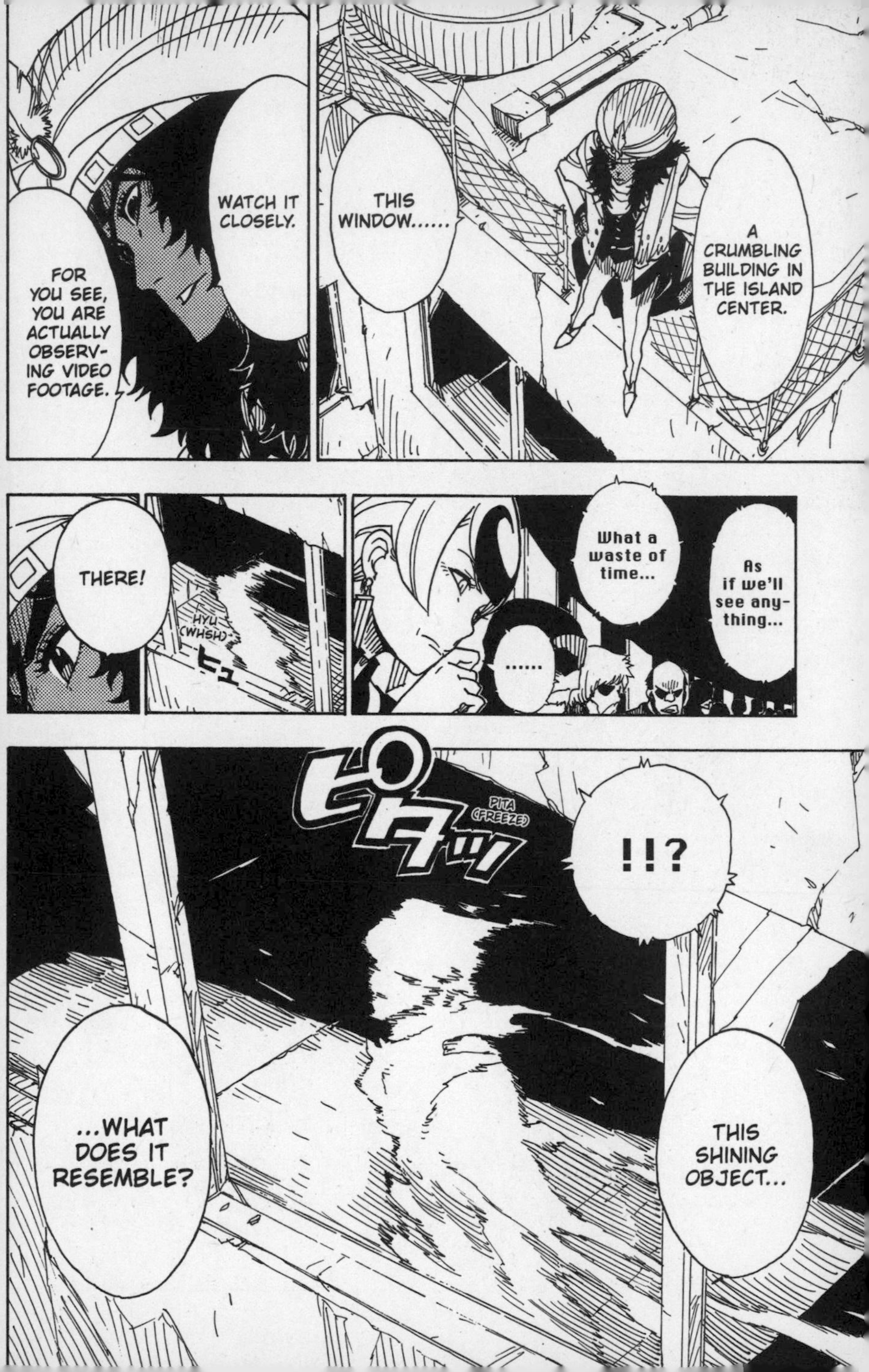
A CRUMBLING BUILDING IN THE ISLAND CENTER.
THIS WINDOW......
WATCH IT CLOSELY.
FOR YOU SEE, YOU ARE ACTUALLY OBSERVING VIDEO FOOTAGE.
As if we'll see anything...
What a waste of time...
......
ヒュ
HYU (WHSH)
THERE!
ピタッ
PITA (FREEZE)
!!?
THIS SHINING OBJECT...
...WHAT DOES IT RESEMBLE?

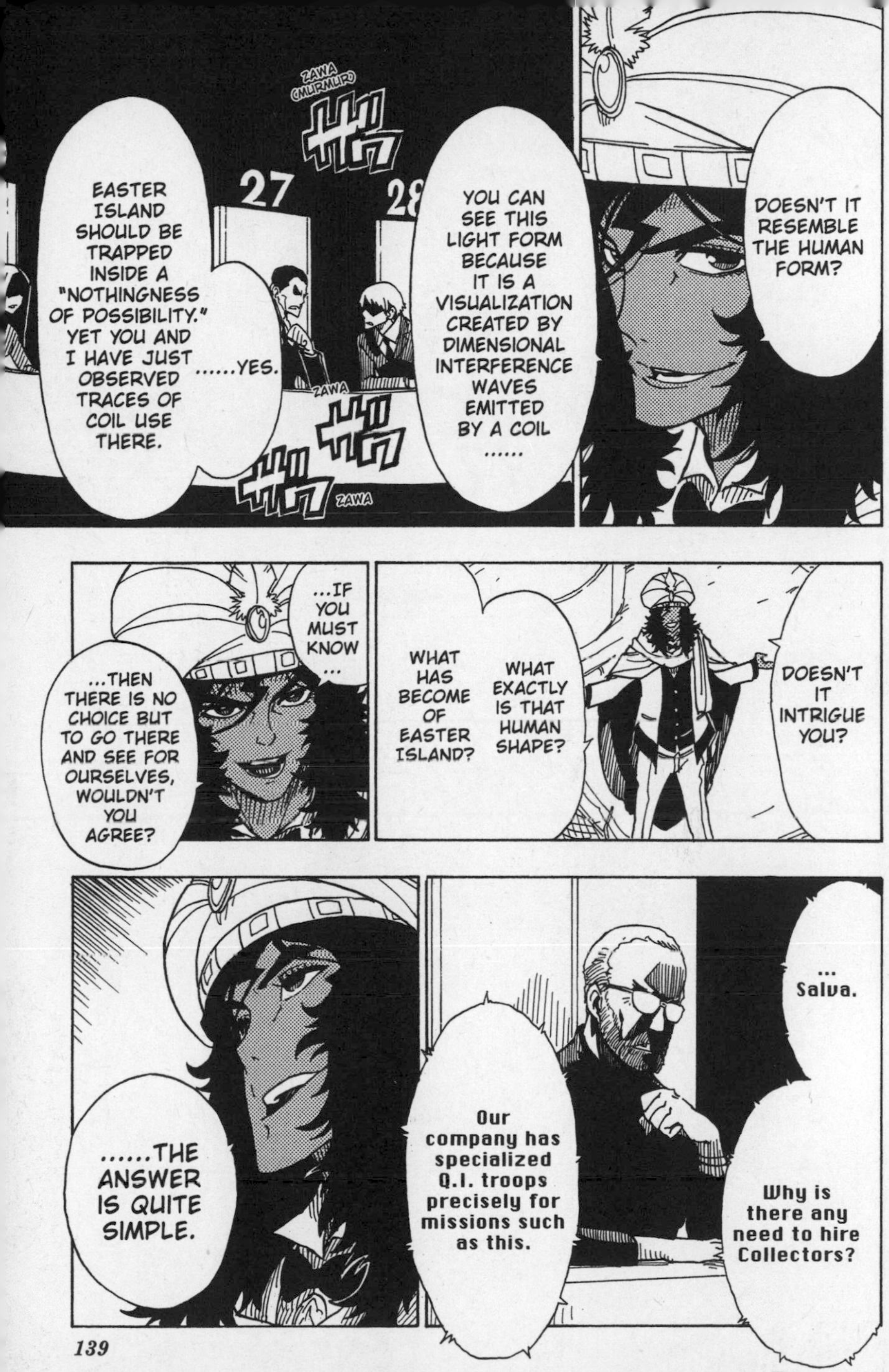
DOESN'T IT RESEMBLE THE HUMAN FORM?
YOU CAN SEE THIS LIGHT FORM BECAUSE IT IS A VISUALIZATION CREATED BY DIMENSIONAL INTERFERENCE WAVES EMITTED BY A COIL ......
ZAWA (MURMUR)
EASTER ISLAND SHOULD BE TRAPPED INSIDE A "NOTHINGNESS OF POSSIBILITY." YET YOU AND I HAVE JUST OBSERVED TRACES OF COIL USE THERE.
......YES.
ZAWA
ZAWA
DOESN'T IT INTRIGUE YOU?
WHAT EXACTLY IS THAT HUMAN SHAPE?
WHAT HAS BECOME OF EASTER ISLAND?
...IF YOU MUST KNOW ...
...THEN THERE IS NO CHOICE BUT TO GO THERE AND SEE FOR OURSELVES, WOULDN'T YOU AGREE?
... Salva.
Why is there any need to hire Collectors?
Our company has specialized Q.I. troops precisely for missions such as this.
......THE ANSWER IS QUITE SIMPLE.

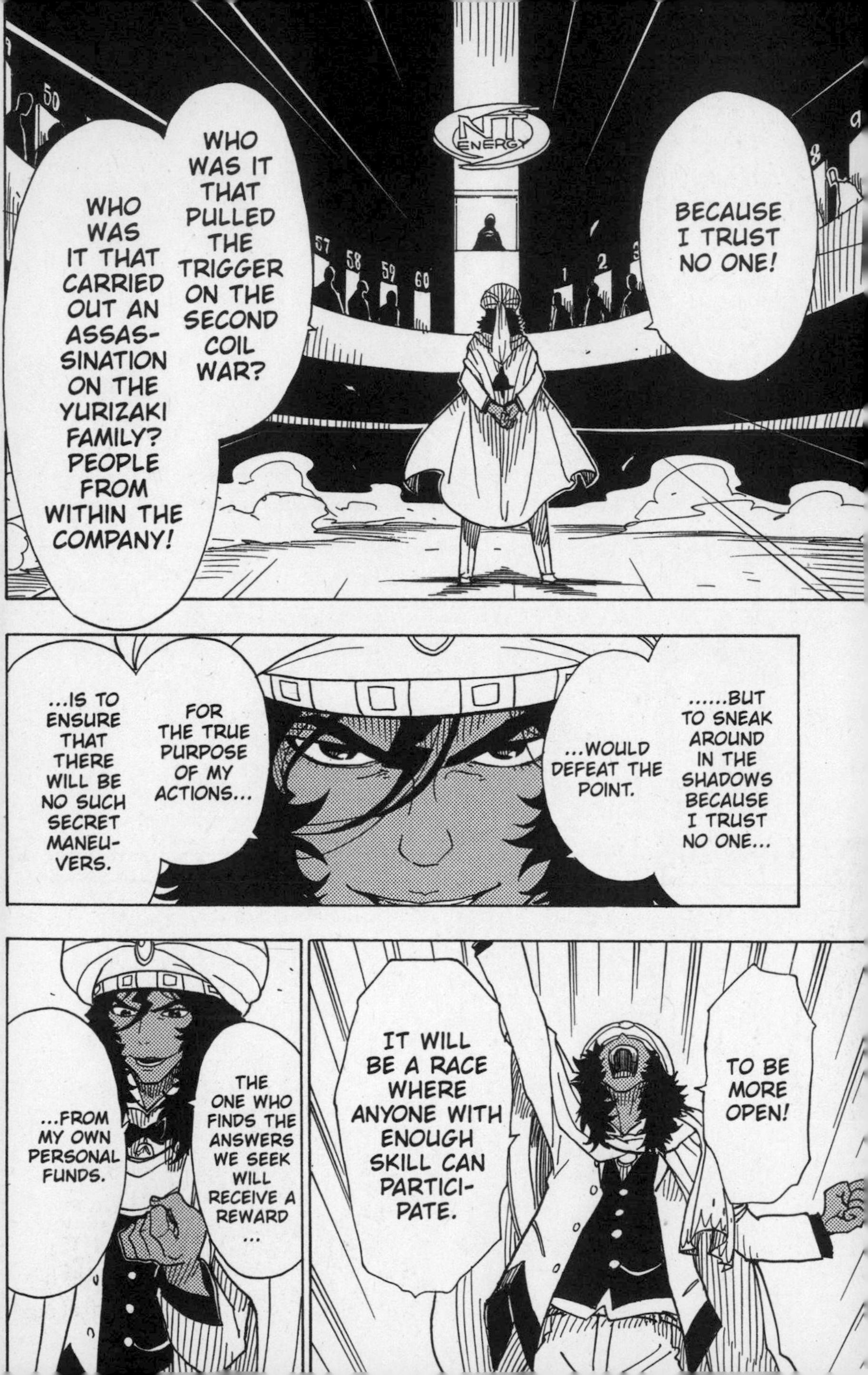
NT ENERGY
BECAUSE I TRUST NO ONE!
WHO WAS IT THAT PULLED THE TRIGGER ON THE SECOND COIL WAR?
WHO WAS IT THAT CARRIED OUT AN ASSAS-SINATION ON THE YURIZAKI FAMILY? PEOPLE FROM WITHIN THE COMPANY!
......BUT TO SNEAK AROUND IN THE SHADOWS BECAUSE I TRUST NO ONE...
...WOULD DEFEAT THE POINT.
FOR THE TRUE PURPOSE OF MY ACTIONS...
...IS TO ENSURE THAT THERE WILL BE NO SUCH SECRET MANEU-VERS.
TO BE MORE OPEN!
IT WILL BE A RACE WHERE ANYONE WITH ENOUGH SKILL CAN PARTICI-PATE.
THE ONE WHO FINDS THE ANSWERS WE SEEK WILL RECEIVE A REWARD...
...FROM MY OWN PERSONAL FUNDS.

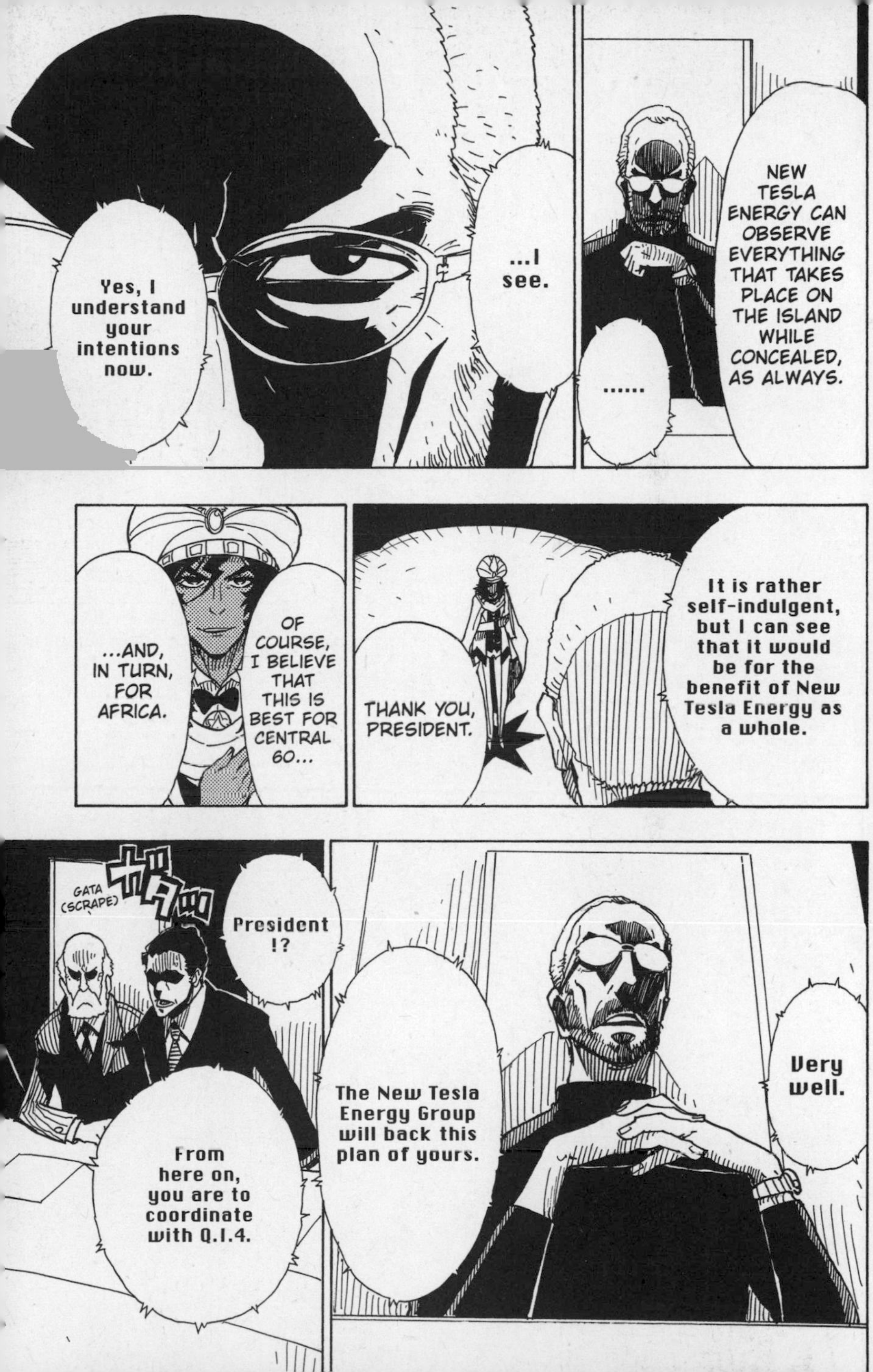
NEW TESLA ENERGY CAN OBSERVE EVERYTHING THAT TAKES PLACE ON THE ISLAND WHILE CONCEALED, AS ALWAYS.
......
...I see.
Yes, I understand your intentions now.
It is rather self-indulgent, but I can see that it would be for the benefit of New Tesla Energy as a whole.
THANK YOU, PRESIDENT.
OF COURSE, I BELIEVE THAT THIS IS BEST FOR CENTRAL 60...
...AND, IN TURN, FOR AFRICA.
Very well.
The New Tesla Energy Group will back this plan of yours.
From here on, you are to coordinate with Q.I.4.
GATA (SCRAPE)
President !?

President!

HYUN
(FSST)

KURU
(SPIN)

ZUBUBU
(ZBB)

GATA
(SCRAPE)

President!

This meeting is adjourned.

......

YOUR ORDERS ARE DULY NOTED.

46

47

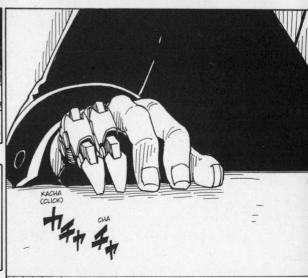

KACHA
(CLICK)

CHA

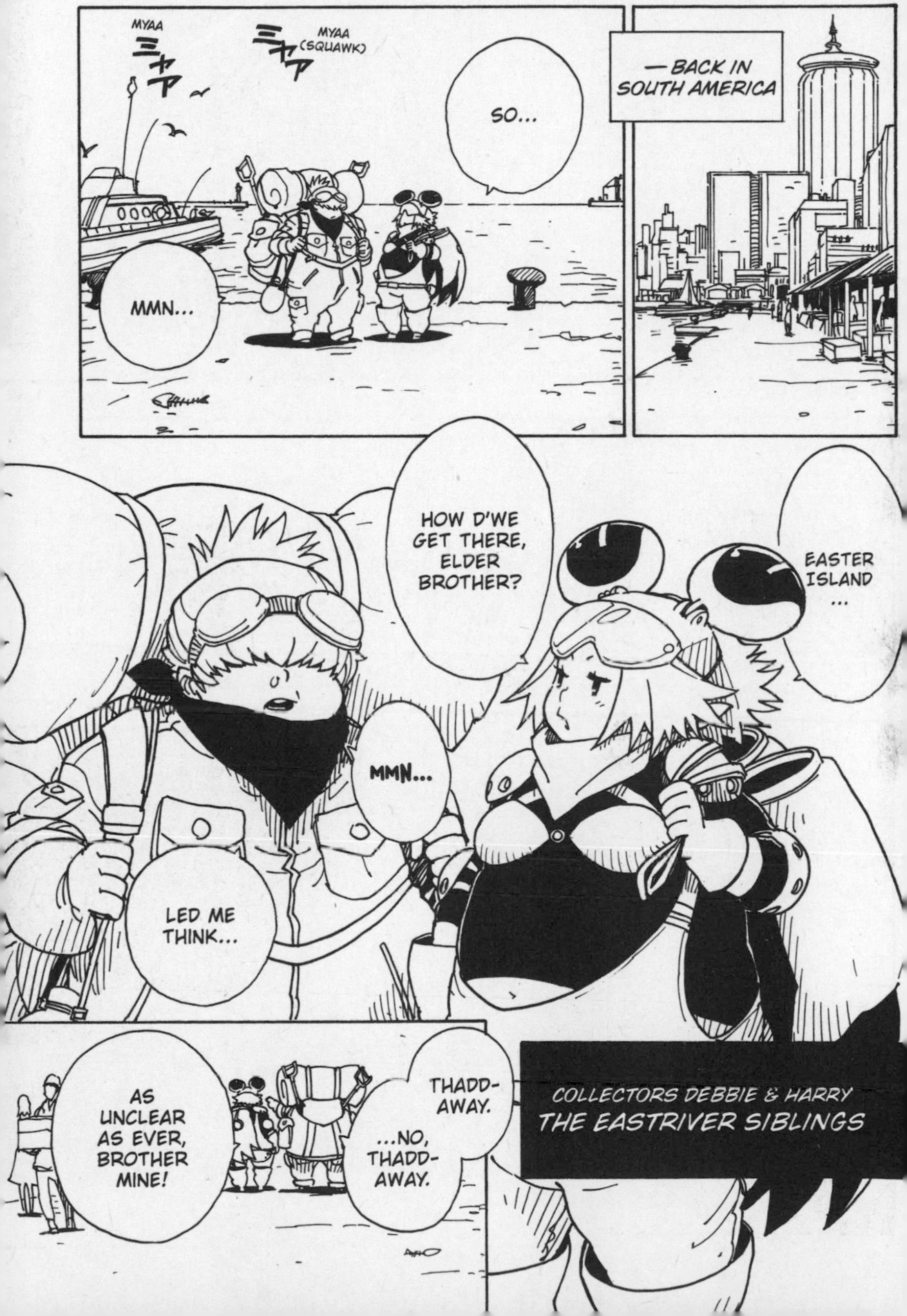
— BACK IN SOUTH AMERICA
SO...
ミャア
MYAA (SQUAWK)
ミャア
MYAA
MMN...
EASTER ISLAND ...
HOW D'WE GET THERE, ELDER BROTHER?
MMN...
LED ME THINK...
COLLECTORS DEBBIE & HARRY
THE EASTRIVER SIBLINGS
THADD-AWAY.
...NO, THADD-AWAY.
AS UNCLEAR AS EVER, BROTHER MINE!

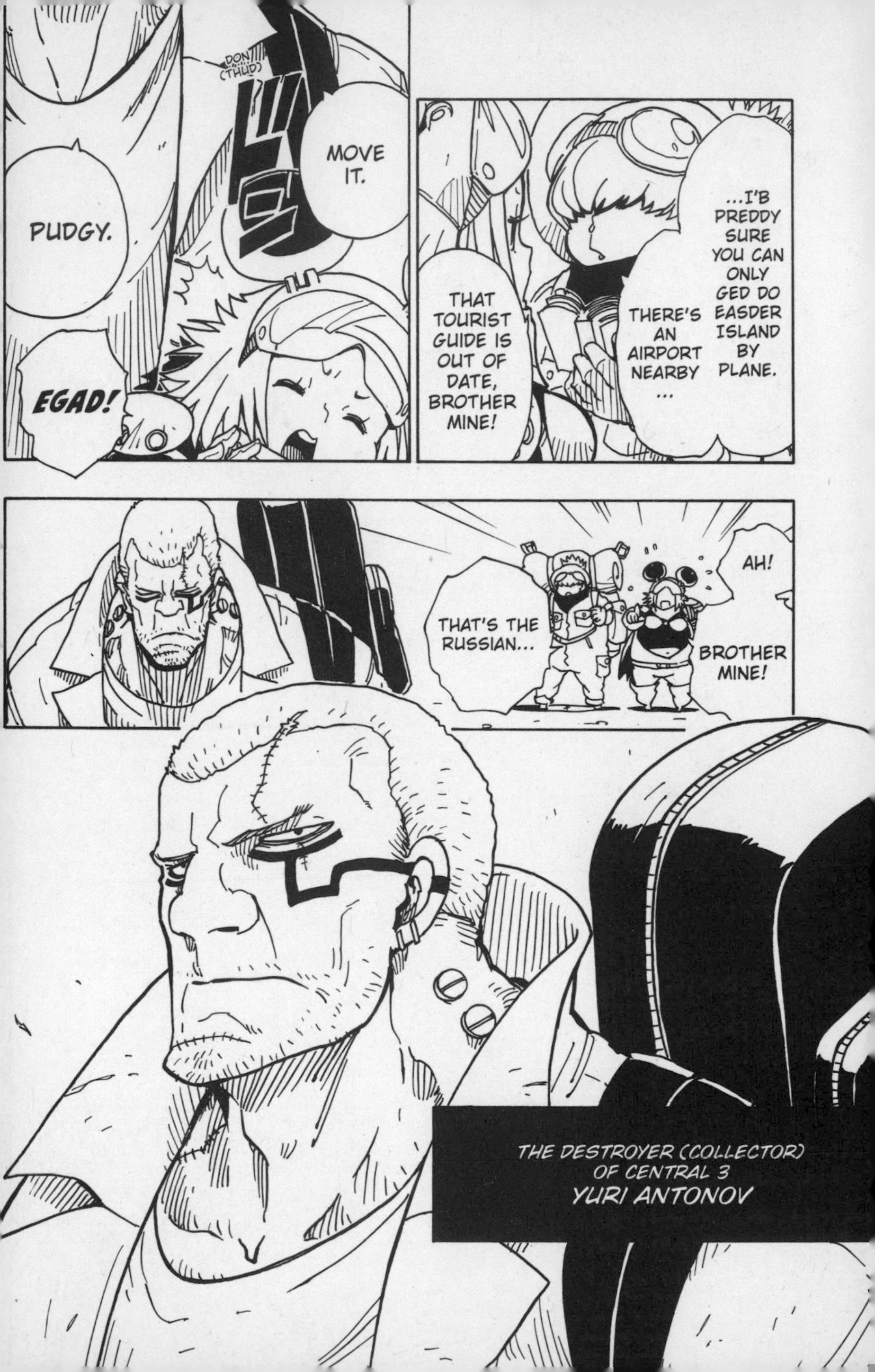
...I'B PREDDY SURE YOU CAN ONLY GED DO EASDER ISLAND BY PLANE.
THERE'S AN AIRPORT NEARBY ...
THAT TOURIST GUIDE IS OUT OF DATE, BROTHER MINE!
DON (THUD)
MOVE IT.
PUDGY.
EGAD!
AH!
BROTHER MINE!
THAT'S THE RUSSIAN...
THE DESTROYER (COLLECTOR) OF CENTRAL 3 YURI ANTONOV

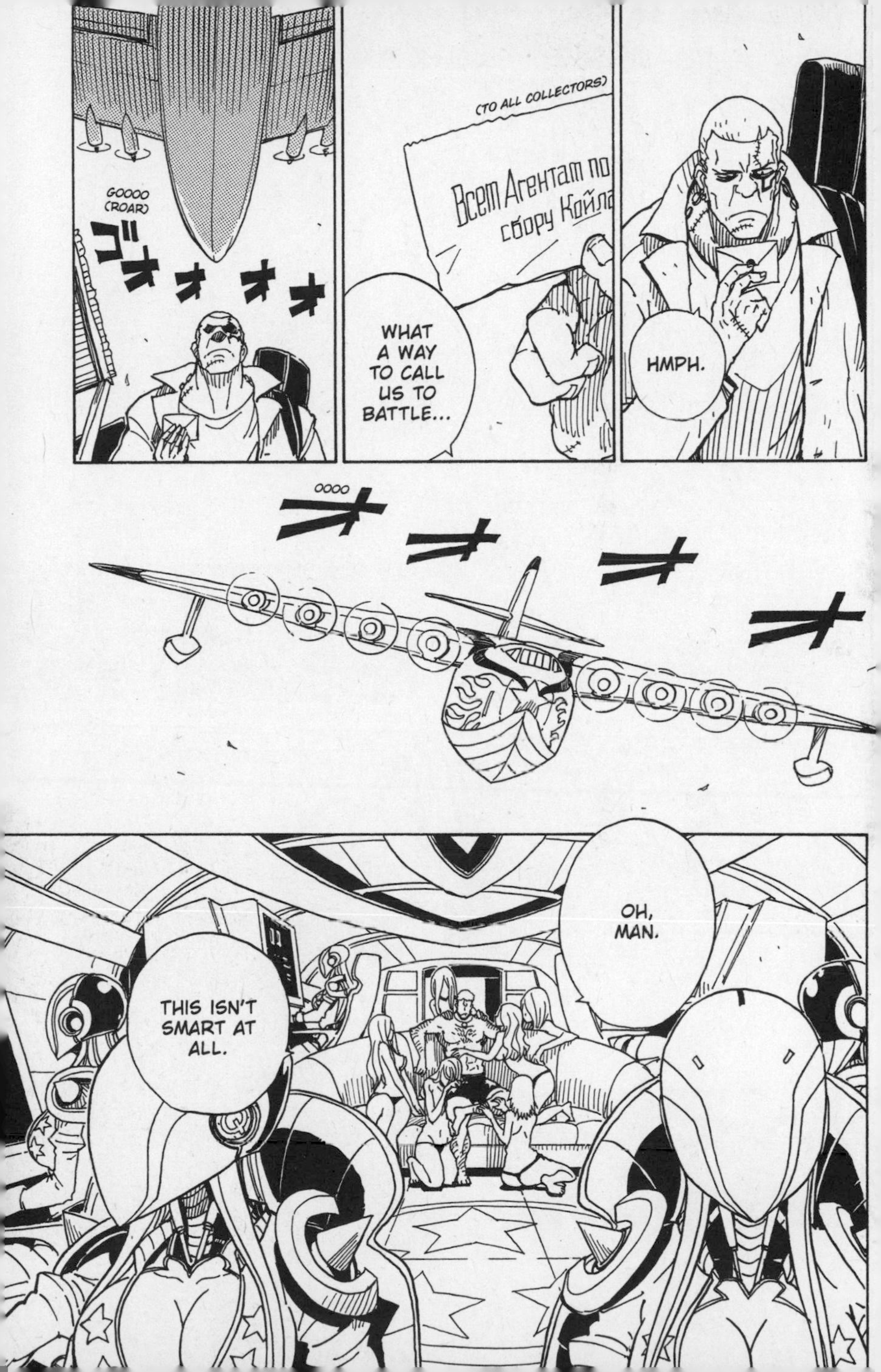
HMPH.
Всем Агентам по сбору Койла
(TO ALL COLLECTORS)
WHAT A WAY TO CALL US TO BATTLE...
ゴオオオオ
GOOOO (ROAR)
オオオオ
OOOO
OH, MAN.
THIS ISN'T SMART AT ALL.

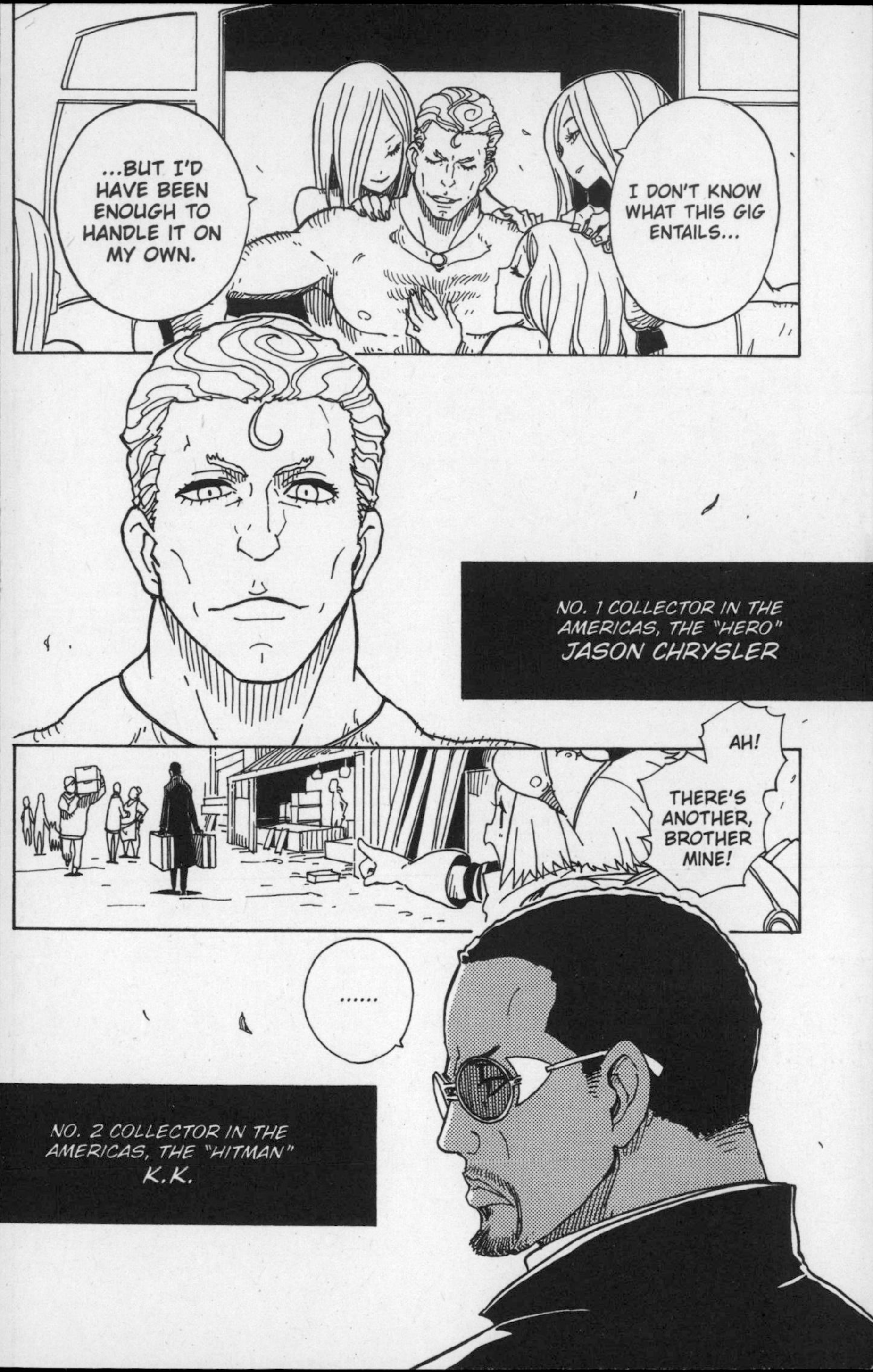
I DON'T KNOW WHAT THIS GIG ENTAILS...
...BUT I'D HAVE BEEN ENOUGH TO HANDLE IT ON MY OWN.
NO. 1 COLLECTOR IN THE AMERICAS, THE "HERO" JASON CHRYSLER
AH!
THERE'S ANOTHER, BROTHER MINE!
......
NO. 2 COLLECTOR IN THE AMERICAS, THE "HITMAN" K.K.

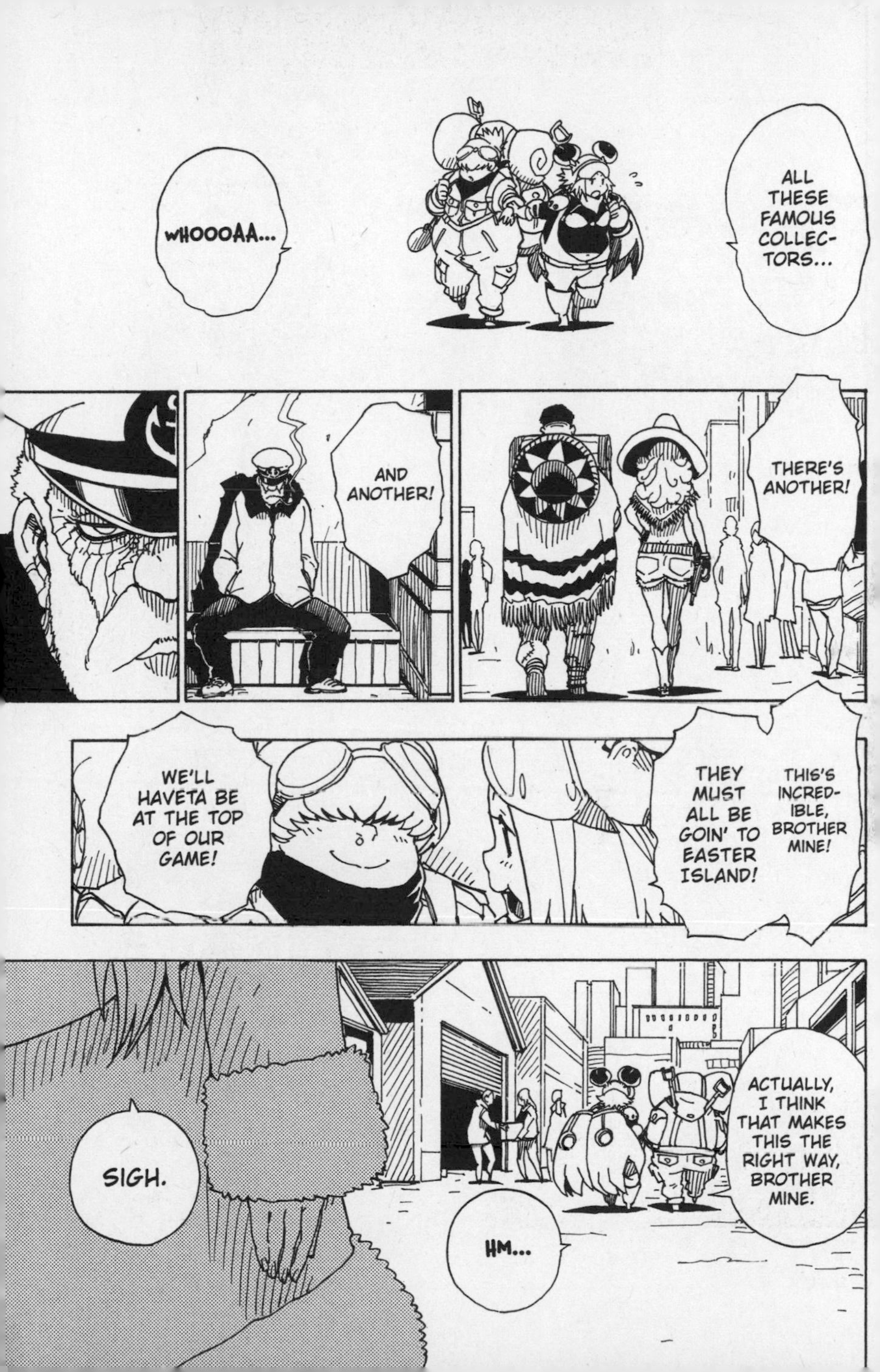
ALL THESE FAMOUS COLLECTORS...
WHOOOAA...
THERE'S ANOTHER!
AND ANOTHER!
THIS'S INCREDIBLE, BROTHER MINE!
THEY MUST ALL BE GOIN' TO EASTER ISLAND!
WE'LL HAVETA BE AT THE TOP OF OUR GAME!
ACTUALLY, I THINK THAT MAKES THIS THE RIGHT WAY, BROTHER MINE.
HM...
SIGH.

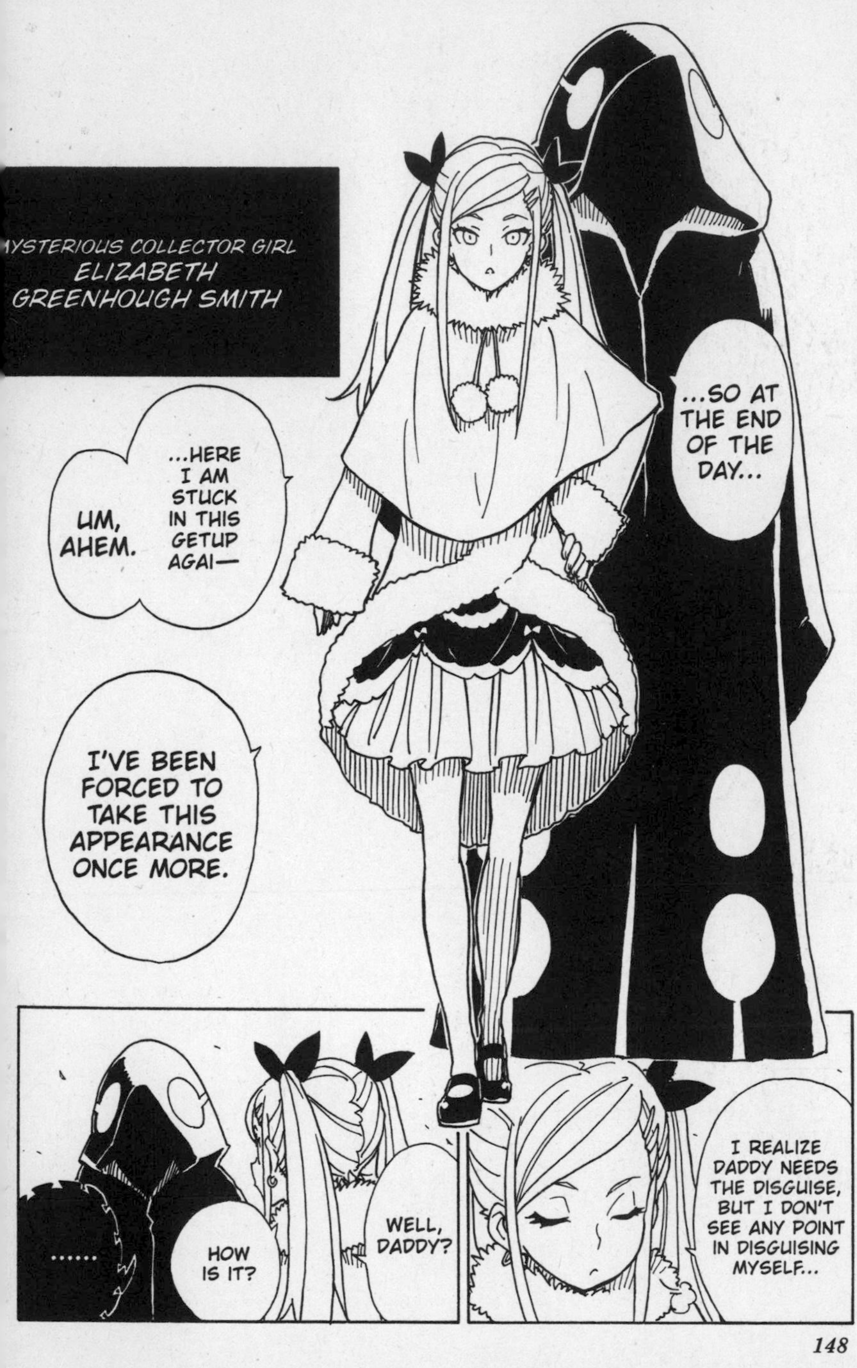
MYSTERIOUS COLLECTOR GIRL
ELIZABETH GREENHOUGH SMITH
...SO AT THE END OF THE DAY...
...HERE I AM STUCK IN THIS GETUP AGAI—
UM, AHEM.
I'VE BEEN FORCED TO TAKE THIS APPEARANCE ONCE MORE.
I REALIZE DADDY NEEDS THE DISGUISE, BUT I DON'T SEE ANY POINT IN DISGUISING MYSELF...
WELL, DADDY?
HOW IS IT?
......

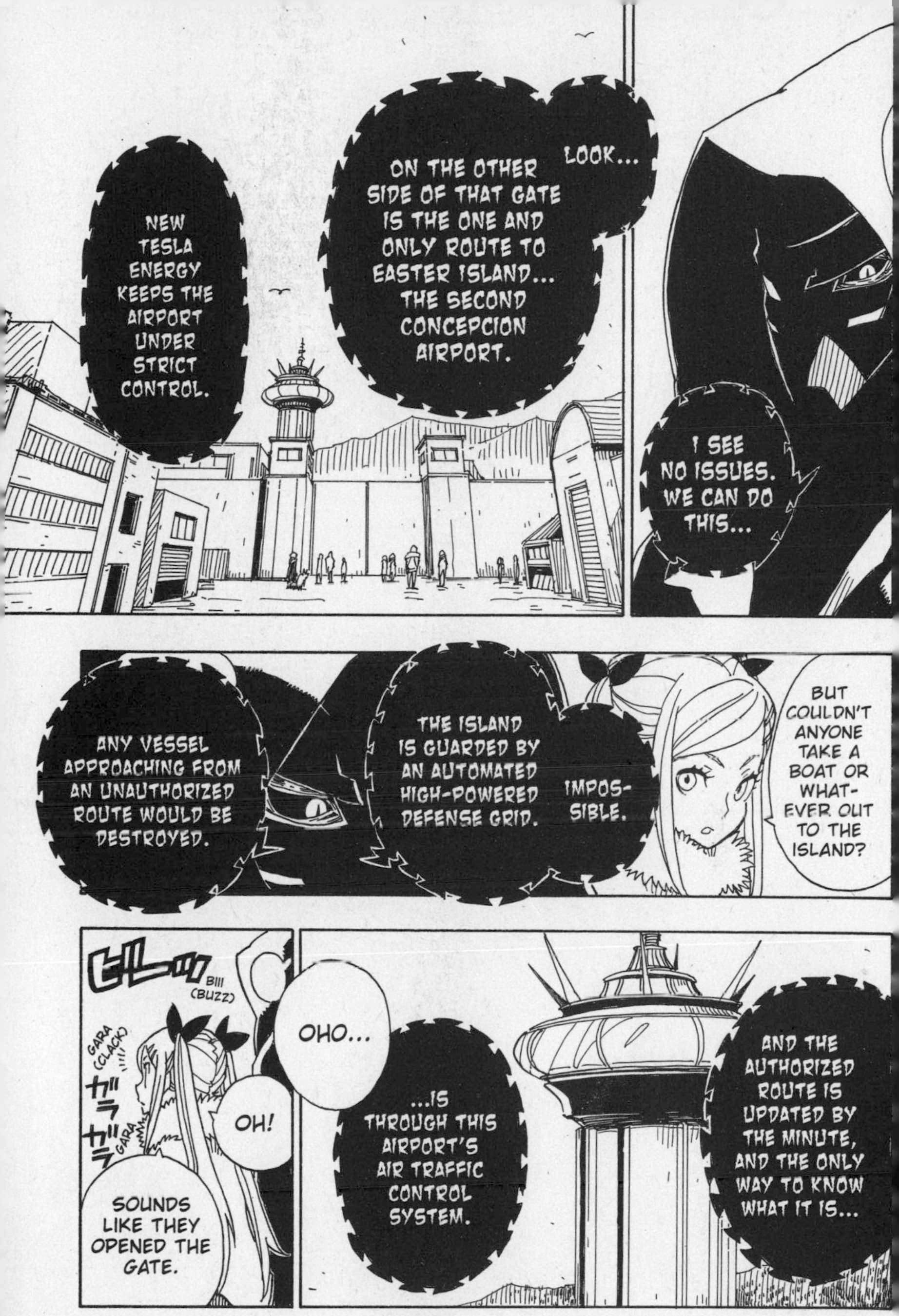
I SEE NO ISSUES. WE CAN DO THIS...
LOOK...
ON THE OTHER SIDE OF THAT GATE IS THE ONE AND ONLY ROUTE TO EASTER ISLAND... THE SECOND CONCEPCION AIRPORT.
NEW TESLA ENERGY KEEPS THE AIRPORT UNDER STRICT CONTROL.
BUT COULDN'T ANYONE TAKE A BOAT OR WHATEVER OUT TO THE ISLAND?
IMPOSSIBLE.
THE ISLAND IS GUARDED BY AN AUTOMATED HIGH-POWERED DEFENSE GRID.
ANY VESSEL APPROACHING FROM AN UNAUTHORIZED ROUTE WOULD BE DESTROYED.
AND THE AUTHORIZED ROUTE IS UPDATED BY THE MINUTE, AND THE ONLY WAY TO KNOW WHAT IT IS...
...IS THROUGH THIS AIRPORT'S AIR TRAFFIC CONTROL SYSTEM.
OHO...
BIII (BUZZ)
GARA (CLACK)
GARA
OH!
SOUNDS LIKE THEY OPENED THE GATE.

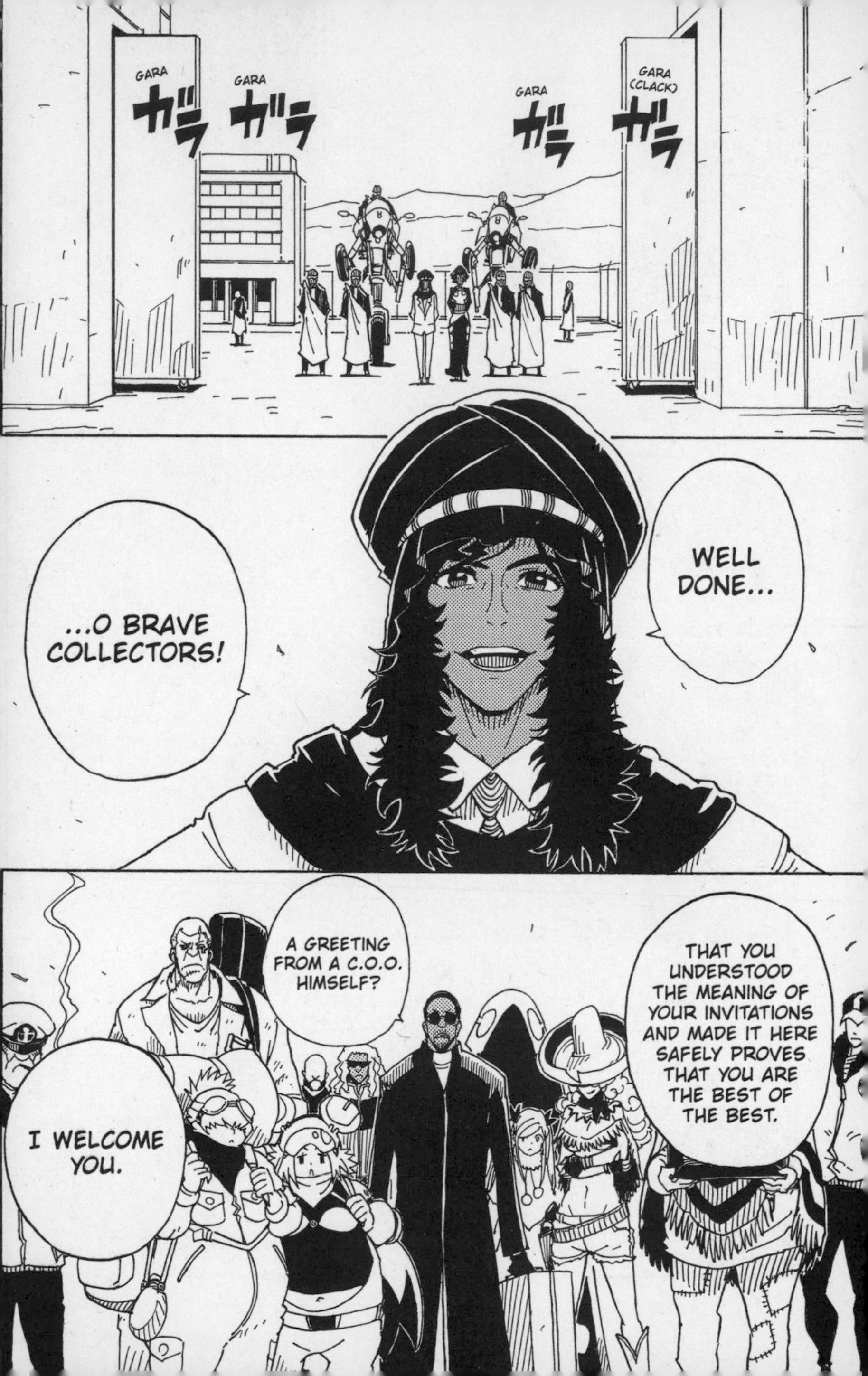
GARA (CLACK)
ガラ
GARA
ガラ
GARA
ガラ
GARA
ガラ
WELL DONE...
...O BRAVE COLLECTORS!
THAT YOU UNDERSTOOD THE MEANING OF YOUR INVITATIONS AND MADE IT HERE SAFELY PROVES THAT YOU ARE THE BEST OF THE BEST.
A GREETING FROM A C.O.O. HIMSELF?
I WELCOME YOU.

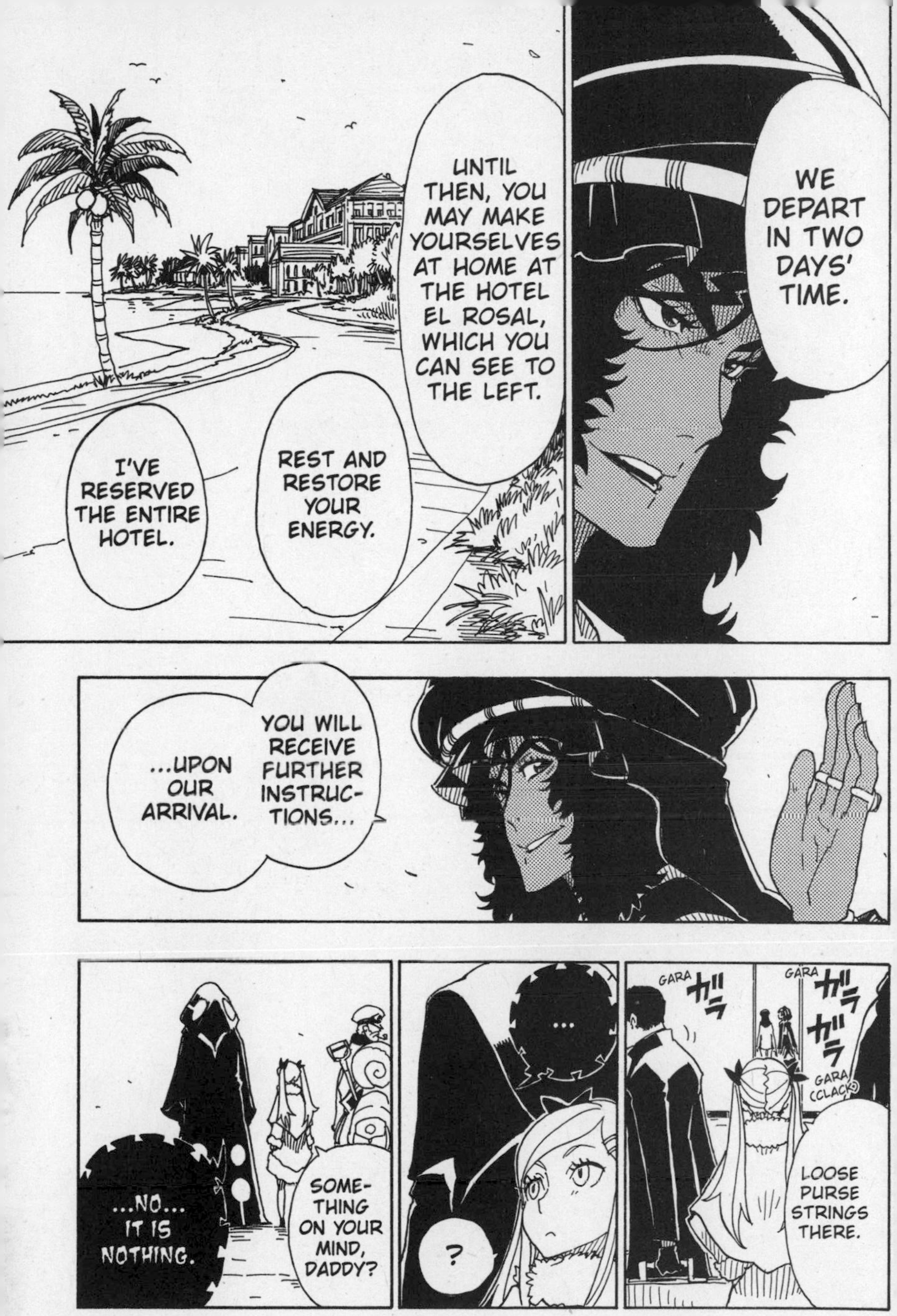
WE DEPART IN TWO DAYS' TIME.
UNTIL THEN, YOU MAY MAKE YOURSELVES AT HOME AT THE HOTEL EL ROSAL, WHICH YOU CAN SEE TO THE LEFT.
REST AND RESTORE YOUR ENERGY.
I'VE RESERVED THE ENTIRE HOTEL.
YOU WILL RECEIVE FURTHER INSTRUC- TIONS...
...UPON OUR ARRIVAL.
GARA
GARA
GARA (CLACK)
LOOSE PURSE STRINGS THERE.
...
?
SOME- THING ON YOUR MIND, DADDY?
...NO... IT IS NOTHING.

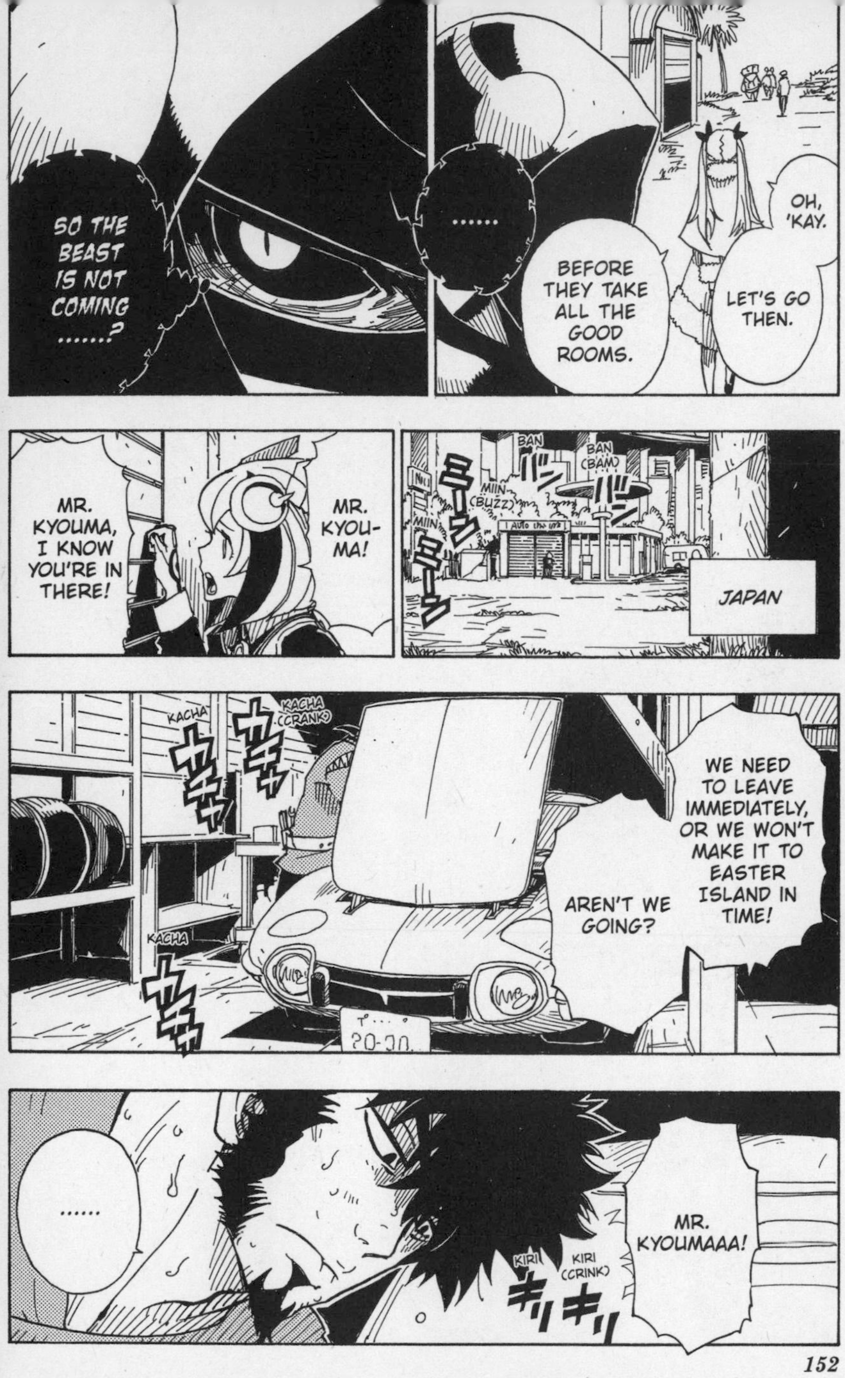

OH, 'KAY.
LET'S GO THEN.
BEFORE THEY TAKE ALL THE GOOD ROOMS.
......
SO THE BEAST IS NOT COMING......?
BAN
BAN (BAM)
MIIN (BUZZ)
MIIN
JAPAN
MR. KYOU-MA!
MR. KYOUMA, I KNOW YOU'RE IN THERE!
WE NEED TO LEAVE IMMEDIATELY, OR WE WON'T MAKE IT TO EASTER ISLAND IN TIME!
AREN'T WE GOING?
KACHA (CRANK)
KACHA
KACHA
MR. KYOUMAAA!
KIRI (CRINK)
KIRI
......

FILE.38
A PAST LIFE

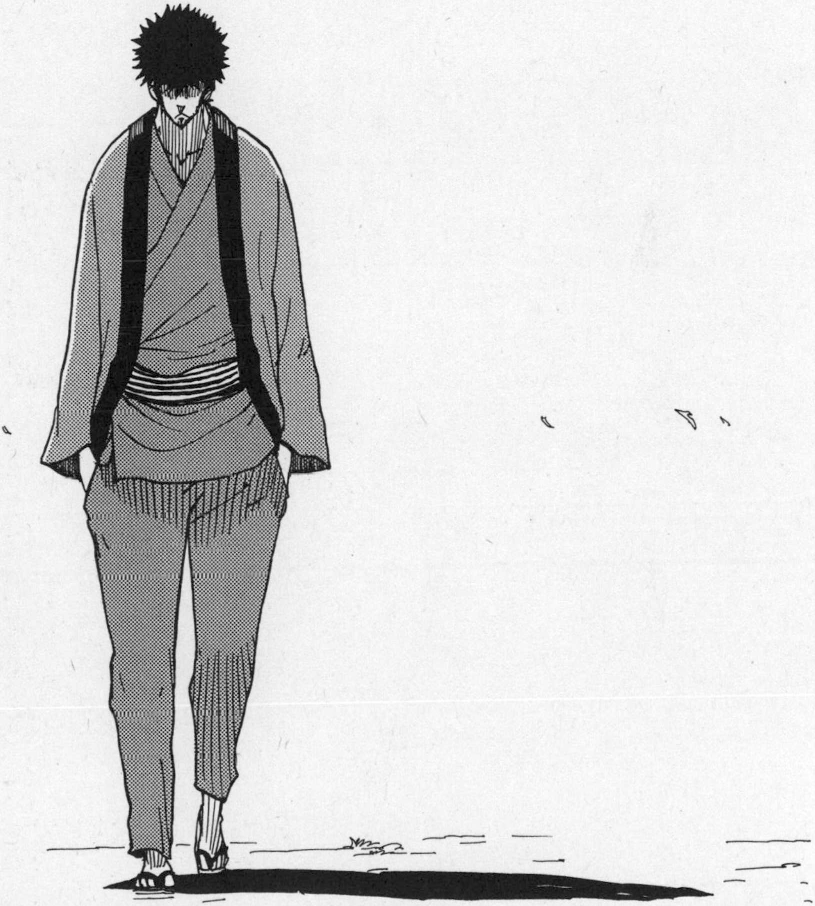

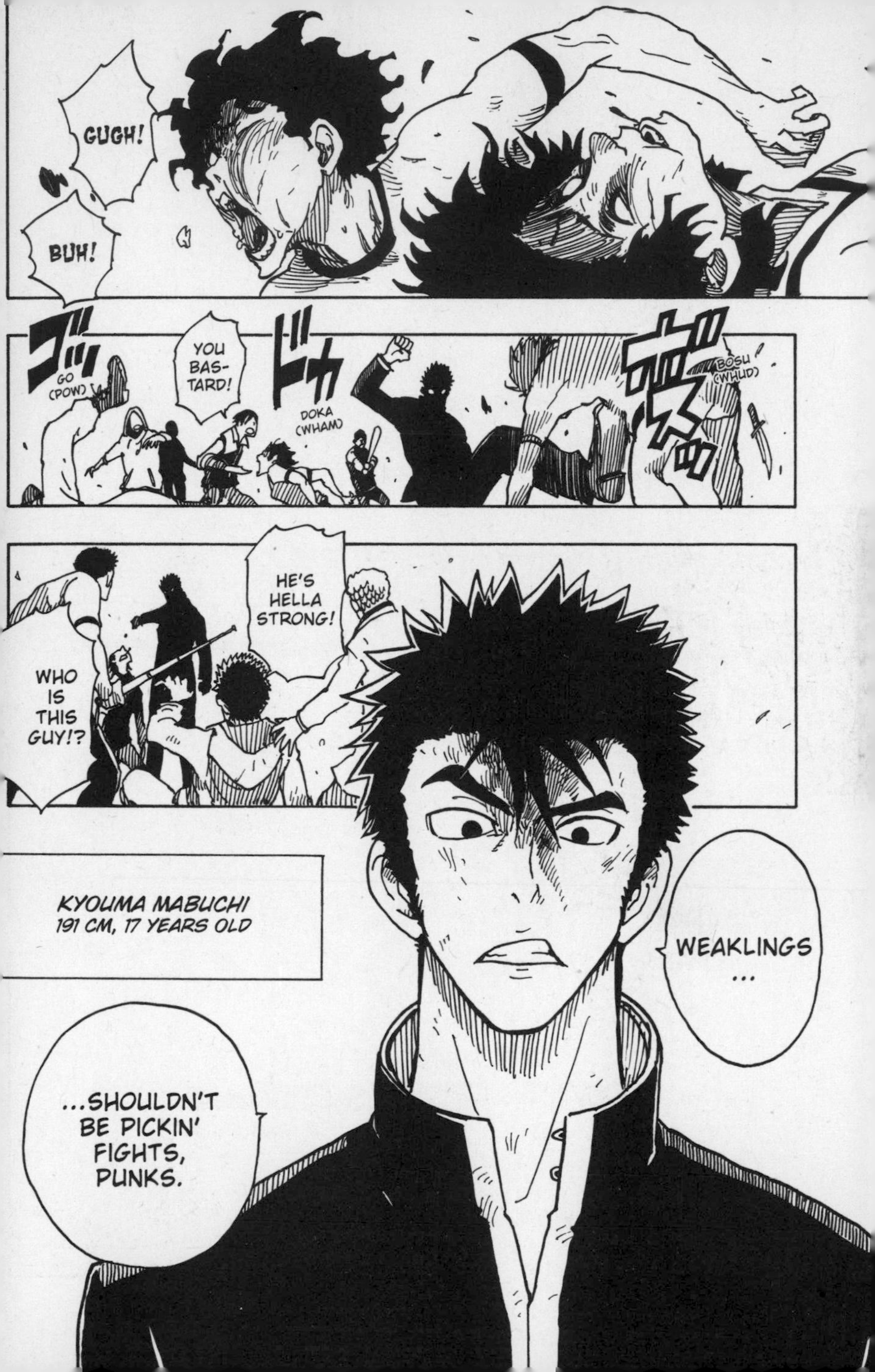
GUGH!
BUH!
BOSU (WHUD)
DOKA (WHAM)
YOU BASTARD!
GO (POW)
HE'S HELLA STRONG!
WHO IS THIS GUY!?
WEAKLINGS ...
KYOUMA MABUCHI
191 CM, 17 YEARS OLD
...SHOULDN'T BE PICKIN' FIGHTS, PUNKS.

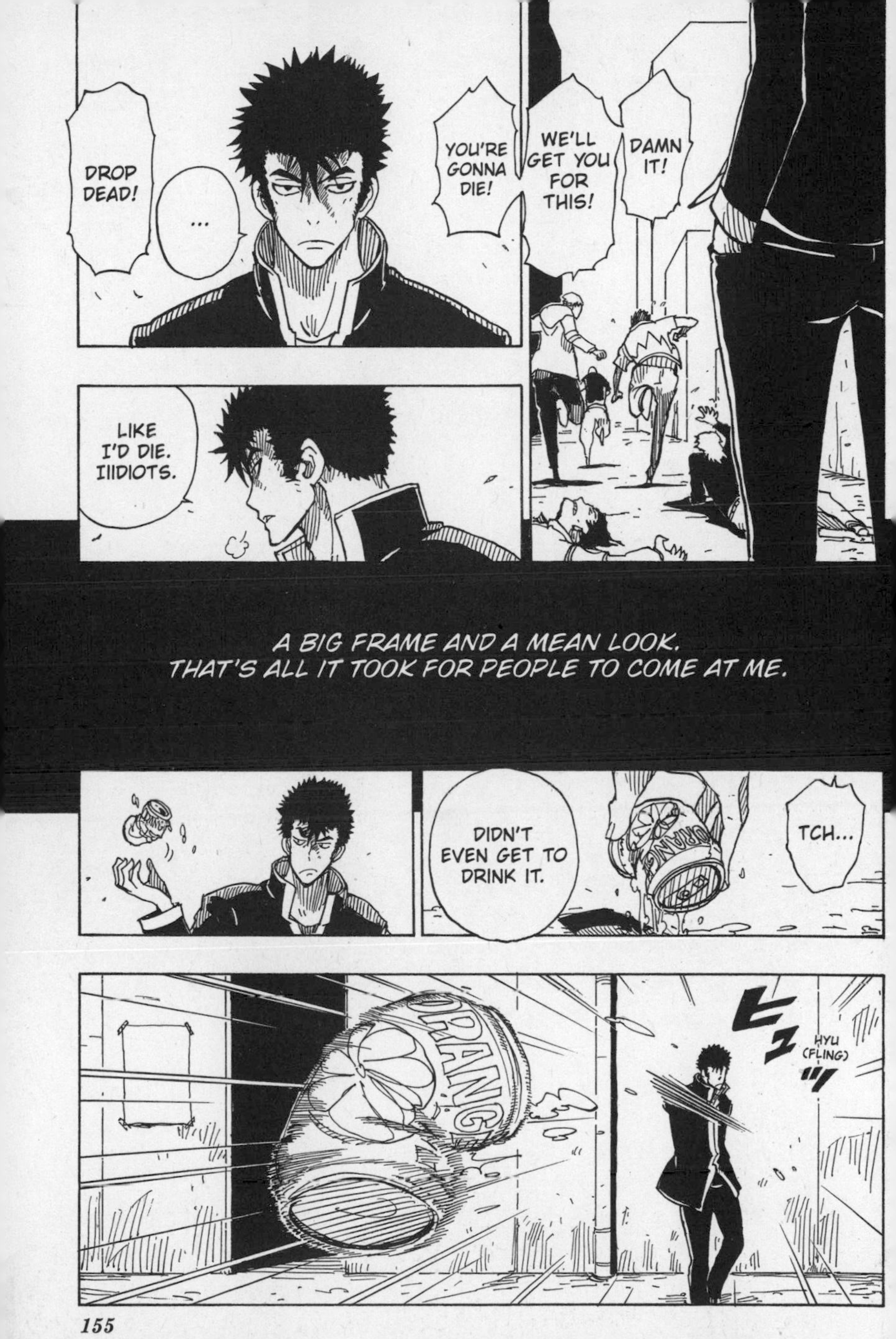
DAMN IT!
WE'LL GET YOU FOR THIS!
YOU'RE GONNA DIE!
DROP DEAD!
...
LIKE I'D DIE. IIIDIOTS.
A BIG FRAME AND A MEAN LOOK. THAT'S ALL IT TOOK FOR PEOPLE TO COME AT ME.
TCH...
DIDN'T EVEN GET TO DRINK IT.
HYU (FLING)

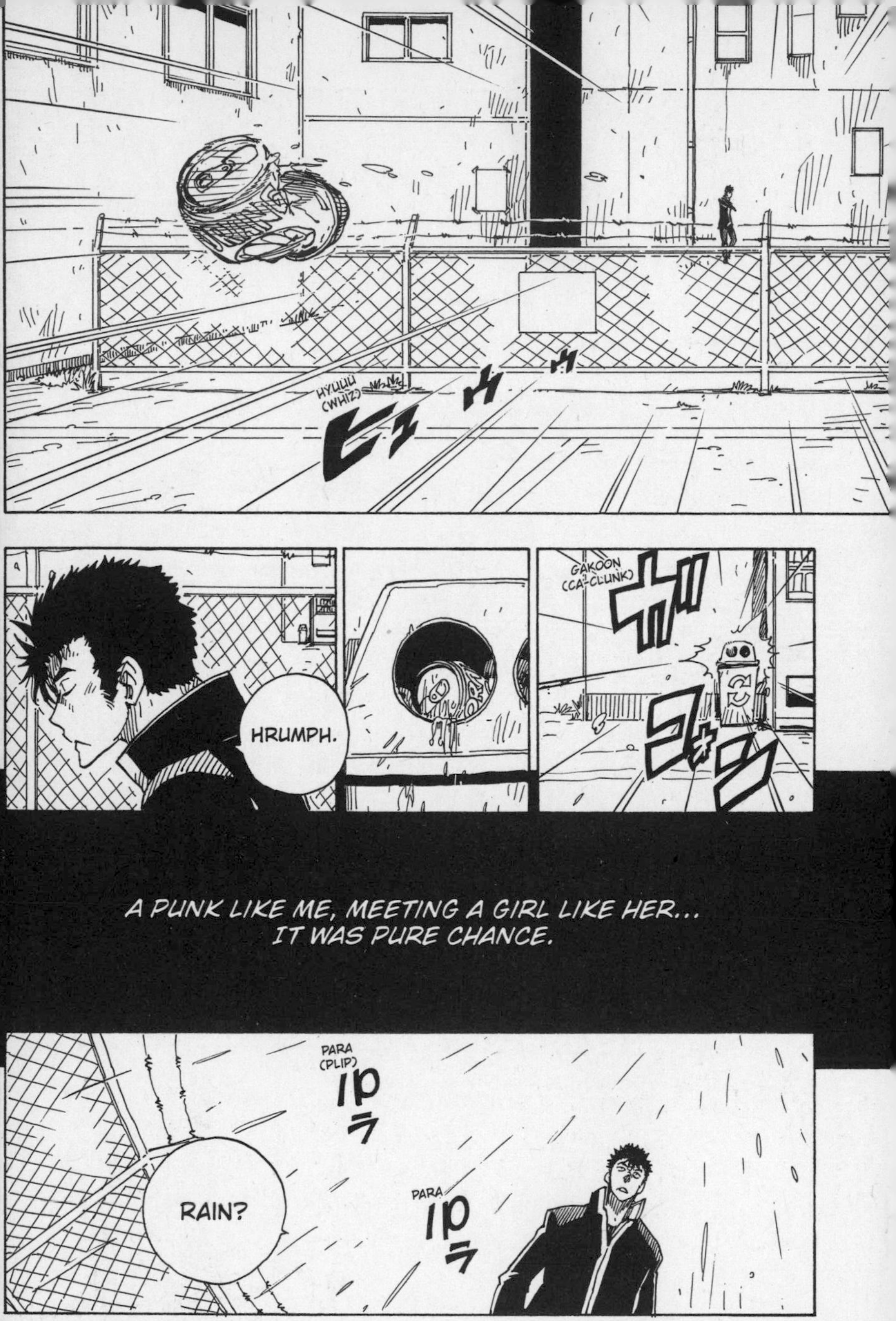
HYUUU (WHIZ)
GAKOON (CA-CLUNK)
HRUMPH.
A PUNK LIKE ME, MEETING A GIRL LIKE HER... IT WAS PURE CHANCE.
PARA (PLIP)
RAIN?
PARA

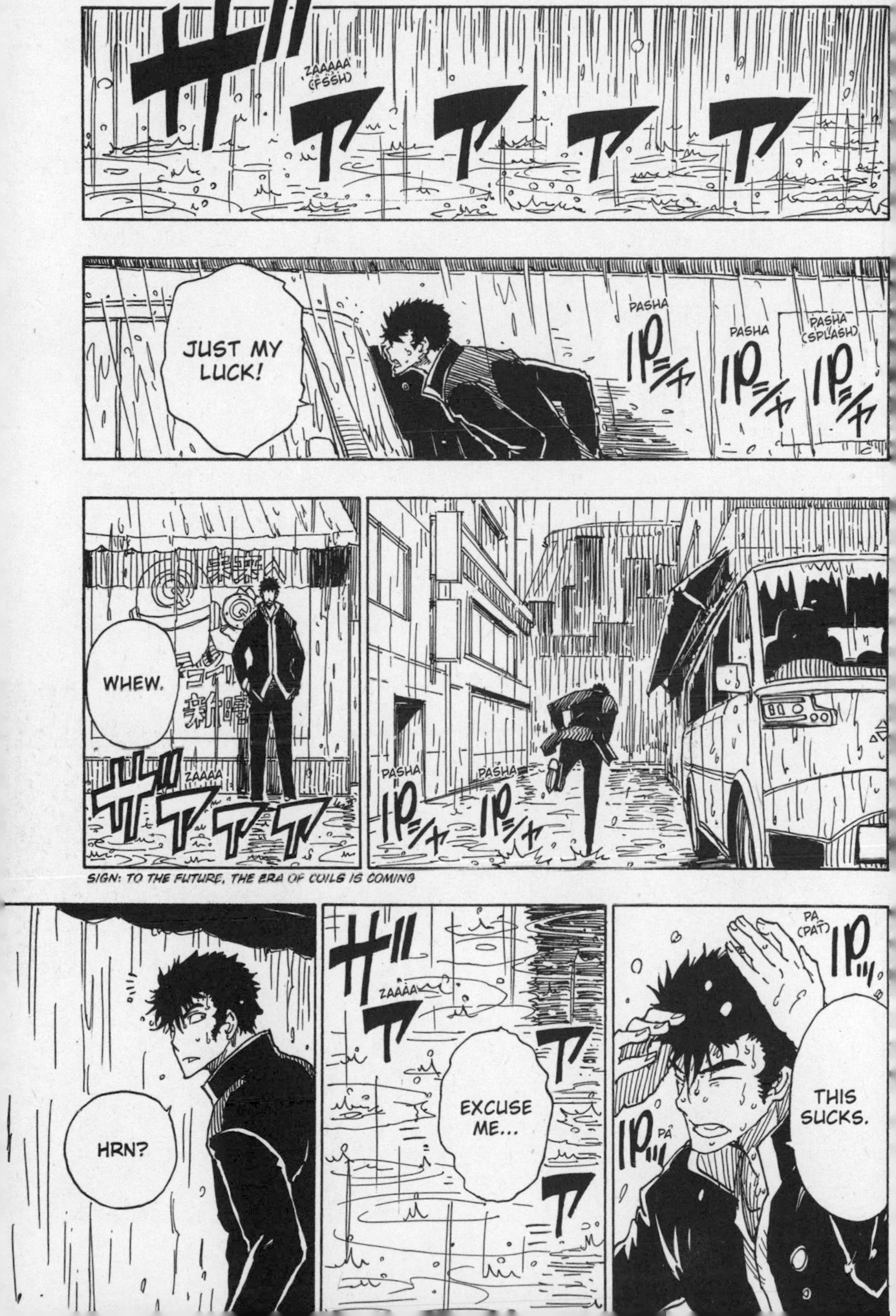
ZAAAAA (FSSH)
PASHA (SPLASH)
PASHA
PASHA
JUST MY LUCK!
PASHA
PASHA
ZAAAA
WHEW.
SIGN: TO THE FUTURE, THE ERA OF COILS IS COMING
PA (PAT)
THIS SUCKS.
PA
ZAAAA
EXCUSE ME...
HRN?

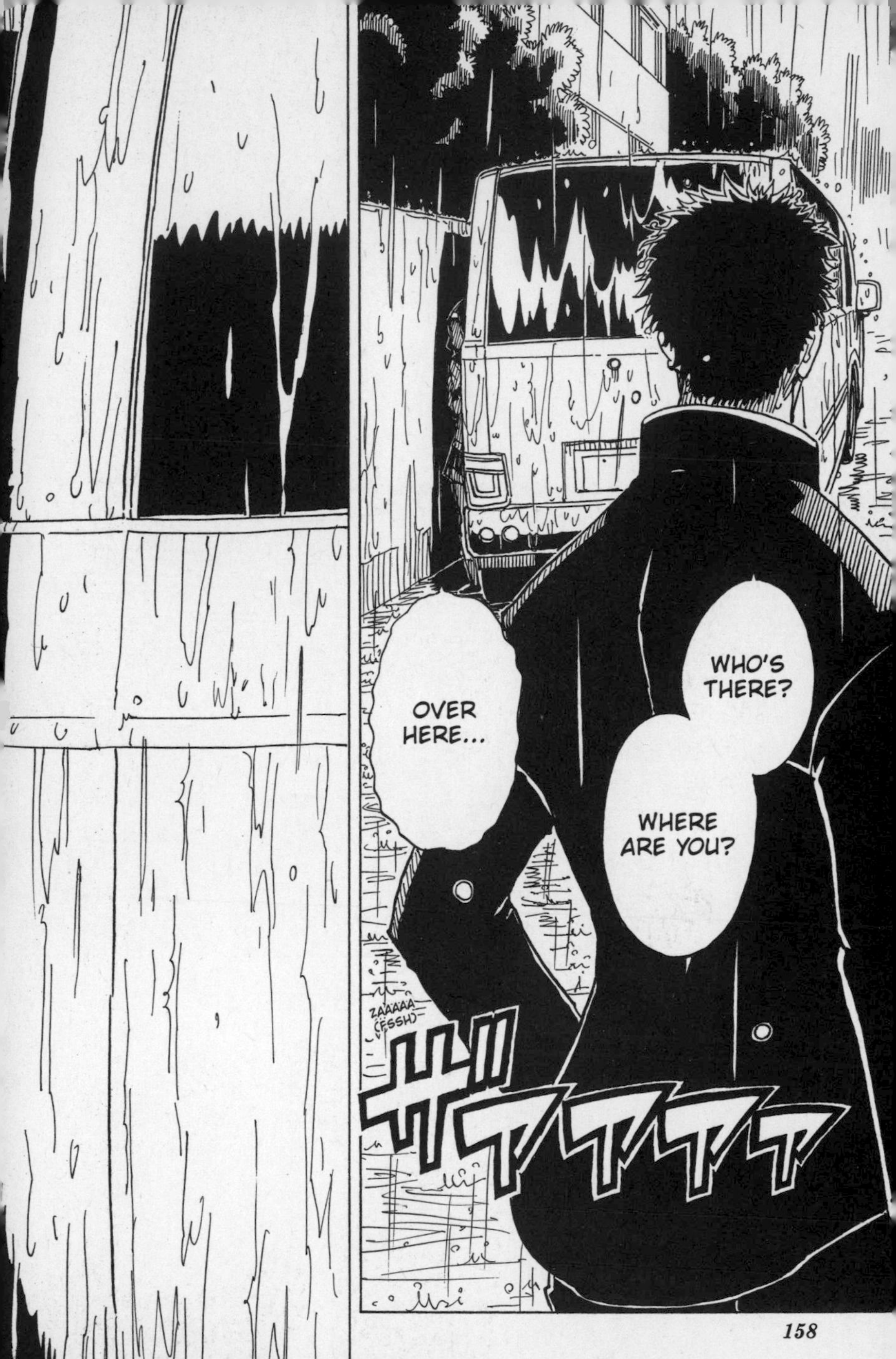
WHO'S THERE?
WHERE ARE YOU?
OVER HERE...
ZAAAAA (FSSH)

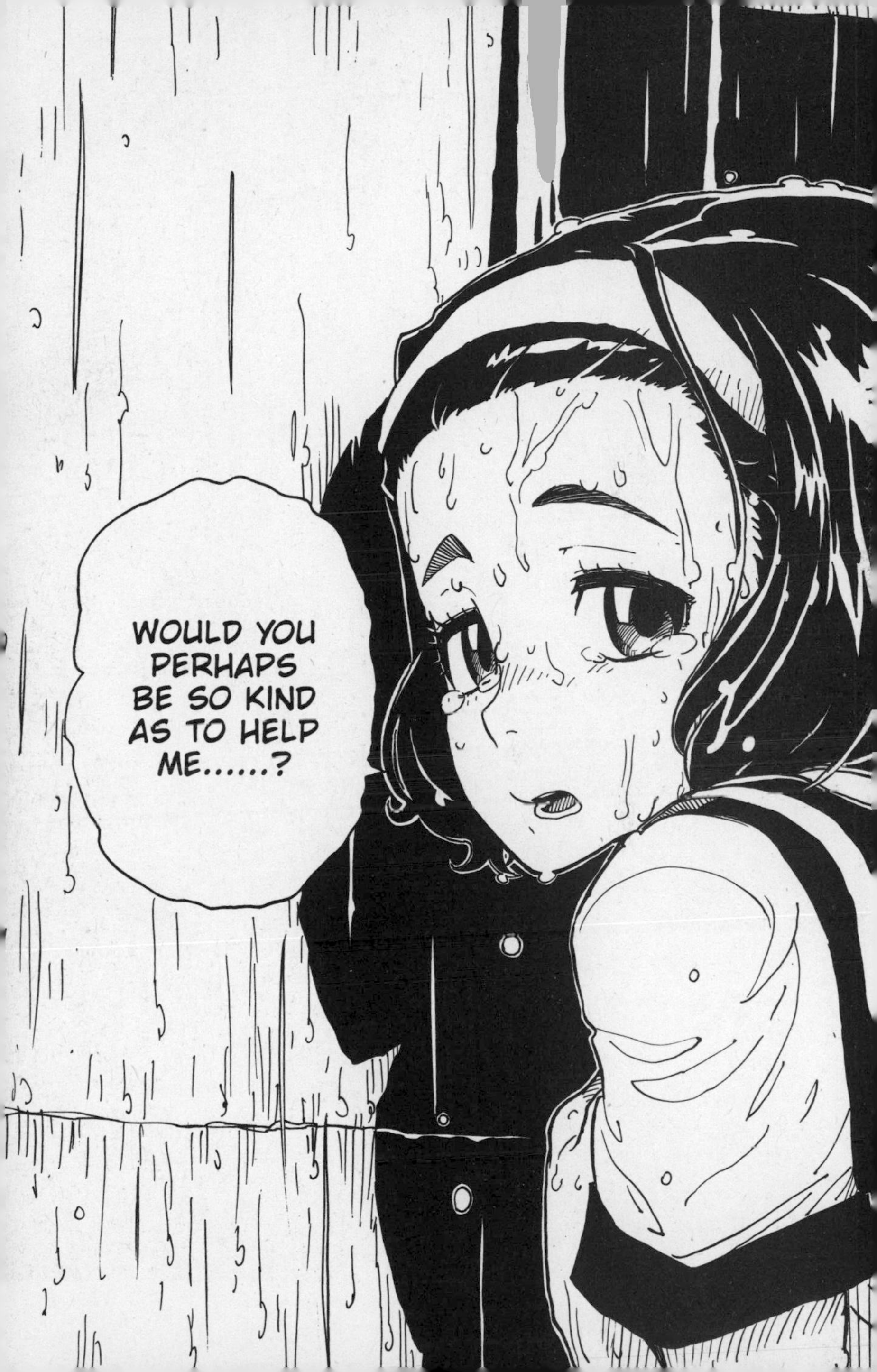
WOULD YOU PERHAPS BE SO KIND AS TO HELP ME......?

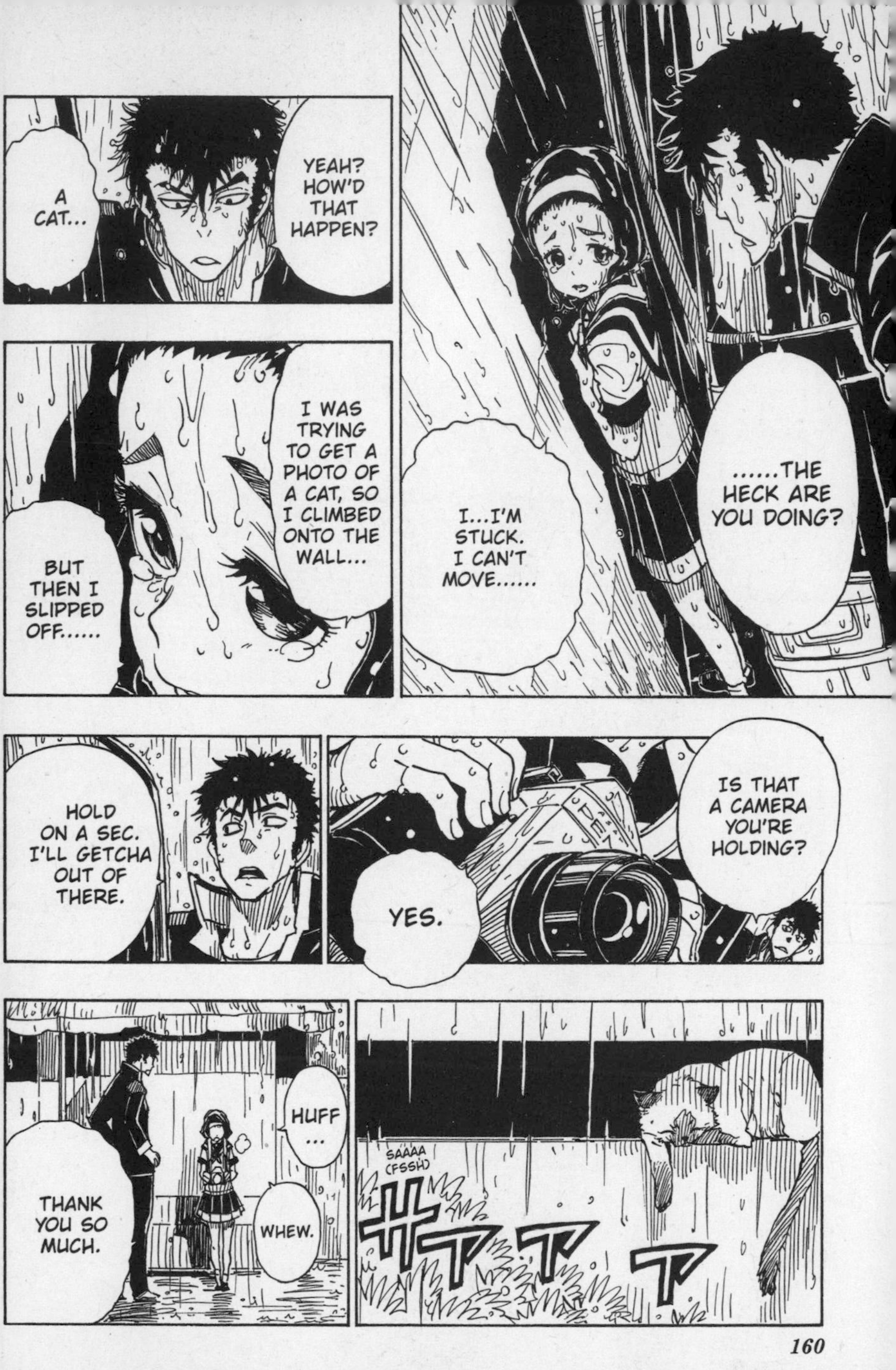
......THE HECK ARE YOU DOING?
I...I'M STUCK. I CAN'T MOVE......
YEAH? HOW'D THAT HAPPEN?
A CAT...
I WAS TRYING TO GET A PHOTO OF A CAT, SO I CLIMBED ONTO THE WALL...
BUT THEN I SLIPPED OFF......
IS THAT A CAMERA YOU'RE HOLDING?
YES.
HOLD ON A SEC. I'LL GETCHA OUT OF THERE.
SAAAA (FSSH)
HUFF...
WHEW.
THANK YOU SO MUCH.

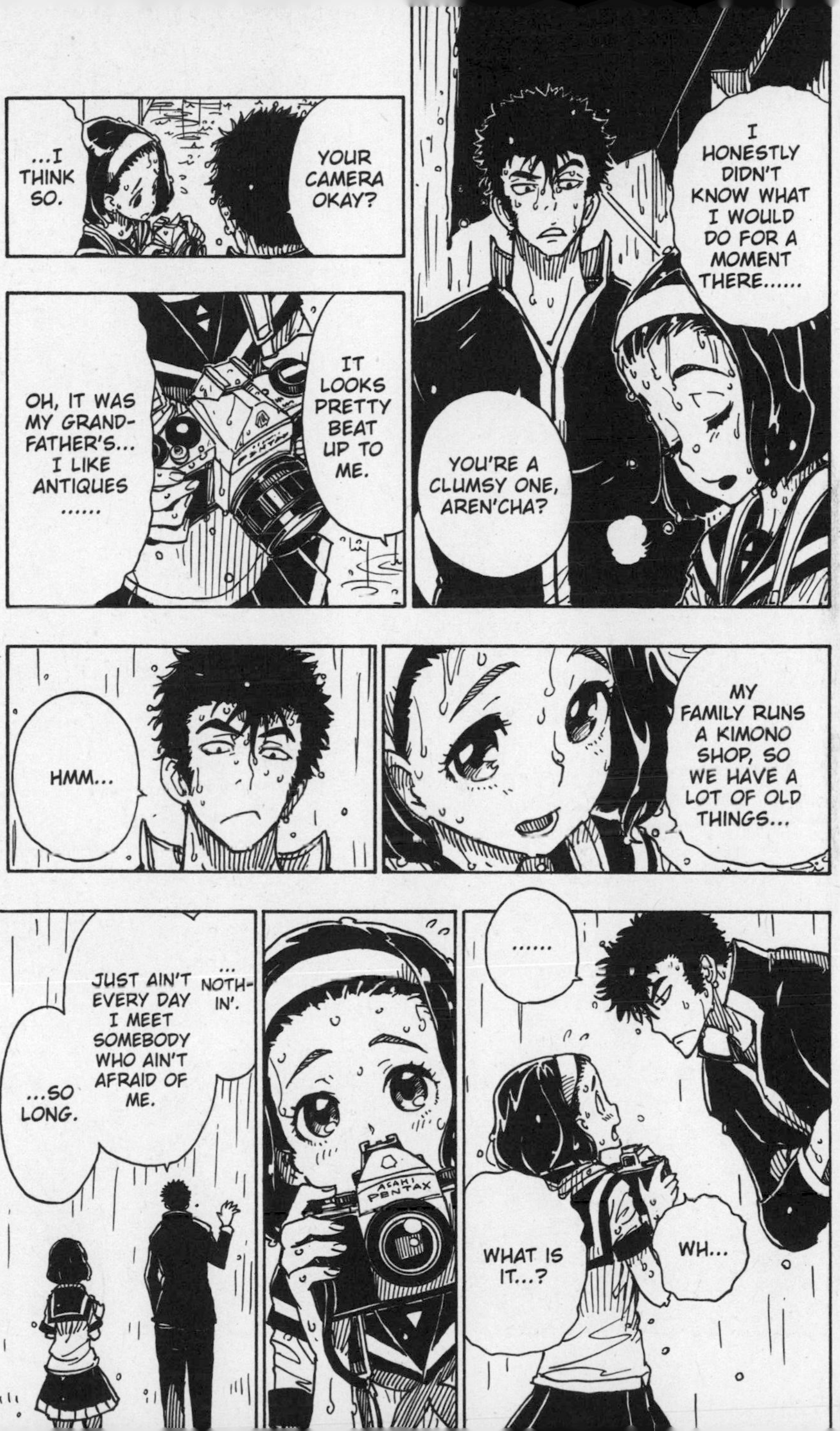
I HONESTLY DIDN'T KNOW WHAT I WOULD DO FOR A MOMENT THERE......
YOU'RE A CLUMSY ONE, AREN'CHA?
YOUR CAMERA OKAY?
...I THINK SO.
IT LOOKS PRETTY BEAT UP TO ME.
OH, IT WAS MY GRAND-FATHER'S... I LIKE ANTIQUES ......
MY FAMILY RUNS A KIMONO SHOP, SO WE HAVE A LOT OF OLD THINGS...
HMM...
......
WH...
WHAT IS IT...?
ASAHI PENTAX
...NOTHIN'.
JUST AIN'T EVERY DAY I MEET SOMEBODY WHO AIN'T AFRAID OF ME.
...SO LONG.

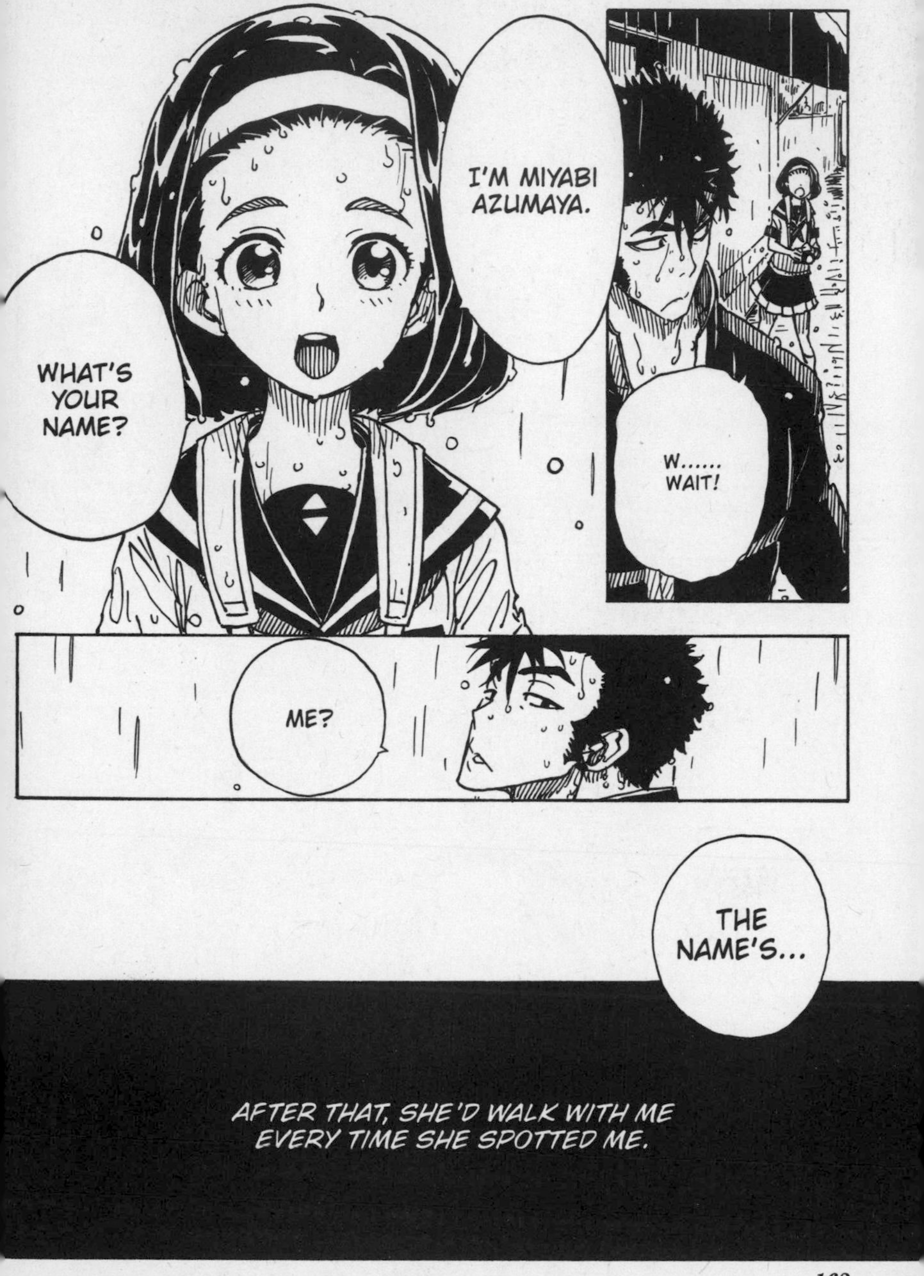
W...... WAIT!
I'M MIYABI AZUMAYA.
WHAT'S YOUR NAME?
ME?
THE NAME'S...
AFTER THAT, SHE'D WALK WITH ME EVERY TIME SHE SPOTTED ME.

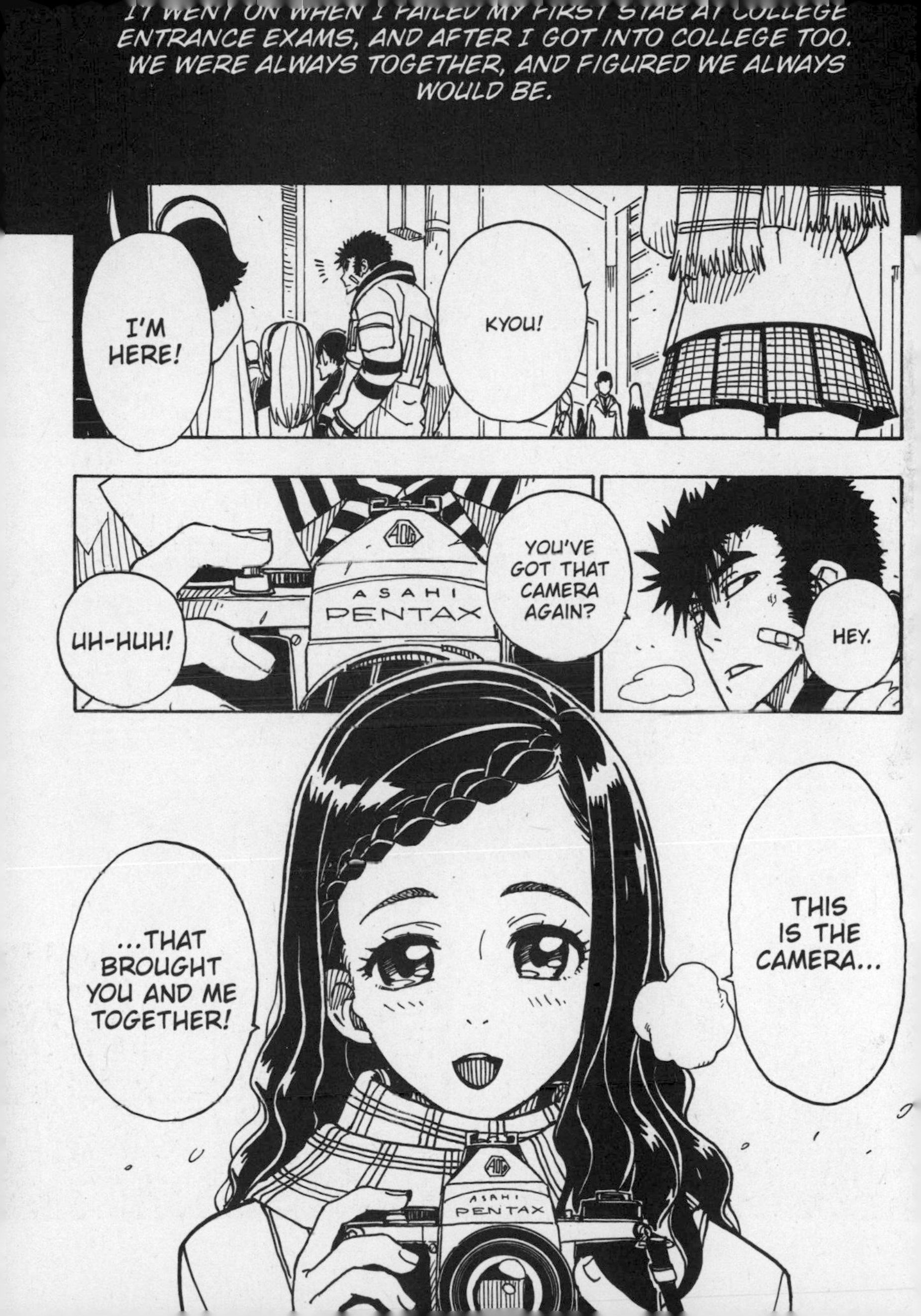
IT WENT ON WHEN I FAILED MY FIRST STAB AT COLLEGE ENTRANCE EXAMS, AND AFTER I GOT INTO COLLEGE TOO. WE WERE ALWAYS TOGETHER, AND FIGURED WE ALWAYS WOULD BE.
KYOU!
I'M HERE!
HEY.
YOU'VE GOT THAT CAMERA AGAIN?
ASAHI PENTAX
UH-HUH!
THIS IS THE CAMERA...
...THAT BROUGHT YOU AND ME TOGETHER!
ASAHI PENTAX

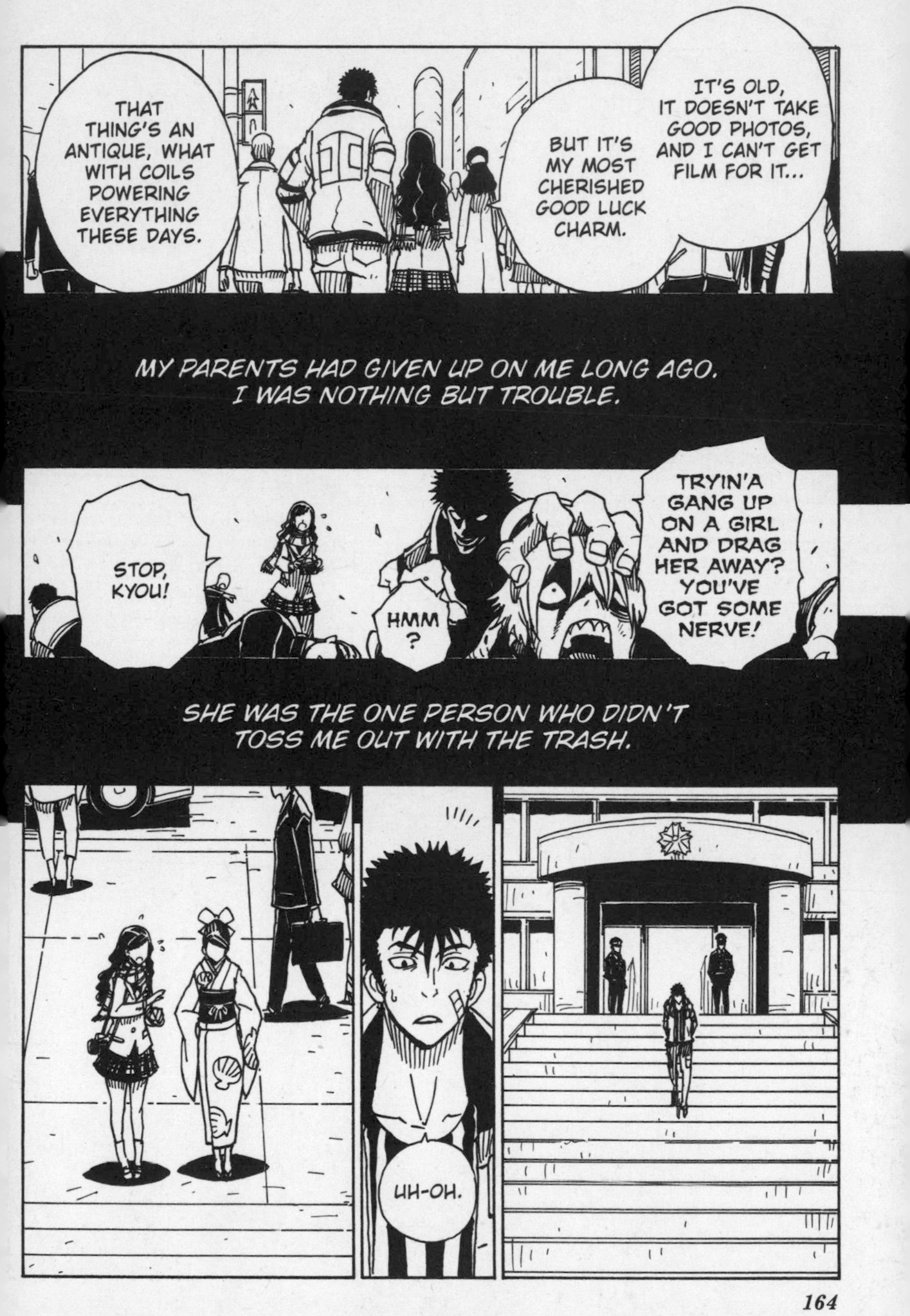
IT'S OLD, IT DOESN'T TAKE GOOD PHOTOS, AND I CAN'T GET FILM FOR IT...
BUT IT'S MY MOST CHERISHED GOOD LUCK CHARM.
THAT THING'S AN ANTIQUE, WHAT WITH COILS POWERING EVERYTHING THESE DAYS.
MY PARENTS HAD GIVEN UP ON ME LONG AGO. I WAS NOTHING BUT TROUBLE.
TRYIN'A GANG UP ON A GIRL AND DRAG HER AWAY? YOU'VE GOT SOME NERVE!
HMM?
STOP, KYOU!
SHE WAS THE ONE PERSON WHO DIDN'T TOSS ME OUT WITH THE TRASH.
UH-OH.

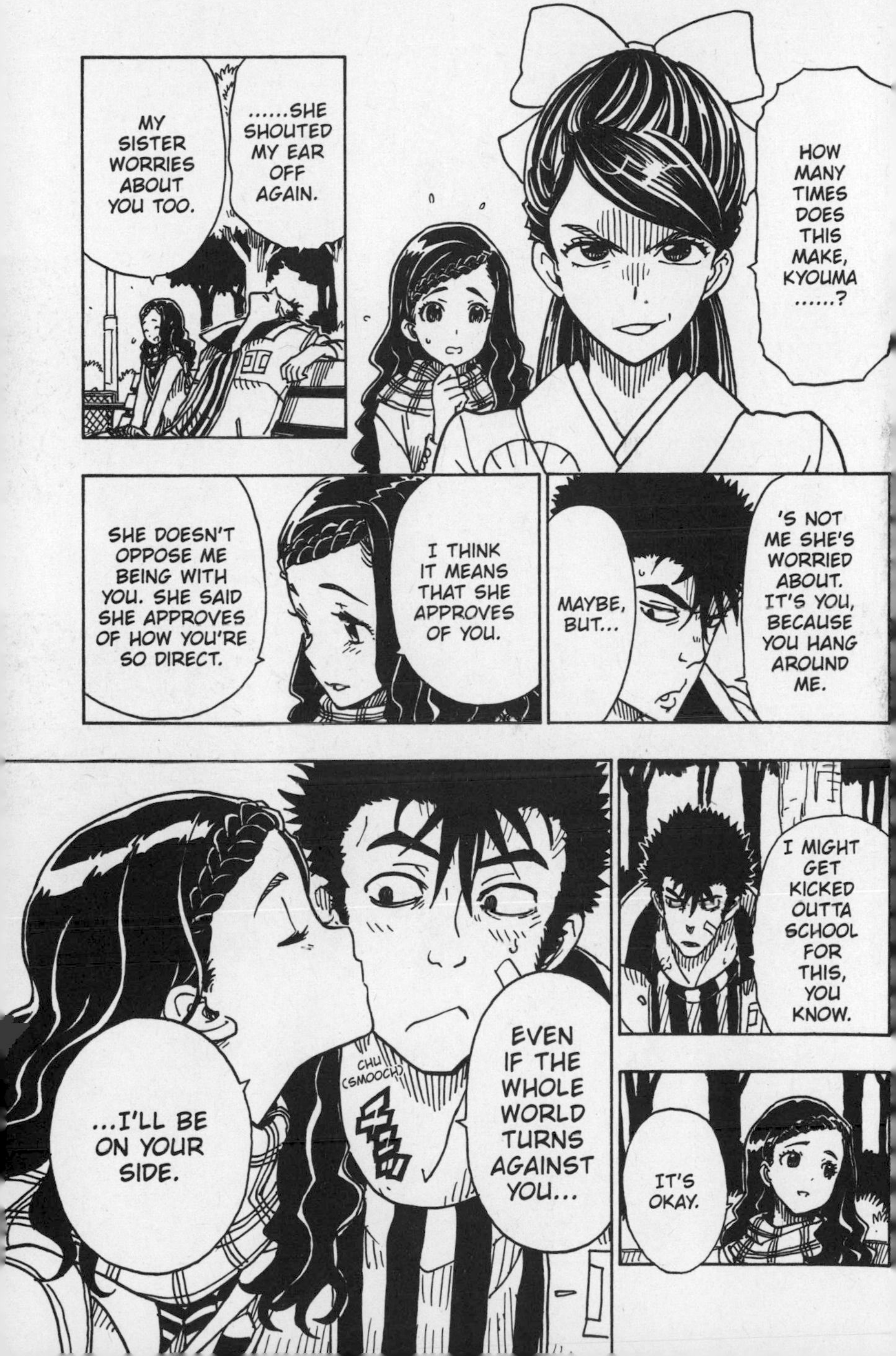
HOW MANY TIMES DOES THIS MAKE, KYOUMA ......?
......SHE SHOUTED MY EAR OFF AGAIN.
MY SISTER WORRIES ABOUT YOU TOO.
'S NOT ME SHE'S WORRIED ABOUT. IT'S YOU, BECAUSE YOU HANG AROUND ME.
MAYBE, BUT...
I THINK IT MEANS THAT SHE APPROVES OF YOU.
SHE DOESN'T OPPOSE ME BEING WITH YOU. SHE SAID SHE APPROVES OF HOW YOU'RE SO DIRECT.
I MIGHT GET KICKED OUTTA SCHOOL FOR THIS, YOU KNOW.
IT'S OKAY.
EVEN IF THE WHOLE WORLD TURNS AGAINST YOU...
CHU (SMOOCH)
...I'LL BE ON YOUR SIDE.

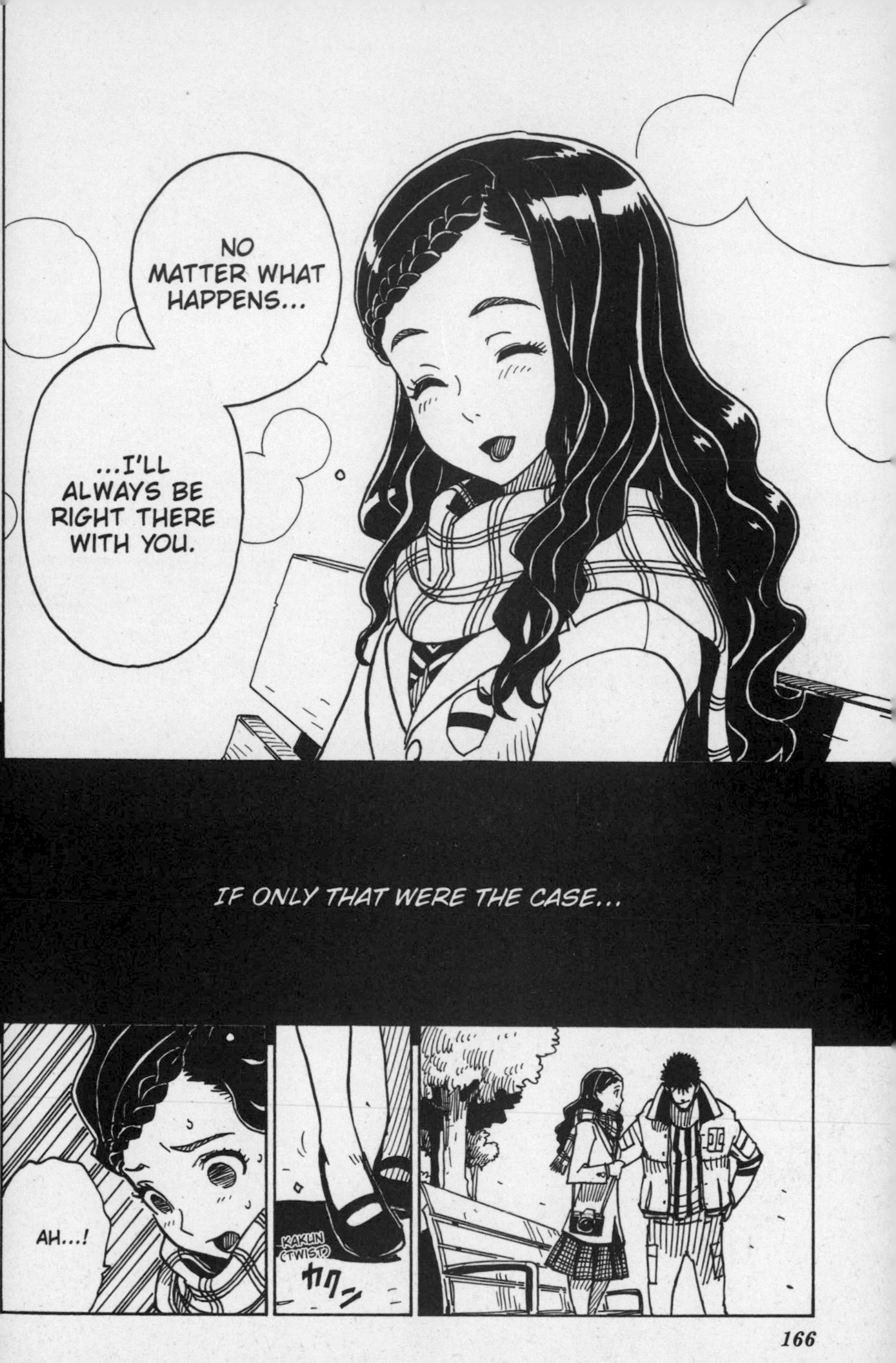
NO MATTER WHAT HAPPENS...
...I'LL ALWAYS BE RIGHT THERE WITH YOU.
IF ONLY THAT WERE THE CASE...
KAKUN (TWIST)
カクン
AH...!

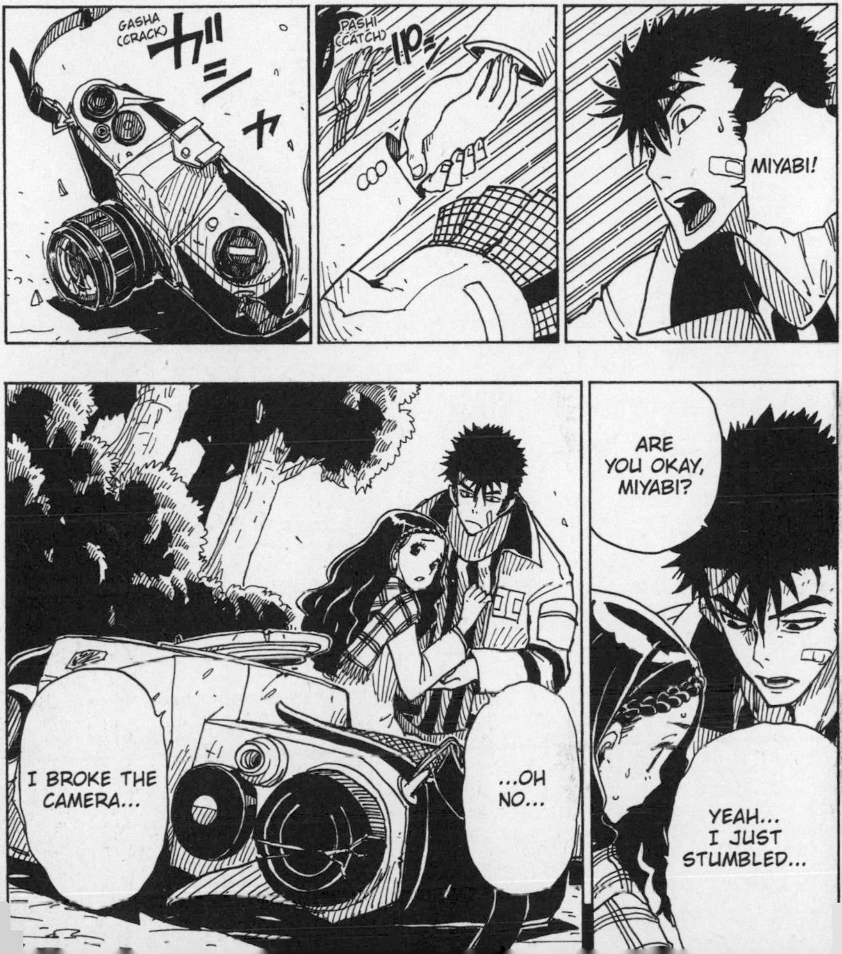
MIYABI!
PASHI (CATCH)
GASHA (CRACK)
ガシャ
ARE YOU OKAY, MIYABI?
YEAH... I JUST STUMBLED...
...OH NO...
I BROKE THE CAMERA...

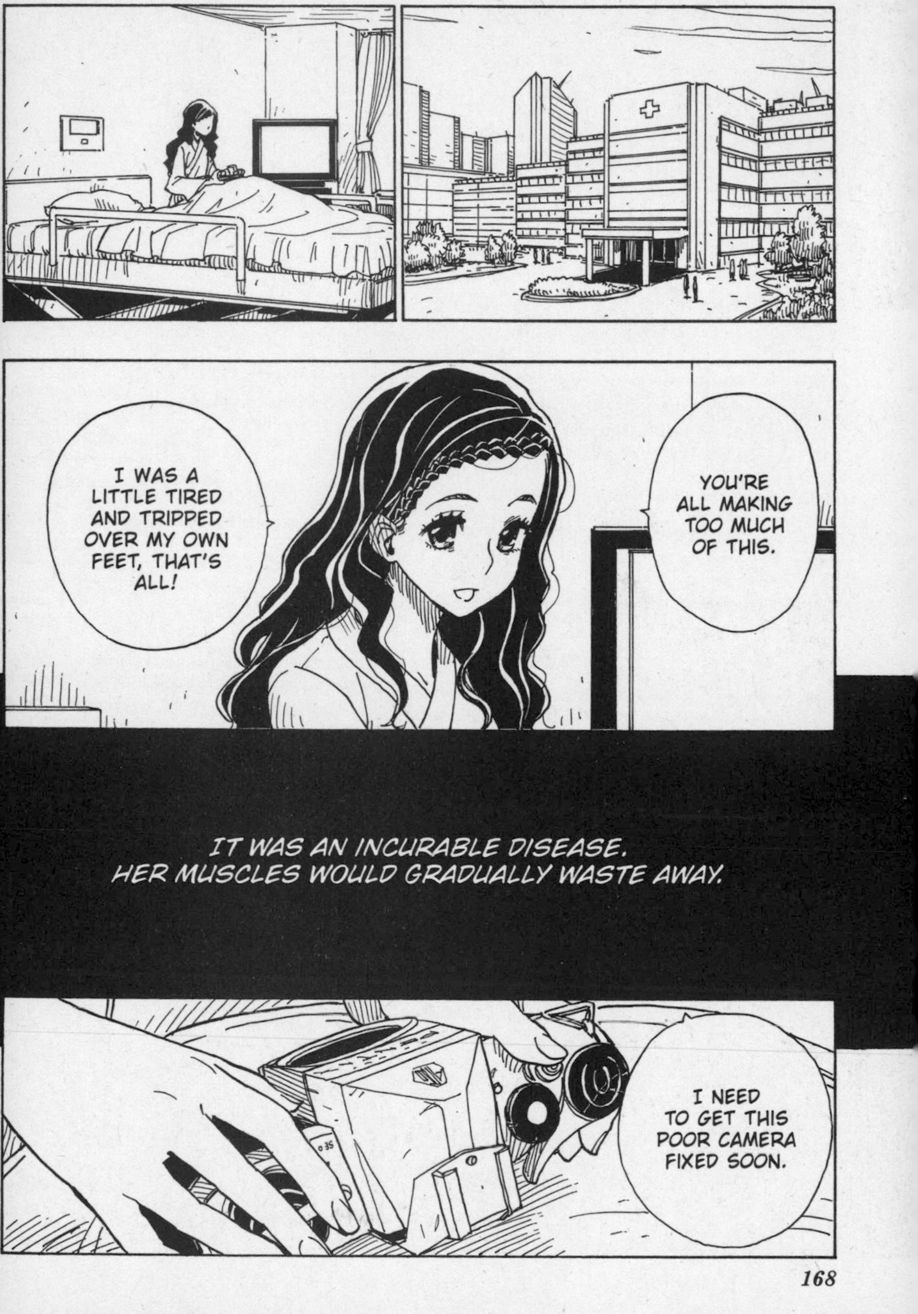
YOU'RE ALL MAKING TOO MUCH OF THIS.
I WAS A LITTLE TIRED AND TRIPPED OVER MY OWN FEET, THAT'S ALL!
IT WAS AN INCURABLE DISEASE. HER MUSCLES WOULD GRADUALLY WASTE AWAY.
I NEED TO GET THIS POOR CAMERA FIXED SOON.

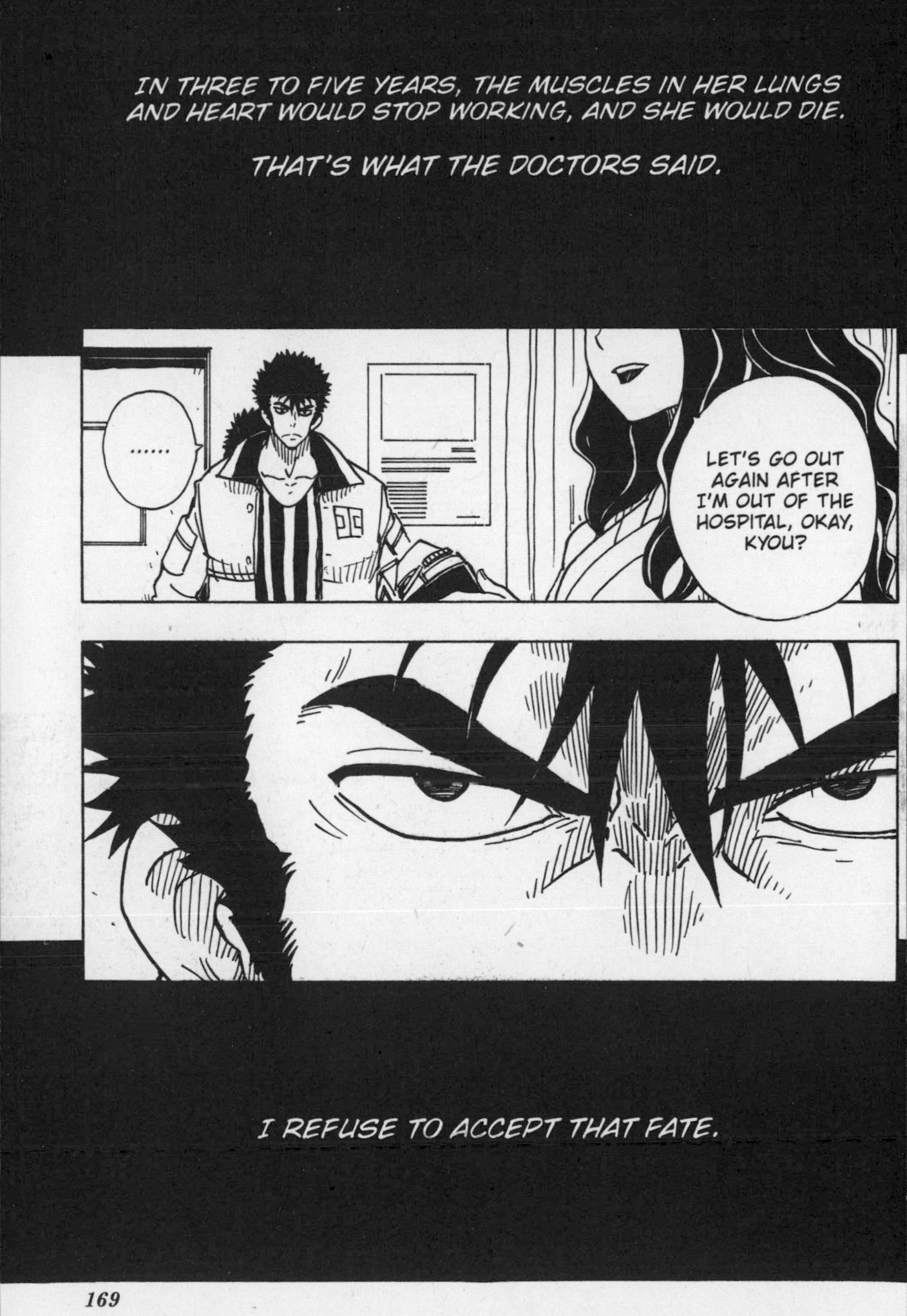
IN THREE TO FIVE YEARS, THE MUSCLES IN HER LUNGS AND HEART WOULD STOP WORKING, AND SHE WOULD DIE.
THAT'S WHAT THE DOCTORS SAID.
LET'S GO OUT AGAIN AFTER I'M OUT OF THE HOSPITAL, OKAY, KYOU?
......
I REFUSE TO ACCEPT THAT FATE.

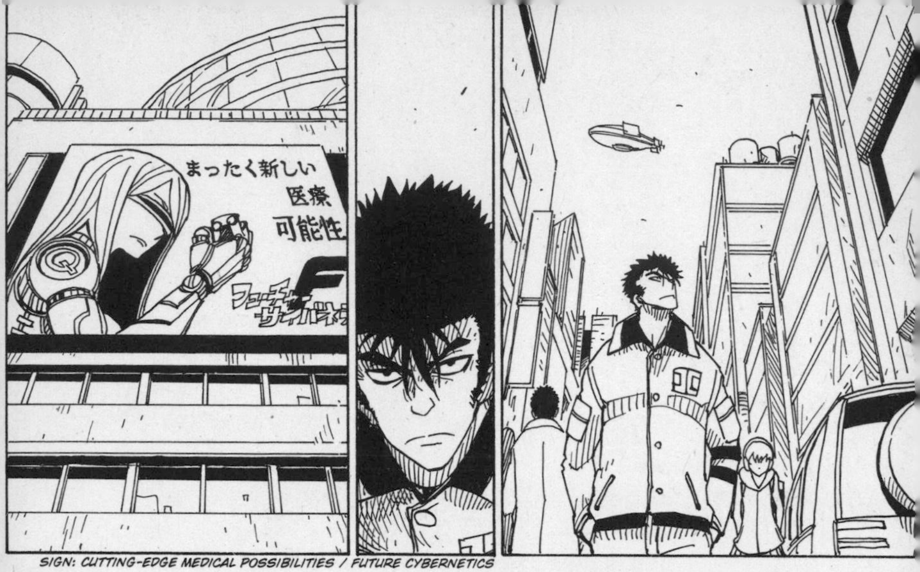
まったく新しい
医療
可能性
SIGN: CUTTING-EDGE MEDICAL POSSIBILITIES / FUTURE CYBERNETICS

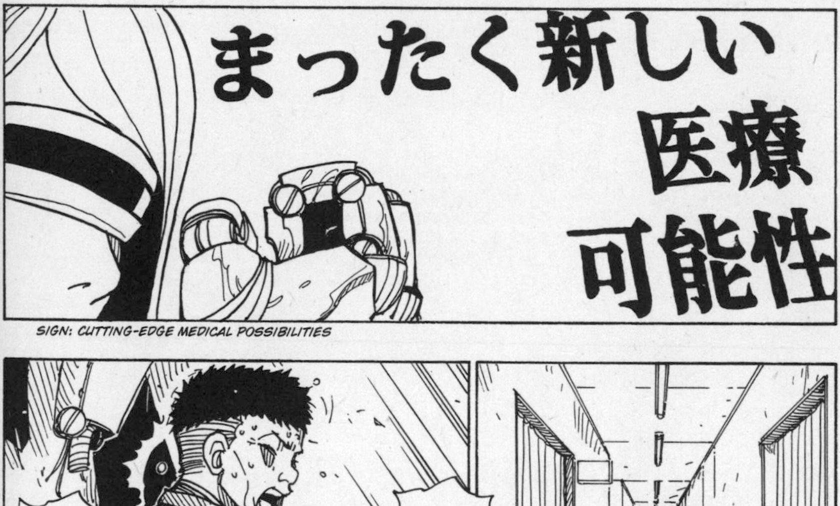
まったく新しい
医療
可能性
SIGN: CUTTING-EDGE MEDICAL POSSIBILITIES

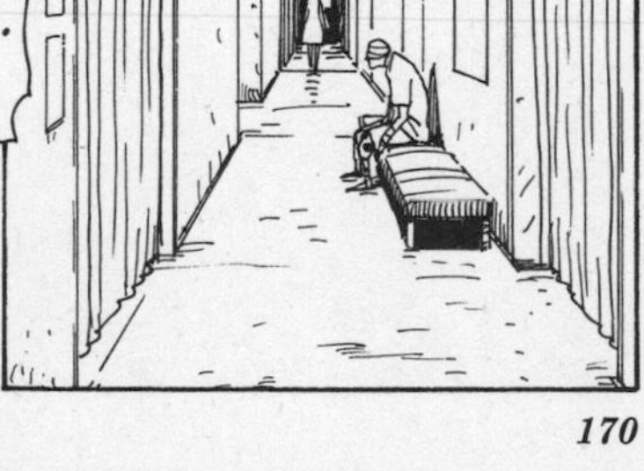

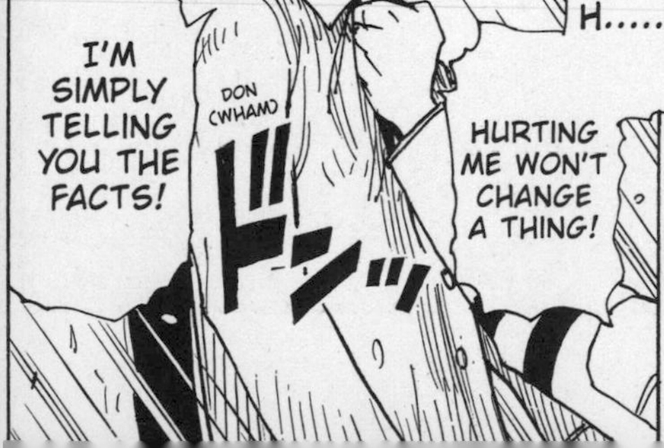
H......
HURTING ME WON'T CHANGE A THING!
DON (WHAM)
ドンッ
I'M SIMPLY TELLING YOU THE FACTS!

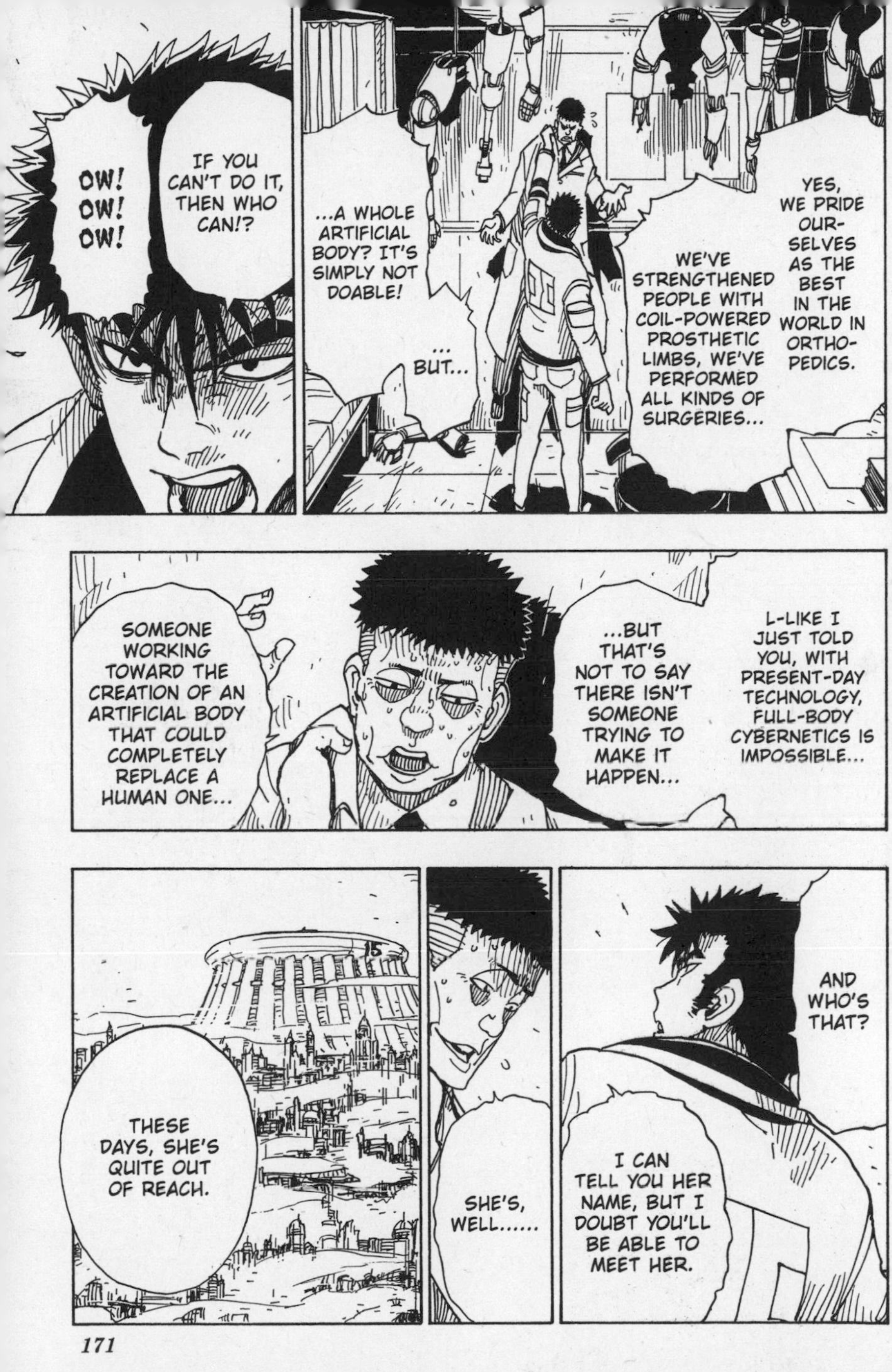
YES, WE PRIDE OURSELVES AS THE BEST IN THE WORLD IN ORTHOPEDICS.
WE'VE STRENGTHENED PEOPLE WITH COIL-POWERED PROSTHETIC LIMBS, WE'VE PERFORMED ALL KINDS OF SURGERIES...
... BUT...
...A WHOLE ARTIFICIAL BODY? IT'S SIMPLY NOT DOABLE!
IF YOU CAN'T DO IT, THEN WHO CAN!?
OW! OW! OW!
L-LIKE I JUST TOLD YOU, WITH PRESENT-DAY TECHNOLOGY, FULL-BODY CYBERNETICS IS IMPOSSIBLE...
...BUT THAT'S NOT TO SAY THERE ISN'T SOMEONE TRYING TO MAKE IT HAPPEN...
SOMEONE WORKING TOWARD THE CREATION OF AN ARTIFICIAL BODY THAT COULD COMPLETELY REPLACE A HUMAN ONE...
AND WHO'S THAT?
I CAN TELL YOU HER NAME, BUT I DOUBT YOU'LL BE ABLE TO MEET HER.
SHE'S, WELL......
THESE DAYS, SHE'S QUITE OUT OF REACH.

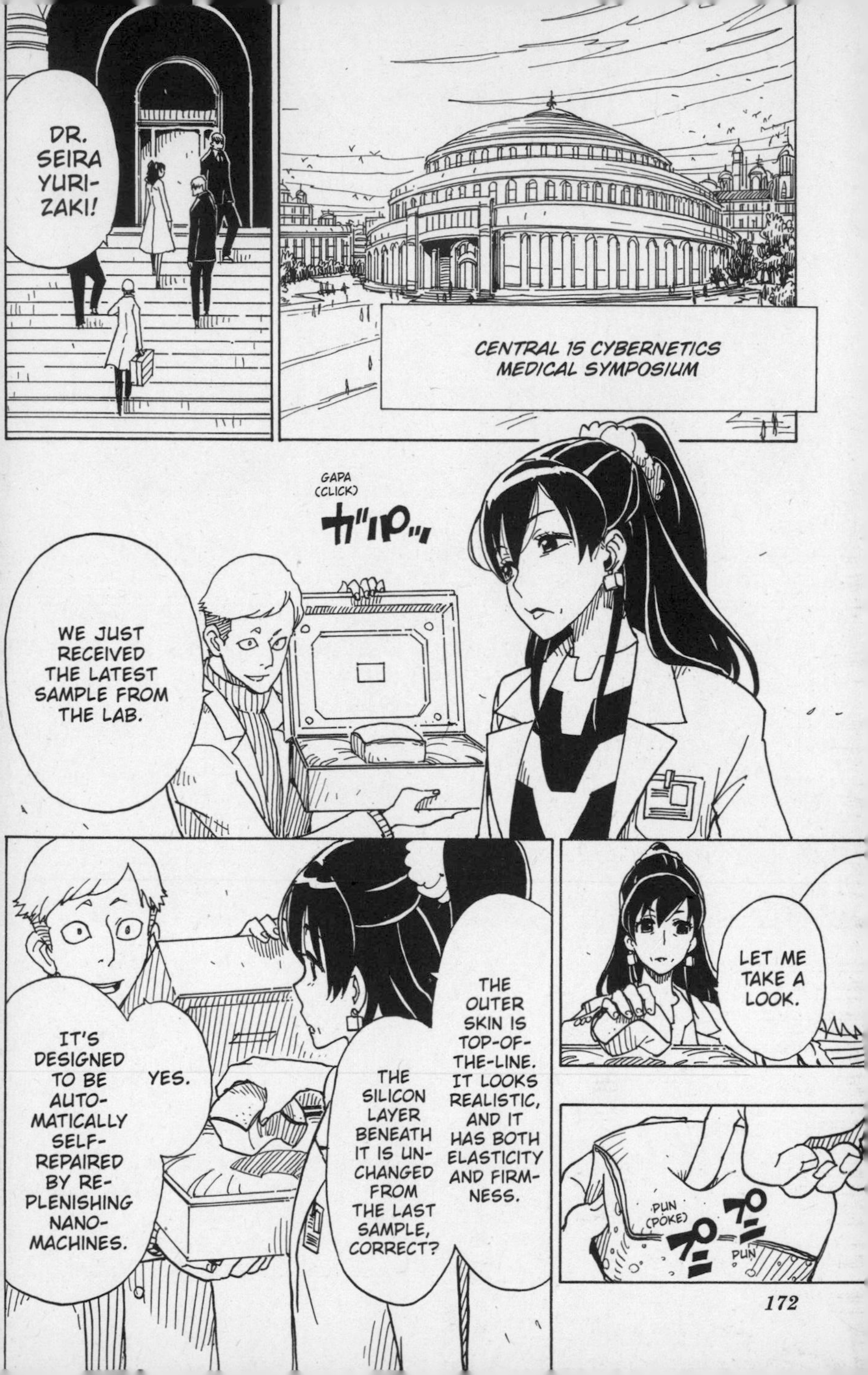
CENTRAL 15 CYBERNETICS MEDICAL SYMPOSIUM
DR. SEIRA YURI-ZAKI!
GAPA (CLICK)
WE JUST RECEIVED THE LATEST SAMPLE FROM THE LAB.
LET ME TAKE A LOOK.
PUN (POKE)
PUN
THE OUTER SKIN IS TOP-OF-THE-LINE. IT LOOKS REALISTIC, AND IT HAS BOTH ELASTICITY AND FIRM-NESS.
THE SILICON LAYER BENEATH IT IS UN-CHANGED FROM THE LAST SAMPLE, CORRECT?
YES.
IT'S DESIGNED TO BE AUTO-MATICALLY SELF-REPAIRED BY RE-PLENISHING NANO-MACHINES.

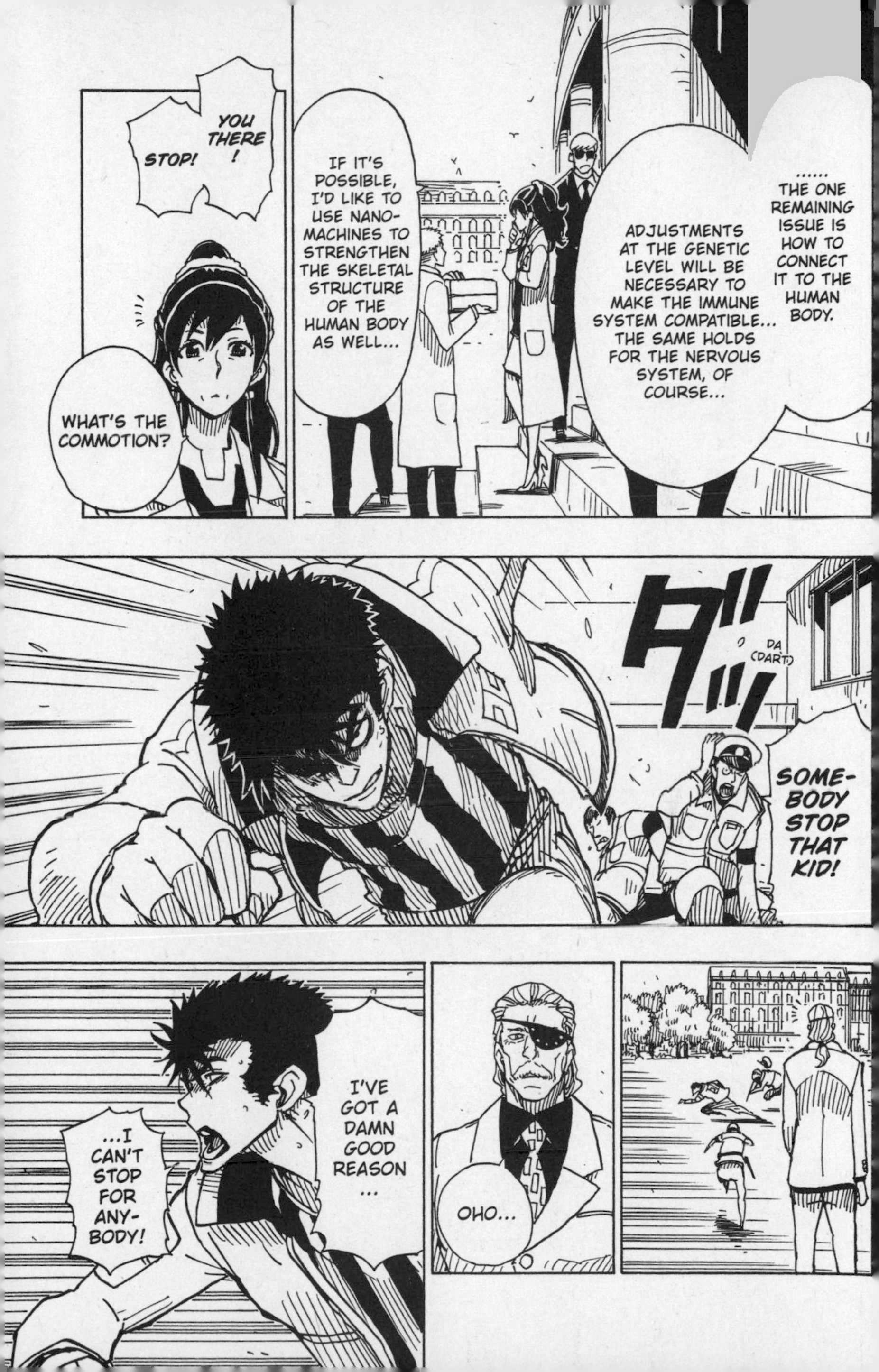
...... THE ONE REMAINING ISSUE IS HOW TO CONNECT IT TO THE HUMAN BODY.
ADJUSTMENTS AT THE GENETIC LEVEL WILL BE NECESSARY TO MAKE THE IMMUNE SYSTEM COMPATIBLE... THE SAME HOLDS FOR THE NERVOUS SYSTEM, OF COURSE...
IF IT'S POSSIBLE, I'D LIKE TO USE NANO-MACHINES TO STRENGTHEN THE SKELETAL STRUCTURE OF THE HUMAN BODY AS WELL...
YOU THERE!
STOP!
WHAT'S THE COMMOTION?
ダッ
DA (DART)
SOME-BODY STOP THAT KID!
OHO...
I'VE GOT A DAMN GOOD REASON...
...I CAN'T STOP FOR ANY-BODY!

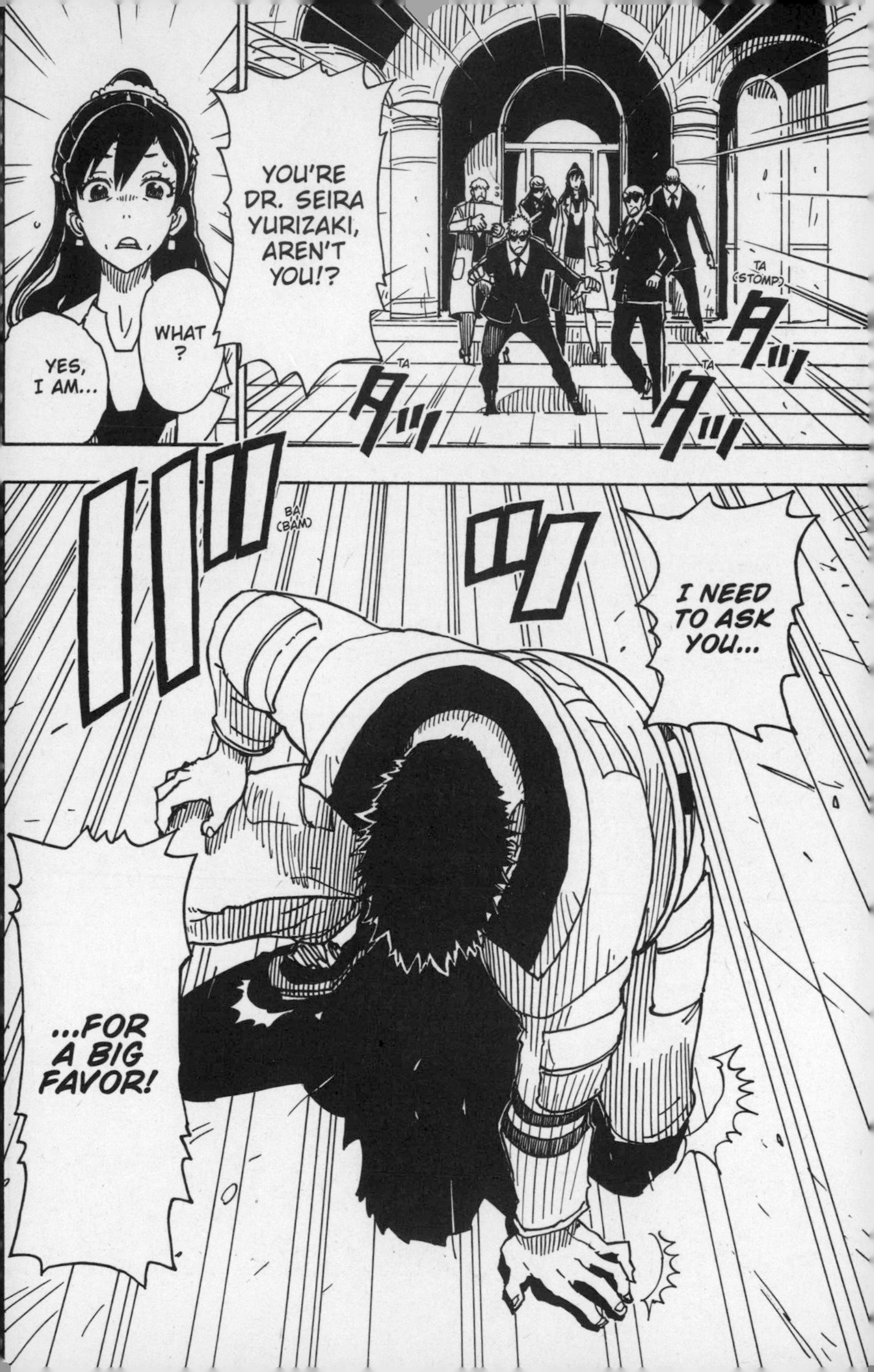
YOU'RE DR. SEIRA YURIZAKI, AREN'T YOU!?
TA (STOMP)
TA
TA
WHAT?
YES, I AM...
BA (BAM)
I NEED TO ASK YOU...
...FOR A BIG FAVOR!

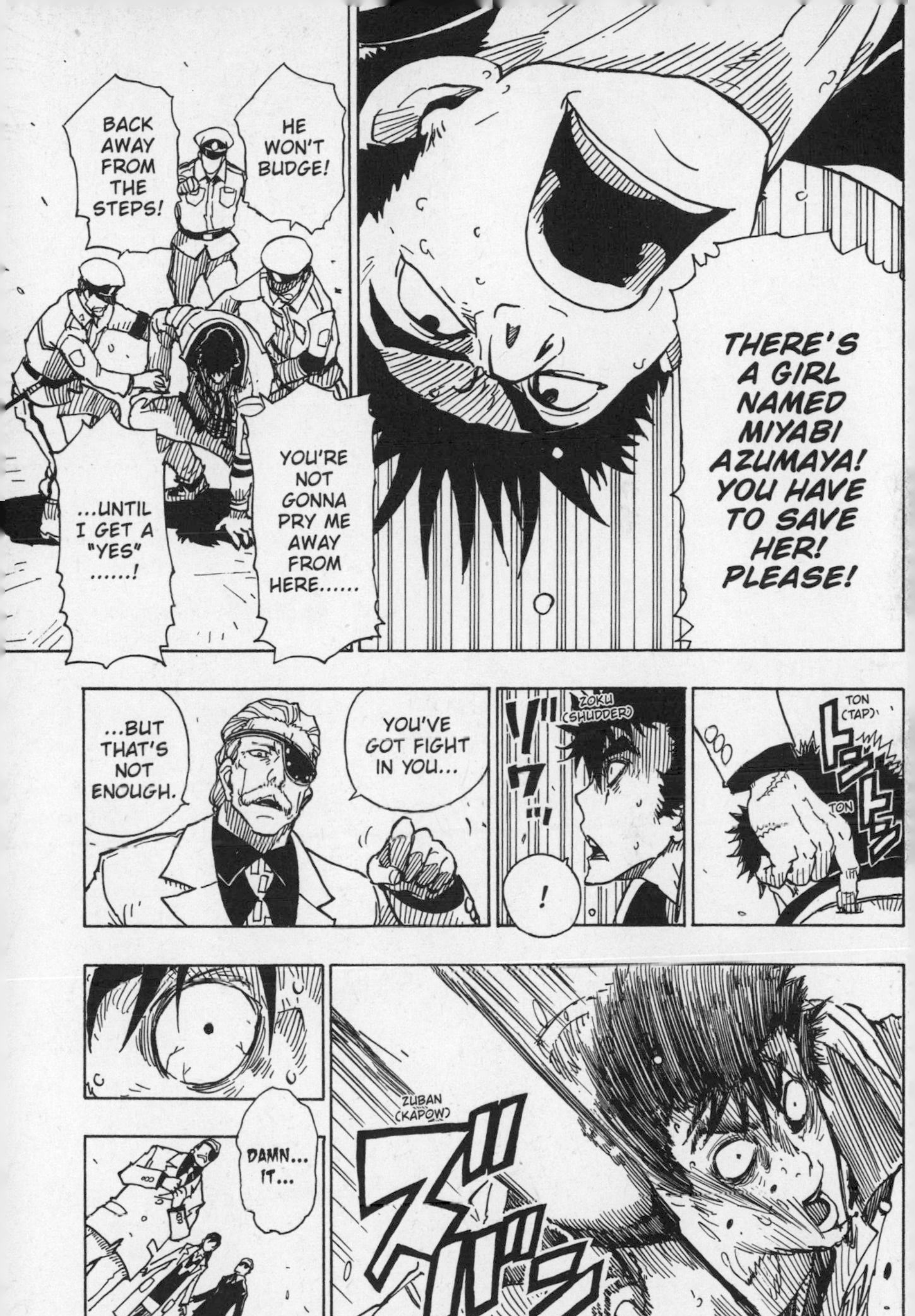
THERE'S A GIRL NAMED MIYABI AZUMAYA! YOU HAVE TO SAVE HER! PLEASE!
HE WON'T BUDGE!
BACK AWAY FROM THE STEPS!
YOU'RE NOT GONNA PRY ME AWAY FROM HERE......
...UNTIL I GET A "YES" ......!
TON (TAP)
TON
ZOKU (SHUDDER)
!
YOU'VE GOT FIGHT IN YOU...
...BUT THAT'S NOT ENOUGH.
ZUBAN (KAPOW)
DAMN... IT...

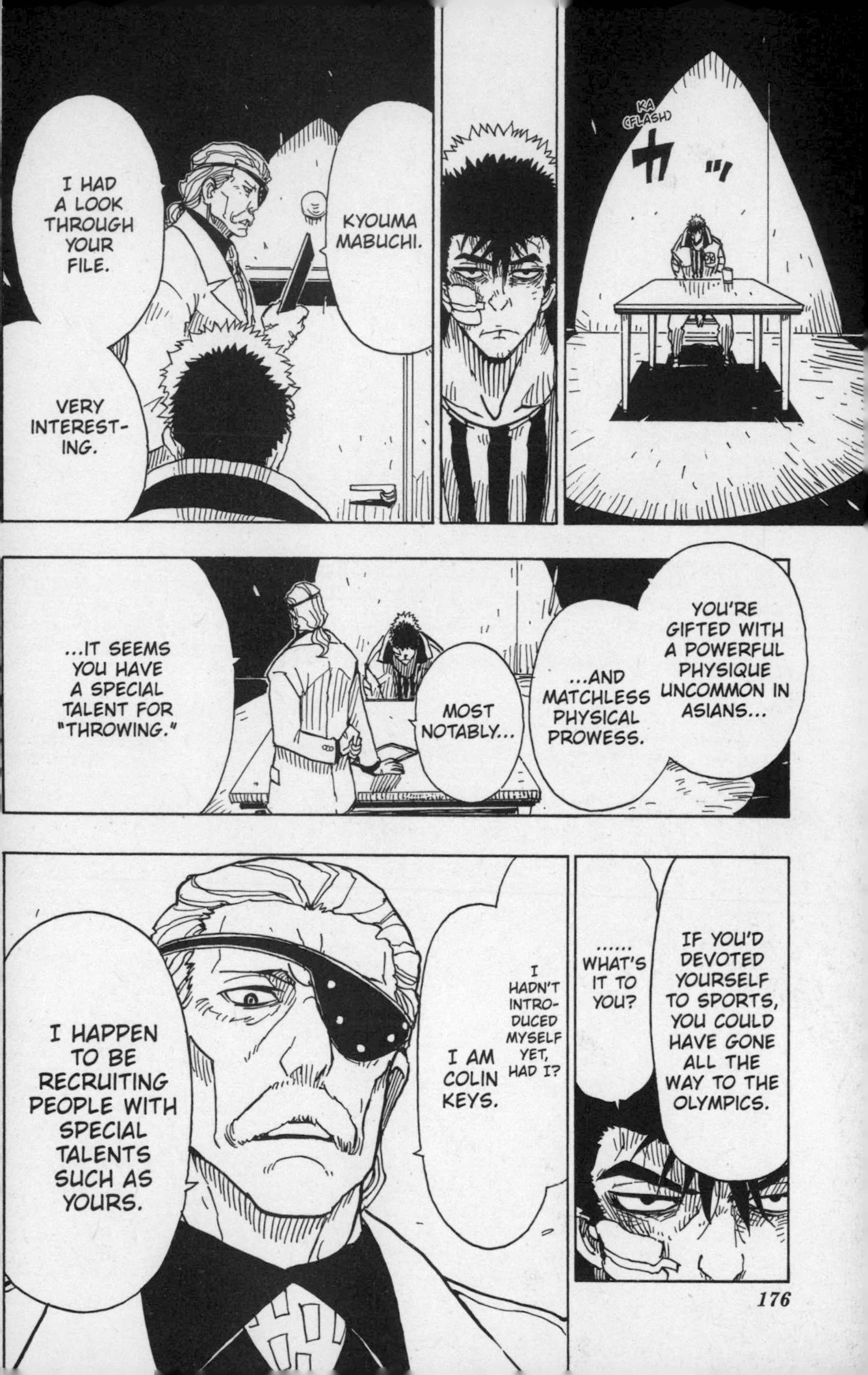
KA (FLASH)
KYOUMA MABUCHI.
I HAD A LOOK THROUGH YOUR FILE.
VERY INTEREST-ING.
YOU'RE GIFTED WITH A POWERFUL PHYSIQUE UNCOMMON IN ASIANS...
...AND MATCHLESS PHYSICAL PROWESS.
MOST NOTABLY...
...IT SEEMS YOU HAVE A SPECIAL TALENT FOR "THROWING."
IF YOU'D DEVOTED YOURSELF TO SPORTS, YOU COULD HAVE GONE ALL THE WAY TO THE OLYMPICS.
...... WHAT'S IT TO YOU?
I HADN'T INTRO-DUCED MYSELF YET, HAD I?
I AM COLIN KEYS.
I HAPPEN TO BE RECRUITING PEOPLE WITH SPECIAL TALENTS SUCH AS YOURS.

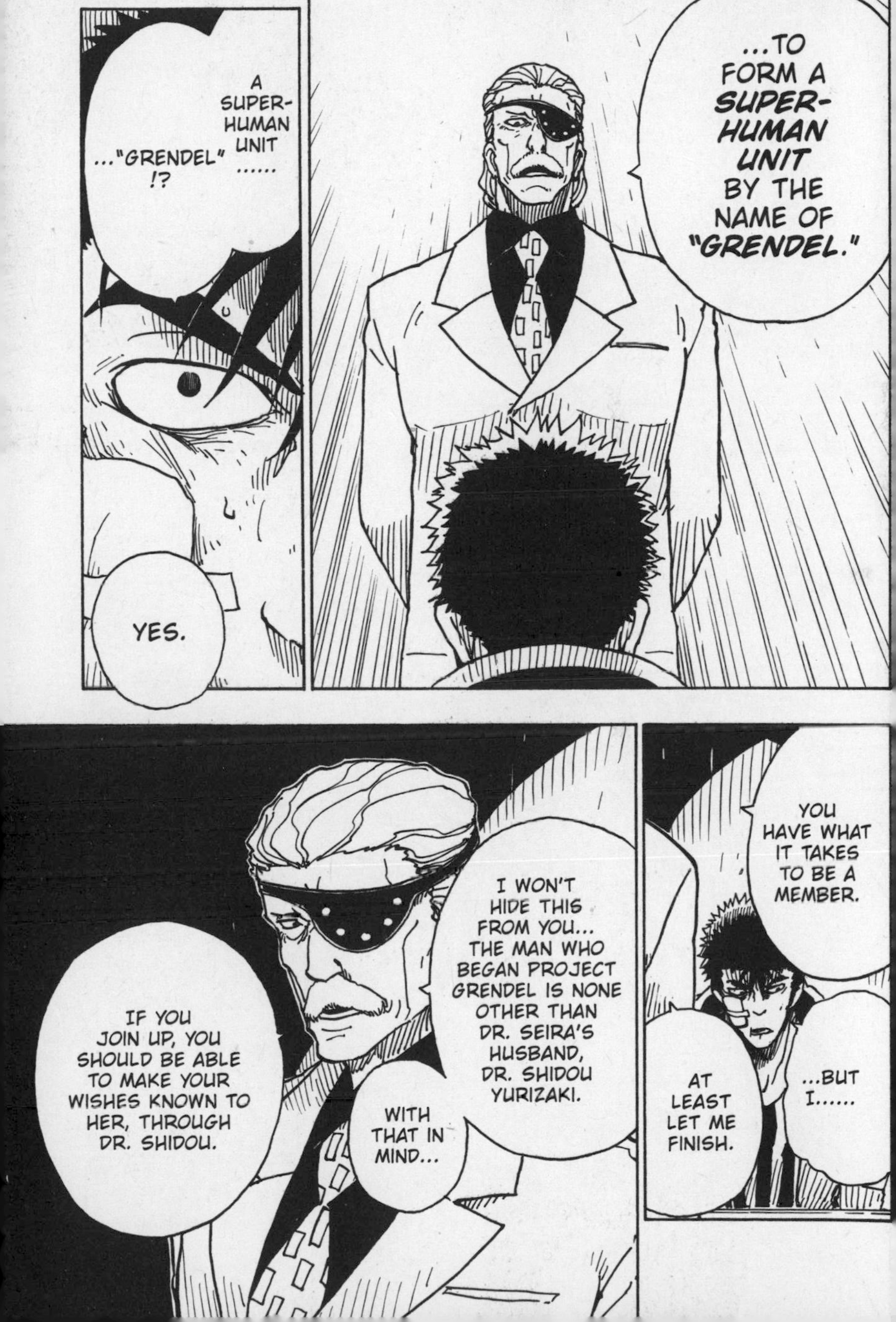
...TO FORM A SUPER-HUMAN UNIT BY THE NAME OF "GRENDEL."
A SUPER-HUMAN UNIT ......
..."GRENDEL" !?
YES.
YOU HAVE WHAT IT TAKES TO BE A MEMBER.
...BUT I......
AT LEAST LET ME FINISH.
I WON'T HIDE THIS FROM YOU... THE MAN WHO BEGAN PROJECT GRENDEL IS NONE OTHER THAN DR. SEIRA'S HUSBAND, DR. SHIDOU YURIZAKI.
WITH THAT IN MIND...
IF YOU JOIN UP, YOU SHOULD BE ABLE TO MAKE YOUR WISHES KNOWN TO HER, THROUGH DR. SHIDOU.

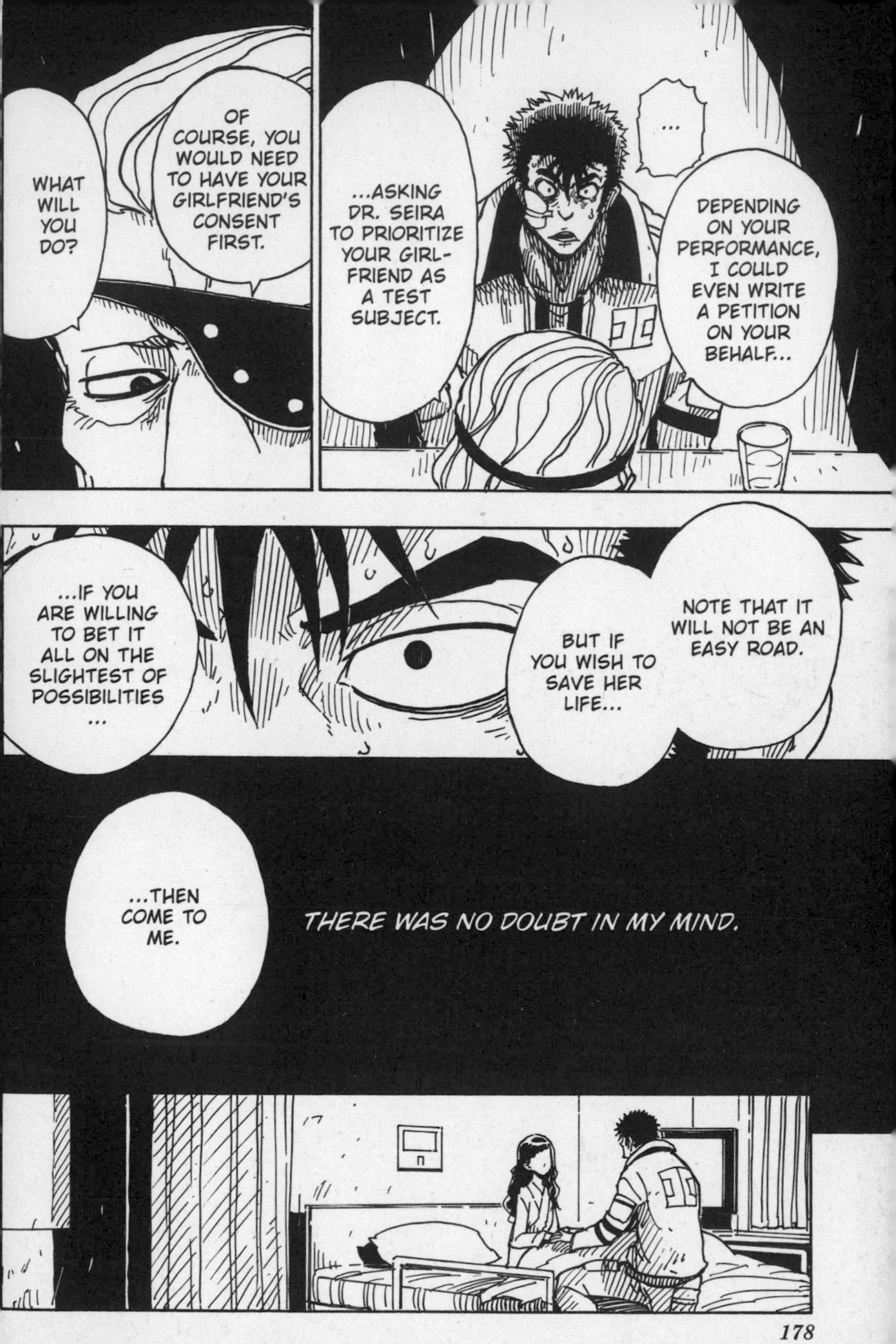
...
DEPENDING ON YOUR PERFORMANCE, I COULD EVEN WRITE A PETITION ON YOUR BEHALF...
...ASKING DR. SEIRA TO PRIORITIZE YOUR GIRL-FRIEND AS A TEST SUBJECT.
OF COURSE, YOU WOULD NEED TO HAVE YOUR GIRLFRIEND'S CONSENT FIRST.
WHAT WILL YOU DO?
NOTE THAT IT WILL NOT BE AN EASY ROAD.
BUT IF YOU WISH TO SAVE HER LIFE...
...IF YOU ARE WILLING TO BET IT ALL ON THE SLIGHTEST OF POSSIBILITIES...
...THEN COME TO ME.
THERE WAS NO DOUBT IN MY MIND.

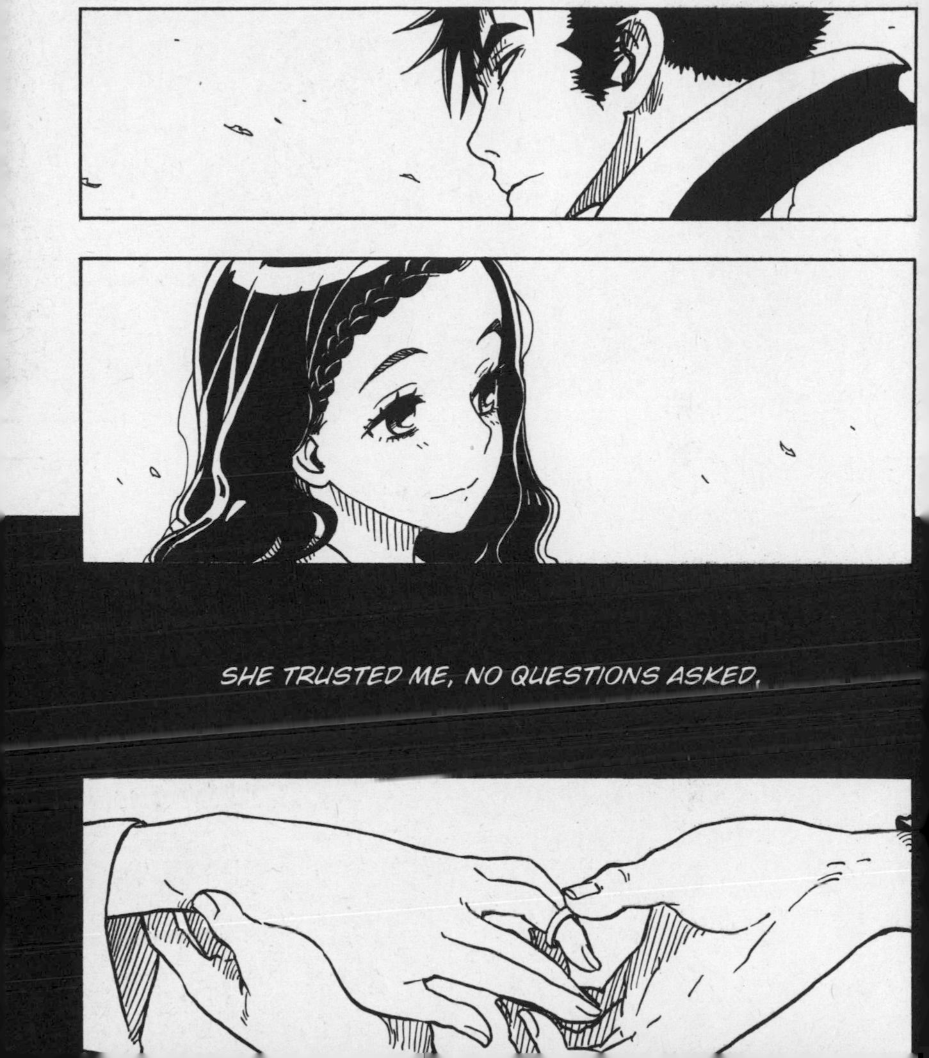
SHE TRUSTED ME, NO QUESTIONS ASKED.

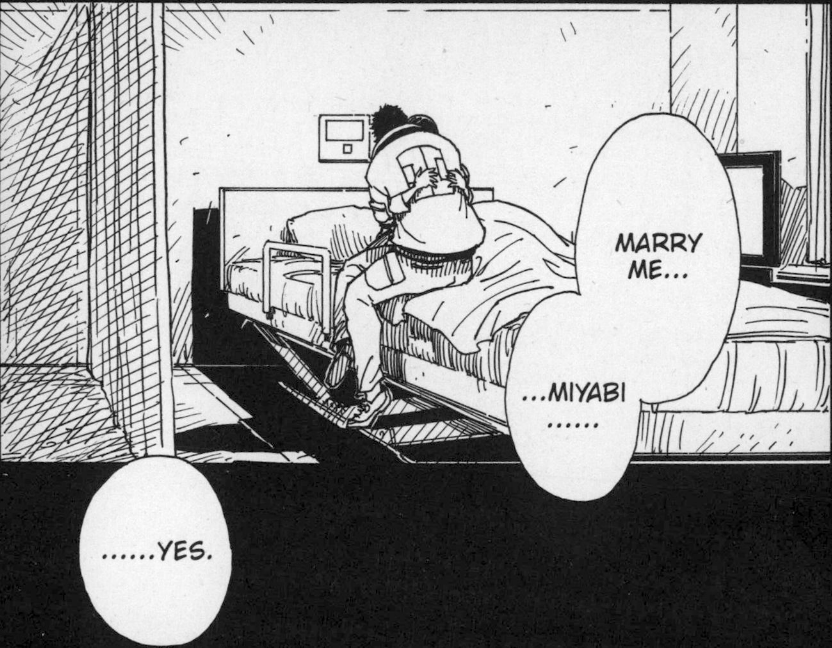
MARRY ME...
...MIYABI ......
......YES.

FILE.39

TO DISAPPEAR INTO DARKNESS

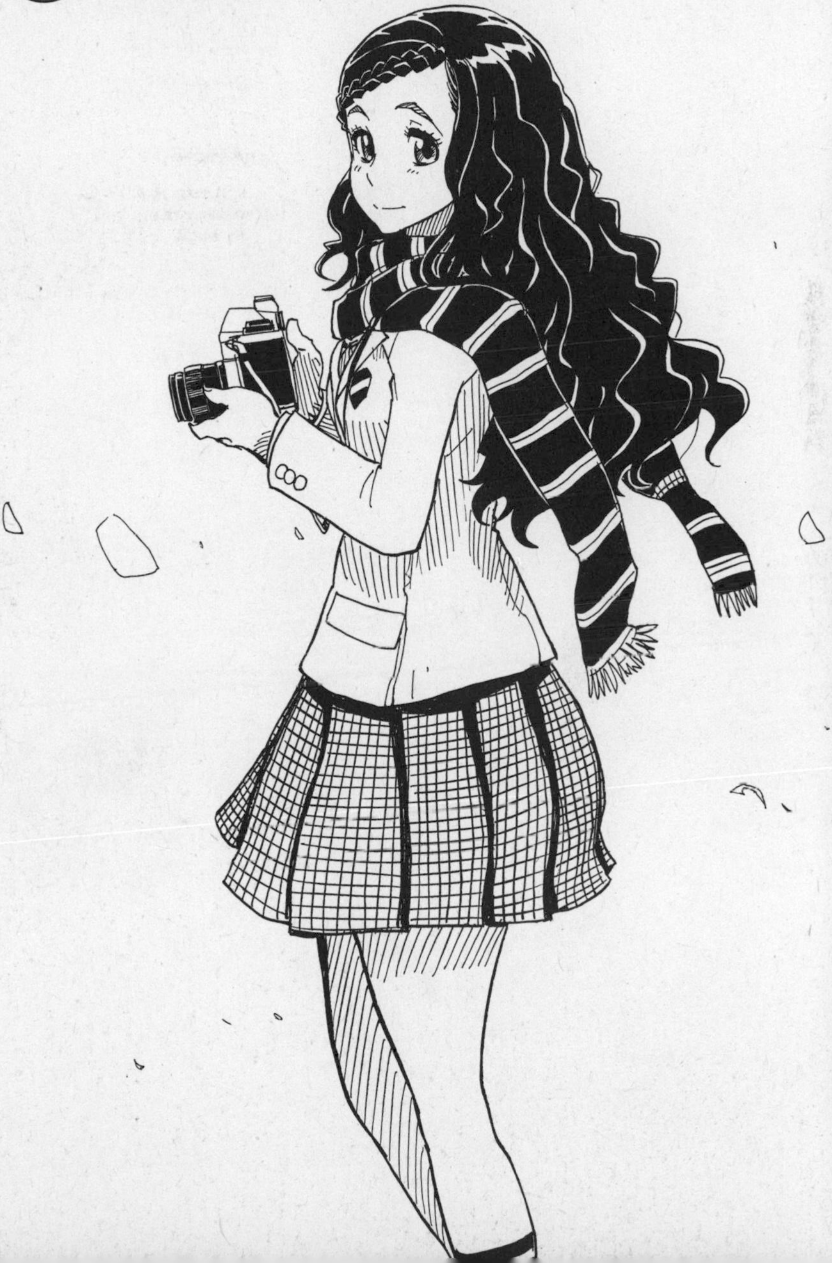

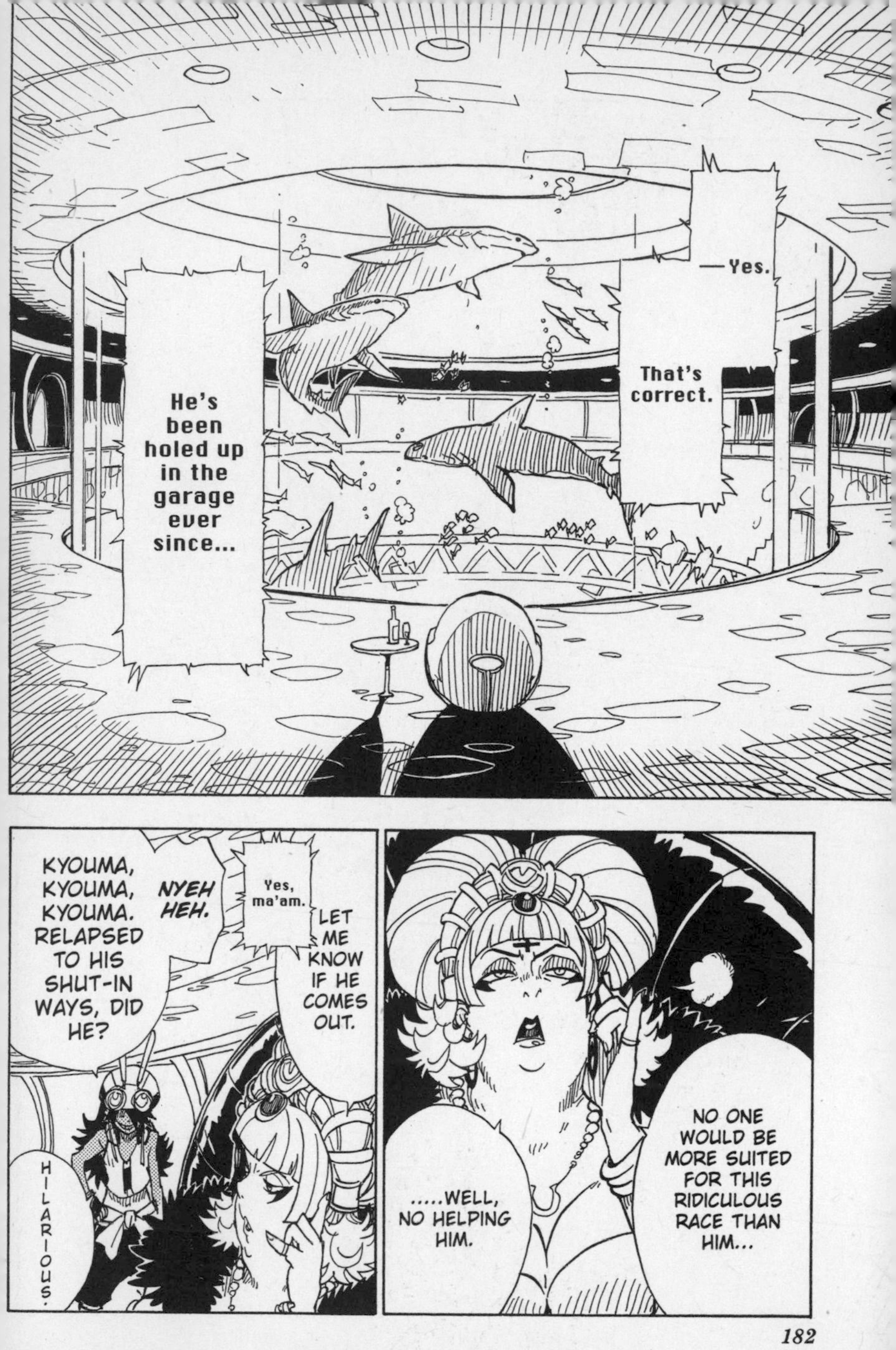
—Yes.
That's correct.
He's been holed up in the garage ever since...
NO ONE WOULD BE MORE SUITED FOR THIS RIDICULOUS RACE THAN HIM...
.....WELL, NO HELPING HIM.
LET ME KNOW IF HE COMES OUT.
Yes, ma'am.
NYEH HEH.
KYOUMA, KYOUMA, KYOUMA. RELAPSED TO HIS SHUT-IN WAYS, DID HE?
HILARIOUS.

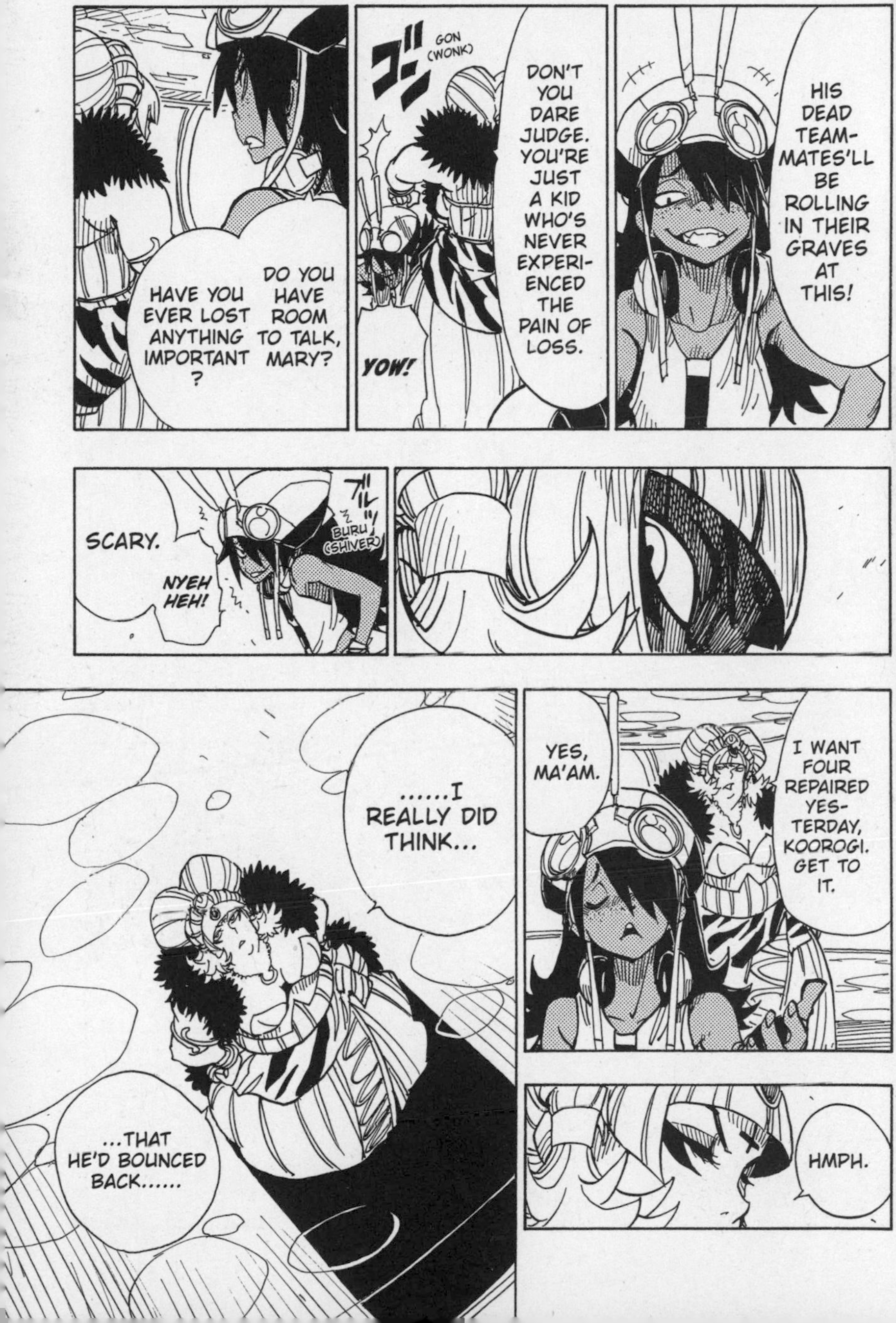
HIS DEAD TEAM-MATES'LL BE ROLLING IN THEIR GRAVES AT THIS!
DON'T YOU DARE JUDGE. YOU'RE JUST A KID WHO'S NEVER EXPERIENCED THE PAIN OF LOSS.
GON (WONK)
YOW!
DO YOU HAVE ROOM TO TALK, MARY?
HAVE YOU EVER LOST ANYTHING IMPORTANT?
BURU (SHIVER)
SCARY.
NYEH HEH!
I WANT FOUR REPAIRED YES-TERDAY, KOOROGI. GET TO IT.
YES, MA'AM.
HMPH.
......I REALLY DID THINK...
...THAT HE'D BOUNCED BACK......

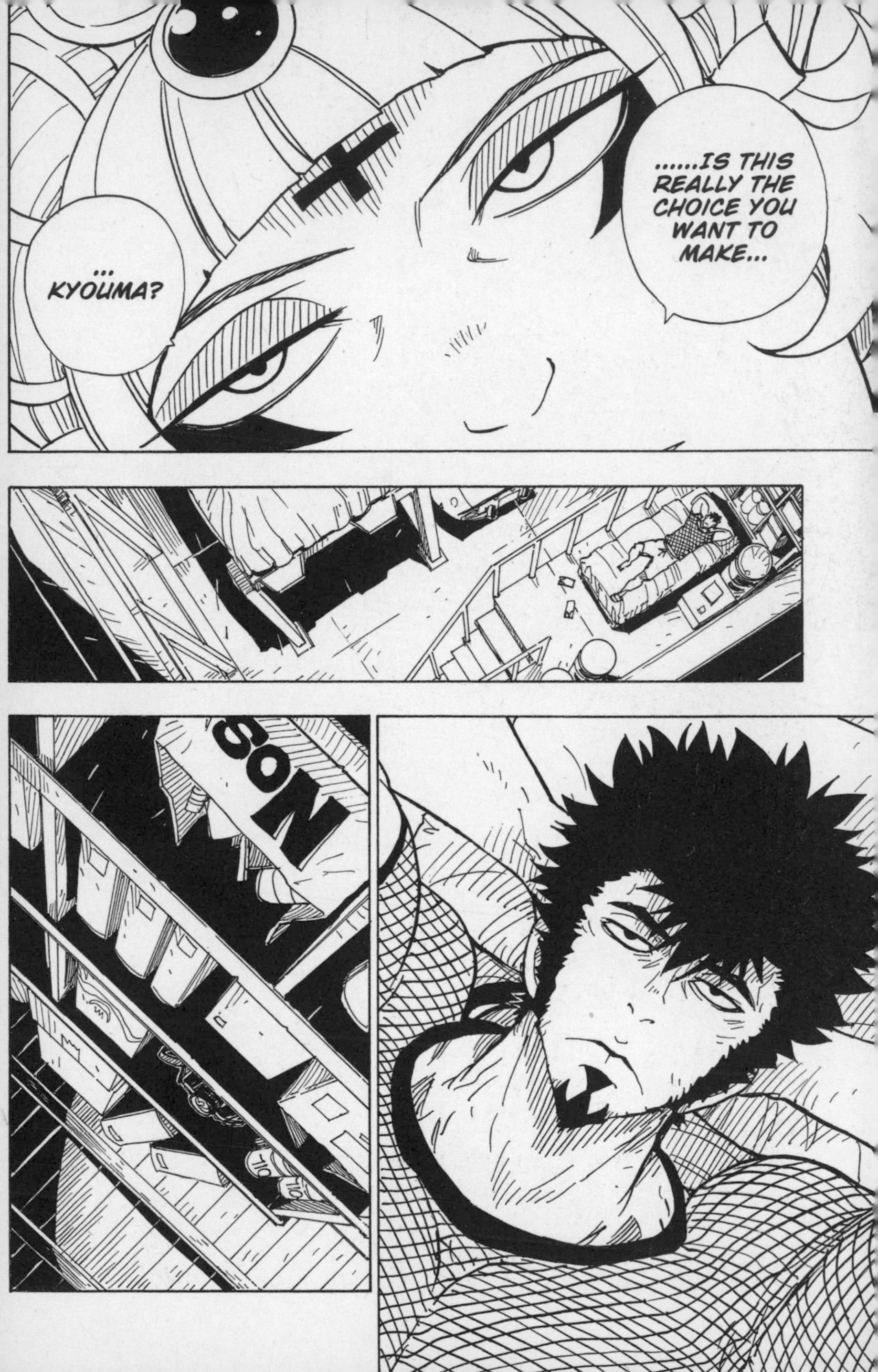
......IS THIS REALLY THE CHOICE YOU WANT TO MAKE...
... KYOUMA?

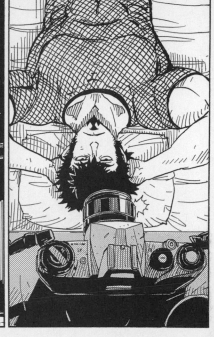

......

GABA
(THUD)

KAN
(CLANG)

ASAHI
PENTAX

KAN

KAN

OIL

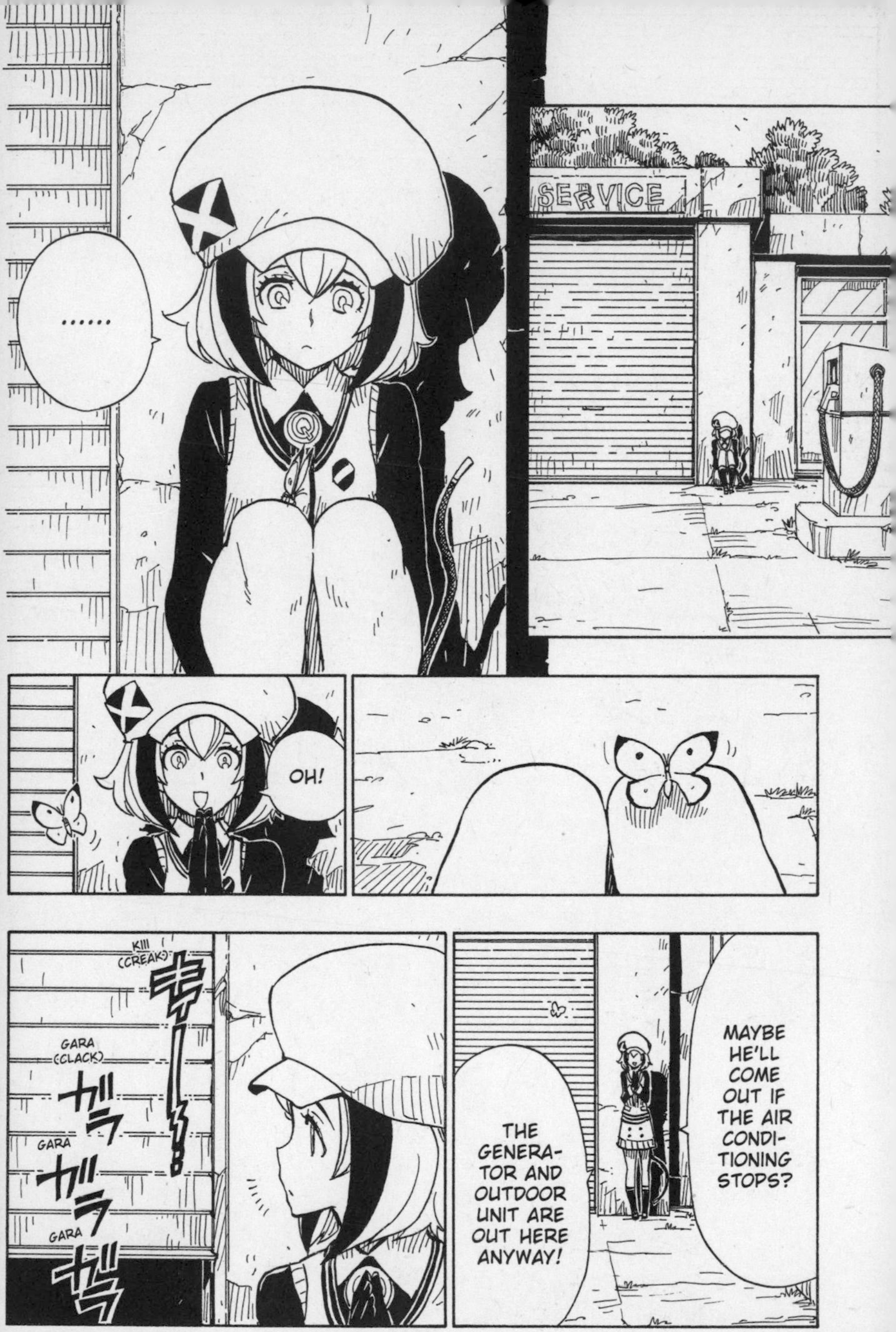
SERVICE
......
OH!
MAYBE HE'LL COME OUT IF THE AIR CONDITIONING STOPS?
THE GENERATOR AND OUTDOOR UNIT ARE OUT HERE ANYWAY!
KIII (CREAK)
GARA (CLACK)
GARA
GARA

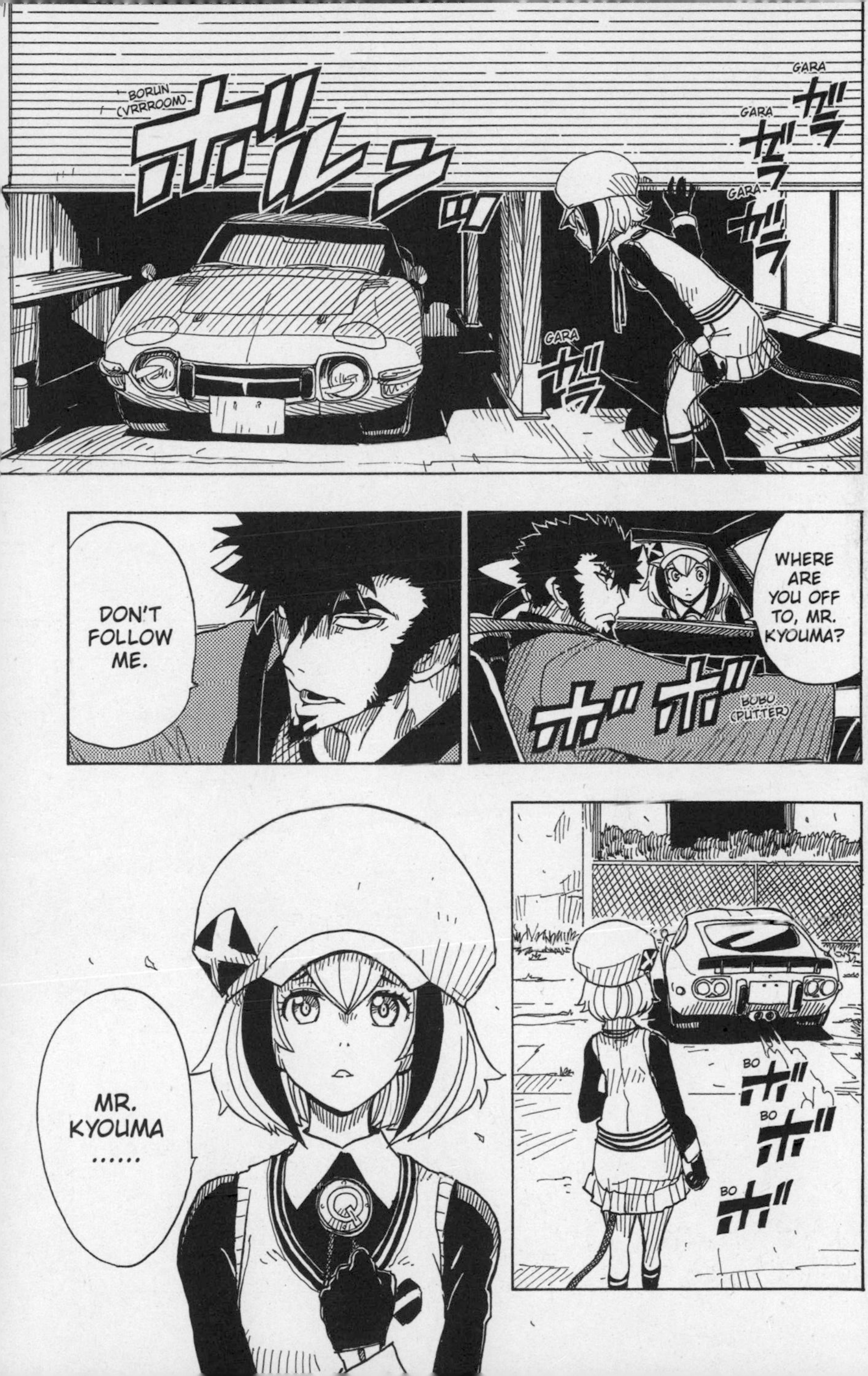
GARA
GARA
GARA
BORUN (VRRROOM)
GARA
WHERE ARE YOU OFF TO, MR. KYOUMA?
BOBO (PUTTER)
DON'T FOLLOW ME.
BO
BO
BO
MR. KYOUMA ......

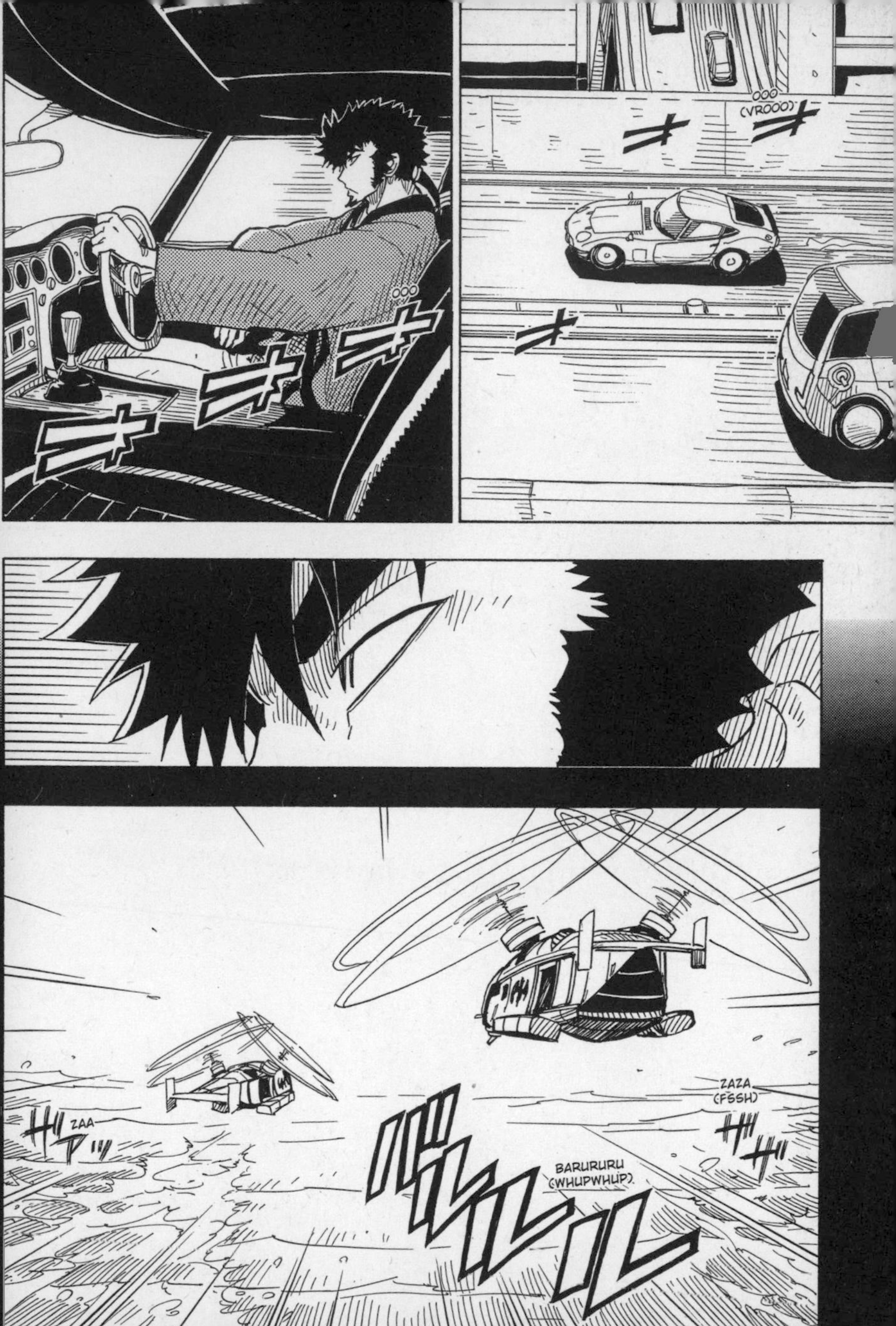
OOO
(VROOO)
ZAZA
(FSSH)
BARURURU
(WHUPWHUP)
ZAA

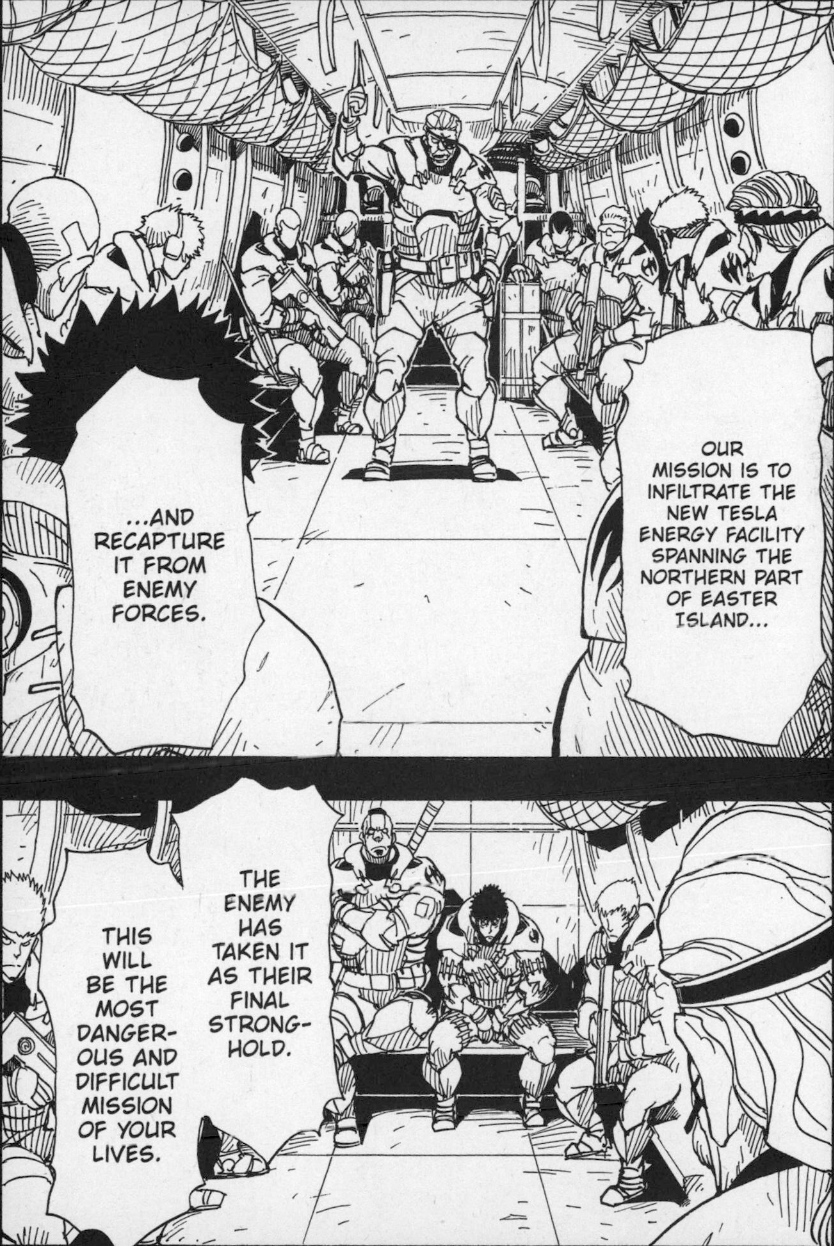
OUR MISSION IS TO INFILTRATE THE NEW TESLA ENERGY FACILITY SPANNING THE NORTHERN PART OF EASTER ISLAND...
...AND RECAPTURE IT FROM ENEMY FORCES.
THE ENEMY HAS TAKEN IT AS THEIR FINAL STRONG-HOLD.
THIS WILL BE THE MOST DANGER-OUS AND DIFFICULT MISSION OF YOUR LIVES.

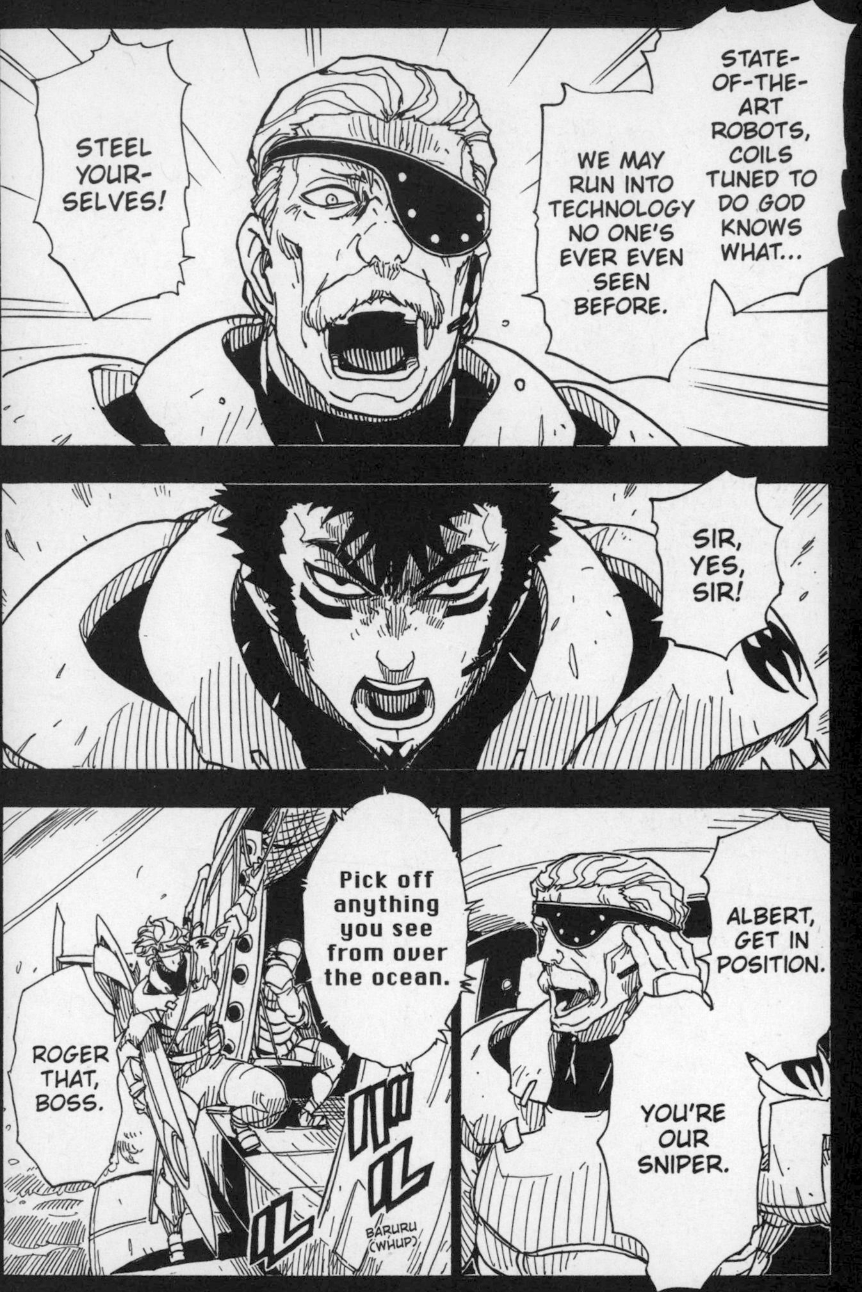
STATE-OF-THE-ART ROBOTS, COILS TUNED TO DO GOD KNOWS WHAT...
WE MAY RUN INTO TECHNOLOGY NO ONE'S EVER EVEN SEEN BEFORE.
STEEL YOUR-SELVES!
SIR, YES, SIR!
ALBERT, GET IN POSITION.
YOU'RE OUR SNIPER.
Pick off anything you see from over the ocean.
ROGER THAT, BOSS.
BARURU (WHUP)

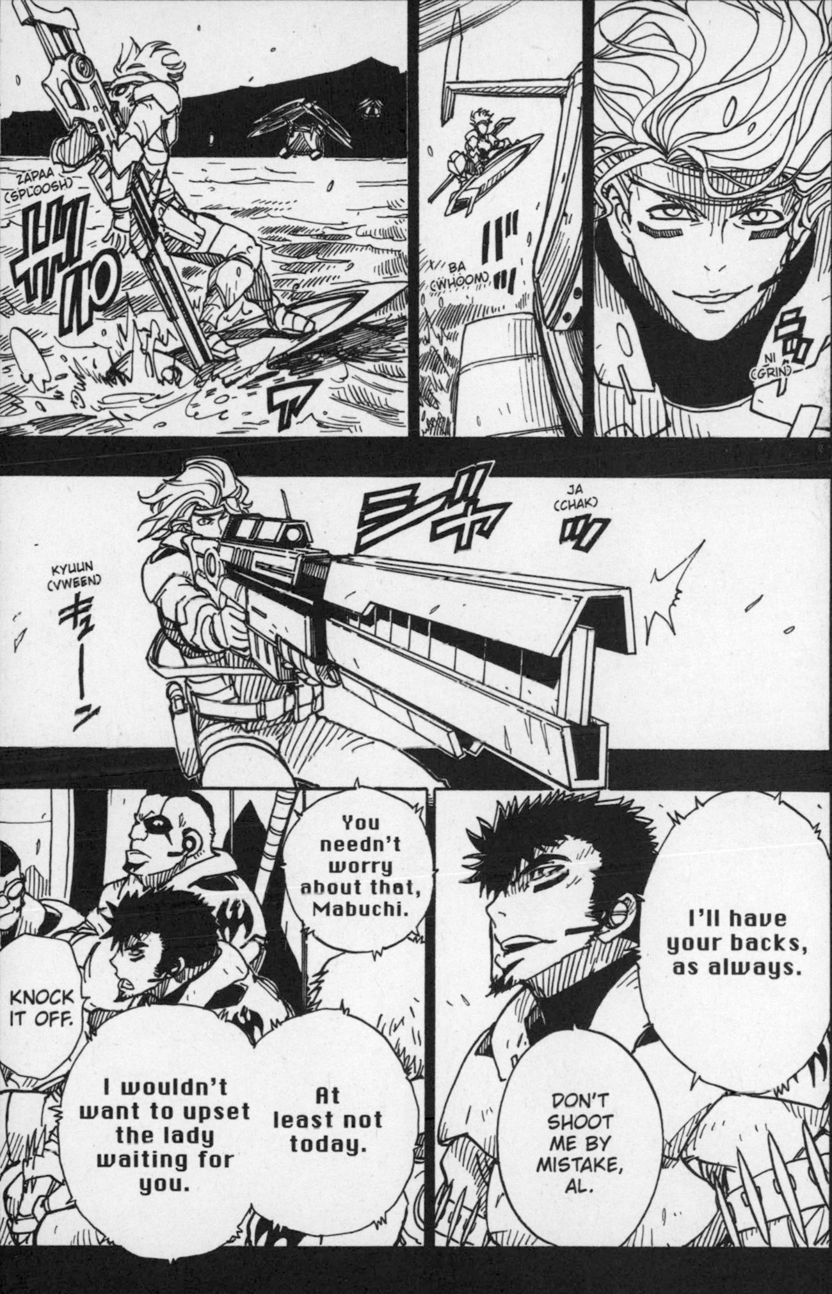
NI
(GRIN)
BA
(WHOOM)
ZAPAA
(SPLOOSH)
JA
(CHAK)
KYUUN
(VWEEN)
I'll have your backs, as always.
DON'T SHOOT ME BY MISTAKE, AL.
You needn't worry about that, Mabuchi.
At least not today.
I wouldn't want to upset the lady waiting for you.
KNOCK IT OFF.

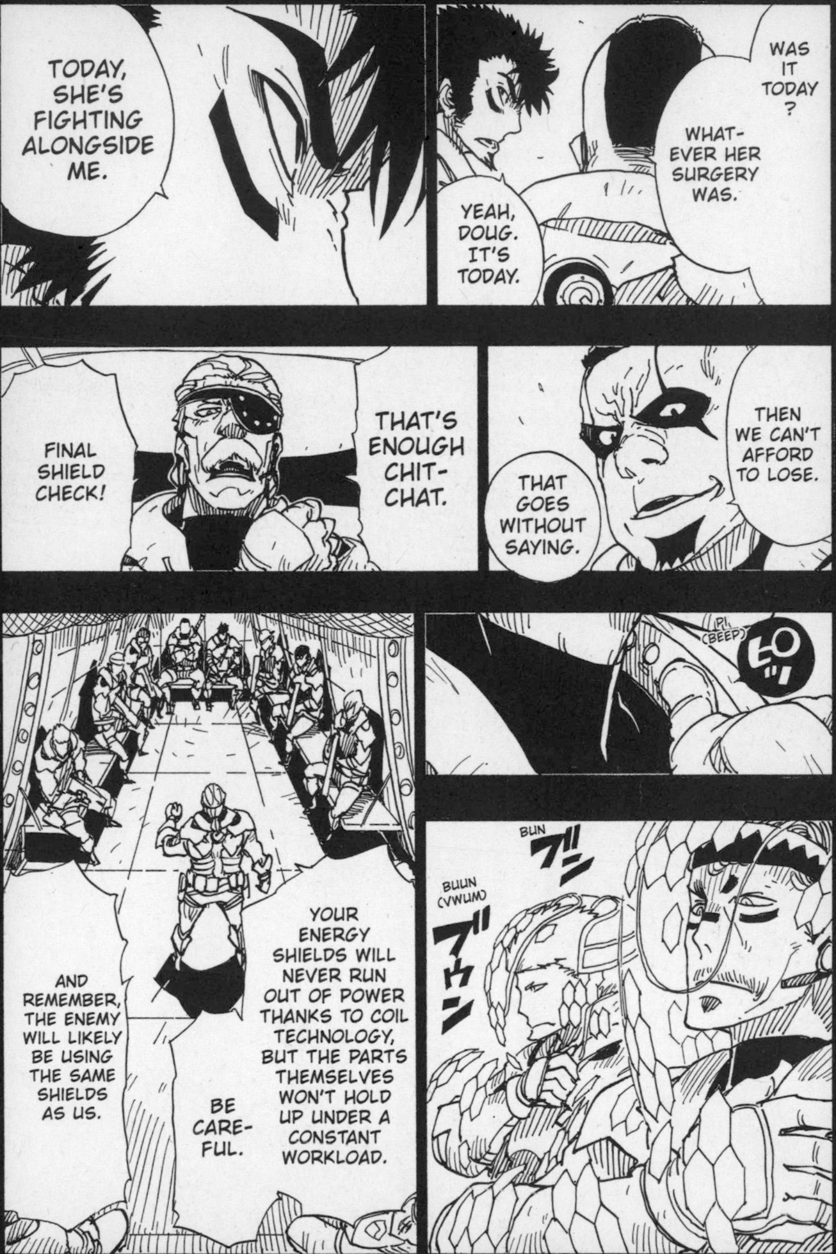
WAS IT TODAY?
WHAT-EVER HER SURGERY WAS.
YEAH, DOUG. IT'S TODAY.
TODAY, SHE'S FIGHTING ALONGSIDE ME.
THEN WE CAN'T AFFORD TO LOSE.
THAT GOES WITHOUT SAYING.
THAT'S ENOUGH CHIT-CHAT.
FINAL SHIELD CHECK!
PI (BEEP)
BUN
ブン
BUUN (VWUM)
ブウン
YOUR ENERGY SHIELDS WILL NEVER RUN OUT OF POWER THANKS TO COIL TECHNOLOGY, BUT THE PARTS THEMSELVES WON'T HOLD UP UNDER A CONSTANT WORKLOAD.
BE CARE-FUL.
AND REMEMBER, THE ENEMY WILL LIKELY BE USING THE SAME SHIELDS AS US.

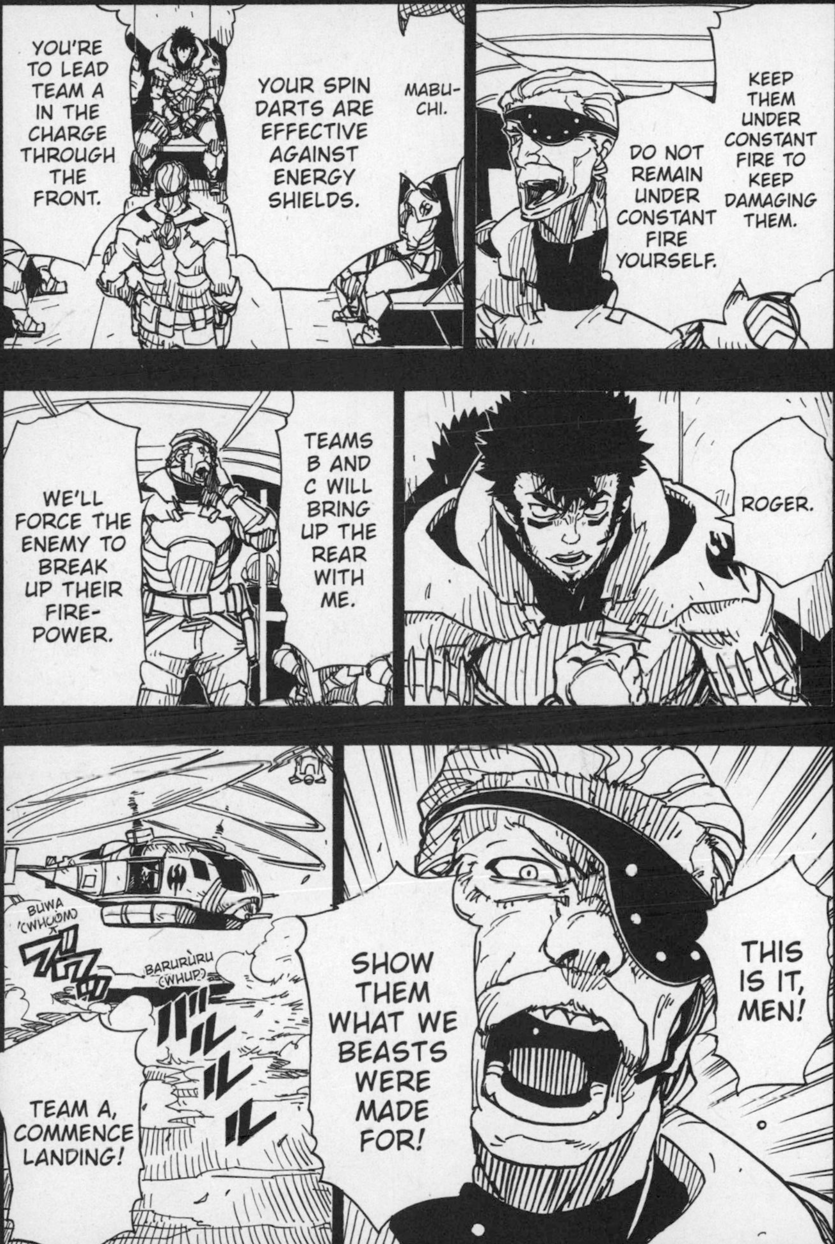
KEEP THEM UNDER CONSTANT FIRE TO KEEP DAMAGING THEM.
DO NOT REMAIN UNDER CONSTANT FIRE YOURSELF.
MABU-CHI.
YOUR SPIN DARTS ARE EFFECTIVE AGAINST ENERGY SHIELDS.
YOU'RE TO LEAD TEAM A IN THE CHARGE THROUGH THE FRONT.
ROGER.
TEAMS B AND C WILL BRING UP THE REAR WITH ME.
WE'LL FORCE THE ENEMY TO BREAK UP THEIR FIRE-POWER.
THIS IS IT, MEN!
SHOW THEM WHAT WE BEASTS WERE MADE FOR!
BUWA (WHOOM)
BARURURU (WHUP)
TEAM A, COMMENCE LANDING!

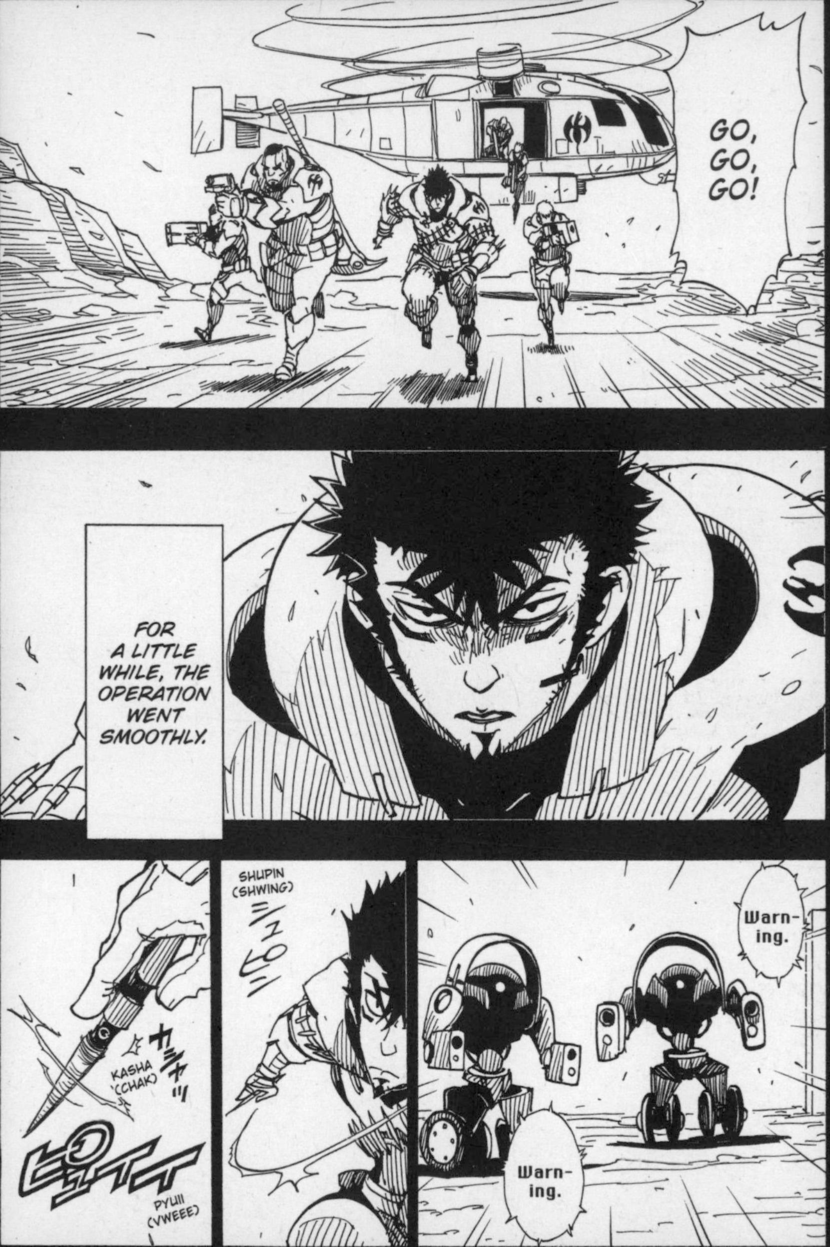
GO, GO, GO!
FOR A LITTLE WHILE, THE OPERATION WENT SMOOTHLY.
Warn-ing.
Warn-ing.
SHUPIN (SHWING)
KASHA (CHAK)
PYUII (VWEEE)

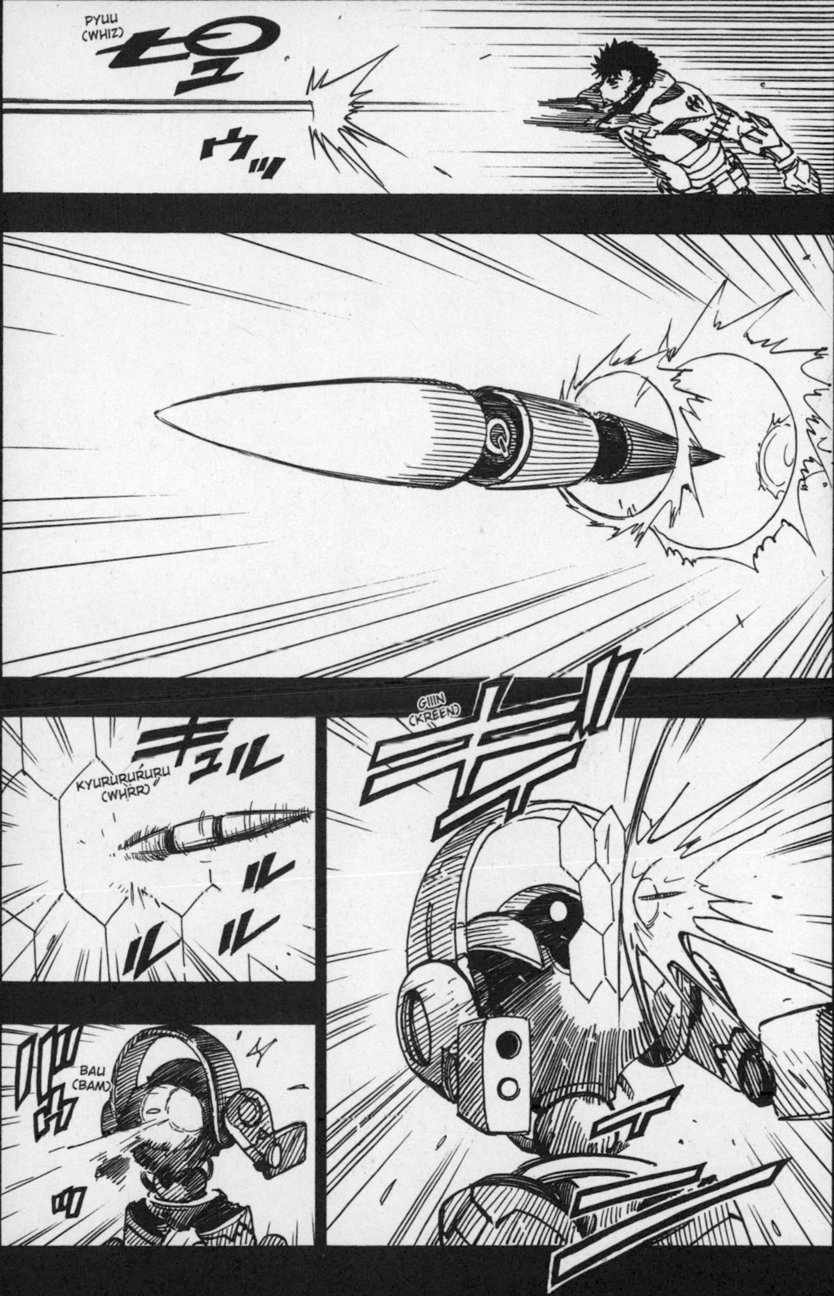
PYUU (WHIZ)
ピュ
ウッ
GIIN (KREEN)
ギ
キュル
KYURURURURU (WHRR)
ルル
BAU (BAM)

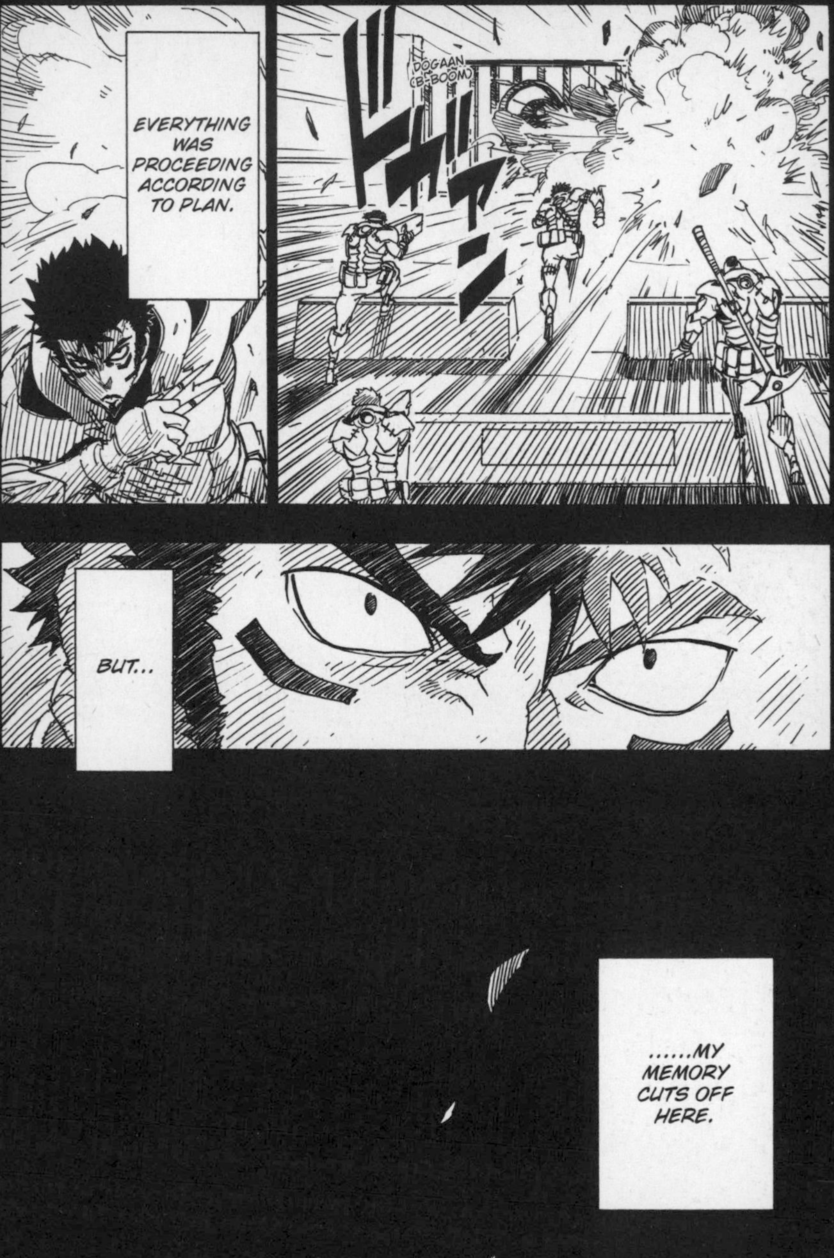

DOGAAN (B-BOOM)
EVERYTHING WAS PROCEEDING ACCORDING TO PLAN.
BUT...
......MY MEMORY CUTS OFF HERE.

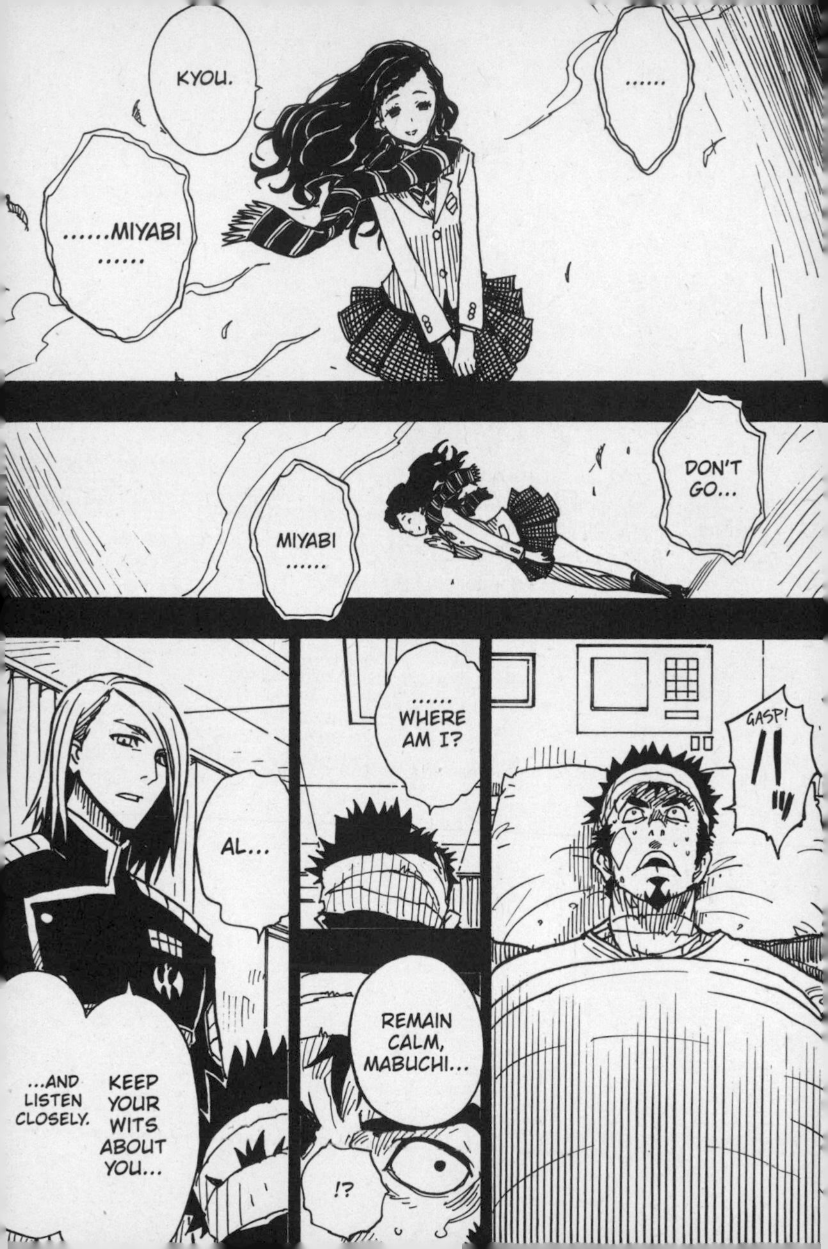
......
KYOU.
......MIYABI ......
DON'T GO...
MIYABI ......
GASP!
!!
...... WHERE AM I?
REMAIN CALM, MABUCHI...
!?
AL...
KEEP YOUR WITS ABOUT YOU...
...AND LISTEN CLOSELY.

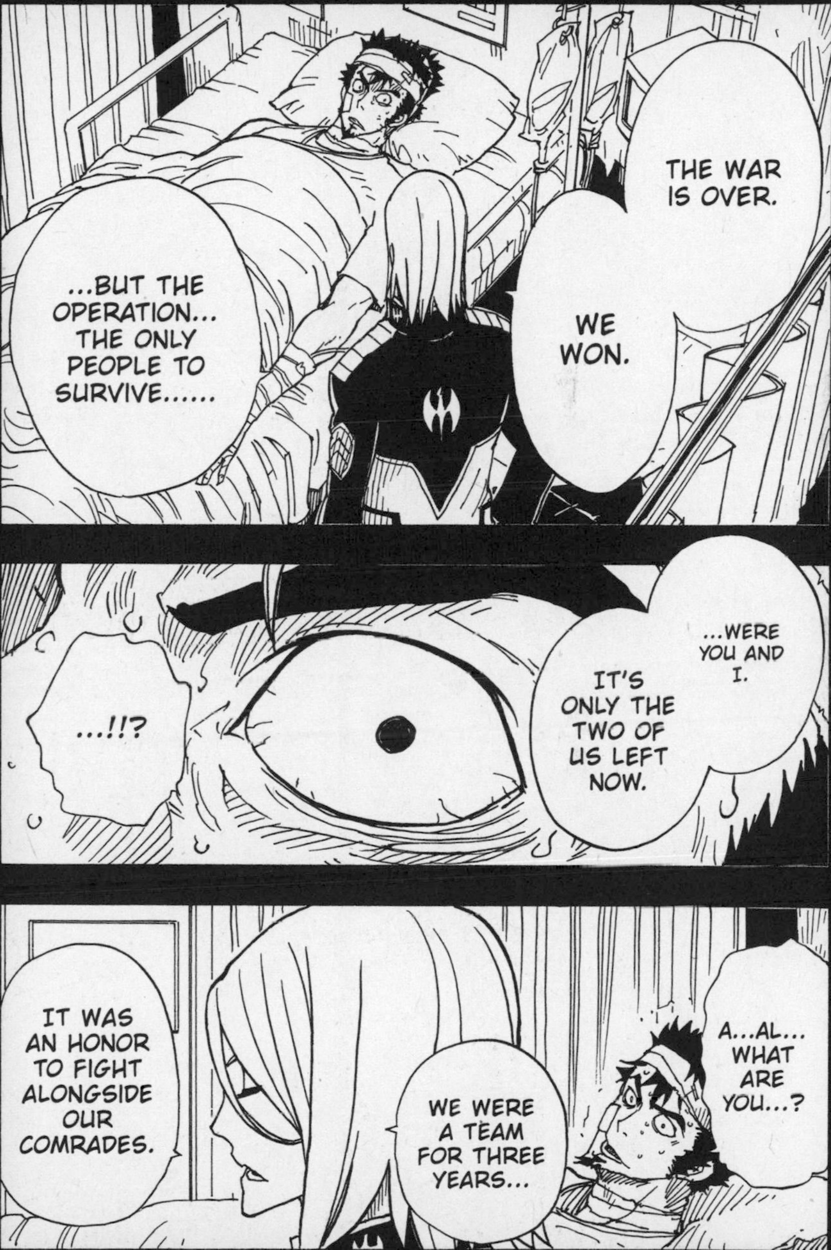
THE WAR IS OVER.
WE WON.
...BUT THE OPERATION... THE ONLY PEOPLE TO SURVIVE......
...WERE YOU AND I.
IT'S ONLY THE TWO OF US LEFT NOW.
...!!?
A...AL... WHAT ARE YOU...?
WE WERE A TEAM FOR THREE YEARS...
IT WAS AN HONOR TO FIGHT ALONGSIDE OUR COMRADES.

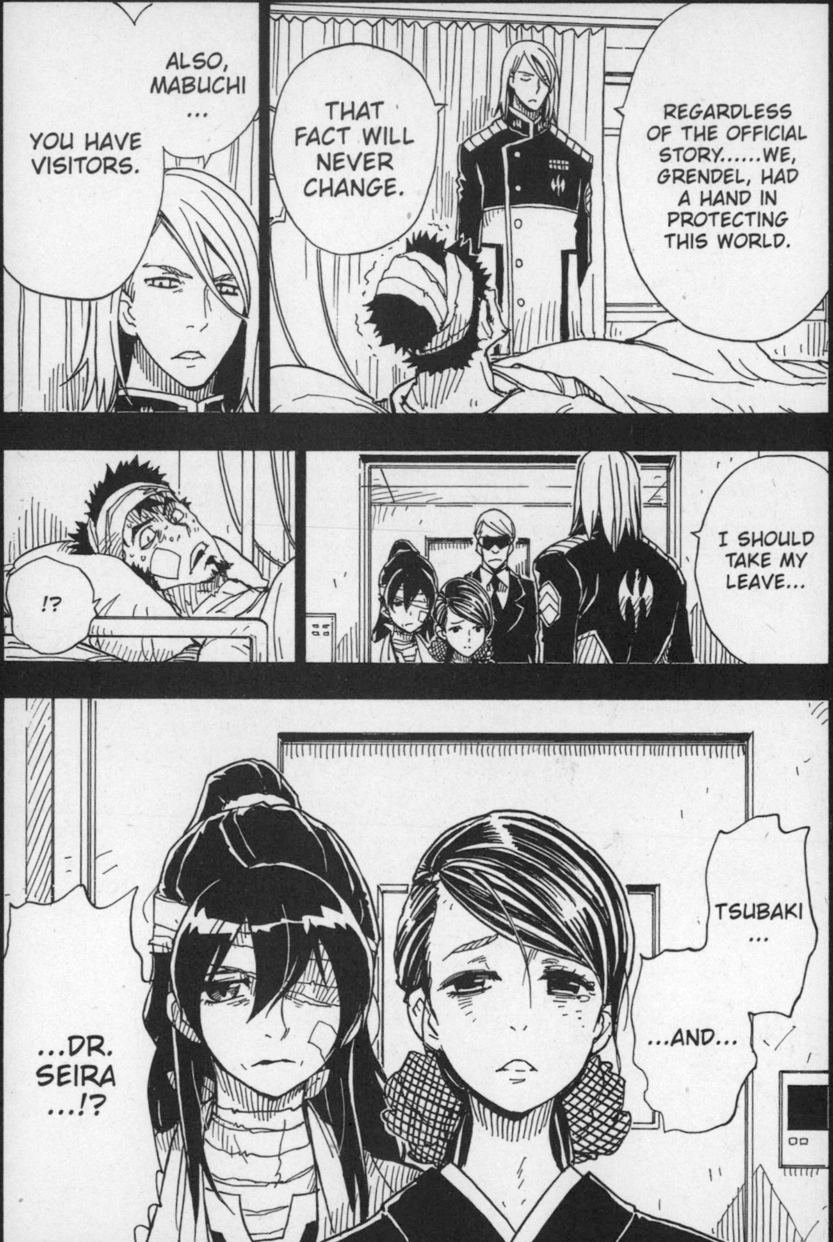
REGARDLESS OF THE OFFICIAL STORY......WE, GRENDEL, HAD A HAND IN PROTECTING THIS WORLD.
THAT FACT WILL NEVER CHANGE.
ALSO, MABUCHI ...
YOU HAVE VISITORS.
I SHOULD TAKE MY LEAVE...
!?
TSUBAKI ...
...AND...
...DR. SEIRA ...!?

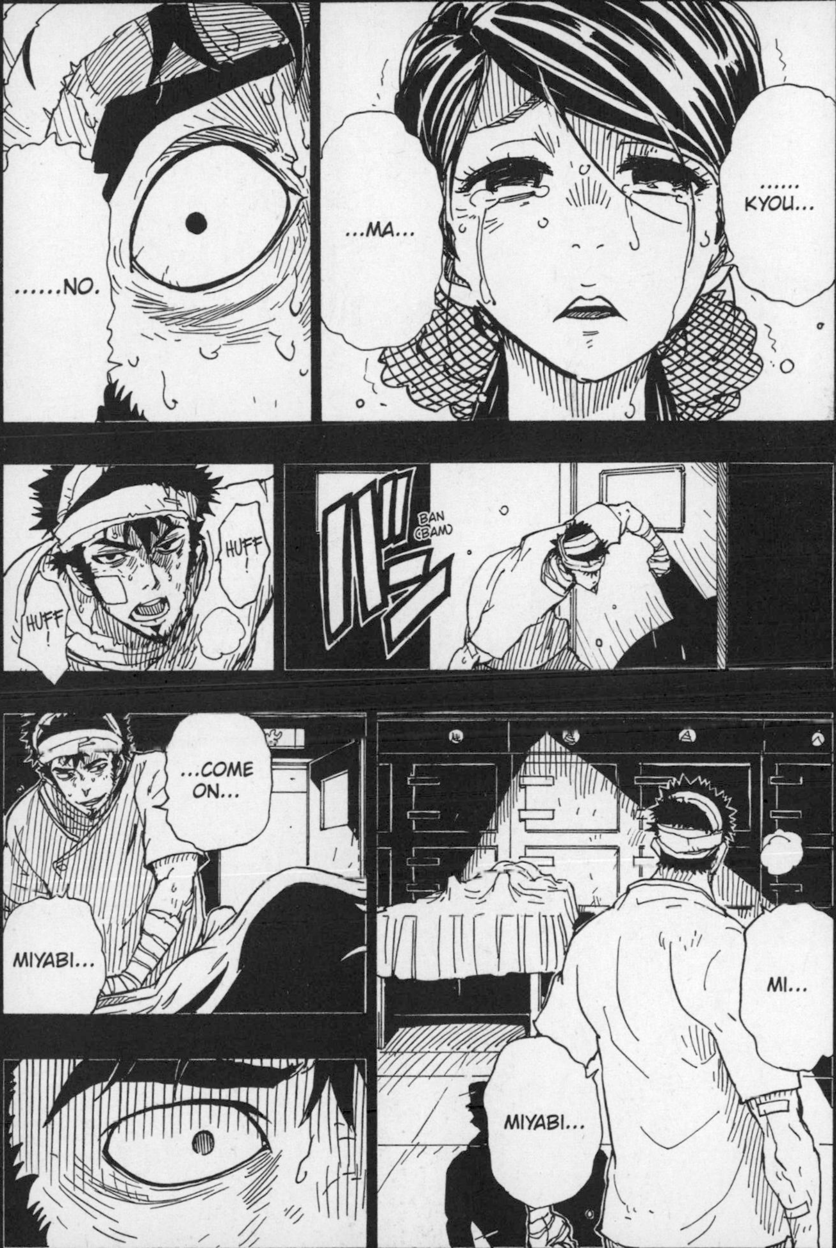
......KYOU...
...MA...
......NO.
BAN (BAM)
HUFF!
HUFF!
MI...
MIYABI...
...COME ON...
MIYABI...

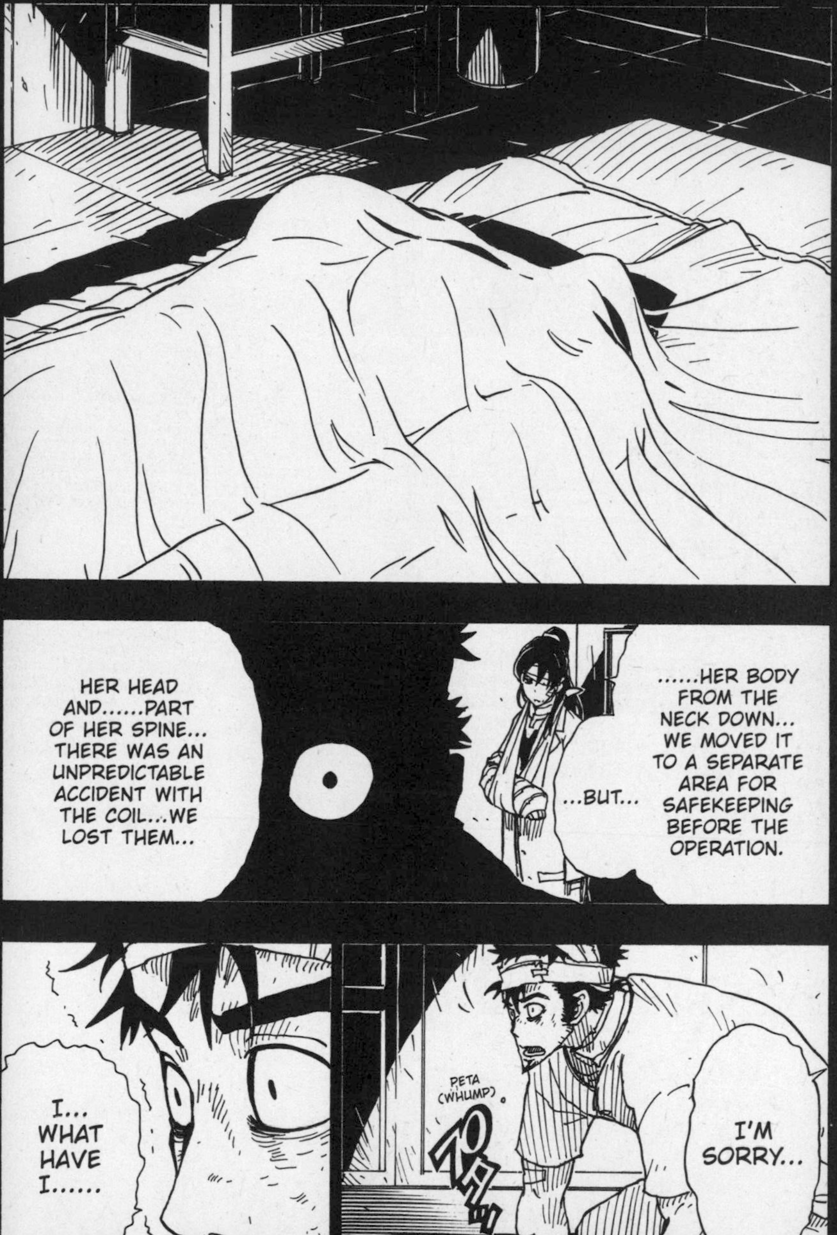
......HER BODY FROM THE NECK DOWN... WE MOVED IT TO A SEPARATE AREA FOR SAFEKEEPING BEFORE THE OPERATION.
...BUT...
HER HEAD AND......PART OF HER SPINE... THERE WAS AN UNPREDICTABLE ACCIDENT WITH THE COIL...WE LOST THEM...
I'M SORRY...
PETA (WHUMP)
I... WHAT HAVE I......

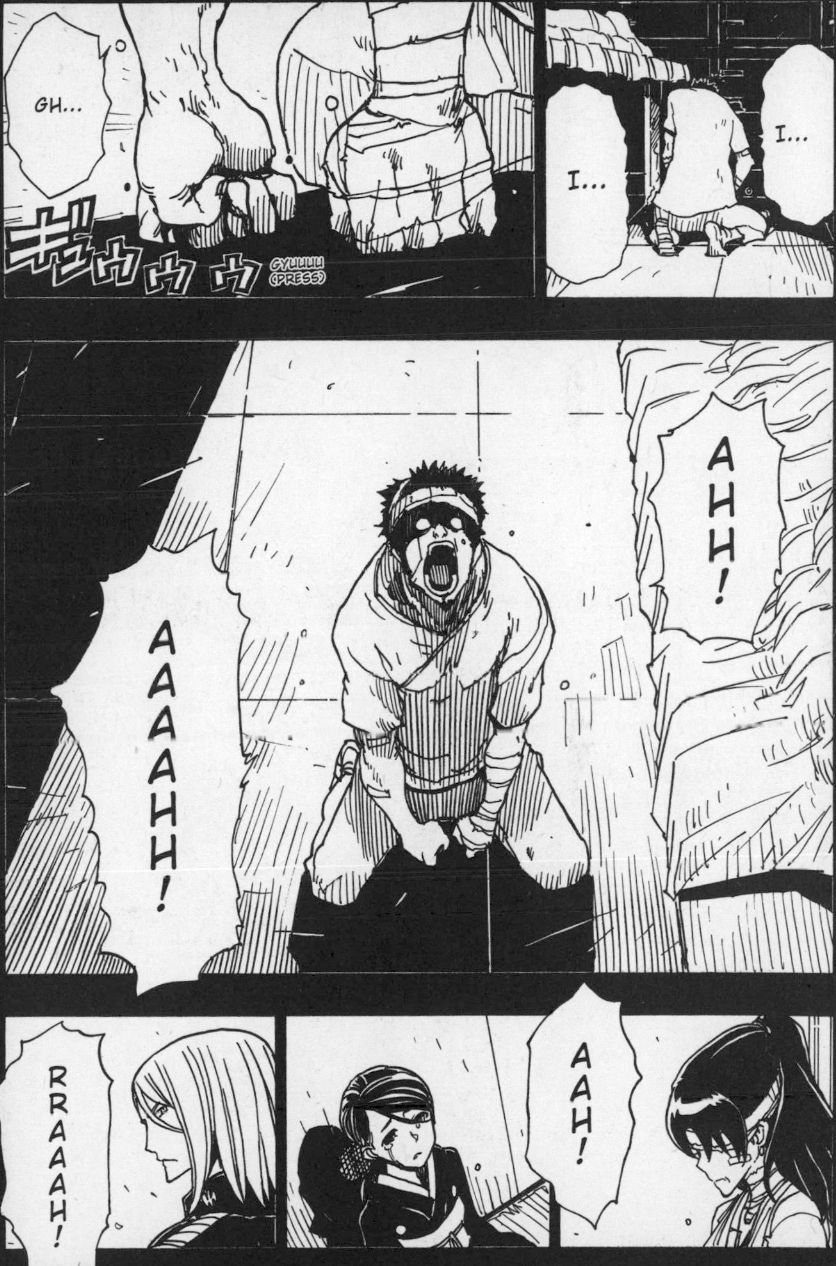
I...
I...
GH...
GYUUUU (PRESS)
AHH!
AAAAAHH!
AAH!
RRAAAAH!

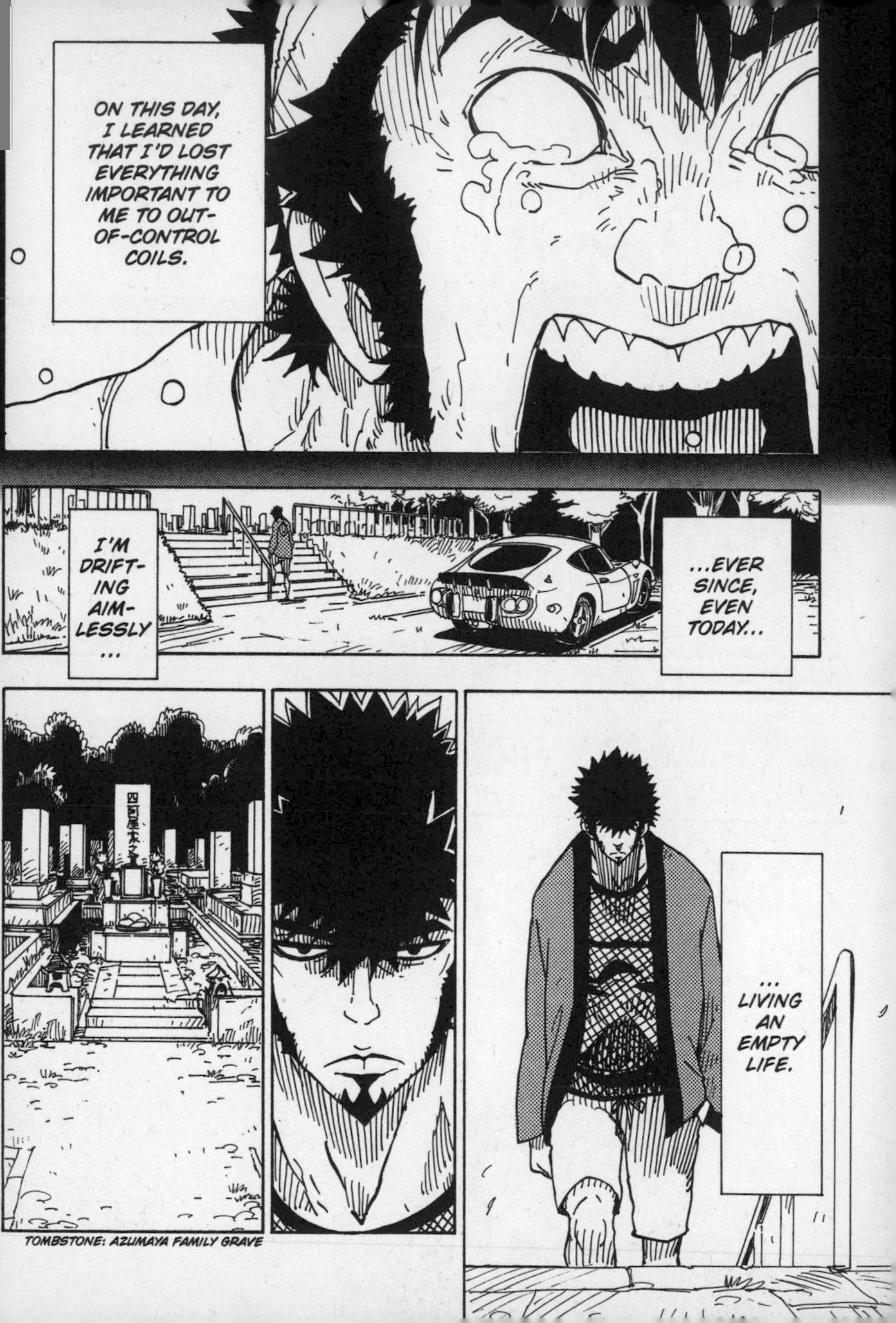
ON THIS DAY, I LEARNED THAT I'D LOST EVERYTHING IMPORTANT TO ME TO OUT-OF-CONTROL COILS.
...EVER SINCE, EVEN TODAY...
I'M DRIFTING AIMLESSLY...
...LIVING AN EMPTY LIFE.
TOMBSTONE: AZUMAYA FAMILY GRAVE

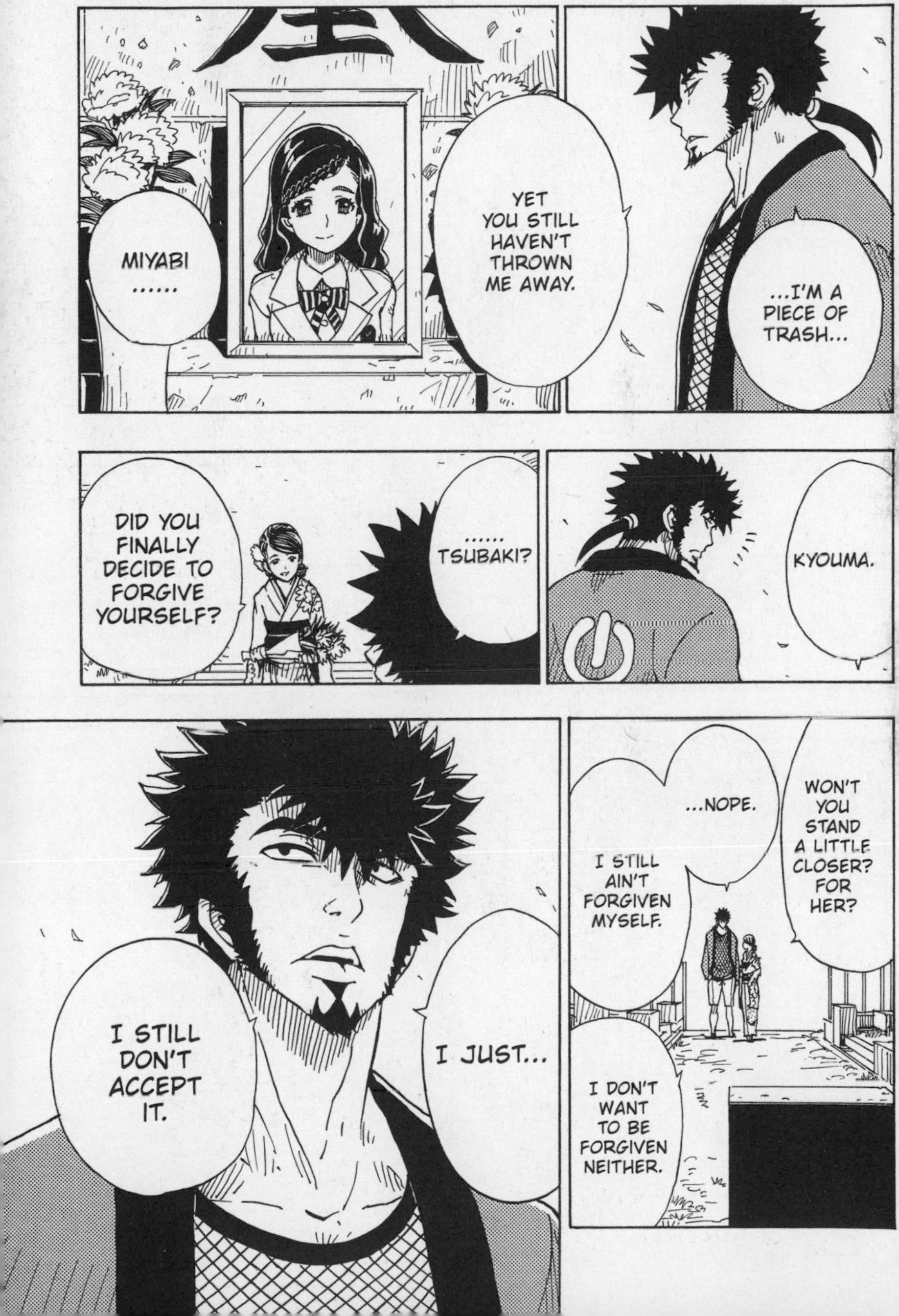
...I'M A PIECE OF TRASH...
YET YOU STILL HAVEN'T THROWN ME AWAY.
MIYABI ......
KYOUMA.
...... TSUBAKI?
DID YOU FINALLY DECIDE TO FORGIVE YOURSELF?
WON'T YOU STAND A LITTLE CLOSER? FOR HER?
...NOPE.
I STILL AIN'T FORGIVEN MYSELF.
I DON'T WANT TO BE FORGIVEN NEITHER.
I JUST...
I STILL DON'T ACCEPT IT.

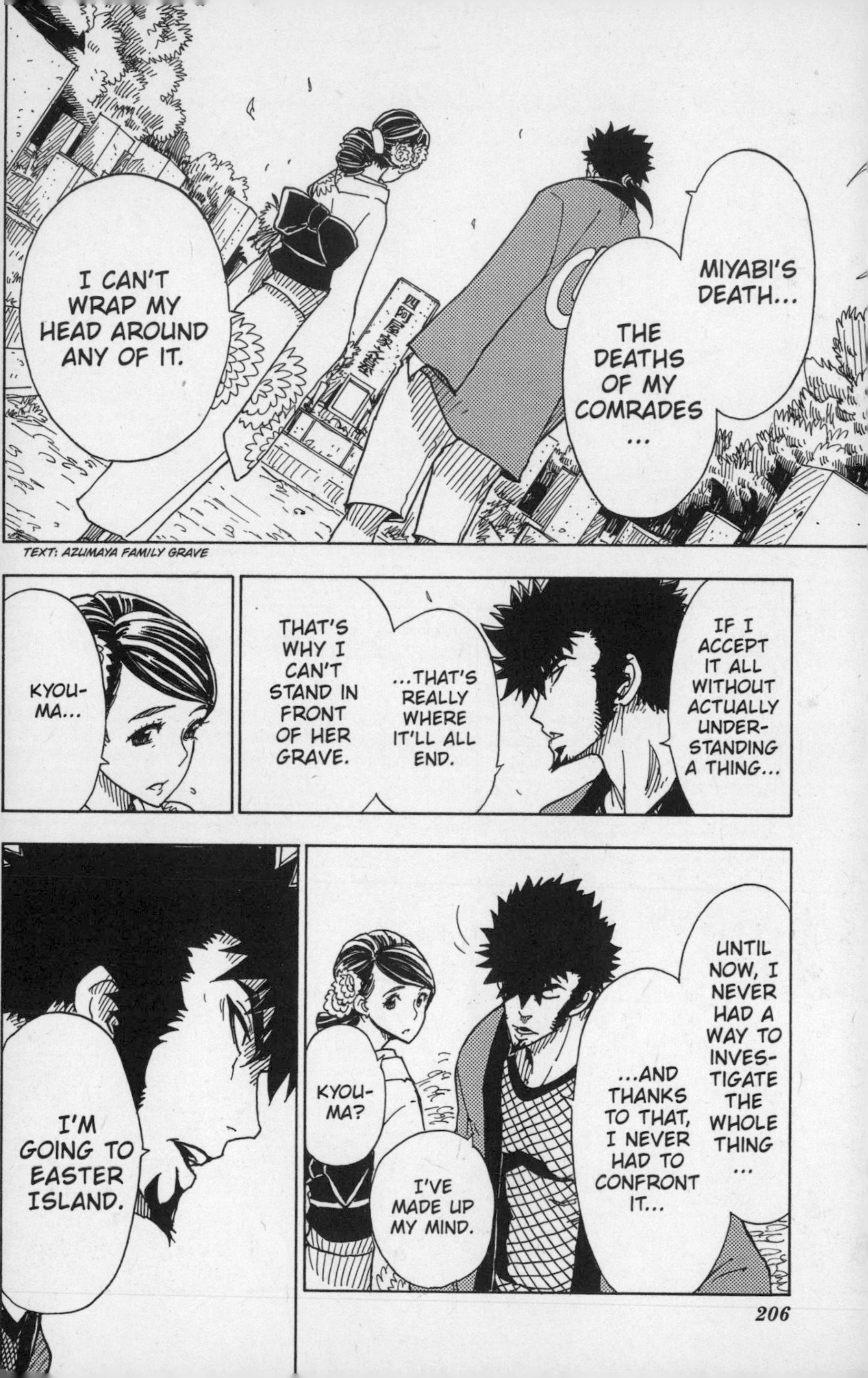
MIYABI'S DEATH...
THE DEATHS OF MY COMRADES ...
I CAN'T WRAP MY HEAD AROUND ANY OF IT.
TEXT: AZUMAYA FAMILY GRAVE
IF I ACCEPT IT ALL WITHOUT ACTUALLY UNDERSTANDING A THING...
...THAT'S REALLY WHERE IT'LL ALL END.
THAT'S WHY I CAN'T STAND IN FRONT OF HER GRAVE.
KYOUMA...
UNTIL NOW, I NEVER HAD A WAY TO INVESTIGATE THE WHOLE THING ...
...AND THANKS TO THAT, I NEVER HAD TO CONFRONT IT...
KYOUMA?
I'VE MADE UP MY MIND.
I'M GOING TO EASTER ISLAND.

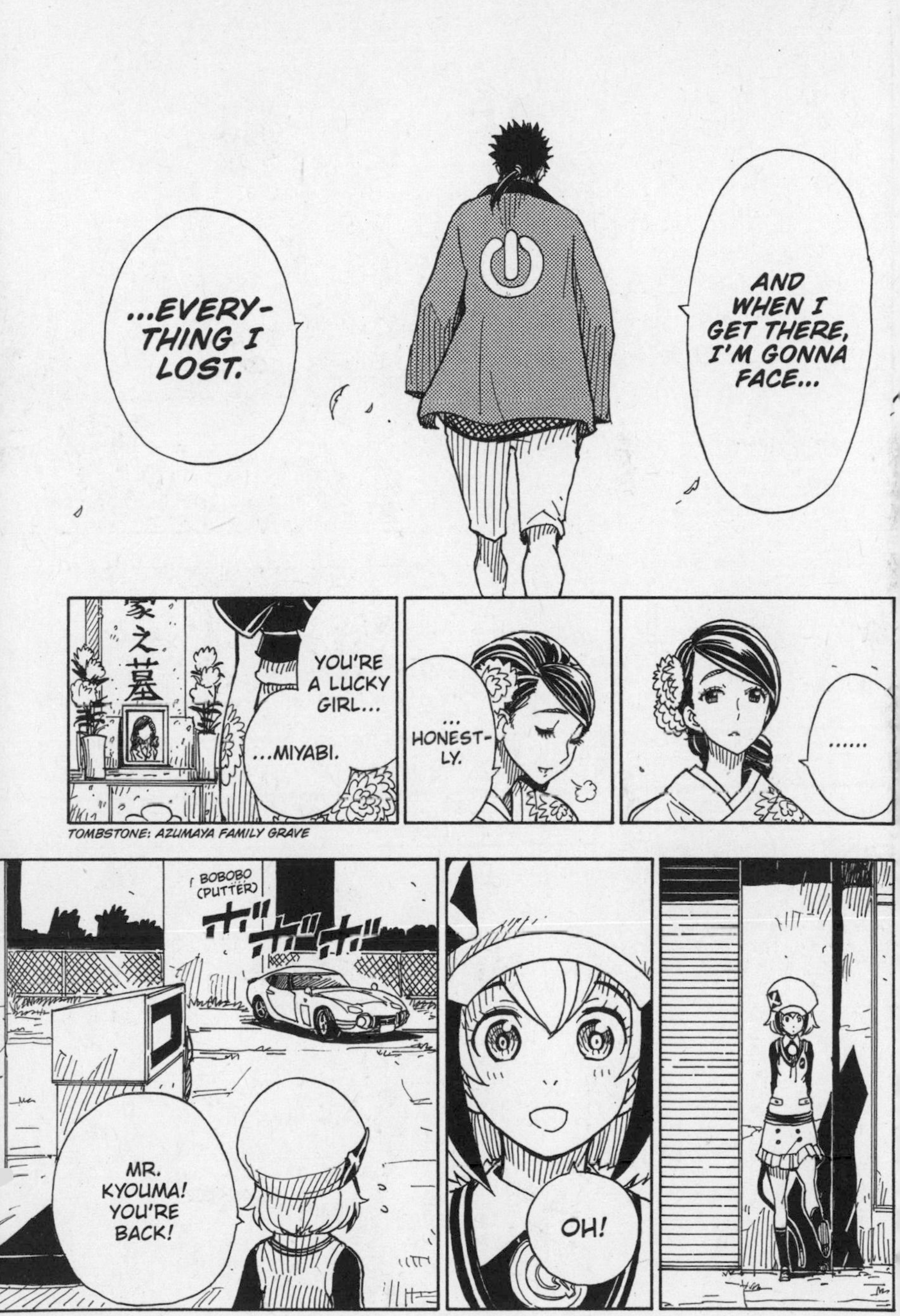
AND WHEN I GET THERE, I'M GONNA FACE...
...EVERY-THING I LOST.
......
... HONEST-LY.
YOU'RE A LUCKY GIRL...
...MIYABI.
家之墓
TOMBSTONE: AZUMAYA FAMILY GRAVE
OH!
BOBOBO (PUTTER)
MR. KYOUMA! YOU'RE BACK!

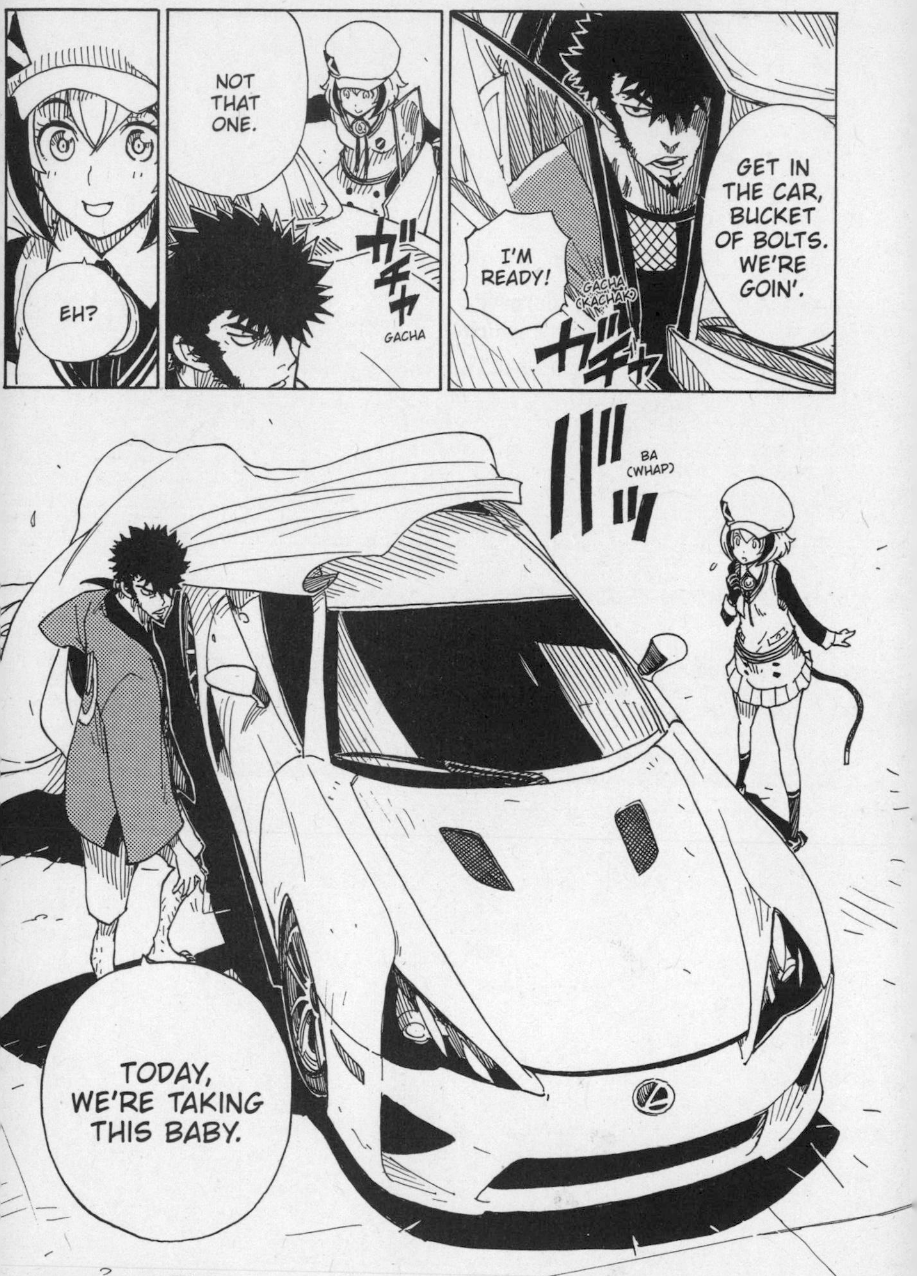
GET IN THE CAR, BUCKET OF BOLTS. WE'RE GOIN'.
I'M READY!
GACHA (KACHAK)
NOT THAT ONE.
GACHA
EH?
BA (WHAP)
TODAY, WE'RE TAKING THIS BABY.

DIMENSION W 5 END

APPENDIX.01
TRANSLATION NOTES

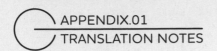

PAGE 36

Nippon: An older way of referring to the country of Japan in the Japanese language. The more common term is *Nihon.*

PAGE 85

Obon: A holiday honoring the spirits of one's ancestors, during which people visit and clean their ancestors' graves. One Obon tradition is to float paper lanterns down a river on the last day of the festival, to guide the spirits of the dead back to the afterlife.

PAGE 151

El Rosal: Spanish for "the rosebush."

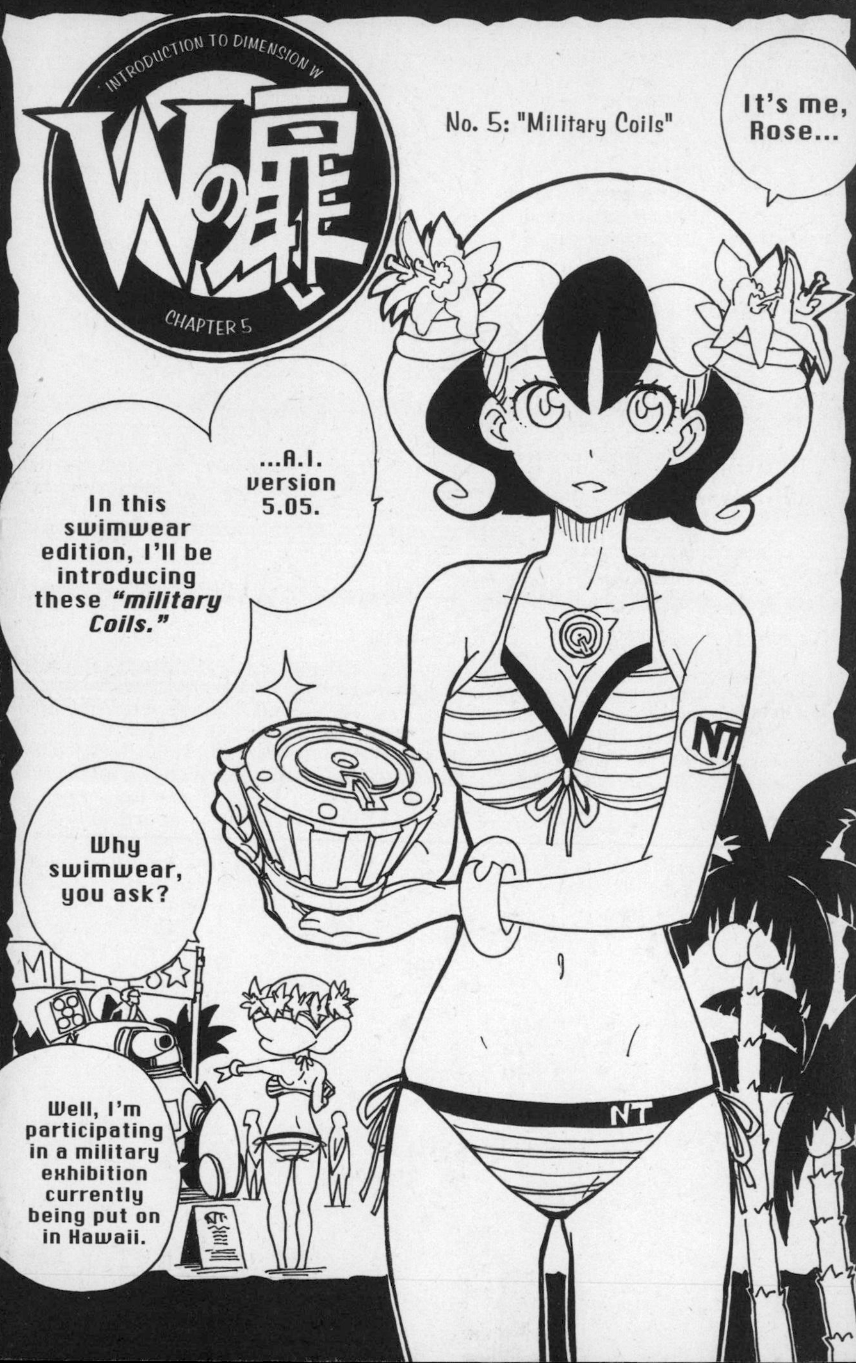
INTRODUCTION TO DIMENSION W
CHAPTER 5
No. 5: "Military Coils"
It's me, Rose...
...A.I. version 5.05.
In this swimwear edition, I'll be introducing these *"military Coils."*
Why swimwear, you ask?
Well, I'm participating in a military exhibition currently being put on in Hawaii.

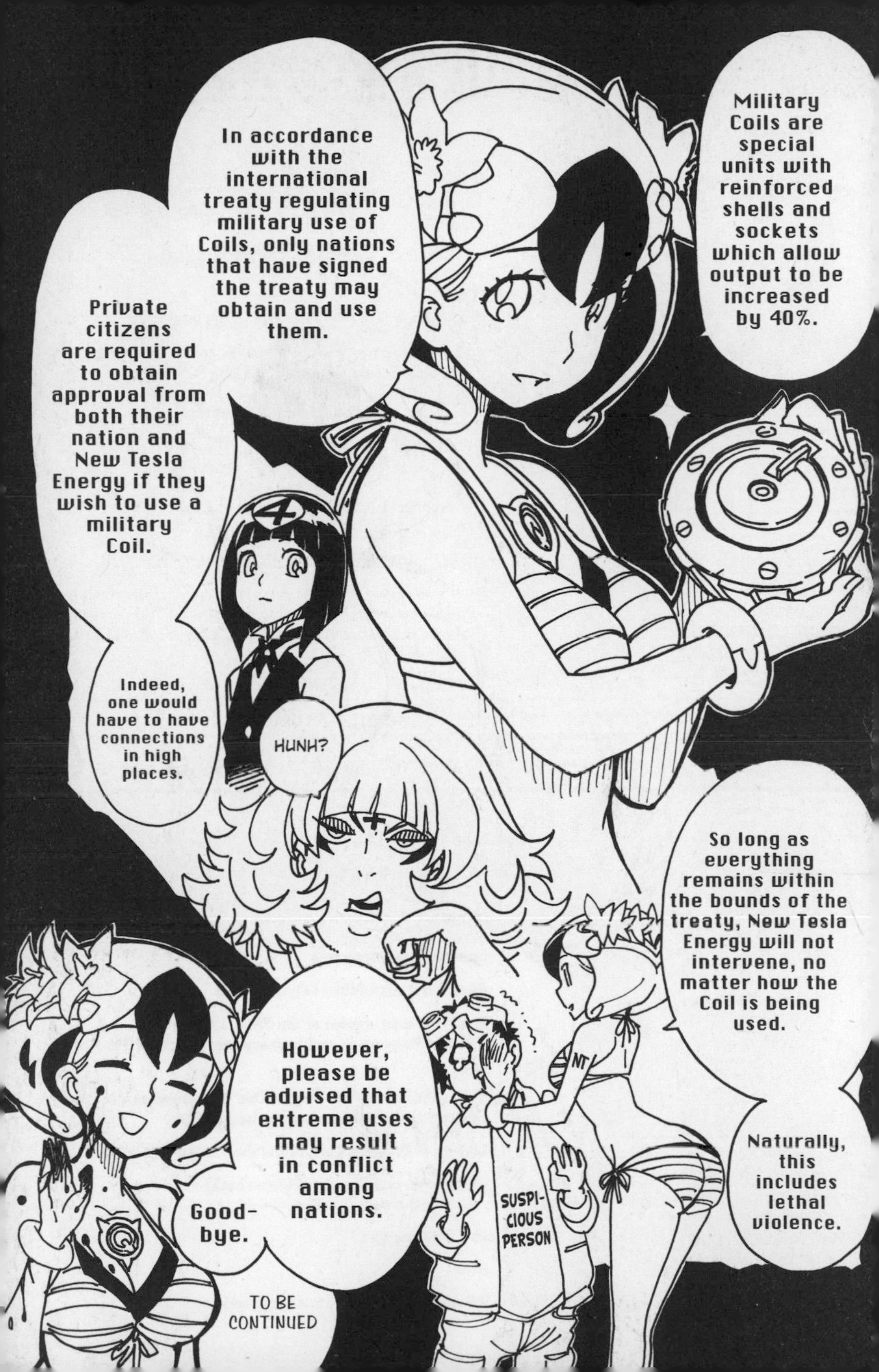

Military Coils are special units with reinforced shells and sockets which allow output to be increased by 40%.
In accordance with the international treaty regulating military use of Coils, only nations that have signed the treaty may obtain and use them.
Private citizens are required to obtain approval from both their nation and New Tesla Energy if they wish to use a military Coil.
Indeed, one would have to have connections in high places.
HUNH?
So long as everything remains within the bounds of the treaty, New Tesla Energy will not intervene, no matter how the Coil is being used.
Naturally, this includes lethal violence.
NT
SUSPI-CIOUS PERSON
However, please be advised that extreme uses may result in conflict among nations.
Good-bye.
TO BE CONTINUED

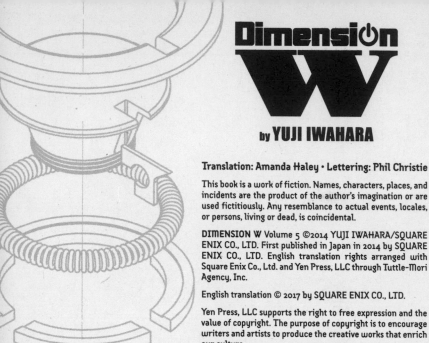

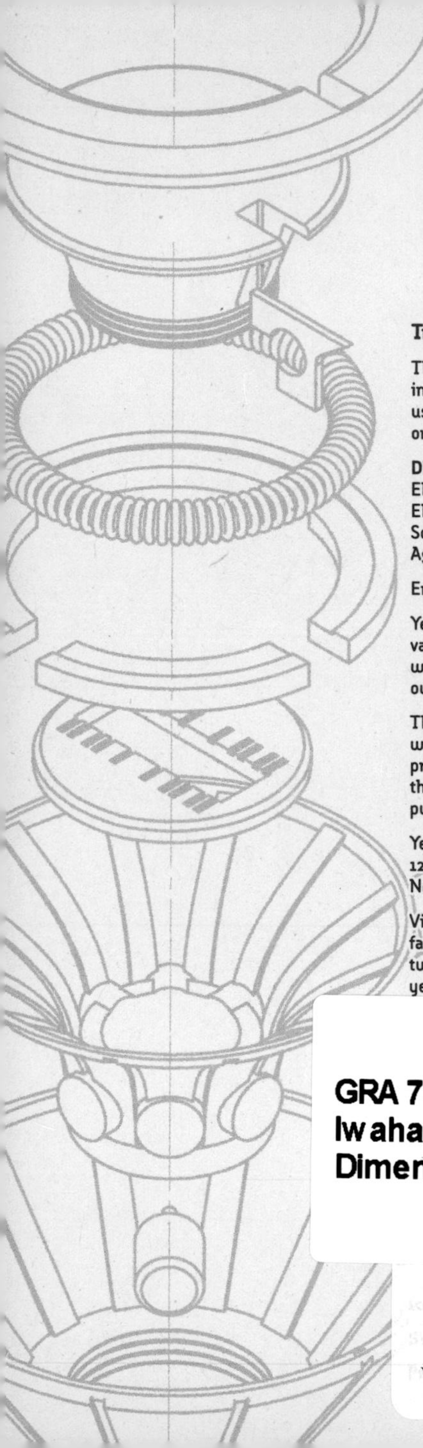

Dimension

W

by YUJI IWAHARA

Translation: Amanda Haley • Lettering: Phil Christie

DIMENSION W Volume 5 ©2014 YUJI IWAHARA/SQUARE ENIX CO., LTD. First published in Japan in 2014 by SQUARE ENIX CO., LTD. English translation rights arranged with Square Enix Co., Ltd. and Yen Press, LLC through Tuttle-Mori Agency, Inc.

English translation © 2017 by SQUARE ENIX CO., LTD.

Yen Press
1290 Avenue of the Americas
New York, NY 10104

Visit us at yenpress.com
facebook.com/yenpress
twitter.com/yenpress
yenpress.tumblr.com